Dr. John Doran

Lives of the Queens of England of the House of Hanover

Vol. II

Dr. John Doran

Lives of the Queens of England of the House of Hanover
Vol. II

ISBN/EAN: 9783337150426

Printed in Europe, USA, Canada, Australia, Japan

Cover: Foto ©ninafisch / pixelio.de

More available books at **www.hansebooks.com**

LIVES

OF THE

QUEENS OF ENGLAND

OF THE

HOUSE OF HANOVER

BY

DR. DORAN, F.S.A.

AUTHOR OF 'TABLE TRAITS' 'HABITS AND MEN' ETC.

FOURTH EDITION

CAREFULLY REVISED AND MUCH ENLARGED

IN TWO VOLUMES

VOL. II.

LONDON

RICHARD BENTLEY & SON, NEW BURLINGTON STREET

Publishers in Ordinary to Her Majesty

1875

CONTENTS
OF
THE SECOND VOLUME.

CHARLOTTE SOPHIA—Cont.

CHAPTER IV.

BIRTHS, DEATHS, AND MARRIAGES.

PAGE

Death of the Duke of Cumberland—His military career—The *soubriquet* of the Butcher given him—Anecdotes of him—Marriage of Caroline Matilda—Her married life unhappy—Dr. Struensee—*Mésalliances* of the Dukes of Gloucester and Cumberland—The Duke of Cumberland and Lady Grosvenor—The Royal Marriage Act—Olivia Serres—Lord Clive's present of diamonds to the Queen—Disgusting correspondence of the Duchess of Orleans and Queen Caroline—The Prince of Wales's juvenile Drawing-room—Simple life of the Royal Family at Kew—Prince Frederick and his cottage beauty—Paton and his naval pictures—Royal births—The custom of cake and caudle observed—Petty larcenists—Sarah Wilson and her subsequent life—Death of Princess Mary; and of Princess Augusta, the King's mother—The Earl of Bute—Neglected education of George III.—Petronilla, Countess Delitz—The Countess of Chesterfield, her conversion by Whitfield—Efforts of Lady Huntingdon to convert the gay Earl of Chesterfield—Mr. Fitzroy—George III. at Portsmouth—Jacob Bryant's 'golden rule'—Witty remark of Queen Charlotte—Attendant bards on Royalty; Mark Smeaton, Thomas Abel, David Rizzio—The Princess under the guardianship of Lady Charlotte Finch—The Queen's benevolence—Satirists. 1

CHAPTER V.

PERILS, PROGRESS, AND PASTIMES.

The American War—Dr. Dodd—The Duchess of Queensberry and the 'Beggar's Opera'—Royal Progress—Royal Visit to Bulstrode—Mrs. Delany and Queen Charlotte—Birth of Prince Octavius—Strange, the Engraver—The Riots of London—Lady Sarah Lennox—The Prince and his Sire—The Prince's Preceptors—Errors committed in the education of the Princes—The Prince's favourite, Perdita Robinson—Marie Antoinette's present to her—Separate establishment granted to the Prince—Lord North's facetious remark—Parliamentary provision for the Prince—The Prince's presence in the House of Commons not acceptable—His pursuit of pleasure—The Duke of Clarence described by Walpole—The Prince of Wales overwhelmed with debts—Dissension in the Royal Family—Marriage proposed to him to extricate him from his debts—The Prince's connection with Mrs. Fitzherbert—The Prince's marriage disclaimed by Mr. Fox—The Prince's behaviour to Mrs. Fitzherbert—The Prince acknowledges his marriage to the Queen . . 31

CHAPTER VI.

COURT FORMS AND COURT FREEDOMS.

Loss of the American Colonies—Political Struggle—The King's health unsatisfactory—Life of the Royal Family at Windsor—Mrs. Delany—The Queen and the Widow—Early service in the Chapel Royal at Windsor—Rev. Tom Twining and Miss Burney—Miss Burney's Reception by the Queen—Promenade of the Royal Family on the terrace—The Queen's 'dressing'—The Queen's partiality for Snuff—Country life of the Royal Family at Kew—Princess Amelia; the King's great affection for her—Scene on the birthday of the Princess—Margaret Nicholson's attempt to assassinate the King—The Queen's dread—Her fondness for Diamonds—Mrs. Warren Hastings—The present from the Nizam of the Deccan—Unpopularity of the King and Queen—Their affection for each other—The Queen's tenderness to Mrs. Delany—Reconciliation of the King and the Prince—A pleasant scene—Another Court Incident 54

CHAPTER VII.

SHADOWS IN THE SUNSHINE.

The Princess Amelia—Her connection with the Duke of Grafton—Beau Nash and the Princess—Her despotism as Ranger of Richmond Park—Checked by Mr. Bird—A scene at her Loo-table—

Her fondness for stables—Her eccentric Costume—Inordinate love of Snuff—Her Death—Conduct of the Princes—The King's Illness—Graphic picture of the state of affairs—Lord Thurlow's treachery—Heartlessness of the Prince—Deplorable condition of the Queen—The King delirious—Particulars of his Illness—Dr. Warren—Melancholy scene—The King wheedled away to Kew—Placed under Dr. Willis—The Prince and Lord Lothian eavesdroppers—The King's Recovery—The King unexpectedly encounters Miss Burney 72

CHAPTER VIII.

THE 'FIRST GENTLEMAN' AND HIS PRINCIPLES.

Inconsistency of the Whigs—The Tories become radical reformers—Party spirit—A restricted Regency scorned by the Prince—Compelled to accept it—The King's rapid recovery—Incredulity of the Princes in regard to the King's recovery—A family scene at Kew—Ball at White's Club on the King's recovery, and unbecoming conduct of the Princes—Thanksgiving at St. Paul's—Indecent conduct of the Princes—Grief of the King—Expectations of the Prince disappointed—Caricatures and satires 92

CHAPTER IX.

ROYALTY UNDER VARIOUS PHASES.

Bishop Watson a partisan of the Prince—The bishop's reception by the Queen—The Prince's patronage of the bishop—Bishop Watson's views on the Regency—Laid on the shelf—The Prince and the bishop's 'Apology'—Ball given on the King's recovery by Brookes's Club—Mrs. Siddons, as Britannia—The Queen's Drawing-room on the occasion—Mrs. Siddons's readings at Buckingham House—Gay life of the Duke of York—Popularity of the Duke of Clarence—His boundless hospitality at the Admiralty—Duel between the Duke of York and Colonel Lennox—Littleness of spirit of the Princes—Royal Visit to Lulworth Castle—Assault on the King—Caricatures of the day—Marriage of the Duke of York—Ceremonious royal visit to the young couple—Caricatures of the Duchess of York—Unhappy in her marriage—The Duchess and Monk Lewis—Alleged avarice of the King and Queen—Dr. Johnson's opinion of the King—Etiquette at Court—The Sailor Prince 'too far gone' for a minuet—The Royal Family at Cheltenham—The mayor and the master of the ceremonies—Questionable taste of the Queen in regard to the drama—Moral degradation of England during the reign of the first two Georges—Mrs. Hannah More's

ideas on morality; and Rev. Sydney Smith's witty remark on it—
A delicate hint by the Queen to Lady Charlotte Campbell—The
Prince's pecuniary difficulties—The Prince and affairs of the heart
—*Mésalliance* of the Duke of Sussex 102

CHAPTER X.

LENGTHENING SHADOWS.

The Prince of Wales's marriage to the Princess Caroline of Brunswick
—Her character—The Prince's behaviour at the marriage ceremony
—Lord Holland's two accounts of the Princess irreconcileable—The
Prince's hatred of the Princess—Propriety of the Queen's Court—
Unpopularity of the King—Pelted by the mob—Birth of the Princess
Charlotte—Strict observance of Court etiquette—Marriage of
the Princess Royal to the Prince of Wurtemburg—First book
stereotyped in England—The Volunteer mania—Attempted assassination
of the King—Archbishop Cornwallis's drums, and Lady
Huntingdon's efforts to induce him to discontinue—Her hot reception
by Mrs. Cornwallis—Lady Huntingdon induces the King to
aid her—The King's letter to the archbishop—Conduct of the
clergy—Incident of the Drawing-room—The Prince a Radical—
—The King's illness—His excitement—Feeling exhibited by the
Duke of York—The Prince of Wales incredulous of the recovery of
the King—Conversation between the King and Dr. Willis—The
Queen's anxiety—Particulars of the King's Illness—Recovery of
the King—Home scene at Windsor Castle 128

CHAPTER XI.

THE END OF GREATNESS.

Queen as an author—Domestic life of the Royal Family—Return of
the King's Illness—His continual agitation—Dr. Symonds not the
medical officer for the King—Capricious changes made by the
King in his household—His humorous eccentricities—Contest
between the King and the Prince—The Queen's conduct—Scant
courtesy to the royal invalid—Errors committed by the King—
Wellesley and Nelson—Gradual decay of the King—His eccentricity
at the installation of Knights of the Garter—Picture of the
daily life of the Royal Family—Position of the Queen—The King's
resignation on his blindness—Distress of his mind—Renewal of
the Regency question—Extraordinary assertion to Lord Eldon—
The King's person confided to the Queen—The Queen's letters to
Lord Eldon—Her merry letter to him—A touching incident—The
Queen's unpopularity—Marriage of the Princess Charlotte—Decline

                                                                    PAGE
of the Queen's health—Disgraceful reception of her by the City—
Her death—Considered as a parent—Her political influence—The
debts of Prince of Strelitz—The Court on George III.'s ceasing
to exercise authority—Regal retinue about the old King dismissed—The Queen's funeral—Her will—Her diamonds—Death
of the Duke of Kent—Death of the King—Visit of the Emperor
of the French to the Duchess of Gloucester 151

CAROLINE OF BRUNSWICK,
WIFE OF GEORGE IV.

CHAPTER I.

MOTHER AND DAUGHTER.

Marriage of Princess Augusta to the Prince of Brunswick—His reception at Harwich—Wedding performed with maimed rites—The
Prince at the opera—A scene—Old mode of travelling of the bride
and bridegroom—Issue of this marriage—Dashing replies of Princess Caroline—Her mother the Duchess a weak and coarse-minded
woman—Education of German princesses—Infamous conduct of
the Duke of York—Lord Malmesbury sent to demand Princess
Caroline in marriage for the Prince of Wales—His account of the
Princess—Eloquence of the Duchess on the virtues of the Princess—
The Duke's mistress, and picture of the Court of Brunswick—The
Duchess's stories of bygone times—The marriage by proxy—Celebration of the wedding-day—The marriage treaty—Eccentricity of
the Duke—Education of the Princess neglected—The courtesan
champion of morality—The Duke's fears for the Princess—Lady
Jersey and the Queen—Lord Malmesbury's advice to the Princess
—Madame de Hertzfeldt's portrait of the Princess—The Princess's
exuberant spirits at a court masquerade—More admonitions by
Lord Malmesbury—Madame de Waggenheim's taunt, and Lord
Malmesbury's thrust *en carte* 183

CHAPTER II.

THE NEW HOME.

The Princess desires to have Lord Malmesbury as her lord chamberlain—The Duchess a coarse-minded woman—The Duke of Clarence
her bitter enemy—The Duke and Duchess's caution to Lord

Malmesbury, and his dignified reply—The Abbess of Gandersheim's opinion of mankind—Difficult question proposed by the Princess, and Lord Malmesbury's gallant reply—The Abbess without human sympathy—A state dinner, and a mischievous anonymous letter—The Princess's departure for England—Her indifference to money—Instances—Ignorance of the Duchess—Difficulties of the journey—The Princess's design to reform the Prince of Wales—Indefatigable care of Lord Malmesbury—Story of the Princess at Hanover—Care as to her toilette recommended—Presents given by the Princess—Her arrival in England—Ridiculed by Lady Jersey—Reproof administered to her ladyship by Lord Malmesbury—The first interview of the Prince and Princess—Cold reception of the bride—Flippant conduct of the Princess—Lord Malmesbury reproached by the Prince of Wales . . . 209

CHAPTER III.

THE FIRST YEAR OF MARRIED LIFE.

The Princess's letters to her family intercepted—Unkindness exhibited to her—The Prince seeks a separation—Acceded to by the Princess—She removes to Blackheath—Her income settled—Merry hours spent by the Princess at Blackheath—Intercourse between the Princess and her daughter—The Princess's unfortunate acquaintance with Lady Douglas—The boy Austin—Lady Douglas's communication to the Prince attacking the Princess—The *delicate investigation*—Witnesses examined—The Princess hardly dealt with—Her memorial to the King—Delay in doing her justice—The Monarch's decision—Exculpated from the grave charges—Comparison of Caroline Queen of George II. and Caroline of Brunswick—The Prince and Lady Hertford—Miss Seymour, and the Prince's subornation of witnesses—Persecution of the Princess by her husband—Her appeal to the King—Menace of publishing THE BOOK—The Princess received at the Queen's Drawing-room—Meeting of the Prince and Princess—Death of the Duke of Brunswick at the battle of Jena—The Duchess a fugitive—The Princess's debts 235

CHAPTER IV.

MOTHERS AND DAUGHTERS.

Imbecility finally settled on the mind of George III.—Intercourse between the Princess and her daughter obstructed—The Whigs betrayed by the Prince—Sketch of the Duchess of Brunswick—The Princess's Court at Kensington diminished—Her pleasant dinners there—Lively outbreaks of the Princess—Her sketches of character—Her indiscretion—An adventure—Description of the Princess Charlotte—The Princess of Wales's demeanour to her mother—Thoughtlessness of the Duchess of Brunswick—Popularity of the Princess on the wane—Her determination to bring her wrongs before the public—She becomes more melancholy—An incident—Continued agitation of the Princess—She becomes querulous—The poet Campbell presented to her—A humorous fault of orthography—The Prince and John Kemble . . . 263

CHAPTER V.

HARSH TRIALS AND PETTY TRIUMPHS.

The Princess again in public—Restricted intercourse between the Princess and her daughter—Sealed letters addressed by the Princess to the Prince—Published—The Princess's appeal to Parliament—Bitterness on both sides—Meeting of the Princess and her daughter—The Princess at Vauxhall—Death of the Duchess of Brunswick—Last interview between the Duke of Brunswick and the Princess—Her depressed spirits—Unnoticed during the festivities of 1814—Sacrifice made by the Princess—Unnoticed by the Emperor of Russia and the King of Prussia—The Princess at the opera—A scene—Not invited to the great City banquet—Mr. Whitbread's advice to the Princess—A freak—Reception of the Regent in the City—The Princess excluded from the Drawing-rooms—Correspondence between the Queen and the Princess—Her letter to the Regent—Discussed in the House of Commons . 277

CHAPTER VI.

A DOUBLE FLIGHT.

The Prince of Orange proposes to the Princess Charlotte—His suit declined—Dr. Parr—A new household appointed for the Princess Charlotte—Her astonishment and immediate flight—Alarm and pursuit—Princess Charlotte removed to Cranbourne Lodge—The Princess of Wales determines to leave England—Her departure from Worthing—The Regent's continued hatred of her . . 299

CHAPTER VII.

THE ERRANT ARIADNE.

The Princess arrives at Hamburgh—Assumes the title of Countess of Wolfenbüttel—Travels in Switzerland—Meeting of the Princess with the ex-Empress Maria Louisa and the divorced wife of the Grand

Duke Constantine—The Princess at Milan—Her English attendants fall off—Her reception by the Pope—At a masked ball at Naples—Her imprudence—Her festivals at Como—The Princess at Palermo—Bergami her chamberlain—The Princess at Genoa—Corresponds with Murat—Personal vanity of Queen Charlotte—The Pope visits the Princess—Surrounded by Italians—Her roving life—Proceeds to Syracuse—At Jericho—Lands at Tunis and visits the Bey—Liberates European slaves—The Princess at Athens—At Troy—At Constantinople—At Ephesus—At Acre—Stopped at Jaffa—Enters Jerusalem—Her reception by the Capuchin Friars—Institutes a new order of chivalry—Life on board the polacca—The Princess and Countess Oldi at Como—Private theatricals a favourite pastime—Agents and spies—Innocent incidents converted into crimes—Bergami divested of his knighthood—The Princess at Carlsruhe—Contemptuously neglected at Vienna—The chamberlain her only attendant—The Princess in public—Deeply affected by the death of Princess Charlotte—As uncircumspect as ever . 313

CHAPTER VIII.

THE RETURN TO ENGLAND.

Report of the Milan Commissioners—The Princess's determination to return to England—Studied neglect of her by Louis XVIII.—Lord Hutchinson's proposal to her to remain abroad—Her indignant refusal—Bergami's anger on the refusal of the proposition—Discourtesy of the French authorities to the Princess—Her reception in England—The Regent's message to Parliament—The green bag—Sympathy with the Queen—Desire for a compromise evinced; meeting for the purpose at Lord Castlereagh's—The contending parties in Parliament—Mr. Wilberforce as Mr. Harmony—Mr. Brougham the Queen's especial advocate—The Queen's name in the Liturgy demanded—Mr. Denman's argument for it—Address of the House of Commons to the Queen—Her reply, and appeal to the nation—A secret inquiry protested against—The Queen at Waithman's shop—Violence of party spirit 334

CHAPTER IX.

QUEEN, PEERS, AND PEOPLE.

The secret committee on the Queen's conduct—Encounter between the Queen and Princess Sophia—Bill of Pains and Penalties brought into the House of Lords—The Queen demands to know the charges against her—Her demand refused—The Queen again petitions—Lord Liverpool's speech—The Queen's indignant message to the Lords—Money spent to procure witnesses against her—

Public feeling against the Italian witnesses—Dr. Parr's advice to the Queen—His zealous advocacy of her cause—Lord Erskine's efforts in her favour—Her hearty protest against legal oppression—Gross attack on her in a provincial paper—Cruel persecution of her—Her sharp philippic against Ministers—Lord John Russell's letter to Mr. Wilberforce, and petition to the King—The Queen at Brandenburgh House—Death of the Duchess of York—Her eccentricities—Her character—Addresses to the Queen, and her replies 349

CHAPTER X.

THE QUEEN'S TRIAL.

The Queen's reception by the House of Lords—Royal progress to the House—The Queen's enthusiastic reception by the populace—Their treatment of the King's party—Marquis of Anglesea—The Duke of Wellington's reply to them—The Attorney-General's opening speech—Examination of Theodore Majocchi—The Queen overcome at the ingratitude of this knowing rogue—Disgusting nature of the evidence—Other witnesses examined—Mr. Brougham's fearless defence of the Queen—Mr. Denman's advocacy not less bold—His denunciation of the Duke of Clarence—Question of throwing up the bill entertained by Ministers—Stormy debates—Lords Grey and Grosvenor in favour of the Queen—Duke of Montrose against her—Ministerial majority—The Queen protests against the proceedings—The Ministers in a minority—The bill surrendered by Lord Liverpool—Reception of the news by the Queen—Her unspeakable grief 365

CHAPTER XI.

'TRISTIS GLORIA.'

The result of the Queen's trial advantageous to neither party—The Queen's application to Parliament for a residence—Lord Liverpool's reply—Royal message from the Queen to Parliament, and its discourteous reception—The Queen goes to St. Paul's to return thanks—Uncharitable conduct of the Cathedral authorities—Their unseemly behaviour rebuked by the Lord Mayor—Revenue for the Queen recommended by the King—Accepted by her—The Coronation of George IV.—The Queen claims a right to take part in the ceremony—Her right discussed—Not allowed—Determines to be present—The Queen appears at the Abbey, and is refused admittance—With a broken spirit retires—Her sense of degradation—The King labours to give *éclat* to his Coronation—The Coronation-festival in Westminster Hall described—Appearance of the Duke of Wellington—His banquet to the King—The King's

speech on the occasion—True greatness of the Duke—Anecdote of
Louis XIV. and Lord Stair—Regal banquet to the foreign ministers
—The Duke of Wellington appears as an Austrian general—
Incident of the Coronation—Lord Londonderry's banquet to the
minister of Louis Napoleon 381

CHAPTER XII.
A CROWN LOST, AND A GRAVE WON.

The Queen's agitation—Her illness—Her sufferings—Desires her diary
may be destroyed—Her death—Sketch of her life—Her mother a
foolish woman—Every sense of justice outraged by the King—
Inconsistency of the Whigs—The Queen persecuted even after
death—Disrespect shown to her remains by the Government—
Protest against a disgraceful haste to remove her remains—Course of
the funeral procession interrupted by the people—Collision between
the military and the populace—Effort to force a way through the
people ineffectual—The procession compelled to pass through the
City—The plate on the Queen's coffin removed—The funeral reaches
Harwich—The Queen's remains taken to Brunswick—Funeral
oration—Tombs of the illustrious dead there 401

ADELAIDE OF SAXE-MEINENGEN,
WIFE OF WILLIAM IV.

The pocket Duchy—Old customs—Early training—The Father of the
Princess Adelaide—Social life at the Ducal Court—Training of the
Princess Adelaide—Marriage Preliminaries—English Parliament—
The Duke of Clarence—Arrival in London of the Princess—Quaint
royal weddings—At home and abroad—Duke and Duchess of
Clarence at Bushey—'State and Dirt' at St. James's—William
IV. and Queen Adelaide—Course of life of the new Queen-consort
—King's gallantry to an old love—Royal simplicity—The Sovereigns and the Sovereign people—Court anecdotes—Drawing-rooms
—Princess Victoria—The Coronation—Incidents of the day—Coronation finery of George IV.—Princess Victoria not present—Revolutionary period—Reform question—Unpopularity of the Queen—
Attacks against her on the part of the press—Violence of party spirit
—Friends and foes—Bearing of the King and Queen—Duchess of
Angoulême—King a republican—His indiscretion—Want of temper
—Continental press adverse to the Queen—King's declining health
—Conduct of Queen Adelaide—King William's death—Declining
health of the Queen—Her travels in search of health—Her last
illness—Her will—Death—And funeral 419

LIVES

OF THE

QUEENS OF ENGLAND.

CHARLOTTE SOPHIA.—Cont.

CHAPTER IV.

BIRTHS, DEATHS, AND MARRIAGES.

Death of the Duke of Cumberland—His military career—The *soubriquet* of the Butcher given him—Anecdotes of him—Marriage of Caroline Matilda—Her married life unhappy—Dr. Struensee—*Mésalliances* of the Dukes of Gloucester and Cumberland—The Duke of Cumberland and Lady Grosvenor—The Royal Marriage Act—Olivia Serres—Lord Clive's present of diamonds to the Queen—Disgusting correspondence of the Duchess of Orleans and Queen Caroline—The Prince of Wales's juvenile drawing-room—Simple life of the Royal Family at Kew—Prince Frederick and his cottage beauty—Paton and his naval pictures—Royal births—The custom of cake and caudle observed—Petty larcenists—Sarah Wilson and her subsequent life—Death of Princess Mary; and of Princess Augusta, the King's mother—The Earl of Bute—Neglected education of George III.—'Petronilla,' Countess Delitz—The Countess of Chesterfield, her conversion by Whitfield—Efforts of Lady Huntingdon to convert the gay Earl of Chesterfield—Mr. Fitzroy—George III. at Portsmouth—Jacob Bryant's 'golden rule'—Witty remark of Queen Charlotte—Attendant bards on Royalty; Mark Smeaton, Thomas Abel, David Rizzio—The Princes under the guardianship of Lady Charlotte Finch—The Queen's benevolence—Satirists.

THE favourite son of Caroline, and the favourite brother of the Princess Amelia, died on the last day of October,

His health had long been precarious: he had, like his mother, grown extremely corpulent, and his sight had nearly perished. Indeed, he could only see, and that very imperfectly, with one eye—and yet he was comparatively but a young man; not more than forty-four years of age. His course of life, both in its duties, and its so-called pleasures, had made an old man of him before his time. He had had a paralytic stroke, was much afflicted with asthma, and suffered continually from a wound in the leg, which he had received in his first great battle, at Dettingen, and which had never healed.

He was born when his mother was yet Princess of Wales. She loved him because he was daring and original; qualities which he evinced by his replies to her when she was lecturing him as a wayward child. For the same reasons was he liked by his grandfather, at whose awkward English the graceless grandson laughed loudly, and mimicked it admirably.

It is not astonishing that his mother loved him, for as he grew in years he (up to a certain time) grew in grace and dignity. In outward bearing, as in mental endowments, he was very superior to his brother, the Prince of Wales: he was gentlemanlike without affectation; and accomplished without being vain of his accomplishments. Never was a prince so popular, so winning in his ways, as William of Cumberland during his minority.

He was but twenty-two years of age when he accompanied George II. to the field and shared in the bloody honours of the day at Dettingen. The honours he reaped here, however, were fatal to him. They led to his being placed in chief command of an army before he was fitted to do more than lead a brigade. In '45, when the French invested Tournay under Marshal Saxe, the son of Aurora Königsmark, the Duke of Cumberland was placed in command of the English and Dutch forces, numerically very inferior to the foe, and charged with leading them to force the enemy to raise the siege. The attempt was made in the great battle of Fontenoy, where we gained a victory, and yet were vanquished. We beat the enemy, but, through want of caution, exposed ourselves to a cross fire of batteries, against which valour was impotent. It cost us ten thousand men and unmerited loss of reputation.

The rose which had fallen from his chaplet the duke replaced at Culloden, where he fought one of the battles whereby the hopes of the Stuarts were crushed in half an hour. The alleged severity of the young general, after the battle, gave him the name of the 'Butcher.' The duke was not ashamed of the name. He wore it with as much complacency as though it had been a decoration. With regard to his severities, it may be said that, terrible as they were, they had the effect of deterring men from rushing into another rebellion, which would have cost more blood than the duke ever caused to be shed by way of prevention.

But not from his contemporaries. For himself and his troops the popular heart beat high with admiration and sympathy; and while the public hand scattered rewards in profuse showers upon the army, parliament increased the duke's reward, and colleges offered him their presidential chairs. He was familiarly called 'the Duke,' as Marlborough had been before him, and as Wellington was after him.

As he grew in manhood his heart became hardened; he had no affection for his family, nor fondness for the army, for which he had affected attachment. When his brother died, pleasure, not pain, made his heart throb, as he sarcastically exclaimed, 'It is a great blow to the country, but I hope it will recover in time.' The death, if it did not place him next to the throne, at least gave him hopes of being regent should his sire die before the young heir was of age.

It was, however, the bloody Mutiny Act, of which he was really the author, which brought upon him the universal execration. 'The penalty of death,' says Walpole, 'came over as often as the curses of the commination on Ash Wednesday.' He who despised popularity was philosophically content when deprived of it. He was dissolute and a gambler. He hated marriage, and escaped from being united with a Danish princess by the adroit manœuvre of getting his friends to insist upon a large settlement from the royal father, too avaricious to grant it.

If he was lashed into fury by his name being omitted from the Regency Bill, he was more sensitively wounded still, by being made to feel that English uncles had, before this, murdered the nephews who were heirs to the throne. He was incapable of the crime, for it could have profited him nothing. The knowledge, however, that popular opinion stigmatised him as being capable of committing an offence so sanguinary was a torture to him. One day, Prince George, his nephew, entered his room. It was a soldier's apartment, hung with arms. He took down a splendid sword to exhibit it to the boy. The future husband of Charlotte turned pale, evidently suspecting that his uncle was on sanguinary thoughts intent. The duke was dreadfully shocked, and complained to the Princess-dowager of Wales that scandalous prejudices had been instilled into the child against him.

In 1757 he reluctantly assumed the command of the army commissioned to rescue Hanover from the threatened invasion of the French. His opponent was Marshal D'Estrées, from before whom he fell back at the Rhine, and to whom he disgracefully surrendered Hanover, by the infamous convention of Klosterseven. When the King saw him enter Kensington Palace, after his peremptory recall, the monarch exclaimed, 'Behold the son who has ruined me and disgraced himself!' That son, who declared he had written orders for all he did, and who certainly was invested with very full powers, resigned all his posts; and the hero of Dettingen and pacificator of North Britain became a private gentleman, and took to dice, racing, and other occupations natural then, or common at least, to gentlemen with more money than sense or principle. There is a good trait remembered of him at this period of his career. He had dropped and lost his pocket-book at Newmarket; and declined to make any more bets, saying that 'he had lost money enough for that day.' In the evening the book was brought to him by a half-pay officer who had picked it up. 'Pray keep it, sir,' said the duke, 'for if you had not found it, the contents would, before this, have been in the hands of the blacklegs.' Another favourable trait was his desire to give commissions to men who earned them on the field. He felt that while any 'fool' might purchase a commission, it was hard to keep it back from the man who had fought for it. He once promoted a sergeant to an ensigncy, and, finding him very coolly treated by his brother officers, the duke refused to dine with Lord Ligonier unless—pointing to the ensign—he might bring his 'friend' with him. This recognition settled the question.

The duke, cheated by his father's will, and sneered at by Marshal Saxe; with no reputation but for bravery, and no merit as a country gentleman but that of treating his labourers with some liberality, lived on as contentedly as though he were quietly enjoying all possible honour. His good-humoured gallantry was of a hearty nature. When George III., in 1762, complimented Lady Albemarle, in full drawing-room, on the victories achieved by her husband, the Duke of Cumberland stepped across the room to her and enthusiastically exclaimed, 'If it was not in the drawing-room I would kiss you.' He was a constant attendant at these ceremonies. On the morning of the 31st of October he had been to court, and had conversed cheerfully with Queen Charlotte. It was the last time she ever beheld him. He subsequently dined in Arlington Street with Lord Albemarle, and appeared in good health, although the day before, when playing at picquet with General Hodgson, he had been confused and mistook his cards. Early in the evening he was at his town-house, 54, Upper Grosvenor Street, when the Duke of Newcastle and Lord Northington called upon him. As they entered the room he was seized with a suffocation. One of his valets, who was accustomed to bleed him, was called, and prepared to tie up his arm; but the duke exclaimed, 'It is all over!' and immediately expired in Lord Albemarle's arms.

Thus died the favourite son of Caroline of Anspach, to place a crown on whose brow she would have sacrificed her own life. He was an indifferent general, who outlived the reputation he acquired at Culloden, where it was impossible that he should be beaten. Where to be vanquished was possible he never had the good luck of being victor. But he cared as little for fame as he did for money; and his neglect in the latter case is testified by the fact that nearly eighteen hundred pounds, in bank notes, were found in the pocket of one of his cast-off suits, of which a present had been made, after the duke's death, to one of his hussars. The hussar had the honesty to return the money.

The King behaved with appropriate delicacy on this occasion. When Lord Albemarle, the duke's executor, presented to the King the key of his uncle's cabinet, George III. returned it, bidding Lord Albemarle use his own discretion in examining all private papers, and in destroying all such as the duke himself probably would not have wished to be made public. On the 28th of December the death of his Majesty's youngest brother, Prince Frederick, at the early age of sixteen years, threw additional gloom on the circle of the royal family. At least, so say the journalists of the period.

At this time the King and Queen resided chiefly at Richmond, in very modest state, and with very few servants. Their chief amusement, amid the turmoil of politics and the crush of factions, consisted in 'going about to see places,' as Walpole describes their visits to such localities as Oatlands and Wanstead; and the 'call' of the Queen at Strawberry Hill, which the sovereign lady could not see, for the sufficient reason that the sovereign lord was in bed and unable to perform the necessary honours.

The youngest daughter of Frederick, Prince of Wales, was married by proxy on the 1st of October 1766, in the Chapel Royal, St. James's, to Christian VII., King of Denmark. Queen Charlotte was not present, she having given birth, only two days previously, to Charlotte Augusta, Princess Royal, and subsequently Duchess of Wurtemburg.

The King of Denmark was an exceedingly small, but not an ill-made, a weakly, not an ill-favoured man. His character was, however, in every respect detestable; and when poor Caroline Matilda passed on in tears, amid the congratulations of the court of Queen Charlotte, her tears were better founded than their smiles. She was speedily treated with cruelty, and abandoned at home while her lord travelled in foreign countries and indulged in profligacy. Queen Charlotte accorded him a more hearty reception than he deserved when he came over to England, two years subsequent to the marriage. At that time his absurdly pompous airs were the ridicule of the circle at the Queen's and at Carlton House, the residence of the Princess-dowager of Wales.

After spending some years in travel, he returned, neither a wiser nor a better man, to Denmark. In his suite was the German physician, Struensee. This man enjoyed his master's utmost confidence. He soon gained that of the young Queen also, who sought by his means to be reconciled to the King. He was, on the other hand, hated by the Queen-mother and other branches of the royal family; particularly in his character of reformer of political abuses. They contrived to overthrow him, procured a warrant for his execution from the King, and involved the young Queen in his ruin, on the ground of an improper familiarity between them. The triumphant enemies of Struensee would have put Caroline Matilda also to death but for the appearance in the Baltic of a British fleet under Admiral Keith, by whom she was carried off to Zell, where she died in 1775, neglected, unhappy, and under the weight of accusation of a charge of which she has never been proved guilty.

It may be stated here, that of all the children of Frederick, Prince of Wales, George III. can be said to have been the only one happily married. The second son, William Henry, the amiable, assiduous, brave, but not over-accomplished Duke of Gloucester (born in 1743), scandalised Queen Charlotte and the court by a *mésalliance* which he contracted, in 1766, with Maria, Countess-dowager of Waldegrave. This marriage was not, indeed, especially unhappy to the contractors of it, except inasmuch as they were embarrassed by being obliged for some time to keep it secret, and that when discovered, the royal husband and his noble wife were for a long period banished from court. They resided during a portion of their time of exile in Italy; and at Rome, the

Pope himself had so much esteem for the Prince that his Holiness, on one occasion, declined to take precedence of him when their carriages encountered in the streets. The Holy Father drew on one side, and courteously waited while the Prince, in obedience to the bidding of the Universal Bishop, passed on. The children of this union were subsequently acknowledged as the legal heirs of their parents. The duke died in 1805.

The third son of Frederick, Prince of Wales, Henry, Duke of Cumberland (after the death of his uncle 'the Duke'), born in 1744, more grievously offended Queen Charlotte by a *mésalliance* than his brother. He was fierce of temper, frivolous of character, and foppish in his dress. In the year 1770 the attentions of the duke to Lady Grosvenor were so marked, and so ridiculous, that everybody talked about them, except her husband. The lady, when a Miss Vernon, had been first seen by Lord Grosvenor as she and a companion were leaving Kensington Gardens, flying under sudden and heavy rain. He looked at and pitied the shower-bearing nymphs, as Aristophanes styles maidens so molested, and he offered them an asylum in his carriage. Soon after, Miss Vernon was the married mistress of his house; and the union would have been happy had not the foolish prince appeared to disturb it. He speedily contrived to seduce Lady Grosvenor from her duty. He followed her about in disguises, often betraying himself by his fopperies and imbecility, slept whole nights in woods like any Corydon not subject to the infirmities of nature, and subsequently had 10,000*l.* to pay for the ruin he brought to Lord Grosvenor's hearth. But this guilt did not so much flurry Queen Charlotte as the marriage of the duke in the following year with Mrs. Horton, a widow, daughter of Lord Carhampton, who was much older than the senseless and coarse-minded prince, her husband.

This act of folly caused him to be permanently banished

from court. The Queen would never consent to a reconciliation; and the King, to prevent such unions in future, brought in the Royal Marriage Act. By this act no prince or princess of the blood could marry without consent of the Sovereign before the age of twenty-five. After that age the royal sanction was still to be applied for; but if withheld the prince or princess had a resource in the privy council. To this body the name of the individual to whom the English member of the royal family desired to be married was to be given, and if parliament made no objection within the year the enamoured parties were at liberty to enter into the holy bond of matrimony. Queen Charlotte, who was exceedingly 'nice' on such matters, thought that she at least prevented all such alliances among her own children. She little thought how one of her sons would twice offend.

The duke died childless and a widower in 1790, but a paternity derived from him was claimed by 'Olivia Serres,' who professed to be the daughter of a second marriage. Her claim was never heeded, but she used to patronise the cheaper minor theatres, whose bills announced her presence as that of 'H.R.H. the Princess Olivia of Cumberland.' She was as much a princess as the counterfeits upon the stage, but not more so.

There are two more children of Frederick yet to be mentioned. These are Edward, Duke of York, the second son, born in 1739, and the Princess Louisa Anne, born ten years later. Neither of these was married. A report, nevertheless, was long prevalent that the weak (he voted against ministers on the American Stamp Act) but witty duke was privately married to a lady at Monaco, where he died in 1767. The Princess Louisa, his sister, was almost from her birth the victim of slow consumption, which finally ended her life when she was in the eighteenth year of her age.

A circumstance occurred in 1767 which was not advantageous to the memory or reputation of Queen Caroline, and which did not raise her in the opinion of Queen Charlotte. The latter, however, was too much occupied in contemplating with delight the Indian presents brought over to her by Lord Clive to trouble herself much about the character of Caroline. These consisted of two diamond drops worth twelve thousand pounds. In the year just named the Duchess of Brunswick's repositories were examined by her executors, and among other things discovered therein were not less than eight hundred letters addressed by the Duchess of Orleans, second wife of the brother of Louis XIV., to Caroline Wilhelmina Dorothea, Princess of Wales, and to Ulric, Duke of Brunswick. From this correspondence selections have been published, which have disgusted most persons who have read them. The portions suppressed must have been edifying indeed. But even if no more had come under the eyes of the wife of George Augustus than what publishers have ventured to print, there would still be evidence enough to show that, although Caroline conversed with philosophers, her mind could descend to be dragged through the filthiest pollution. There was not much refinement in the age, it is true; but, impure as it may have been, the fact that Caroline could submit to have such letters addressed to her, or to read a second, is proof that it was more radically rotten and profoundly unclean than has been generally supposed.

The most interesting domestic event of the following year was the juvenile drawing-room held by the Prince of Wales and the Princess Royal. The boy heir-apparent was, perhaps, too early initiated into the solemnities of festivals and gorgeous ceremonies. On this occasion he was attired in a crimson suit, his brother of York in one of blue and gold, while the Princess Royal and the younger branches of the family were grouped together on a sofa in Roman togas. The happy mother looked upon them with delight, and thought the scene worthy of a painter. The public did not share the enthusiasm nor approve of the royal taste for extensive displays; and when the youthful Prince of Wales gave a ball and supper this year at the Queen's House the mob broke into the court-yard, drove a hearse round it, and saluted the revellers, old and young, with anything but shouts of compliment or congratulation.

But if the town life of the royal family was one of considerable display, private life at Kew was of the very simplest aspect. Their Majesties were early risers, an example which, forcible as the fashion is which royalty deigns to offer, was not followed very generally even by their own household, except such persons whose services were needed. A king and queen rising at six and spending the first two hours of the day emphatically as their own, undisturbed by business of state, afforded a singular spectacle to those who could remember the indolent habits of the late court, for it was only on rare occasions that George II. was an early riser. Caroline was never so by choice. At eight o'clock there was a joyous family breakfast, at which the Sovereigns were surrounded by the Prince of Wales, the Bishop of Osnaburgh, as the second son was called before he was created Duke of York, the Princes William and Edward, and the Princess Royal. At this morning festival the children were not bound to the silence which they always observed in presence of their parents in public. After breakfast the younger children were brought in, and with these the King and Queen spent an hour of amusement, while the elder princes were away at exercise of body or mind.

Queen Charlotte generally, and often in company with the King, presided at the children's early dinner. Such attendance was the forerunner of the early dinners which the King subsequently took himself. A weekly holiday was passed by the whole family in Richmond Gardens. This was, in some sort, a continuation of a custom commenced by George II. His custom, however, had not so pure a motive as that observed by George III. and Queen Charlotte, who took innocent delight in witnessing innocent enjoyment. In the cottage there, erected from her own design, she would ply the needle (Queen Adelaide was not a more indefatigable worker) while the King read aloud to her, generally from Shakspeare. The Sovereign loved the poet as deeply as the great Duke of Marlborough did, who knew nothing of English history, save what he had gathered from the not altogether indisputable authority of the great poet. 'Whatever charms,' says an 'observer,' with more enthusiasm than elegance, ' ambition or folly may conceive to surround so exalted a station, it is neither on the throne nor in the drawing-room, in the splendour or the joys of sovereignty, that the King and Queen place their felicity. It is in social and domestic gratifications, in breathing the free air, admiring the works of nature, tasting and encouraging the elegances of art, and in living without dissipation. In the evening all the children pay their duty at Kew House before retiring to bed; after which the King reads to her Majesty; and having closed the day with a joint act of devotion, they retire to rest. This is the order of each revolving day, with such exceptions as are unavoidable in their high stations.

'The Sovereign is the father of the family; not a grievance reaches his knowledge that remains unredressed, nor a character of merit or ingenuity disregarded; his private conduct, therefore, is as exemplary as it is amiable.'

Alexander Young, referring to the period when the Prince of Wales was not above twelve years old, furnishes us with a picture that represents the Queen's sons as so many Cincinnati at the plough, or rather like Diocletian cultivating cabbages; only that *he* did not take to the healthy pursuit until he had lost a throne, whereas the English heir-apparent had not yet gained one. The young princes were, perhaps, more like the royalty of Cathay, whose greatest glory was to cultivate the soil, and delude itself into the idea that it was being useful to mankind. Nevertheless the royal pursuits of the Prince of Wales and his brother of York were harmless at least. 'A spot of ground in the garden at Kew was dug by his royal highness the Prince of Wales and his brother the Duke of York, who sowed it with wheat, attended the growth of their little crop, weeded, reaped, and harvested it, solely by themselves. They thrashed out the corn and separated it from the chaff; and at this period of their labour were brought to reflect from their own experience upon the various labours and attention of the husbandman and farmer. The princes not only raised their own crop, but they also ground it; and, having parted the bran from the meal, attended the whole process of making it into bread, which it may well be imagined was eaten with no slight relish. The King and Queen partook of the philosophical repast, and beheld with pleasure the very amusements of their children rendered the source of useful knowledge.'

The second son of Charlotte was not very far advanced in his teens when he carried his love of rustic pursuits to rustic persons. He so especially admired one cottage beauty in the neighbourhood of Kew or Windsor that his absences from home became rather too numerous and too prolonged to escape notice. The royal truant was less narrowly watched than strictly looked after upon being missed. On one of these occasions something more powerful than conjecture took the enquirers to a certain cottage door, and on looking into the room upon which it opened there sat the second son of Queen Charlotte, Duke of York and Bishop of Osnaburgh, upon a wooden stool shelling peas!

Reference has been made to the patronage which both Queen Charlotte and King George extended to art. Their patronage of painters was not, generally speaking, on a liberal scale. They requested Paton to bring to the palace, for their inspection, the naval pictures intended for Saint Petersburgh. The artist obeyed, but at a cost of fifty pounds for carriage. He was repaid in thanks, but he received no pecuniary compensation. On another occasion twenty-five pounds was given to an artist for a picture worth four times the sum. The artist had a friend in Dr. Wolcot, and the satires of Peter Pindar avenged the disappointed painter.

It was the excuse of both King and Queen that their increasing family prevented them from exercising all the liberality they could wish. However the fact may or may not have influenced the plea, it could not be denied that the circle round the royal hearth was annually enlarging. In 1767 was born Edward, afterwards Duke of Kent; and in the following year the Princess Augusta Sophia. At this period the old custom was still observed of admitting the public to 'cake and caudle.' Among the loyal young ladies who flocked to the palace to see the infant princess were two who partook so plentifully of the caudle as to lose their discretion, and to walk away with the cup in their keeping. They were detected, and were pardoned after kneeling to ask for forgiveness. The inequality in the application of the law was as marked then as it is now. Petty larcenists of high birth, as these young ladies were, were permitted to escape; not so a poor Sarah Wilson, who, yielding to a strong temptation in the year 1771, filched one or two of the Queen's jewels, and was condemned to be executed. It was considered almost a violation of justice that the thief should be saved from the halter, and be transported instead of hanged. She was sent to America, where she was allotted as slave or servant to a Mr. Dwale, Bud Creek, Frederick County. Queen Charlotte would have thought nothing more of her had her Majesty not heard, with some surprise, that her own sister, Susannah Caroline Matilda, was keeping her court in the plantations. Never was surprise more genuine than the Queen's; it was exceeded only by her hilarity when it was discovered that the Princess Susannah was simply Sarah Wilson at large. That somewhat clever girl, having stolen a queen's jewels, thought nothing, after escaping from the penal service to which she was condemned, of passing herself off as a queen's sister. The Americans—so in love were some of them with the greatness they affected to despise—paid royal honours to the clever impostor. She passed the most joyous of seasons before she was consigned again to increase of penalty for daring to pretend relationship with the consort of King George. The story of the presuming girl, whose escapades, however, were not fully known in England at the time, served, as far as knowledge of them had reached the court, to amuse the 'gossips' who had assembled in 1770 about the cradle of the young Elizabeth, and still more those who, in the following year, greeted the new Prince Ernest, one of the three sons of Charlotte destined to wear a crown.

The fourth daughter of Caroline and George II. died on the 14th of June in this year, 1771. She was born on the 22nd of February, 48 years before. Before she had completed her eighteenth year she was married to Frederick, Prince of Hesse, a man whose naturally brutal temperament was rendered still more brutal after his passing over from Protestantism to Romanism. This aggravation of a naturally bad temper was not the immediate result of the change of religion, but of the political restrictions to which such change subjected him. Never had wife a more vicious and unfeeling husband than poor Mary; never had husband a more submissive and uncomplaining wife than Frederick of Hesse. His death relieved her of a most inhuman tyrant, and her last days were spent in a happy tranquillity.

The person of Her Majesty at this period is described as having been easy and graceful, rather than striking or majestic. They who could not call her handsome, which she *never* was, compromised the matter by describing the contour of her face as delicate and pleasing. Her well-shaped forehead and her beautiful teeth, no inconsiderable items in a face, were her chief beauties. Her bright chestnut-coloured hair would have been an additional beauty to have been reckoned, but that it was generally hidden under thick layers of powder—so long, at least, as powder was in fashion. Of her hands and arms the royal lady was proud to a very late period of her life; and amateurs, in the early term of her reign, eulogised the beauties of a neck, which soon very well bore the discreet veil with which it was wisely and modestly covered. Her countenance was naturally benignant, except when flushed, as it could sometimes be, by an offended feeling; and it was naturally pallid, 'except,' says an anonymous writer '(which happened not unfrequently), when a blush of diffidence suffused her modest cheek.'

The succeeding year to that last named brought mourning with it, for the death of the mother of George III. On the death of her husband she was appointed the chief guardian of her eldest son, in case of the demise, before that son's majority, of the king, his grandfather. In the meantime she was really his guardian during that king's lifetime. This office, however, she shared with Lord Bute, who, according to the scandal-mongers, was less attached to the pupil than to the pupil's mother. Of this attachment the Prince of Wales himself is said to have had full knowledge, and did not object to Lord Bute taking solitary walks with the Princess, while *he* could do the same with Lady Middlesex. However this may be, the Princess and Lord Bute kept the Prince George in very strict seclusion after his father's death. The future husband of Charlotte had, however, abundance of teachers, but a paucity of instruction. One taught him '*deportment*,' another imbued him with Jacobitism. Dr. Thomas did honestly his little ineffective best. Lord Bute superintended Dr. Thomas, and the Princess said the boy was slow, and the masters indifferent.

The boy would probably have been an accomplished scholar had his preceptors been more careful in their training. There was the *stuff* and also the taste in him; but he was neglected, and the lost ground was never recovered. His affection for his mother was strong, and she deserved it. She was not a favourite with the people, and she did *not* deserve her unpopularity. George III. and Queen Charlotte visited her regularly every evening at eight o'clock. After one of these filial visits, in February 1772, when her health had been long declining, she expressed a hope that she might pass a good night. The hope was fulfilled, but death came in the morning. Never was woman more praised or censured than she. Her merit lay, perhaps, between both. Her son adored her, Queen Charlotte respected her, and a commercial country should reverence the memory of a woman who, out of her own jointure, paid off all the debts which her husband left at his decease. During the illness of the Dowager-Princess of Wales, her daughter, the Princess of Brunswick, arrived in England, on her mother's invitation. The Princess was coolly treated by her brother, George III., and by Queen Charlotte. She was ill lodged in a furnished house in Pall Mall, while the Prince of Mecklenburg had apartments in the royal palace. Charlotte was jealous of Augusta, her sister-in-law, and could not help showing it unbecomingly. At the Court held on the Queen's birthday Augusta was attended by Lady Gower, an old friend, and one of her former ladies-in-waiting. Lady Gower followed the Princess into the ball-room, and sat next to her—Lady Gower's friend, the Duchess of Argyle, courteously making way for her. The Queen was excessively angry. A few days later, all her ladies being present, Her Majesty said, crossly, to the Duchess of Argyle, ' Duchess, I must reprimand you for letting Lady Gower take place of you as lady to the Princess of Brunswick. I had a mind to speak to you on the spot, but would not, for fear of saying anything I should repent of, *though I should have thought it.* The Princess of Brunswick has nothing to do here, and I insist on your recovering the precedence you gave up. One day or other my son will be married, and then I shall have his wife's ladies pretending to take place in my palace, which they shall not do.' The Princess of Brunswick left England in a naturally angry mood. The King, reluctantly and tardily, paid both her journeys, and gave her 1,000*l.* besides. Her mother left her nothing.

The death of a woman of less note caused some conversation in Queen Charlotte's circle, soon after the demise of the Princess-dowager of Wales, and it may be fittingly noticed here.

Petronilla Melusina was the illegitimate daughter of George I. and Mdlle. von der Schulenburg (Duchess of Kendal). It was the discovery of her birth (in 1693) that stirred Sophia Dorothea to the resolution to leave Hanover. Petronilla came to England, passed as her mother's niece, and was created Countess of Walsingham. She became acquainted in this country with Lady Huntingdon, and that good, active, eccentric, but earnest apostle of the Gospel, Whitfield. With the latter Petronilla maintained a long correspondence, and she is spoken of as being a gem in the crown which metaphor placed upon the preacher's brow.

In 1733, this lady married the Earl of Chesterfield, and in her name her husband is said to have compelled George II. to pay him a very large sum, which also, according to report, was bequeathed her by George I. in the will which was destroyed. She led as gay and careless a life as her lord, but not for so long a period as he. She was in the very height of her enjoyment of the splendour of the great world, when, attracted by curiosity to the obscurely lighted drawing-room of Lady Huntingdon, where Whitfield was preaching, she learned, for the first time, to heed as well as hear the story of the brighter splendour of a greater, and the night and anguish of a more terrible, world than the one in which she was the chief lady of the revels, and the fascinator, not to be resisted, of every man in it except her husband. It was here she first felt that all was not so well with her heart, nor so safe for her soul, as should be. She was a woman of strong mind, and she at once braved all the storm with which fools and fine gentlemen pelted her, by boldly declaring the difference which had come over her views, and that which should in future mark her practice. She would fain have retired altogether from the world, but in obedience to her husband, who exacted from her a service which he never repaid, she went occasionally to court. At each visit it was remarked that her costume diminished in finery, but increased in taste. At her last visit among the gay and panting throng she appeared in a plain but elegant dress of sober brown brocade, 'powdered with silver flowers.' A smile may mock this humility of a court lady, but the costly and continental simplicity was encountered by her half-brother the King (for it was in George II.'s time that this occurred) with a frown. He had not yet learned to honour pious men or women of any creed, and he had little respect for Lady Huntingdon or Whitfield. He accordingly made two or three steps in advance to the shrinking lady, and rather rudely remarked, 'I know who selected that gown for you; it must have been Mr. Whitfield. I hear you have been a follower of his for this year and a half.' Lady Chesterfield mildly replied, 'I have, and very well do I like him,' and withdrew; but she afterwards used to regret that she had not said more when she had so excellent an opportunity for uttering a word in season with effect.

Lady Huntingdon hoped, for some time, that a sense of religion might soon touch the heart of the Earl, who continued to be polite and impious to the last. He laughingly called death a leap in the dark, and he obstinately refused the light which would have saved him from leaping to his destruction. The nearest approach he ever made to being converted by Lady Huntingdon was when he once sent her a subscription towards building a chapel, and earnestly implored her not to expose him to ridicule by revealing the fact!

His noble wife—for she *was* a wife—true woman, rising above the shame of her birth, and resolute to save even him who was resolute and resigned to perish, was most assiduous at the death-bed of a husband who was as anxious as Charles II. to be courteous and civil, even in death. His last day on earth was the 24th of March, 1773; and his courtesy had well-nigh failed him when he heard that his wife had sent for Mr. Rowland Hill to attend him. 'Dear Lady Chesterfield,' says Lady Huntingdon, in one of her letters detailing 'the blackness of darkness' which had thickened round his dying moments, 'Dear Lady Chesterfield could not be persuaded to leave his room for an instant. What unmitigated anguish has she endured! But her confidential communications I am not at liberty to disclose. The curtain has fallen; his immortal part has passed to another state of existence. Oh, my soul, come not thou unto *his* end!'

This wife, the illegitimate daughter of George I., was not even mentioned incidentally in a will which recognised the services of menials, and rewarded them with ostentation. But after Chesterfield's death the mansion in May Fair, and its great room, and its dark, mysterious boudoirs, curtained with blue and silver tissue, and slightly echoing the rustle of silks that were not worn by the wife of the lord of the house—over all these there came a change. The stage remained, but the actors and audiences were different, and now we see that once little girl who usurped in Hanover a love to which she was not legitimately entitled, a sober woman grown, throwing open her saloons to Rowland Hill and the eager multitude who thronged to hear that hearty, honest, and uncompromising man. In March 1777, Horace Walpole wrote: 'Lady Chesterfield has had a stroke of palsy, but may linger some time longer.' In September of the following year, the record is: 'Lady Chesterfield is dead, at above fourscore. She was not a girl when she came over with George I.' 'She was very like him,' Walpole writes, in the following month to Cole, 'as her brother, General Schulenburg, is, in black, to the late King.'

Such was the end of that lady whose birth in 1693 had so severely wounded the pride and self-dignity of Sophia Dorothea. 'I was with her to the last,' says Lady Huntingdon, 'and never saw a soul more humbled in the dust before God, on account of her own vileness and nothingness, but having a sure and steadfast hope of the love and mercy of God in Christ, constantly affirming that his blood cleanseth from all sin. The last audible expressions which fell from her a few moments before her final struggle were, " Oh, my friend, I have hope, a strong hope—through grace." Then, taking my hand, and clasping it earnestly between hers, she exclaimed with much energy, " God be merciful to me, a sinner ! " '

Between the period of the birth of the last child of Queen Charlotte and the date last named Her Majesty had presented other claimants upon the love and liberality of the people. These were Augustus (Sussex), born in 1773; Adolphus (Cambridge), in 1774; Mary, in 1776; and Sophia, in 1777. Walpole compares a Mrs. Fitzroy with the Queen. ' Mrs. Fitzroy,' he writes, ' has got a seventh boy. Between her and the Queen, London will be like the senate of old Rome, an assembly of princes. In a few generations there will be no joke in saying, " *Their Highnesses the Mob.*" ' Meanwhile a Queen, thus constantly occupied, performed all household and matronly duties in a way that won respect even from those who detected in her faults of temper or errors in politics. Of her method and success in training some of her children we have this evidence. The King took frequent excursions, while the Queen kept house at home. Of one of these, a visit to the fleet at Portsmouth, Walpole writes: ' All England is gone to meet King George at Portsmouth. The Duchess of Northumberland gives forty guineas for a bed, and must take her chambermaid into it. I did not think she would pay so dear for such company. His Majesty, because the post-chaises of gods are as immortal as their persons, would not suffer a second chaise to be sent for him; and therefore, if his could and did break down, he would enter Portsmouth in triumph in a hack.'

When the youngest of the daughters of Her Majesty was about six years old, the well-known Jacob Bryant heard the Queen make a remark to the child which he (the author of the 'Treatise on the Authenticity of the Scriptures and Truth of the Christian Religion') considered and cited as high authority for a mode of reasoning which he adopted when speaking of the obstacles that encumber the way even of the seekers after truth. He is alluding to those who are discouraged because the truth they would fain seize is not yet obvious to them; and he bids them wait with patience and not be discouraged. 'I have high authority,' he says, 'for this mode of reasoning, which I hope I may take the liberty to produce. When a great personage some years ago was visiting the royal nursery, a most amiable princess (the Princess Mary, afterwards Duchess of Gloucester), then about six years old, ran with a book in her hand, and tears in her eyes, and said, "Madam, I cannot comprehend it! I cannot comprehend it!" Her Majesty, with true parental affection, looked upon the princess, and bade her not to be alarmed. "What you cannot comprehend to-day, you may comprehend to-morrow; and what you cannot attain to this year, you may arrive at the next. Do not therefore be frightened with little difficulties, but attend to what you do know, and the rest will come in time."' This was good common sense, and Mr. Bryant calls it 'a golden rule, well worthy our observation.' Charlotte, too, could say a witty as well as a wise thing. The year 1775 was unmarked by the birth of an heir or heiress in Brunswick's line. The Queen's own birthday drawing-room was all the more brilliant. 'The crowd,' says Walpole, 'was excessive, and had squeezed, and shoved, and pressed upon the Queen in the most hoyden manner. As she went out of the drawing-room, somebody said, in flattery, that "the crowd was very great." "Yes," said the Queen, "and wherever one went, the Queen was in everybody's way."'

Her Majesty displayed even more readiness in

patronising such men as the author above named than she did in the patronage of musicians, fond as she and her royal consort were of the really tuneful art. In old days the honour of British queens was said to be most safe when it had a bard for its attendant protector. At a comparatively early period the Queen furnished the grateful Prince of Wales with a chaplain, whose chief duty was comprised in daily reading prayers in the young prince's presence, and, if we may judge by the result, not very much to the young prince's profit. Among those who were candidates for the office was the too celebrated Dr. Dodd; but though the Queen was in some degree interested in him, on account of his reported ability, she united heartily with the King in refusing to nominate him to the responsible duty. The elder princes were, as early as 1773, located at Carlton House, under the guardianship of Lady Charlotte Finch, almost daily superintended by the Queen. The latter was, however, always glad to escape from town to Kew, which had come into the King's possession on the death of his mother, and for which the residence at Old Richmond had been abandoned. It was at Kew that she received Beattie, for whom she had procured a pension of 200*l.* a-year, right royal reward, for his indifferent work on the Immutability of Truth. The well-recompensed author was in too good a humour with the royal lady to see any fault in her. He even pronounced her English 'fair,' and herself as 'most agreeable.' The portraits of her, he thought, hardly rendered her justice, and the expression of her eye and of her smile was declared by him to be most engaging.

She was not so favourably considered by some of her own court. Thus, the wearers of the fashionable long feathers denounced her bad taste when the Queen issued her decree against their being worn at court. The decree, however, was not issued without great provocation, a dowager-duchess having appeared at a drawing-room with a head-dress of feathers a yard and a quarter in height. The sight was so ridiculous that Charlotte would, for a long time, neither tolerate them in others nor wear them herself. The maids of honour grumbled as heartily at this as they did at the rule of the Queen's household which did not provide them with supper. The fair ladies' remonstrance on this latter subject almost amounted to a mutiny. The affair was ended by compromise. Their salary was raised, and each maid received on her marriage a gift of 1,000*l.* from the Queen.

The latter frowned when the heavy bargain was concluded, but she changed the frown for a smile on being told that the Prince of Wales had corrected Lord Bruce for making a false quantity. Next to his being a gentleman she hoped he would be a scholar, and here was a prospect of her hopes being realised!

As a sample of the Queen's benevolence we may cite the following record. In the action off Brest, in which the adversaries fought with a valour which did honour to both parties and enhanced the glory of the victors, there was no ship more distinguished in the fray than the gallant but luckless *Quebec*. This vessel blew up in the action, and out of her numerous crew only seventeen persons escaped. Among the latter was a master's mate, named William Moore, afterwards Captain Moore. He was desperately wounded in the shoulder and leg, and he conceived little hopes of ever being, like the old commodore in the song, fit for sea again. Meanwhile, however, he had a friend at court, in the person of a kinsman named Ashburner, who was mercer to the Queen. The kind-hearted tradesman was exhibiting his wares to Her Majesty, when amid his commendations of them he contrived to introduce his cousin's name and condition, with some commiserating comment upon his hard fate. The Queen was extremely judicious in her acts of charity, and she simply told the mercer to send the master's mate down to Windsor, if he were well enough to bear the journey. The very command was sovereign spermaceti to his wounds, and in a day or two the sadly battered sailor was comfortably lodged at Windsor, the patient of the Queen's own surgeon and physician. He took some time to cure, but the desired result was achieved at last, and the master's mate now stood in presence of the Queen to thank her, which the pale sailor did with faltering expression of gratitude, for the royal benevolence which had again made a man of him. To a query from the royal lady, he protested that he felt perfectly equal for the performance of duty again. 'So I hear from the doctor,' said Queen Charlotte. 'And I have spoken about you to the King, and there, Mr. Moore, is His Majesty's acknowledgments for your gallantry and sufferings when afloat.' Mr. Moore thought the Queen and King an exceedingly civil couple to say so much about the performance of a matter of duty, and he was about to retire from the presence, when the Queen said, smilingly, 'Mr. Moore, will not you see what His Majesty says?' The master's mate obeyed, and was rewarded for his obedience by finding that he had been promoted to a lieutenancy on board the *Mercury*. This was a good deed gracefully enacted. Not less so was another of which the Queen was the author, whereby she procured for the widow and large family of Captain Farmer, who fell in the *Quebec*, an annuity which made really princely provision for the widow and children of the slain commander.

The poets of 1779 were not addicted to satire, except in jest. Thus one, in a rhymed dialogue, makes one of his interlocutors say to the other—

I own your satire's just and keen;
Proceed, and satirise the Queen.

To which the reply is—

With all my heart.—The Queen, they say,
Attends her nurs'ry every day;
And, like a common mother, shares
In all her infants' little cares.
What vulgar, unamusing scene,
For George's wife and Britain's queen.
'Tis whispered also at the palace
(I hope 'tis but the voice of malice)
That (tell it not in foreign lands)
She works with her own royal hands;
And that our sovereign's sometimes seen
In vest embroidered by his queen.
This might a courtly fashion be
In days of old Andromache;
But modern ladies, trust my words,
Seldom sew tunics for their lords.
What secret next must I unfold?
She hates, I'm confidently told—
She hates the manners of the times
And all our fashionable crimes,
And fondly wishes to restore
The golden age, and days of yore,
When silly, simple women thought
A breach of chastity a fault,
Esteem'd those modest things, divorces,
The very worst of human curses;
And deem'd assemblies, cards, and dice
The springs of every sort of vice.
Romantic notions! all the fair
At such absurdities must stare;
And, spite of all her pains, will still
Love routs, adultery, and quadrille.

Well, is that all you find to blame,
Sir Critic, in the royal dame?

All I could find to blame? no, truly!
The longest day in June and July
Would fail me ere I could express
The half of Charlotte's blemishes.
Those foolish and old-fashioned ways
Of keeping holy Sabbath days,

That affectation to appear
At church, the Word of God to hear:
That poor-like plainness in her dress,
So void of noble tawdriness:
That affability and ease
That can her menial servants please,
But which incredibly demean
The state and grandeur of a queen:
These, and a thousand things beside,
I could discover and deride.
But here's enough; another day
I may, perhaps, renew my lay.
Are you content?

        Not quite, unless
You put your satire to the press.
For sure a satire in this mode
Is equal to a birthday ode.

No doubt of it! and much better written and applied than any of the birthday odes of the period. The fact was, that if there were strong prejudices, there were also simple virtues at court. The King would have no ode sung to him, as his predecessors had, on New Year's day; and the Queen would not allow Twelfth Night to be celebrated by the usually ruinous play at 'hazard.' No wonder the poets praised her.

The King loved Kew, and hated Hampton Court because George II. had once struck him there. Of the royal domestic life at the former place a contemporary observer has given a sketch, when the royal parents were still young and their offspring still children:—

'Their Majesties rise at 6 o'clock in the morning, and enjoy the two succeeding hours in a manner which they call their own. At 8 o'clock the Prince of Wales, the Bishop of Osnaburg, the Princess Royal, and the Princes William and Edward are brought from their respective apartments to breakfast with their illustrious parents. At 9 o'clock the younger children attend to lisp or smile their good-morrows; and while the five eldest are closely applying to their tasks, the little ones and their nurses pass the whole morning in Richmond Gardens. The King and Queen frequently amuse themselves with sitting in the room while the children dine, and once a week, attended by the whole offspring in pairs, make the little delightful tour of Richmond Gardens. In the afternoon, while the Queen works, the King reads to her. In the evening all the children again pay their duty at Kew House before they retire to bed, and the same order is observed through each returning day. Exercise, air, and light diet are the grand fundamentals in the King's idea of health. His Majesty feeds chiefly on vegetables, and drinks but little wine. The Queen is what many private gentlewomen would call whimsically abstemious; for, at a table covered with dishes, she prefers the plainest and simplest dish, and seldom eats of more than two things at a meal. Her wardrobe is changed every three months; and while the nobility are eager to supply themselves with foreign trifles, her care is that nothing but what is English shall be provided for her wear.'

CHAPTER V.

PERILS, PROGRESS, AND PASTIMES.

The American War—Dr. Dodd—The Duchess of Queensberry and the 'Beggars' Opera'—Royal Progress—Royal Visit to Bulstrode—Mrs. Delany and Queen Charlotte—Birth of Prince Octavius—Strange, the Engraver—The Riots of London—Lady Sarah Lennox—The Prince and his Sire—The Prince's Preceptors—Errors committed in the education of the Princes—The Prince's favourite, Perdita Robinson—Marie Antoinette's present to her—Separate establishment granted to the Prince—Lord North's facetious remark—Parliamentary provision for the Prince—The Prince's presence in the House of Commons not acceptable—His pursuit of pleasure—The Duke of Clarence described by Walpole—The Prince of Wales overwhelmed with debts—Dissension in the Royal Family—Marriage proposed to him to extricate him from his debts—The Prince's connection with Mrs. Fitzherbert—The Prince's Marriage disclaimed by Mr. Fox—The Prince's behaviour to Mrs. Fitzherbert—The Prince acknowledges his Marriage to the Queen.

THERE had been, during the recent years of Charlotte's married life, no lack of either private or public trials and misfortunes. The struggles of the government at home against the press had signally failed ; and that against the American colonies, wherein France, Spain, and Holland were arrayed against England, ended in the acknowledgment, on our part, of the independence of the United States. The unpopularity of the King, who applied for and received 100,000*l.* per annum in addition to the 400,000*l.* granted to him at his accession, was extended to the Queen. The King was insulted by a female, said to be insane, as he was proceeding in his chair to the Haymarket Theatre. This circumstance rendered the Queen ill at ease for several days. Her sympathy could at no time, however, induce the King to grant her a favour, if he thought it was against his sense of right. Thus, few persons more interested themselves to rescue the Reverend Dr. Dodd, the forger, from the hands of the executioner, than Queen Charlotte. Her respect for the sacred office was so great that it seemed to be something shocking that a clergyman should be hanged. But George III. remarked that Dodd's offence was rendered the more grievous from the fact of his being a clergyman, and that the law must take its course.

During the year 1778 many royal 'progresses' were made to the fleet, to the fortified towns on the coast, to the various camps, and to the mansions of the nobility. A general air of festivity was exhibited about the Queen and court, but there was nothing in the condition of the affairs of the kingdom to warrant the apparent joy. By sea and land our flag, though not dishonoured, was not triumphant; and for the moment the most unpopular man in the kingdom was the King himself—obstinate in his determination to govern as well as reign, and daily verging towards that disturbed state of mind which ended at last in hopeless insanity.

Meanwhile, however, the home enjoyments of the court were placid and unexciting. In her 'progresses' with the King, Charlotte was not reluctant to maintain the state of a Queen. Her ideas on this subject seem strange to us now. Thus, when she held a court in the old royal city of Winchester, her costume consisted of a scarlet riding-habit, faced with blue, and covered with rich gold embroidery. In the same dress, with the addition of a black hat and a large cockade, she accompanied the King on his visits to the various camps established in the south. Nothing, however, could be more simple than the way of life of this royal pair when really 'at home.' Its simplicity extracted from a foreigner who witnessed it the remark that such citizen-like plainness was injurious to royalty, and an encouragement to republicanism.

Adopting as far as possible the descriptions of eye-witnesses of scenes in which the sovereigns enacted the principal part, we will now turn to the gossiping Mrs. Delany's letters for the report of a visit made in 1779 by the Queen and her royal consort and family to the Duke of Portland's, at Bulstrode. 'The royal family,' says the writer, 'ten in all, came to Bulstrode at twelve o'clock. The King drove the Queen in an open chaise, with a pair of white horses. The Prince of Wales and Prince Frederick rode on horseback; all with proper attendants, but no guards. Princess Royal and Lady Weymouth in a post-chaise. Princess Augusta, Princess Elizabeth, Prince Adolphus (about seven years old), and Lady Charlotte Finch, in a coach. Prince William, Prince Edward, Duke of Montague, and the Bishop of Lichfield, in a coach; another coach full of attendant gentlemen; among others, Mr. Smelt, whose character sets him above most men and does great honour to the King, who calls him his friend, and has drawn him out of his solitude (the life he had chosen), to enjoy his conversation every leisure moment. These, with all their attendants in rank and file, made a splendid figure as they drove through the park and round the court, up to the house. The day was as brilliant as could be wished, the 12th of August, the Prince of Wales's birthday. The Queen was in a hat, and in an Italian night-gown of purple lustring, trimmed with silver gauze. She is graceful and genteel. The dignity and sweetness of her manner, the perfect propriety of everything she says or does, satisfies everybody she honours with her instructions so much that beauty is by no means wanting to make her perfectly agreeable; and though awe and long retirement from court made me feel timid on my being called to make my appearance, I soon found myself perfectly at ease; for the King's conversation and good humour took off all awe but what one must have for so respectable a character, severely tried by his enemies at home as well as abroad. The three princesses were all in frocks. The King and all the men were in uniform, blue and gold. They walked through the great apartments, which are in a line, and attentively observed everything, the pictures in particular. I kept back in the drawing-room, and took that opportunity of sitting down, when the Princess Royal returned to me and said the Queen missed me in the train. I immediately obeyed the summons with my best alacrity. Her Majesty met me half-way, and seeing me hasten my steps, called out to me, " Though I desired you to come, I did not desire you to run and fatigue yourself." They all returned to the great drawing-room, where there were only two arm-chairs, placed in the middle of the room for the King and Queen. The King placed the Duchess Dowager of Portland in his chair, and walked about, admiring the beauties of the place. Breakfast was offered, all prepared in a long gallery that runs the length of the great apartments (a suite of eight rooms and three closets). The King and all his royal children and the rest of the train chose to go to the gallery, where the well-furnished tables were set, one with tea, coffee, and chocolate, another with their proper accompaniments of eatables, rolls, cakes, &c. Another table with fruits and ices in their utmost perfection, which with a magical touch had succeeded a cold repast. The Queen remained in the drawing-room. I stood at the back of her chair, which, happening to be one of my working, gave the Queen an opportunity to say many obliging things. The Duchess Dowager of Portland brought Her Majesty a dish of tea on a waiter, with biscuits, which was what she chose. After she had drunk her tea, she would not return her cup to the Duchess, but got up and would carry it to the gallery herself; and was much pleased to see with what elegance everything was prepared. No servants but those out of livery made their appearance. The gay and pleasant appearance they all made, and the satisfaction all expressed, rewarded the attention and politeness of the Duchess of Portland, who is never so happy as when she gratifies those she esteems worthy of her attentions and favours. The young royals seemed quite happy, from the eldest to the youngest, and to inherit the gracious manners of their parents. I cannot enter upon their particular address to me, which not only did me honour, but showed their humane and benevolent respect for old age. The King desired me to show the Queen one of my books of plants. She seated herself in the gallery, a table and a book laid before her. I kept my distance till she called me to ask some questions about the mosaic paper work; and as I stood before Her Majesty, the King set a chair behind me. I turned with some confusion and hesitation on receiving so great an honour, when the Queen said, "Mrs. Delany, sit down, sit down; it is not every lady that has a chair brought her by a King." So I obeyed. Amongst many gracious things, the Queen asked me why I was not with the Duchess when she came, for I might be sure she would ask for me. I was flattered, though I knew to whom I was obliged for this distinction, and doubly flattered by that. I acknowledged it in as few words as possible, and said I was particularly happy at that moment to pay my duty to Her Majesty, as it gave me an opportunity to see so many of the royal family, which age and obscurity had deprived me of. "Oh, but," said Her Majesty, "you have not seen all my children yet." Upon which the King came up and asked what we were talking about, which was repeated, and the King replied to the Queen, "You may put Mrs. Delany in the way of doing that by naming a day for her to drink tea at Windsor Castle." The Duchess of Portland was consulted, and the next day fixed upon, as the Duchess had appointed the end of the week for going to Weymouth.'

In 1779 was born the short-lived Prince Octavius. Before the death of this happy little Prince, Strange, the engraver, consented to engrave his portrait. The Queen did not like the politics of the artist, for he was the most determined Jacobite in the kingdom—except his wife. He was so successful, however, with his 'plate' of Octavius, that George III. knighted him; and even his wife thought the better of the 'Elector and Electress of Hanover' for having made her what 'the King over the water' had never thought of doing—Lady Strange.

The following year was that of the riots of London. While that popular tumult was raging the King behaved with courage and common sense; and the Queen, left almost entirely alone at Buckingham House with her children, with equal calmness and intrepidity. The 'ladies' who *ought* to have been in attendance had hurried homeward with their jewels. The Queen did not lose heart at this desertion, but was amply comforted by the frequent yet brief visits of the King, who spent two entire nights, holding council with the heads of the army, in the Queen's Riding House.

In the September of this year another prince, Alfred —who shared with his brother Octavius the advantages of dying early—was added to the family of George and Charlotte. This increase, perhaps, inspired her with increase of sympathy for others. In the fall of this year she very warmly seconded the project of Mr. Raikes for the foundation of Sunday Schools. The project was sneered at, snubbed, and satirised by a public who, however, were ultimately wise enough to be grateful.

In 1780, Walpole affords us a glimpse of the alleged rival of Queen Charlotte in company with the Queen's son. 'The Prince of Wales has lately made a visit to Lady Cecilia Johnstone, where Lady Sarah Napier was.' She was the Lady Sarah Lennox who had touched the heart of the King some twenty years before. 'She did not appear, but he insisted on seeing her, and said, "She was to have been there," pointing to Windsor Castle. When she came down he said he did not wonder at his father's admiring her, and was persuaded she had not been more beautiful then.'

In 1781, at the age of nineteen, the Prince of Wales became 'lord of himself.' His mother had been his first governess; and at eight years of age he had been delivered by his father to Dr. Markham and Cyril Jackson, with the injunction to treat him as they would any private gentleman's son, and to flog him whenever he deserved it. Markham acted up to his instructions. The Prince never bore any ill-will to either preceptor or sub-preceptor for their severity; but he took the earliest opportunity of showing his antagonism against his father. In 1772, when the struggle was going on between Wilkes and the crown—for such were the real adversaries— the young Prince made his sire's ears tingle indignantly with the popular cry of 'Wilkes and "forty-five" for ever!'

The young Prince's preceptors were changed in 1776. Lord Bruce became governor in place of Lord Holdernesse; but he retired almost immediately, vexed, it is said, at the Prince having detected him in the commission of a false quantity. Bishop Hurd and the Rev. Mr. Arnold, under the superintendence of the oatmeal-porridge-loving Duke of Montague, were now entrusted to

impart what instruction they might to the Prince and his
next brother Frederick. They adopted the old plan of
severity; but on endeavouring to carry it into effect,
when the high-spirited boys were considerably advanced
in their teens, one or both of the royal pupils turned on
their preceptor, Arnold, who was about most grossly to
castigate them, tore the weapon from his hand, and
roughly administered to him the punishment with which
they themselves had been threatened.

Excess of restraint marred the education of the two
elder sons of Charlotte. Even when the Prince was considered of age, and was allowed his own establishment at
Kew, the system of seclusion was still maintained. Such
a system had its natural consequences. The Prince, ill at
ease with his parents, sought sympathy elsewhere; and
he was not yet out of his teens when Charlotte was
horrified at hearing his name coupled with that of the
most bewitching actress of the day.

Had the father of Miss Darby, the maiden name of
Mrs. Robinson, been a man of less philanthropic principles, his daughter, probably, would have been a more
virtuous and a more happy woman. She was born at
Bristol in 1758, and was looked upon as a little heiress,
till her father lost the whole of a not inconsiderable
fortune by speculating in an attempt to civilise the Esqui-
maux Indians!

Miss Darby was, for some time, a pupil of Miss
Hannah More; but was herself compelled to turn instructress as early as in her fourteenth year. She was,
however, a precocious beauty; and the year previous she
had received an offer of marriage, which she had declined. The young teacher worked hard and cheerfully,
in order that she might be the better enabled to support
her mother. The proceeds of this labour also enabled
her to increase the number of her own accomplishments;

among others, dancing. Her master was a Covent Garden ballet-master, who introduced her to Garrick, and Roscius brought her out on the stage, in the character of Cordelia with success.

Before she had terminated her sixteenth year she married Mr. Robinson, an articled clerk in an attorney's office, with a good fortune, upon which the youthful couple lived in splendour till it was gone, and the husband was arrested. His wife then spent fifteen months with him in prison, and then misery drove her again to Garrick, who gave her some instruction, rehearsed Romeo to her Juliet, and, bringing her out in the latter character, gave to the stage one of the handsomest and youngest and most captivating of actresses who had ever charmed the town.

Her Juliet was admirable, but her Perdita, in the 'Winter's Tale,' set the town mad. On the 3rd of December 1779 she played the character in presence of George III., Queen Charlotte, the Prince of Wales, and other members of the royal family, and a numerous audience. When she entered the green-room, dressed for the part, she looked so bewitching that Smith exclaimed, 'By Jove! you will make a conquest of the Prince, for you look handsomer than ever.' Smith's prediction was true; and letters from the Prince, signed 'Florizel,' were delivered to Perdita by no less noble a go-between than the Earl of Essex.

The position of Perdita Robinson at this time was peculiar: her husband was living in profligacy upon the wages of her labour, and she had refused the most brilliant offers made to her on condition of separating from him. She refused them all; but lent too ready an ear to the princely suitor, who now besieged her with indifferently-written letters and promises of never-dying affection. An interview was contrived, first in a boat moored off Kew, and afterwards in Kew Gardens by moonlight, at which the Bishop of Osnaburgh was present —by way of playing propriety, perhaps—and at which there appears to have been little said, but much feared, lest the parties should be found out.

The prince and Perdita became so attached to each other after a few more interviews that *she* declared she should never forget the magic with which she was wooed, and *he* presented her with a bond for 20,000*l.*, to be paid on his coming of age. When that period arrived—it happened in a few months—'Florizel' would not pay the money, and had grown weary of the lady. To modify her despair, he granted a last interview, in which he declared that his affection for her was as great as ever; and the poor lady, who trusted in the declaration, was passed by on the following day, in the park, without a sign of recognition on the part of her princely betrayer. The remark which she made on this conduct was worthy of Talleyrand for its sting, smartness, and application—but it is as well, perhaps, to leave it unquoted.

She had quitted the stage to please him, and now, in her embarrassment, sought refuge abroad, living in straitened circumstances in Paris, till, by the intervention of Mr. Fox, an annuity was settled upon her of 500*l.* a-year. With this she maintained some splendour, and she was even noticed by Marie Antoinette as *La belle Anglaise.* The gift of a purse netted by the royal hand of that unfortunate Queen, and conferred by her on Perdita, showed at once the sovereign lady's admiration and lack of judgment and propriety.

For some time she resided alternately in England and France, but ultimately she settled at Brighton, about the time that Mrs. Fitzherbert was there in the brightest of her beauty and the height of her splendour. The ex-actress wrote pretty poetry, and was the authoress of a dozen novels: poetry and romances are now forgotten; but the former does not want for tenderness of sentiment and expression, nor the latter for power and good sense. Finally, in 1799, she undertook the poetical department of the *Morning Post*, retained her office for a few months, and died in the year 1800.

Perdita was not without her grievous faults; but she had her virtues, too. She was the loving and helping child of her mother, and she was the loving and helping mother of her child. For her mother and her daughter she worked at her literary occupations with unwearied fervour, and even Hannah More may have refrained from casting reproach on her erring and yet not worthless pupil.

In 1783 the Prince of Wales had allotted to him a separate establishment. He could have none more appropriate than that old Carlton House which had been the residence of his grandfather, Frederick Prince of Wales— a man whom he resembled in many respects. The old house was originally built on a part of the royal garden around St. James's Palace, a lease whereof was granted for that purpose by Queen Anne to Henry Boyle, Lord Carlton. This was in 1709. Sixteen years subsequently, on the death of Lord Carlton, the house was occupied by his heir and nephew, Richard Boyle (Lord Burlington, the architect), who seven years later (1732) gave it to his mother, the Dowager Lady Burlington, by whom, in the same year, it was made over to Frederick Prince of Wales, father of George III. The gardens, laid out by Kent, like Pope's grounds at Twickenham, extended westward as far as Marlborough House. The first change that Frederick made was to construct a bowling-green, the healthy exercise of bowls being then fashionable; and he inaugurated his entry by a grand ball, given, as the *Daily Post* says, 'to several persons of quality and distinction of both sexes.'

George Prince of Wales found the old house rather antiquated as to fashion and dilapidated as to condition, and he employed Holland, the architect, to correct these defects. The artist did that, and more. He added the Ionic screen, some of the pillars of which are now in Queen Charlotte's favourite gardens at Kew, and the Corinthian portico, the columns of which, when the house was taken down in 1827, were transferred to the National Gallery. On the two residences of the two eldest sons of Queen Charlotte, Southey, in his 'Espriella's Letters,' has a remark worth quoting. The Duke of York's mansion (Melbourne House, Whitehall), now known as Dover House, was distinguished by a circular court, which served as a sort of entrance-hall. It still remains, and may be seen from the street. The distinguishing feature of Carlton House was the row of pillars in front. 'These two buildings being described to the late Lord North, who was blind in the latter part of his life, he facetiously remarked, "Then the Duke of York, it should seem, has been sent to the round-house, and the Prince of Wales is put in the pillory."'

Meanwhile, despite the Prince's escapades, the least innocent of which was his visiting a Quaker's meeting disguised as a female Friend—where he was betrayed by the appearance of his leather breeches, seen through the pocket-hole of the gown—despite these and other escapades, the Queen's affection for her son was in no wise diminished. In 1782 she had brought tambouring into fashion by embroidering for him, with her own hands, a waistcoat, which he wore at the first ball at which his sister, the princess royal, appeared in public. The Queen, however, had more serious subjects for her consideration. She had to mourn over the death of the infant Alfred, and for the loss of a sister. We find also, this year, the first direct proof of her having interfered in politics. It was in 1782 that Charlotte commissioned Hutten, the Moravian, to enter into correspondence with Franklin, with a view of conciliating matters with the United States.

The eldest son of Queen Charlotte began life very amply provided for; Parliament gave him 100,000*l*. as an outfit, and 50,000*l*. annually by way of income. Three months after the birth of his youngest sister, Amelia, in November 1783, he took his seat in the House of Peers, joined the opposition, gave himself up to the leading of the opposition chiefs, whether in politics or vices, was praised by the people for his spirit, and estranged from the King, who did not like the principles of those who called themselves his son's friends, and who held in horror the vices and follies for which they were distinguished. He was as often present under the gallery of the Commons as in his seat in the Lords. Such a presence is never acceptable, in such a place, to the representatives of the people. It perhaps influences the votes, and certainly affects the liberty of debate. As much was hinted to the Prince, when he used to watch the struggle in the Commons between the Coalition and Pitt. He made the hint his excuse for being disgusted with politics, and thereupon devoted himself to but one pursuit—the love of pleasure. But if he had only one pursuit, it had many varieties and objects. He hunted after what was called ' pleasure' in every form, squandered fortunes in not finding it, and made what he called ' love ' and extraordinary presents to two ladies at one and the same time. Mrs. Crouch, the actress, and Mrs. Fitzherbert (whom he married), were the Lucy and Polly to whom this light-of-heart prince gaily sang his ' How happy could I be with either ! '

Walpole speaks very highly (in 1783) of the Prince's brother, William Henry, whom he met at Gunnersbury, the suburban seat of the old Princess Amelia. ' He had been with the Princess in the morning,' writes Walpole, 'and returned of his own accord to dinner. She presented me to him, and I attempted, at the risk of tumbling on my nose, to kiss his hand, but he would not let me. You may trust me, madam, who am not apt to be intoxicated with royalty, that he is charming. Lively, cheerful, talkative, manly, well-bred, sensible, and exceedingly proper in all his replies. You may judge how good-humoured he is, when I tell you that he was in great spirits all day, though with us old women; perhaps he thought it preferable to Windsor.'

The Prince of Wales was already overwhelmed with debt. The domestic comfort of the Queen was even more disturbed than that of her consort by the solicitations made by the so-called friends of the Prince of Wales to induce the King to pay the debts of his eldest son. Her Majesty's confidence is said to have been fully placed at this time upon Mr Pitt. A conversation is spoken of as having passed between the Queen and the minister, in which he is reported as having said, 'I much fear, your Majesty, that the Prince, in his wild moments, may allow expressions to escape him that may be injurious to the crown.' 'There is little fear of that,' was the alleged reply of the Queen; 'he is too well aware of the consequences of such a course of conduct to himself. As regards that point, therefore, I can rely upon him.' Mr. Pitt inquired if her Majesty was aware of the intimacy which then existed between Mrs. Fitzherbert and the heir-apparent, and that reports of an intended marriage were current? 'He is now so much embarrassed,' added the minister, 'that at the suggestion of his friend Sheridan he borrows large amounts from a Jew who resides in town, and gives his bonds for much larger amounts than he receives.'

In the family dissensions caused by this unhappy subject neither sire nor son behaved with fairness and candour. In 1784, the Prince had been required to send in an exact account of his debts, with a view to their liquidation. The King had, at least, intimated that he would discharge the Prince's liabilities if this account was rendered. The account *was* rendered; but, after having been kept for months, it was returned as not being exact. The inexactness of this statement consisted of an item of 25,000*l.* being entered without any explanation as to whom it was owing. The Prince refused to make such explanation, on the ground that it was a secret of honour between him and his noble creditor, in whom many persons affected to see the famous, or infamous, Duke of Orleans. The King declared that, if the Prince was ashamed to explain the nature of the debt, his father ought not to be expected to pay it; and there the matter rested.

By the following year his debts amounted to 160,000*l.*, and he could see no chance of relief but by going abroad. His first idea was of a residence in Holland, and he was ready to proceed thither as a private individual, should the King refuse to consent to his leaving England. All that he wished for, according to his own declarations, was to economise, to live in retirement, and remain unknown, until he could appear in a style suitable to his rank. He complained of the unreasonableness of the King's proposition, that he should lay by 10,000*l.* a-year to pay his debts, at a time, he said, when his expenses were twice as great as his income. Such complaint could only come from a radically dishonest man; for it is only such a man who, with an income on which he could very well afford to live—and spare—could complacently talk of even allowing his expenses to exceed his revenue.

The Prince affected to think that he might, perhaps, be able to live in retirement at some of the small German courts, fancying that, under the title of the Earl of Chester, his actions would not be judged of as those of a Prince of Wales. At all events, he declared that to live in England would be ruin and disgrace to him; for that the King hated him, wished to set him at variance with his brothers, and would not even let Parliament assist him till he should marry. The King's hatred for his son, according to the latter, had existed from the time he was seven years old. Reconciliation was deemed by the Prince impossible; for his father, he said, had not only deceived him, but made him deceive others. The son could not trust the father, and the father had no belief in the veracity of the son.

The ministry were not disinclined, at this time, to increase the Prince's allowance, provided only that he would appropriate some portion of it to the payment of his debts, renounce his project of going abroad, and consent to a reconciliation with the King, by ceasing to be a man of political party in opposition to the government. The sum proposed was 100,000*l.* per annum, the half of which was to be reserved for the payment of his debts. The Prince describes the offer as useless, inasmuch as that, though the ministry might sanction it, the King would not hear of it, and Pitt could not carry such a measure in Parliament. The Prince asserted his belief that so rooted was his father's hatred of him that he would turn out Pitt if he ventured to propose such a measure. Further, the Prince refused to abandon Fox and his other political friends. Lord Malmesbury was very anxious to bring the Prince to terms; but the latter still dwelt upon the bitter paternal hatred. In proof of this he exhibited to Lord Malmesbury copies of the correspondence which had passed between himself and his royal sire on the subject. Lord Malmesbury thus describes the letters, and the spirit which animated the writers:—

'The Prince's letters were full of respect and deference, written with great plainness of style and simplicity. Those of the King were also well written, but hard and severe; constantly refusing every request the Prince made, and reprobating in each of them his extravagance and dissipated manner of living. They were void of every expression of parental kindness or affection, and after both hearing them read and perusing them myself, I was compelled to subscribe to the Prince's opinion, and to confess there was very little appearance of making any impression upon His Majesty in favour of His Royal Highness.'

Lord Malmesbury suggested that, as the Queen must have much at heart the bringing about a reconciliation between her son and his father, such might surely be effected through her and his sisters. The Prince thought it impracticable, and only wished that the public knew all the truth and could judge between him and his sire, anticipating a favourable verdict for himself, which, however, the public would not have given even when in possession of all the facts.

Lord Malmesbury then suggested a means of escape from all difficulties by a marriage which would at once reconcile the King and gratify the nation. The Prince, however, emphatically declared that he would never marry; that he had settled that subject with his brother Frederick; and that his resolution was irrevocable. Lord Malmesbury combated such a resolution, but the Prince remained unconvinced. He owed nothing, he said, to the King. Frederick would marry, and his children would inherit the crown. His adviser suggested that a bachelor King, as he would be, would have less hold on the affections of the people than a married heir and father of children, as his brother would be. 'The Prince was greatly struck with this observation. He walked about the room apparently angry;' but, after a few friendly words of explanation, the interlocutors separated, and the scene was at an end.

At the time the Prince said he never would marry he had in his mind that serious marriage which he already had formed with Mrs. Fitzherbert. We may add, with respect to this union and the character of the Prince as a lover, a few words on the authority of Lord Holland.

Never did swain make love so absurdly as the Prince of Wales. For the 'first gentleman in Europe,' he was the greatest simpleton, under the influence of 'passion,' that ever existed. When he was not silly, he was mean, and he sometimes was both, and heartless to boot, even when he most prattled of the heart-anguish he endured. To Perdita Robinson he was little better than a mere bilking knave. In presence of the majestic Mrs. Fitzherbert he was an undignified coxcomb. He insulted her virtue with proposals which even princes ought not to dare to make without bringing personal chastisement upon themselves. Finding his offers declined, and that the lady was going abroad, he acted, and declared he felt, the utmost despair. But his despair was farcical. He went down to his friends the Foxes, at St. Anne's, where he 'cried by the hour, testified the sincerity and violence of his passion and despair by the most extravagant expressions and actions, rolling on the floor, striking his forehead, tearing his hair, falling into hysterics, and swearing he would abandon the country, forego the crown, sell his jewels and plate, and scrape together a competency, to fly with the object of his affections to America.'

The lady proceeded to the continent, but returned in 1785. She came more prepared to listen to the Prince's wooing than when she left. He now proposed a marriage, but she knew that, she being a Romanist, such a marriage could not be legal. Indeed, it was illegal for any prince of the blood to marry without the King's consent, before he had attained the age of twenty-five. After that time he was to notify his intention to Parliament, and if that body did not move the King to withhold his consent within a year, the marriage then might be entered upon. Mrs. Fitzherbert, however, frankly enough said that the ceremony would be all nonsense, and that she was ready to trust to his honour. He insisted, however, and the ceremony was duly performed by an English clergyman. After the solemnisation, the certificate was signed by the clergyman and attested by two witnesses, said to have been Catholics. Mrs. Fitzherbert retained the certificate; but out of a generous fear that harm might come to the witnesses if they should become known she tore off their names. The name of the clergyman (who died before George IV. ascended the throne) remains affixed to the document.

Mr. Fox was *not* present at this ceremony, but reports were so current as to its being about to take place, or to its having taken place, that he addressed to the Prince a very long, a very strong, and a very sensible letter, of which a rough copy (from Fox's MS.) will be found in Lord Holland's 'Memoirs of the Whig Party.' In this manly letter the writer points out the madness of such a scheme, the terrible consequences that might ensue, the illegality of the manner, and the possibility, should the Prince enter subsequently into a legal matrimonial union, and there being issue by both, of a disputed succession. He advised, argued, did all that a bold man and honest friend could do to warn the Prince against this union, which, as we before mentioned, was currently reported to have taken place. The Prince, in reply, declared that his 'dear Charles' might 'make himself easy, as there not only is, but never was, any grounds for such reports.' Armed with this authority, Fox denied in Parliament, on the warrant of the Prince, the assertion of such a union having taken place. The wretched liar who had driven him to assert unconsciously a falsehood was now exposed to a double torment. Mrs. Fitzherbert was angry at the public denial, supposing it to be unauthorised, and urged the Prince to have it announced. The latter prevaricated and promised; appealed to Grey, confessing his marriage, and, when Grey would have nothing to do with it, appealing to Sheridan; the latter made a few remarks in the House wide of the real object, and the marriage remained denied, to the great annoyance of the lady, who continued to be respectfully treated by the royal family. These, if they disbelieved the existence of the connection, must have looked upon Mrs. Fitzherbert as being less worthy of their respect than before. The truth, however, is, that their respect was chiefly manifested when Mrs. Fitzherbert separated herself from her most worthless husband. Documents proving the marriage (long in the possession of Mrs. Fitzherbert's family) have been, since June 1833, actually deposited, by agreement between the executors of George IV. (the Duke of Wellington and Sir William Knighton) and the nominees of Mrs. Fitzherbert (Lord Albemarle and Lord Stourton), at Coutts's bank, in a sealed box, bearing a superscription :—'The property of the Earl of Albemarle; but not to be opened by him without apprising the Duke of Wellington,' or words to that purport.[1]

The author of the Diary illustrative of the court of George IV., referring to the time when the eldest son of Queen Charlotte was subdued by the fascinations of Mrs. Fitzherbert, says that the lady in question 'had a stronger hold over the Regent than any of the other

[1] Lord Holland's 'Memoirs of the Whig Party.'

objects of his admiration, and that he always paid her the respect which her conduct commanded.' She was styled by those who knew her 'the most faultless and honourable mistress that ever a prince had the good fortune to be attached to'—a judgment which abounds in a confusion of terms, and exhibits mental perversion in him who pronounced it. Of the Regent's behaviour to the lady, it may be said that it was as gallant and considerate at first as it was mean and censurable at last. In the early days of their intimacy, when they appeared together at the same parties and were on the point of leaving them, 'the Prince never forgot to go through the form of saying to Mrs. F., with a most respectful bow, "Madam, may I be allowed the honour of seeing you home in my carriage?"' 'It was impossible,' says the same authority, 'to be in his Royal Highness's society and not be captivated by the extreme fascination of his manners, which he inherits from his mother the Queen; for his father has every virtue which can adorn a private character as well as make a king respectable, but he does not excel in courtly grace or refinement.'

It should be added, that the intelligence no sooner reached the ears of the Queen than she commanded the attendance of her son, and insisted on knowing the whole truth. The Prince is declared not only to have acknowledged the fact of the marriage, but to have asserted that no power on earth should separate him from his wife. He is reported to have added, in reference to the King's alleged marriage with Hannah Lightfoot, that his father would have been a happier man had he remained firm in standing by the legality of his own marriage. It would be difficult to say who was at hand to take down the Prince's speech on this occasion; but, according to the author last named, it was substantially as follows:—
'But I beg farther that my wife be received at court,

and proportionately as your Majesty receives her, and pays her attention from this time, so shall I render my attentions to your Majesty. The lady I have married is worthy of all homage, and my very confidential friends, with some of my wife's relations only, witnessed our marriage. Have you not always taught me to consider myself heir to the first sovereignty in the world? Where then will exist any risk of obtaining a ready concurrence from the House in my marriage? I hope, madam, a few hours' reflection will satisfy you that I have done my duty in following the impulse of my inclinations, and, therefore, I await your Majesty's commands, feeling assured you would not blast the happiness of your favourite prince.' The Queen is said to have been softened by his rather illogical reasoning. It is certain that her Majesty received Mrs. Fitzherbert at a drawing-room in the following year with very marked courtesy.

Sixteen years later, and of course long after the marriage of the Prince of Wales with Caroline of Brunswick, Mrs. Fitzherbert was still so high in the Prince's favour that we find the following record in Lord Malmesbury's Diary, under the date of May 25, 1803 :—' Duke of York came to me at five, uneasy lest the Duchess should be forced to sup at the same table as Mrs. Fitzherbert, at the ball to be given by the Knights of the Bath, on the 1st of June. Talks it over with me—says the King and Queen will not hear of it. On the other side, he wishes to keep on terms with the Prince. I say, I will see Lord Henley, who manages the *fête*, and try to manage it so that there shall be two distinct tables, one for the Prince, to which *he* is to invite, another for the Duke and Duchess, to which *she* is to invite her company.' The dislike of Mrs. Fitzherbert for the Duchess of York was as determined as that entertained by the same lady against Fox, whom she never forgave for denying the fact of her marriage with the Prince.

The Prince's pecuniary embarrassments pressed more heavily upon him than the troubles arising from his amours. The Prince, in his difficulties, again had recourse to the Queen. He revealed to her the amount of both his difficulties and debts, and reports credited him with having uttered a menace to the effect that, if the King failed to provide some means for the payment of those debts, there were State secrets which he would certainly reveal, whatever the consequences might be, as, suffering as he did from the treatment he met at his father's hands, he was an object of suspicion or contempt to half the kingdom. The Queen would not engage herself by any promise, but she sent for Mr. Pitt. After this last interview the minister repaired to Carlton House, and the message he bore showed the amount of influence possessed by the Queen. The Prince was assured that means would be found for the discharge of his liabilities. The King promised an additional 10,000*l.* a year out of the civil list, and Parliament subsequently voted the sum of 161,000*l.* to discharge the debts of the Prince, with an additional sum of 20,000*l.* to finish the repairs of Carlton Palace. That mansion had been dull and silent, but it was soon again brilliant, and gaily echoing with the most festive of sounds.

CHAPTER VI.

COURT FORMS AND COURT FREEDOMS.

Loss of the American Colonies—Political Struggle—The King's health unsatisfactory—Life of the Royal Family at Windsor—Mrs. Delany—The Queen and the Widow—Early service in the Chapel Royal at Windsor—Rev. Tom Twining and Miss Burney—Miss Burney's Reception by the Queen—Promenade of the Royal Family on the terrace—The Queen's 'dressing'—The Queen's partiality for Snuff—Country life of the Royal Family at Kew—Princess Amelia; the King's great affection for her—Scene on the birthday of the Princess—Margaret Nicholson's attempt to assassinate the King—The Queen's dread—Her fondness for Diamonds—Mrs. Warren Hastings—The present from the Nizam of the Deccan—Unpopularity of the King and Queen—Their affection for each other—The Queen's tenderness to Mrs. Delany—Reconciliation of the King and the Prince—A pleasant scene—Another Court Incident.

THE loss of the American Colonies, and the triumph of Lord North and Fox, two men whom the King hated, and who forced an Administration upon him, had, in various degrees, a serious effect upon his health. He became dejected, but when Fox's India Bill was thrown out by the Lords he had the firmness—a firmness suggested by the Queen—to turn the obnoxious Cabinet out. Pitt succeeded as prime minister, and no one saw him in that post with greater pleasure than Charlotte.

She continued to support both King and Minister through the tremendous political struggle which followed, and during which Pitt more than once expressed his determination to resign. 'In such case I must resign too,' said the King, adding that he would sooner retire with the Queen to Hanover than submit to a ministry whose political principles he detested. The public admired his firmness, and for a season he was again popular—popular, but not safe. His health was in an unsatisfactory state; and it was at a season when he required to be kept in a state of composure that an attempt was made to stab him by an insane woman named Nicholson, as he was leaving St. James's Palace by the garden entrance, on the 2nd of August, 1786. As he received a paper which she presented, the woman stabbed at him, but with no worse result than piercing his waistcoat.

Before we show how the news of this attempt was received at Windsor, where the Queen was then sojourning, we may glance briefly at the nature of the life passed there. It was generally of a pleasing aspect.

The benevolence of the Queen and her consort was well illustrated in their conduct to Mrs. Delany. The lady in question was a Granville by birth, and in the first flush of her youth and beauty had been married, against her inclination, to a middle-aged squire, named Pendarves, who was much like what middle-aged squires were in those not very refined days. Mr. and Mrs. Pendarves passed much such a life as that described by the young Widow Cheerly as having been that of herself and the squire, her lord; and the lady, too, became a widow almost as early. She was, however, of mature age when she married her old and esteemed acquaintance, Dr. Delany, the friend of Swift. After being a second time a widow, she found a home with the Dowager-duchess of Portland, and when death deprived her of this friend also she found a new home and new friends in Queen Charlotte and King George. They assigned to her a house in Windsor Park, in the fitting-up of which both Queen and King took great personal interest, and the former settled upon her an annuity of 300*l*. When the good old lady went down to take possession of her new habitation the King was there ready to receive her, like a son establishing a mother in a new home. His courtesy was felt, and it was of the right sort, for while it brought him there to welcome the new guest, it would not allow him to stay there to embarrass her. With similar delicacy, when the Queen came down to visit her new neighbour, she put her at once at her ease by her own affability; and when, before leaving, she placed in Mrs. Delany's hands the paper signed by the King, and authorising her to draw her first half-year of her little revenue, it was done with a grace which prevented the object of it from feeling that she was reduced to the condition of a pensioner.

These parties remained, as long as Mrs. Delany lived, on terms of as much equality as could exist between persons so different in rank. In Mrs. Delany's little parlour the Queen would frequently take tea. It was a social banquet in which she delighted; and years afterwards, in her old age, she was as fond of going down to Datchet to take tea with Lord James Murray (afterwards Lord Glenlyon, grandfather of the present Duke of Athol) as she was at this early period of enjoying the same 'dish' with the fine old 'gentlewoman' who was her most grateful pensioner. Queen and widow corresponded with each other, lived as ladies in the country who esteem each other are accustomed to live; and when the doctor's relict had not what was to her, good old soul, the supreme bliss of entertaining the Queen, she enjoyed the inexpressible felicity of receiving at tea the young princes and princesses. A riotous, romping, good-natured group these made; and many a sore headache they must have inflicted on the aged lady, who was too loyal to be anything but proud of such an infliction incurred in such a cause.

The letters of Queen Charlotte to her 'dear friend' are on small subjects, expressed in a small way, and terminating with a mixture of condescension and dignity, with good wishes from 'your affectionate Queen.'

Mrs. Delany speaks in her own letters with well-warranted praise of one circumstance which marked the routine of royal life at Windsor. Every morning throughout the year, at eight o'clock, the Queen, leaning on the King's arm, led her family procession to the Chapel Royal, for the purpose of attending early morning prayer. One of the most pleasing features in the Queen's routine of daily life was to be found in this exemplary practice of hers. The Queen never forced any one to follow her example; she left it to the consciences of all. She was independent, too, in her opinions, and though she joined fervently with the King in the prayer, 'Give peace in our time, O Lord!' and acknowledged (with more truth than the stereotyped expression itself would seem to convey—so illogical is it with its impertinent 'because') that none other fought for us but God alone, yet would she not remain silent, as the King invariably did, when the Athanasian Creed was being repeated. That awful and overwhelm'ng judicatory denunciation at the close shocked the mind of the monarch whose own penal laws, however, were the most sanguinary in Europe. The Queen, as is the case with most ladies in church matters, had less mercy, and she heartily joined in the sentence which so stringently winds up the creed which, after all, was *not* written by Athanasius.

When the Rev. Tom Twining heard that the celebrated Miss Burney was about to be dresser and reader to the Queen, he exclaimed, 'What a fine opportunity you will have of studying the philosophy of human capacity in the highest *sphere* of life!' 'Goodness me! madam!' he exclaims, admiringly; 'are you to take care of the robes yourself?' Miss Burney hardly knew what she would have to do or what her opportunities might be, but she was not long in acquiring the knowledge in question.

Indeed, she picked up much acquaintance with court routine on the first day of her arrival at the Queen's lodge. She found a royal mistress who was extremely anxious to calm the fluttering agitation of her new attendant, and who received her, if not as a friend, yet in no respect as a servant. Gracious as was the reception, the young lady was not sorry to escape to the dinner-table of the ladies and gentlemen in waiting. How graphically does she describe the German officer there who was in waiting on the Queen's brother, Prince Charles of Mecklenburgh: 'He could never finish a speech he had begun, if a new dish made its appearance, without stopping to feast his eyes upon it, exclaim something in German, and suck the inside of his mouth; but all so openly, and with such perfect good-humour, that it was diverting without being distasteful.' The old ceremonious forms had not yet become quite extinct at court. Men did not kneel on serving the Queen, but they never sat down in her presence. How they contrived to dine comfortably at the royal table defies conjecture, if the following paragraph is to be taken literally: 'I find it has always belonged to Mrs. Swellenburgh and Mrs. Haggerdorn to receive at tea whatever company the King or Queen invite to the lodge, as it is only a very select few that can eat with their Majesties, and those few are only ladies; no man, of what rank soever, being permitted to sit in the Queen's presence.' The royal table must then have been the dullest in the palace; and no wonder it is that bishops, peers, officers, *and* gentlemen enjoyed themselves so thoroughly, in less dignity and more comfort, with the maids of honour and ladies of less official greatness.

Nothing was, indeed, more homely and hearty than the promenades made by the illustrious couple, their children all about them, on the terrace of an evening, or when they assembled in the concert-room, where 'nothing was played but Handel.' The time was a transition time; feudality was growing faint, and the best of kings were losing their prestige of infallibility. Still there was much of ceremony both at bed and board; that of the latter has been already mentioned. That at bed-time was not so cumbersome as the ceremony observed at the *coucher* of Marie Antoinette, but it was still of a high and ponderous, yet affectionate, formality. The Queen was handed into her dressing-room by the King, followed by the Princess Royal and the Princess Augusta. The King, on leaving the room, kissed his daughters, who in their turn ceremoniously kissed their royal mother's hand, and bade her 'good-night.' This done, the Queen placed herself in the hands of her 'women,' who, in as brief a time as was consistent with the dignity of her whom they tended, fitted the royal lady for repose. The Queen paid, with a formal curtsey, every sign of respect, by whomsoever offered her, as she passed along.

It is said that Burnet introduced the fashion of high-partitioned pews in the Chapel Royal to prevent the flirting that was constantly going on between the officers and maids of honour. Upon some plea for decorum, rather than because of offence, Queen Charlotte had appointed separate tables for the ladies and gentlemen in waiting; but as she did not forbid them to invite each other, or, as was very often the case with the gentlemen, to invite themselves, the division of tables was only nominally maintained.

The Queen's 'dressing,' deprived as it was of some of the ceremonies of an olden time, was nevertheless not without its formality. Her new 'dresser,' Miss Burney, was not always in time, disliked at first, but wisely got over her dislike, being summoned by a bell, and was so nervous as to mar her services. No maid was permitted to remain in the apartment during the time the Queen was 'tiring.' One lady dresser handed to the other the portions of dress required. ''Tis fortunate for me,' says Miss Burney, 'I have not the handing of them. I should never know which to take first, embarrassed as I am, and should run a prodigious risk of giving the gown before the hoop, and the fan before the neck-kerchief.'

The actual 'dressing for the day' took place at one o'clock, and included the then elaborate matter of powdering. Till the hair-dresser was admitted for the completion of this last matter, the Queen, while being dressed, read the newspapers; but when the powderer came she dismissed the attendants, who had previously covered her up in a peignoir, and was then left alone with the artist, who must have looked very ridiculous in casting, as the Queen must have looked in receiving, the impenetrable clouds of powder which he continued to fling at and about the royal head. But there was another sort of powder patronised by the Queen—the mother of George IV. condescended to take snuff. In the admixture and scent of this she was curiously learned; and Miss Burney filled her boxes and damped the contents when they had got too dry, to her great satisfaction.

There is a fashion in country-towns observed by ladies who go out in chairs to parties, consisting in their carrying with them some portion of their dress, to be adjusted at the locality where they are about to spend the evening. This fashion, too, is a relic of the days of Queen Charlotte. 'On court days,' says Miss Burney, 'the Queen dresses her head at Kew, and puts on her drawing-room apparel at St. James's. Her new attendant dresses all at Kew, except tippet and long ruffles, which she carries in paper to save from dusty roads.' It was the etiquette at St. James's that the finishing of the Queen's dressing there should be the work of the bed-chamber-woman. It consisted of little more than tying the necklace, handing the fan and gloves, and bearing the Queen's train as she left the room. This she did alone, only as far as the anteroom; there the lady of the bed-chamber became the 'first trainbearer,' and the poor Queen had two annoyances to put up with instead of one.

From the cumbrous ceremonies of St. James's the Queen was glad enough to escape to Kew. At the latter place, indeed, ceremony, as far as the royal family was concerned, was left outside the gates. The sovereigns were thoroughly 'at home,' and the Queen enjoyed a 'country life,' not as Marie Antoinette did, a dairymaid in diamonds, at Trianon, but as a simple English country lady. The foreigners who visited the court at this time were disgusted by the republican look which it wore. It was simple and plain enough, at Kew that is, to have pleased even Franklin. The King was really there what he was popularly called everywhere, 'Farmer George;' the Queen was his true dame, the plainest of the plain things around her. The children—that is, the younger portion of them—were as unaffected as their parents, and the little Princess Amelia was the fairy of the place, if one may speak of a fairy in connection with farming. How-ever grave the King might look, through pressure of public events, the little hand of the Princess Amelia, placed by the Queen in his, always touched his heart, and a look into the child's eyes ever brought a smile into his own. Never daughter more closely nestled in a father's heart than Amelia did in that of George III. The Queen loved, but the King adored her. At Kew, father and child appeared more unrestrained in the hearty demonstrations of their love than elsewhere. Indeed, everything at Kew was free and unrestrained; and it was no offence there if any of the attendants *did* pass a room the door of which was open and somebody royal within. In France, they who desired to enter an apartment in which the Queen was, scratched, but never knocked, at the door. In England, at least in Queen Charlotte's time, the etiquette was also not to knock at, but to shake the handle of, the door. Another ceremony was observed in order to *avoid* ceremony. When royal birthdays occurred during the Queen's stay at Windsor the family walked on the terrace, which was crowded with people of distinction, who took that mode of showing respect, to avoid the trouble and fatigue of attending at the following drawing-room. Here is a scene on the birthday of the Princess Amelia, drawn by one who was present:—

'It was really a mighty pretty procession. The little Princess, just turned three years old, in a robe-coat covered with fine muslin, a dressed closed cap, white gloves, and a fan, walked on alone and first, highly delighted in the parade, and turning from side to side to see everybody as she passed; for all the terracers stand up against the walls to make a clear passage for the royal family the moment they come in sight. Then follow the King and Queen, no less delighted themselves with the joy of their little darling.'[1]

The Princess Royal, at this time, is said to have shown more respect and humility to her parents than any of the other children of the family. She passed on in this birthday procession, accompanied by ladies, and her sisters, similarly accompanied, followed her. Happy were they to whom Queen or King addressed a few

[1] Miss Burney's Diary.

words as they stopped on their way; and astounded were the adorers of etiquette when they saw the little Princess Amelia, on recognising Miss Burney, not only go up to kiss her, but actually kissed by her. The Queen herself was probably more surprised than pleased. But it was a birthday! At other seasons etiquette was so rigidly observed (always excepting at Kew) that the children of the royal family never spoke in the presence of the King and Queen, except to answer observations made to them. The Queen, too, as well as she was able, watched over the religious education of her daughters, and always assembled them around her to listen to a course of religious reading by herself. This she did with gravity and good judgment, as became indeed a woman of ordinary good sense.

We have already, incidentally, noticed the attempt made upon the life of the King by Margaret Nicholson. The attack was not known to the Queen till it was announced to her by the King in person. As soon as the poor mad woman had been arrested, the Spanish ambassador posted down to Windsor, to be in readiness to inform her Majesty of the truth, in case of any exaggerated reports reaching her ear. When the King entered the Queen's apartment at Windsor, on his return from London, he wore a rather joyous air, and exclaimed, in a naturally joyous tone, 'Well, here I am, safe and well, though I have had a very narrow escape of being stabbed.' The consternation in the family circle was great; several of the ladies burst into tears, for every one was fond of George III., albeit he was accused of Stuart fondness for the exercise of kingly prerogative. The Queen alone did not at first weep, but pale and agitated she turned round to those who did, and said that she envied them. The relief of tears, however, soon comparatively restored her, and she was enabled, with some outward show of calmness, to listen to the King's details of the occurrence. Into these he entered with the hilarity of a man whose feelings are naturally not very finely strung, but who is strongly persuaded that escape from assassination is rather a matter to be jocund than solemn over. He did not want for a sense of gratitude at his escape, but nothing could prevent his being gay over it. He told the details, therefore, as though they partook something of a joke. He noticed that the knife had slightly cut or grazed his waistcoat; and said he, 'It was great good luck that it did not go further. There was nothing beneath it but some thin linen and a good deal of fat.'

The matter, however, pressed heavily upon the spirits of the Queen. She dreaded lest this attempt should be only a part of a great conspiracy, and feared that the conspirators would not rest satisfied with the mere attempt. The idea was natural at the time, for democracy then was daily barking at, if not biting, kings; and so universally spread was the feeling through one class throughout Europe that the King of England had no cause to deem himself specially exempt from such attempts. George III. had the courageous spirit common to most of the princes of his house, and would not stand aloof from his people because the princes of other houses were at issue with *their* people. The Queen felt greater distrust, but she was partially reassured by the tone taken by the English papers. The pulpit and the press spoke out in tones which showed that, however the country might be divided upon questions connected with politics, it would not tolerate the idea of regicide. These things were known to Queen Charlotte, and comforted the poor lady, who, for a time, could not think of her husband being in London without a spasmodic horror. She pored over the English papers, in order to draw from them comfort and consolation; and it was when reading one of the warmly loyal articles therein, beginning with the words of the coronation anthem, 'Long live the King! may the King live for ever!' that she shed the most copious tears that yet had fallen from her, and drew comfort from what she read. Perhaps the words brought back to her recollection the period, a quarter of a century before, when she had listened to that anthem for the first time, and, glancing back over the long period that had since then elapsed, she perhaps dared to hope that the protection which had been so far vouchsafed would be continued. Another quarter of a century indeed was vouchsafed before the splendour of the reign began to wane in the mental gloom which settled around the King; but already had begun those domestic troubles which were inflicted upon her by the unfilial conduct of her heartless eldest son.

At present, however, she could only think of, and be grateful for, the escape of the King. Loyalty visited her somewhat oppressively in its congratulations, and the next drawing-room was so crowded, and its ceremonies so long, that the Queen was half dead with fatigue before it was over. She found rest and welcome sympathy at ever-pleasant Kew. There the inhabitants welcomed their royal patrons with a zeal, warmth, beer-drinking, and fireworks such as had not been exceeded in any part of the empire. But it was a sort of honour-festival in which the Queen could partake without fatigue. She enjoyed it heartily; and more emphatically than was her wont, even when most pleased, she exclaimed, ' I shall love little Kew for this as long as I live!'

When Charlotte, on her first visit to the City, charmed even the eyes of the fair Quakeresses who surrounded her at the Barclays' by the splendour of her diamonds, she already had the reputation of possessing a desire for acquiring precious stones. Such desire was at one time a mere fashion, like the mania which squandered thousands on a flower, or the madness which at a later period prevailed to be possessed, at whatever cost, of porcelain.

The people were reminded of the Queen's fondness for diamonds at the period when the name of Warren Hastings began to be unpleasantly canvassed in England. The return of that remarkable personage from India was preceded by that of his scarcely less remarkable wife. Soon after her arrival Mrs. Hastings appeared at court, and nothing could exceed the graciousness of the reception she met with from Queen Charlotte. The popular tongue soon wagged audaciously, if not veraciously, on this royal welcome to a lady who was commonly said to have come to England with a lapful of diamonds. For such glittering presents it was said that Queen Charlotte sold her favour and protection. There was, no doubt, much exaggeration in the matter; but the supposed protection of the court, and the alleged manner in which it was said to have been purchased, were as injurious to Hastings as any of the invectives thundered against him by Burke. At the time that the monster impeachment was going on, a present from the Nizam of the Deccan to the King arrived in England. It was a splendid diamond, and was consigned, for presentation, to Warren Hastings, who handed it over to Lord Sydney, but who was present himself at the time when that nobleman duly offered the glittering gift to the King. Its ready acceptance, at a time when Hastings was on his trial, was misconstrued; and that popular voice which so often errs, notwithstanding the assertion that when uttered it is divinely inspired, immediately concluded that at least a bushelful of diamonds, presented to the King and Queen, had bought impunity for the alleged great offender. Ridicule, satire, caricature, violent prose, and execrable rhyme were levelled at both their Majesties in consequence. According to those who were about the person of the Queen, she had better jewels in her virtues than in caskets of precious gems. Miss Burney, in her portrait of the Queen, may be said to contemplate her through pink-coloured spectacles. But, setting aside what predilection induces her to say, enough remains to satisfy an unprejudiced person that there was much amiability, penetration, and good sense in the character of Charlotte. She was more dignified in her visits at the houses of subjects than any of her predecessors had been. She preferred reading the 'Spectator' to reading novels, and indeed had very little regard for novel-writers, and none at all for Madame de Genlis, with whom she very wisely counselled Miss Burney not to correspond.

Of the affection which existed between the Queen and her husband here is a pretty incident :—' The Queen had nobody but myself with her one morning, when the King hastily entered the room with some letters in his hand, and addressing her in German, which he spoke very fast, and with much apparent interest in what he said, he brought the letters up to her and put them into her hand. She received them with much agitation, but evidently of a much pleased sort, and endeavoured to kiss his hand as he held them. He would not let her, but made an effort, with a countenance of the highest satisfaction, to kiss her. I saw instantly in her eyes a forgetfulness at the moment that any one was present, while, drawing away her hand, she presented him her cheek. He accepted her kindness with the same frank affection that she offered it, and the next moment they both spoke English, and talked upon common and general subjects. What they said I am far enough from knowing ; but the whole was too rapid to give me time to quit the room, and I could not but see with pleasure that the Queen had received some favour with which she was sensibly delighted, and that the King, in her acknowledgments, was happily and amply paid.'[1]

This sort of incident, it may be said, is of commonplace frequency in private life, short of the hand-kissing; but it also serves to show that there was an affection existing at this period which, happily, is *not* a rare one in common life. And Charlotte could condescend to the level of that so-called common life, and to them who belonged to it exhibit her natural goodness. Witness for her the directions which she sent on a cold November morning to good old and parcel-blind Mrs. Delany. 'Tell her,' said she, 'that this morning is so very cold and wet that I think she will suffer by going to church. Tell her, therefore, that *Dr. Queen* is of opinion she had better stay and say her prayers at home.' She showed her concern still more when, after having lent to Miss Burney that abominable and absurd tragedy of Horace Walpole's, 'The Mysterious Mother,' she presented her with Ogden's Sermons, wherewith to sweeten her imagination. Perhaps Hurd, Bishop of Worcester, on his visit to Windsor this year, rather underrated the royal power to appreciate sermons. Mrs. Delany asked him for a copy of one which he had preached before their Majesties. The prelate answered that the sermon would not do at all for her. It was a mere plain Christian sermon, he said, made for the King and Queen, but it wouldn't do for a *bel esprit*.

The royal household was sometimes disturbed by family dissensions; thus in 1787 the Prince of Wales would not attend the birthday drawing-room of the Queen, but he sent her written congratulations on the return of the day. The coldness existing between mother and son kept the latter from court. 'I fear it was severely felt by his royal mother,' says Miss Burney, 'though she appeared composed and content.' Of party-spirit

[1] Miss Burney's Diary.

at this time, when party-spirit ran so high and was so fierce and bitter in quality, the Diarist last named asserts that the Queen had but little. She declares her Majesty to have been liberal and nobly-minded, 'beyond what I had conceived her rank and limited connections could have left her, even with the fairest advancements from her early nature; and many things dropped from her, in relation to parties and their consequences, that showed a feeling so deep upon the subject, joined to a lenity so noble towards the individuals composing it, that she drew tears from my eyes in several instances.'

This year saw the reconciliation óf the Prince with his parents, and a public manifestation of this reconciliation of the heir-apparent with his family took place on the terrace at Windsor Castle. The Prince appeared there, chiefly that by his presence he might do honour to a particular incident—the presentation of the Duchesse de Polignac and her daughter, the Duchesse de Guiche, to the King and Queen. The noble visitors themselves, to do honour to the occasion, repaired to the terrace, attired, as they thought, in full English costume—'plain undress gowns, with close ordinary black silk bonnets.' They were startled at finding the Queen and the Princesses dressed with elaborate splendour. For the spectators, however, the most interesting sight was that of the heir-apparent conversing cordially with his illustrious parents. The lookers-on fancied that all, henceforth, would be serene, and that 'Lovely Peace' would reign undisturbedly.

But a pleasanter scene even than this was witnessed shortly after in the Queen's dressing-room. Her Majesty was under the hands of her hair-dresser, and in the room, during the ceremony, were Mr. de Luc, Mr. Turbulent (a pseudonym), and Miss Burney. The Queen conversed with all three. But the sacrilegious and well-named Turbulent, instead of fixing there his sole attention, contrived, 'by standing behind her chair and facing me, to address a language of signs to me the whole time, casting up his eyes, clasping his hands, and placing himself in various fine attitudes, and all with a humour so burlesque that it was impossible to take it either ill or seriously... How much should I have been discountenanced had her Majesty turned about and perceived him, yet by no means so much disconcerted as by a similar Cerberic situation; since the Queen, who, when in spirits, is gay and sportive herself, would be much farther removed from any hazard of misconstruction.'[1] Nor was this the only 'pleasant' incident of the year. It was not long after the above that Lady Effingham, at Windsor, exclaimed to the Queen, 'Oh, ma'am, I had the greatest fright this morning. I saw a huge something on Sir George's throat. "Why, Sir George," says I, "what's that? a wen?" "Yes," says he, " countess, I've had it three-and-twenty years." However, I hear it's now going about—so I hope your Majesty will be careful!'

One more court incident of this year will afford us a specimen of playfulness as understood by the Prince of Wales. The latter was at Windsor with the Duke of York, who had just returned from the Continent, after an absence from England of seven years. His return caused great joy both to the King and Queen; but it was not a joy of long enduring.

'At near one o'clock in the morning, while the wardrobe-woman was pinning up the Queen's hair, there was a sudden rap-tap at the dressing-room door. Extremely surprised, I looked at the Queen, to see what should be done; she did not speak. I had never heard such a sound before, for at the royal doors there is always a particular kind of scratch used, instead of tapping. I heard it, however, again, and the Queen

[1] Miss Burney's Diary.

called out, "What is that?" I was really startled, not conceiving who could take so strange a liberty as to come to the Queen's apartment without the announcing of a page; and no page, I was very sure, would make such a noise. Again the sound was repeated, and more smartly. I grew quite alarmed, imagining some serious evil at hand, either regarding the King or some of the Princesses. The Queen, however, bid me open the door. I did; and what was my surprise to see there a large man, in an immense wrapping great-coat, buttoned up round his chin, so that he was almost hid between cape and hat. I stood quite motionless for a moment; but he, as if also surprised, drew back. I felt quite sick with sudden terror—I really thought some ruffian had broken into the house, or a madman. "Who is it?" cried the Queen. "I do not know, ma'am," I answered. "Who is it?" she called aloud; and then, taking off his hat, entered the Prince of Wales. The Queen laughed very much, and so did I too, happy in this unexpected explanation. He told her eagerly that he only came to inform her there were the most beautiful northern lights to be seen that could possibly be imagined, and begged her to come to the gallery windows.'[1]

[1] Miss Burney's Diary.

CHAPTER VII.

SHADOWS IN THE SUNSHINE.

The Princess Amelia—Her connection with the Duke of Grafton—Beau Nash and the Princess—Her despotism as Ranger of Richmond Park—Checked by Mr. Bird—A Scene at her Loo-table—Her fondness for stables—Her eccentric Costume—Inordinate love of Snuff—Her Death—Conduct of the Princes—The King's Illness—Graphic picture of the state of affairs—Lord Thurlow's treachery—Heartlessness of the Prince—Deplorable condition of the Queen—The King delirious—Particulars of his Illness—Dr. Warren—Melancholy scene—The King wheedled away to Kew—Placed under Dr. Willis—The Prince and Lord Lothian eavesdroppers—The King's Recovery—The King unexpectedly encounters Miss Burney.

ONE event of this year brings us back to the persons and memories of the age of Caroline. Three-quarters of a century had passed away since the day when the then little Princess Amelia Sophia, who was born in Hanover, arrived in London, some three years old, at the period when her parents ascended the throne of England. She was an accomplished and a high-spirited girl, and grew into an attractive and 'lovable' woman. No prince, however, ever came to the feet of Amelia Sophia. She did not, nevertheless, want for lovers of a lower dignity. Walpole, in allusion to this, states of her that she was 'as disposed to meddle' in State matters as her elder sister Anne; and that 'she was confined to receiving court from the Duke of Newcastle, who affected to be in love with her; and from the Duke of Grafton, in whose connection with her there was more reality.'

The latter connection is said to have been more romantic than platonic. The Princess and the Duke were given to riding out in company, conversing together in the recesses of windows, keeping together when out hunting, and occasionally losing themselves together in Windsor Forest and other places convenient for lovers to lose themselves in. This last incident in the love passages of the Princess's life afforded great opportunity for good-natured gossips to indulge in joking, and for ill-natured gossips to indulge in affectedly indignant reproof. The Princess troubled herself very little with the remarks of others on her conduct. It was only when Queen Caroline was worked upon by the ill-natured gossips to notice and to censure the intimacy which existed between the Princess and the Duke that Amelia took the matter somewhat to heart, and wept as a young lady in such circumstances was likely to do at finding a violent end put to her violent delights. The Queen indeed threatened to lay the matter before the King, and it is said that it was only through the good and urgent offices of Sir Robert Walpole that so extreme a course was not taken.

Like her sister Anne, Amelia was rather imperious in disposition, and she never found but one man who openly withstood her. That man was Beau Nash. The Beau had fixed eleven o'clock at which dancing should cease in the rooms at Bath, where he was despotic Master of the Ceremonies. On one occasion, when the Princess was present, the hour had struck, and Nash had raised his jewelled finger, in token that the music was to stop, and the ladies were to 'sit down and cool,' as the Beau delicately expressed it. The imperious daughter of Caroline was not disposed to end the evening so early, and intimated to the *Master* her gracious pleasure that there should be another country dance. Nash looked at her with surprise. He laughed an agitated laugh, shook all the powder out of his wig in signifying his decided refusal, and, muttering something about the laws of the Medes and Persians, set down the Princess as a rather ill-bred person.

In *her* way she was as imperious as Nash; and as Ranger of Richmond Park she was as despotic as the Beau within his more artificial territory at Bath. She kept the park closed, sacred to the pleasure and retirement of royalty and the favoured few. There were, however, some dreadfully democratic persons at Richmond, who had a most obstinate conviction that the public had a right of passage through the park, and they demanded that the right should be allowed them. The royal Ranger peremptorily refused. Democratic cobblers immediately went to law with her, and proved that the right was with them. The Princess yielded to the counsel of her own legal advisers, and, allowing the right of passage, made a very notable concession; she planted rickety ladders against the walls, and bade the ladies and gentlemen of the vicinity pass through the park as they best could by such means. But the persevering people maintained that if they had right of passage the right must be construed in a common-sense way, and that passage implied a *pass* or gate by which such passage might be made. The royal lady thought the world was coming to an end when the vulgar dared thus to 'keep standing on their rights' in presence of a princess. She was in some measure correct; for the age of feudal royalty was coming to a close, and that great shaking-up of equality was beginning from which royalty has never perfectly recovered. The troublesome people, accordingly, kept most vexatiously to the point, and after a fierce struggle they compelled their Ranger to set open a gate whereby they might have free and constant access to their own park. Had this daughter of Caroline been a wise woman, she would have cheerfully gone through this gate with the people, and so, sharing in their triumph, would have won their love. But 'Emily,' as she was often called, was of quite another metal, and was so disgusted at the victory achieved by the vulgar that she threw up her office in disgust, and declared that the downfall of England commenced with the opening of Richmond Park.

The Princess offended more persons than the mere democracy by her arrogance as Ranger. The evidence of Walpole is conclusive on this subject, and is worth citing, often as I have had to quote from his lively pages. In 1752, he writes: 'Princess Emily, who succeeded my brother in the Rangership of Richmond Park, has imitated her brother William's unpopularity, and disobliged the whole country, by refusal of tickets and liberties that had always been allowed. They are at law with her, and have printed in the 'Evening Post' a strong memorial, which she had refused to receive. The high-sheriff of Surrey, to whom she had denied a ticket, but on better thought had sent one, refused it, and said he had taken his part. Lord Brooke, who had applied for one, was told he couldn't have one; and, to add to the affront, it was signified that the Princess had refused one to my Lord Chancellor. Your old nobility don't understand such comparisons. But the most remarkable event happened to her about three weeks ago. One Mr. Bird, a rich gentleman near the palace, was applied to by the late Queen for a piece of ground that lay convenient for a walk she was making. He replied that it was not proper for him to pretend to make a queen a present, but if she would do what she pleased with the ground he would be content with the acknowledgment of a key and two bucks a year. This was religiously observed till the era of her Royal Highness's reign. The bucks were denied, and he himself once shut out, on pretence it was fence month (the breeding-time, when tickets used to be excluded, keys never). The Princess was soon after going through his grounds to town. She found a padlock on his gate. She ordered it to be broken open. Mr. Shaw, her deputy, begged a respite till he could go for the key. He found Mr. Bird at home. "Lord, sir, here is a strange mistake! The Princess is at the gate, and it is padlocked." "Mistake! no mistake at all. I made the road; the ground is my own property. Her Royal Highness has thought fit to break the agreement which her royal mother made with me; nobody goes through my grounds but those I choose should." Translate this to your Florentines,' adds Walpole to our legate in Tuscany; 'try if you can make them conceive how pleasant it is to treat blood royal thus.'

George II., who was more liberal, in many respects, than any of his children, save when these affected liberality for political purposes, finally anticipated the award of law by ordering the park to be thrown open to the public in the month of December 1752. But he could not have kept it closed.

Walpole speaks of the Princess Amelia as if he had never forgotten or forgiven this, or any other of her faults. According to his description, she was for ever prying impertinently into the affairs of other people; silly, garrulous, and importantly communicative of trifles not worth the telling. He paints her as arrogant and insolent; inexcusable, it would seem, in these last respects, simply because she no longer possessed either power or beauty. But these were only eccentricities; there was much of sterling goodness beneath them. She was nobly generous and royally charitable. She was a steady friend and an admirable mistress. In face of such virtues, mere human failings may be forgiven.

Walpole graphically and dramatically describes a scene at her loo-table. The year is 1762, the month December. 'On Thursday,' he says, 'I was summoned to the Princess Emily's loo. *Loo* she called it; *politics* it was. The second thing she said to me was: " How were you the two long days?" "Madam, I was only there the first." " And how did you vote?" " Madam, I went away." " Upon my word, that was carving well!" Not a very pleasant apostrophe to one who certainly never was a time-server. Well, we sat down. She said: " I hear Wilkinson is turned out, and that Sir Edward Winnington is to have his place. Who is he?" addressing herself to me, who sat over against her. " He is the late Mr. Winnington's heir, madam." " Did you like that Winnington?" " I can't but say I did, madam." She shrugged up her shoulders, and continued: " Winnington was originally a great Tory. What do you think he was when he died?" " Madam, I believe what all people are in place." " Pray, Mr. Montague, do you perceive anything rude or offensive in this?" Here then she flew into the most outrageous passion, coloured like scarlet, and said: " None of your wit. I don't understand joking on these subjects. What do you think your father would have said if he had heard you say so? He would have murdered you, and you would have deserved it." I was quite confounded and amazed. It was impossible to explain myself across a loo-table, as she is so deaf. There was no making a reply to a woman and a princess, and particularly for me, who have made it a rule, when I must converse with royalties, to treat them with the greatest respect, since it is all the court they will ever have from me. I said to those on each side of me : " What can I do? I cannot explain myself now." Well, I held my peace; and so did she, for a quarter of an hour. Then she began with me again, examined me upon the whole debate, and at last asked me directly which I thought the best speaker, my father or Mr. Pitt? If possible, this was more distressing than her anger. I replied, it was impossible to compare two men so different; that I believed my father was more a man of business than Mr. Pitt. "Well, but Mr. Pitt's language?" "Madam, I have always been remarkable for admiring Mr. Pitt's language." At last the unpleasant scene ended; but as we were going away I went close to her and said: "Madam, I must beg leave to explain myself. Your Royal Highness has seemed to be very angry with me, and I am sure I did not mean to offend you; all that I intended to say was, that I supposed Tories were Whigs when they got places." "Oh !" said she; "I am very much obliged to you. Indeed, I was very angry." Why she was angry, or what she thought I meant, I do not know to this moment, unless she supposed that I would have hinted that the Duke of Newcastle and the Opposition were not men of consummate virtue, and had not lost their places out of principle. The very reverse was at that time in my head, for I meant that the Tories would be just as loyal as the Whigs when they got anything by it.'

The Princess was not ladylike in her habits. She had a fondness for loitering about her stables, and would spend hours there in attendance upon her sick horses. She of course acquired the ways of those whose lives pass in stables and stable matters. She was manly, too, in her dress. Calamette would have liked to have painted her, as that artist has painted the frock-coat portrait of Madame Dudevant (George Sand). He would have picturesquely portrayed her in the round hat and German riding-habit, 'standing about' at her breakfast, sipping her chocolate, or taking spoonsful of snuff. Of this she was inordinately fond, but she accounted her box sacred. A *Noli me tangere* was engraven on it, but the injunction was not always held sacred. Once, on one of the card-tables in the Assembly Rooms at Bath, her box lay open, and an old general officer standing near inconsiderately took a pinch from it. The indignant Princess immediately called an attendant, who, by her directions, flung the remainder of the contents of the box into the fire.

In June 1786, Walpole, then nearly a septuagenarian, borrowed a dress-coat and sword, in order to dine at Gunnersbury with the Princess. The company comprised the Prince of Wales, the Prince of Mecklenburgh, the Duke of Portland, Lord Clanbrassil, Lord and Lady Clermont, Lord and Lady Southampton, Lord Pelham, and Mrs. Howe. Some of the party retired early. Others, more dissipated, sat up playing commerce till ten. 'I am afraid I was tired,' says Horace. The lively old Princess asked him for some verses on Gunnersbury. 'I pleaded being superannuated. She would not excuse me. I promised she should have an ode on her next birthday, which diverted the Prince; but all would not do. So, as I came home, I made some stanzas not worth quoting, and sent them to her by breakfast next morning.'

In the October following, the daughter of Caroline and George II. died at her house in Cavendish Square, at the east corner of Harley Street. Card-playing and charity were the beloved pursuits of her old age. Her death took place on the last day of October 1786, in the 76th year of her age. Her remains lie in Henry VII.'s chapel in Westminster Abbey.

But the decease of this aged princess appeared a minor calamity compared with the illness which now threatened the King. In presence of this the Queen forgot Mrs. Trimmer and her Sunday Schools; Gainsborough, whom she patronised; public theatricals, and private readings. The illness had been long threatening.

In the 'Memoirs of the Court and Cabinet of George

III.,' by the Duke of Buckingham and Chandos, the elder sons of Queen Charlotte are spoken of, and particularly with reference to this period immediately previous to the King's illness, in a most unfavourable light. The Prince of Wales, we are told, like his two predecessors in the same title, was active in his opposition to the measures of the cabinet and crown. The same spirit, with as little prudence to moderate and more ill-feeling to embitter it, was as lively in the man as in the boy. The Prince was, however, at least consistent in his opposition. 'The Duke of York,' says Lord Bulkeley, writing to the Marquis of Buckingham, 'talks both ways, and I think will end in opposition. His conduct is as bad as possible. He plays very deep and loses, and his company is thought *mauvais ton*. I am told that the King and Queen begin now to feel "how much sharper than a serpent's tooth it is to have an ingrate child." When the Duke of York is completely *done up* in the public opinion, I should not be surprised if the Prince of Wales assume a different style of behaviour. Indeed, I am told, he already affects to see that his brother's style is too bad.'

Public business, as far as its transaction through ministers was concerned, became greatly impeded through the illness which had attacked the King. It had been brought on by his imprudence in remaining a whole day in wet stockings, and it exhibited itself not merely in spasmodic attacks of the stomach, but in an agitation and flurry of spirits which caused great uneasiness to the Queen, and which, both for domestic and political reasons, it was desirous should not be known.

The very attempt at concealment gave rise to various alarming reports. The best answer that could be devised for the latter was to allow the King to appear at the levée at the end of October. The Queen suffered much when this plan was resolved upon; and it had the result, which she expected, of over-fatiguing the King and rendering him worse. At the close of the levée, the King remarked to the Duke of Leeds and Lord Thurlow, the latter of whom had advised him to take care of himself and return to Windsor: 'You then, too, my Lord Thurlow, forsake me, and suppose me ill beyond recovery; but whatever you or Mr. Pitt may think or feel, I, that am born a gentleman, shall never lay my head on my last pillow in peace and quiet as long as I remember the loss of my American Colonies.' This loss appears to have weighed heavily on his mind, and to have been one of the great causes by which it was ultimately overthrown.

Early in November he became delirious, but the medical men, Warren, Heberden, and Sir G. Baker, could not tell whether the malady would turn, at a critical point, for life or death; or whether, if for the former, the patient would be afflicted or not with permanent loss of reason. The disease was now settled in the brain, with high fever. The Princes of the Blood were all assembled at Windsor, in the room next to that occupied by the sufferer, and a regency bestowing kingly power on the Prince of Wales was already talked of.

When the fact of the King's illness could no longer be with propriety concealed, the alarm without the royal residence was great, and the disorder scarcely less within. The most graphic picture of the state of affairs is drawn by Lord Bulkeley. 'The Queen,' he says, 'sees nobody but Lady Constance, Lady Charlotte Finch, Miss Burney, and her two sons, who, I am afraid, do not announce the state of the King's health with that caution and delicacy which should be observed to the wife and the mother, and it is to them only that she looks up. I understand her behaviour is very feeling, decent, and proper. The Prince has taken the command at Windsor, in consequence of which there is no command whatsoever; and it was not till yesterday that orders were given to two grooms of the bedchamber to wait for the future, and receive the inquiries of the numbers who inquire; nor would this have been done if Pitt and Lord Sydney had not come down in person to beg that such orders might be given. Unless it was done yesterday, no orders were given for prayers in the churches, nor for the observance of other forms, such as stopping the playhouses, &c., highly proper (?) at such a juncture. What the consequence of this heavy misfortune will be to government, you are more likely to know than I am; but I cannot help thinking that the Prince will find a greater difficulty in making a sweep of the present ministry in his character of Fiduciary Regent than in that of King. The stocks are already fallen two per cent., and the alarms of the people of London are very little flattering to the Prince. I am told that message after message has been sent to Fox, who is touring with Mrs. Armistead on the continent; but I have not heard that the Prince has sent for him, or has given any orders to Fox's friends to that effect. The system of favouritism is much changed since Lord Bute's and the Princess Dowager's time; for Jack Payne, Master Leigh, an Eton schoolboy, and Master Barry, brother to Lord Barrymore, and Mrs. Fitz, form the cabinet at Carlton House.'

The afflicted King, for a time, grew worse, then the Opposition affected to believe that his case was by no means desperate. Their insincerity was proved as symptoms of amelioration began to show themselves. *Then* they not only denied the fact of the King's improved health, but they detailed all the incidents they could pick up of his period of imbecility, short madness, or longer delirium. But, in justice to the Opposition, it must be remarked that the greatest traitor was not on *that* side, but on the King's. The Lord Chancellor Thurlow was intriguing with the Opposition when he was affecting to be a faithful servant of the crown. His treachery, however, was well known to both parties; but Pitt kept it from the knowledge of George III., lest it should too deeply pain or too dangerously excite him. When Thurlow had, subsequently, the effrontery to exclaim in the House of Lords, 'When I forget my King, may my God forget me!' a voice from one behind him is said to have murmured, 'Forget you! He will see you d—d first.'

There was assuredly no decency in the conduct of the heir-apparent or of his next brother. They were gaily flying from club to club, party to party, and did not take the trouble even to assume the sentiment which they could not feel. 'If we were together,' says Lord Grenville, in a letter inserted in the 'Memoirs,' 'I would tell you some particulars of the Prince of Wales's behaviour towards the King and Queen, within these few days, that would make your blood run cold, but I dare not admit them to paper because of my informant.' It was said that if the King could only recover sufficiently to learn and comprehend what had been said and done during his illness, he would hear enough to drive him again into insanity. The conduct of his elder sons was marked, not only by its savage inhumanity, but by an indifference to public and private opinion which distinguishes those fools who are not only without wits, but who are also without hearts. When the Parliament was divided by fierce party strife, as to whose hands should be confided the power and responsibilities of the regency, the occasion should have disposed those likely to be endowed with that supreme power to seek a decent, if temporary, retirement from the gaze of the world. Not so the Prince of Wales and the Duke of York. They kept open houses, and gaily welcomed every new ally. They were constant guests at epicurean clubs and convivial meetings. They both took to deep play, and both were as fully plucked as they deserved. There was in them neither propriety of feeling nor affectation of it.

The condition of the Queen was deplorable, and a succession of fits almost prostrated her as low as her royal husband. The Prince of Wales himself 'seemed frightened,' says Mr. Neville to the Marquis of Buckingham, 'and was blooded yesterday,' November 6, the second day of the King's delirious condition; but as phlebotomy was a practice of this princely person when in love, one cannot well determine whether his pallor arose from filial or some less respectable affection.

Up to this time the King had grown worse, chiefly through total, or nearly total, loss of sleep. He bewailed this with a hoarse, rapid, yet kindly tone of voice; maintaining that he was well, or that to be so he needed but the blessing of sleep. The Queen paced her apartment with a painful demonstration of impatient despair in her manner; and if, by way of solace, she attempted to read aloud to her children or ladies, any passage that reminded her of her condition and prospects made her burst into tears.

Previous to the first night of the King's delirium he conducted, as he had always been accustomed to do, the Queen to her dressing-room, and there, a hundred times over, requested her not to disturb him if she should find him asleep. The urgent repetition showed a mind nearly overthrown, but the King calmly and affectionately remarked that he needed not physicians, for the Queen was the best physician he could have. 'She is my best friend,' said he; 'where could I find a better?'

The alarm became greater when the fever left the King, after he had three times taken James's powders, but without producing any relief to the brain. The Queen secluded herself from all persons save her ladies and the two eldest Princes. These, as Lord Bulkeley said, did not announce to her the state of the King's health with the caution and delicacy due to the wife and mother who now depended on them. This dependence was so complete that the Prince of Wales, as before said, took the command of everything at Windsor, one result of which was a disappearance of everything like order. The Queen's dependence on such a son was rather compulsory than voluntary. When he first came down to Windsor, from Brighton, the meeting was the very coldest possible, and when he had stated whence he came her first question was when he meant to return. However, it is said that when the King broke out, at dinner, into his first fit of positive delirium, the Prince burst into tears.

The sufferer was occasionally better, but the relapses were frequent. The Queen now slept in a bed-room adjoining that occupied by the King. He once became possessed with the idea that she had been forcibly removed from the bed, and in the middle of the night he came into the Queen's room with a candle in his hand, to satisfy himself that she was still near him. He remained half-an-hour, talking incoherently, hoarsely, but good-naturedly, and then went away. The Queen's nights were nights of sleeplessness and tears.

In the Queen's room could be heard every expression uttered by the King, and they were only such as could give pain to the listener. His state was at length so bad that the Queen was counselled to change her apartments, both for her sake and the King's. She obeyed, reluctantly and despairingly, and confined herself to a single and distant room. In the meanwhile, Dr. Warren was sent for, but the King resolutely refused to see him. He hated all physicians, declared that he himself was only nervous; and that otherwise he was not ill. Dr. Warren, however, contrived to be near enough to be able to give an opinion, and the Queen waited impatiently in her apartment to hear what that opinion might be. When she was told, after long waiting, that Dr. Warren had left the castle, after communicating his opinion to the Prince of Wales, she felt the full force of her altered position, and that she was no longer first in the castle next to the King.

The Prince of Wales, the Duke of York, some of the medical men, and other gentlemen kept a sort of watch in the room adjacent to that in which the King lay, and listened attentively to all he uttered. He surprised them, one night, by suddenly appearing among them, and roughly demanding what they were there for. They endeavoured to pacify him, but in vain. He treated them all as enemies; but not happening to see his second son, who had discreetly kept out of sight, but was present, he said, touchingly, 'Freddy is my friend; yes, *he* is my friend!' Sir George Baker timidly persuaded the poor King to return to his bed-room; but the latter forced the doctor into a corner, and told him that he was an old woman, who could not distinguish between a mere nervous malady and any other. The Prince, by sign and whispers, endeavoured to induce the other gentlemen to lead his father away. All were reluctant, and the King remained a considerable time, till at last a 'Mr. Fairly' took him boldly by the arm, addressed him respectfully but firmly, declaring that his life was in peril if he did not go again to bed, and at length subdued the King, who gave himself up like a wearied child. These details were eagerly made known to the Queen by the Prince with 'energetic violence.' Her Majesty's condition was indeed melancholy, but at its worst she never forgot to perform little acts of kindness to her daughters and others. The conduct of the Princesses was such as became their situation.

They, with their mother, had fallen from their first greatness, and the Prince of Wales was supreme master. Nothing was done but by his orders. The Queen ceased to have any authority beyond the reach of her own ladies. 'She spent the whole day,' says Miss Burney, ' in patient sorrow and retirement with her daughters!'

The King expressed a very natural desire to see these daughters, but he was not indulged. Indeed, the practice observed towards him appears, if the accounts may be trusted, extremely injudicious. The public seem to have thought so; for, on stopping Sir George Baker's carriage, and hearing from him that the King's condition was very bad, they exclaimed, 'More shame for you!'

The Prince of Wales was extremely desirous to remove the King from Windsor to Kew. The King was violently averse from such removal, and the Queen opposed it until she was informed that it had the sanction of the physicians. Kew was said to be quieter and more adapted for an invalid. The difficulty was, how he was to get there. Of his own will he would never go. The Prince and physicians contrived a plan. The Queen and Princesses were to leave Windsor early, and, as soon as the King should be told of their departure, his uneasiness would be calmed by an assurance that he would find them at Kew. The Queen yielded reluctantly, on being told that it would be for her consort's advantage; and she and her daughters proceeded, without state and in profound grief, to Kew. Small accommodation did they find there; for half the apartments were locked up, by the Prince's orders, while on the doors of the few allotted to the Queen and her slender retinue, some illustrious groom of the chambers had scratched in chalk the names of those by whom they were to be occupied! Night had set in before the King arrived. He had been wheedled away from Windsor, on promise of being allowed to see the

Queen and their daughters at Kew. He performed the journey in silent content; and, when he arrived—the promise was broken! The Queen and children were again told that it was all for the best; but a night, passed by the King in violence and raving, showed how deeply he felt the cruel insult to which he had been subjected. In the meantime, preparations to name the Prince regent were going on, the King's friends being extremely cautious that due reserve should be made for their master's rights, in case of what they did not yet despair of—his recovery. His physicians were divided in opinion upon the point; but they all agreed that the malady, which had begun with a natural discharge of humour from the legs, had, by the King's imprudence, been driven to the bowels, and that thence it had been repelled upon the brain. They endeavoured, without too sanguinely hoping, to bring the malady again down to the legs.

Their efforts were fruitless. Addington and Sir Lucas Pepys were more sanguine than their colleagues, of a recovery; but the condition of the patient grew daily more serious, yet with intervals of calm lucidity. It was at this juncture that Dr. Willis, of Lincoln, was called in. This measure gave great relief to the Queen; for she knew that cases of lunacy formed Dr. Willis's *specialité*, and she entertained great hopes from the treatment he should adopt. The doctor was accompanied by his two sons. They were (and the father especially) fine men, full of cheerfulness, firm in manner, entertaining respect for the personal character of the King, but caring not a jot for his rank. They at once took the royal patient into their care, and with such good success—never unnecessarily opposing him, but winning, rather than compelling, him to follow the course best suited for his health—that, on the 10th of December, the Queen had the gratification to see him, from the window of her apartment, walking in the garden alone, the Willises being in attendance at a little distance from him.

There was a party who desired least of all things the recovery of the monarch. The Prince of Wales, during his father's malady, took Lord Lothian into a darkened room, adjacent to that of the King, in order that the obsequious lord might hear the ravings of the sovereign, and depose to the fact, if such deposition should be necessary!

The year 1789 opened propitiously. On its very first morning the poor King was heard praying, aloud and fervently, for his own recovery. A report of how he had passed the night was made to the Queen every morning, and generally by Miss Burney. The state of the King varied so much, and there was so much of painful detail that it was desirable should be concealed, that the task allotted to Miss Burney was sometimes one of great delicacy. On the worst occasions she appears to have spared her royal mistress's feelings with much tact and judgment, and her face was the index of her message whenever she was the bearer of favourable intelligence. The highest gratification experienced by the Queen at the period when hopes revived of the King's recovery, was when she heard that her husband had remembered on the 18th of January that it was her birthday, and had expressed a desire to see her. This joy, however, was forbidden him for a time, and apparently not without reason. A short period only had elapsed after the birthday when the King suddenly encountered Miss Burney in Kew Gardens, where she had ventured to take exercise, under the impression that the sick monarch had been taken to Richmond. As it was the Queen's desire, derived from the physicians, that no one should attempt to come in the King's way, or address him if they did, Miss Burney no sooner became aware of whom she had thus unexpectedly encountered, than she turned round and fairly took to her heels. The King, calling to her by name, and enraptured to see again the face of one whom he knew and esteemed, pursued as swiftly as she fled. The Willises followed hard upon the King, not without some alarm. Miss Burney kept the lead in breathless affright. In vain was she called upon to stop: she ran on until a peremptory order from Dr. Willis, and a brief assurance that the agitation would be most injurious to the King, brought her at once to a stand-still. She then turned and advanced to meet the King, as if she had not before been aware of his presence. *He* manifested his intense delight by opening wide his arms, closing them around her, and kissing her warmly on each cheek. Poor Miss Burney was overwhelmed, and the Willises were delighted. They imagined that the King was doing nothing unusual with him in the days of his ordinary health, and were pleased to see him fulfilling, as they thought, an old observance.

The King would not relax his hold of his young friend. He entered eagerly into conversation, if that may be deemed conversation in which he alone spoke, or was only answered by words sparingly used and soothingly intoned. He talked rapidly, hoarsely, but only occasionally incoherently. His subjects of conversation took a wide range. Family affairs, political business, Miss Burney's domestic interests, foreign matters, music, —these and many other topics made up the staple of his discourse. He was at least rational on the subject of music, for then he commenced singing from his favourite Handel, but with voice so hoarse and ill-attuned that he frightened his audience. Dr. Willis suggested that the interview should close; but this the King energetically opposed, and his medical adviser thought it best to let him have his way. He went on, then, wildly as before, but manifesting much shrewdness; showed that he was aware of his condition, and expressed more than suspicion of assaults made upon his authority during his own incapacity. He talked of whom he would promote when he was fully restored to health; and whom he would dismiss—made allusion to a thousand projects which he intended to realise, and attained a climax of threatening, with a serio-comic expression, that when he should again be King he would rule with a rod of iron.

After various attempts at interruption, the Willises at length succeeded in obtaining his consent to return to the house, and Miss Burney hastened to the Queen's apartment to inform her of all that had passed. The Queen listened to her tale with breathless interest; made her repeat every incident; and augured so well from all she heard, that she readily forgave Miss Burney her involuntary infraction of a very peremptory law. That the Queen's augury was well founded may be seen in the fact that, on the 12th of February following, King and Queen together walked in Kew Gardens—he, happy and nervous; *she*, in much the same condition; and both, as grateful as mortals could be for inestimable blessings vouchsafed to them.

During the progress of the King's illness, while all was sombre and silent at Kew, political intrigue was loud and active elsewhere. The voice of the Queen herself was not altogether mute in this intrigue. She had rights to defend, she had spirit to assert them, and she had friends to afford her aid in enabling her to establish them.

CHAPTER VIII.

THE 'FIRST GENTLEMAN' AND HIS PRINCIPLES.

Inconsistency of the Whigs—The Tories become radical reformers—Party spirit—A restricted Regency scorned by the Prince—Compelled to accept it—The King's rapid recovery—Incredulity of the Princes in regard to the King's recovery—A family scene at Kew—Ball at White's Club on the King's recovery, and unbecoming conduct of the Princes—Thanksgiving at St. Paul's—Indecent conduct of the Princes—Grief of the King—Expectations of the Prince disappointed—Caricatures and satires.

WHEN the Queen first changed her apartments at Windsor, her exclamation, as she entered her new abode, was an assertion of her desolate helplessness, and a deploring hesitation as to what course she was bound to take. She was soon stirred to action. Her eldest son was active in the field against her, and her spirit was speedily aroused to protect and further her own interests. The Parliament had been made acquainted with the condition of the King, by a report from the privy council. With this the legislature was not satisfied. Parliamentary committees sat, before which bodies the King's physicians made detailed depositions, whereby the King's existing incapacity to transact public business was established beyond doubt. Upon this the Whigs, with Fox at their head (he had hurried home from Italy, deplorably ill, to perform this service for the Prince of Wales), declared that the royal incapacity caused the government of the kingdom to fall, as a matter of right, upon the heir-apparent. This assertion, which is a full and complete embracing of the law of divine right, and a trampling under foot of the authority of the parliament, was made in 1788, just one hundred years after the grandfathers of these very Whigs had established the authority of the people in parliament above that of the crown, and made the King who reigned and did not govern, merely the first magistrate of a free people.

On the other hand the Tories, with Pitt for their leader, declared that thus to annihilate the sovereignty of the people in parliament was treason against the constitution, which, in a juncture like the present, bestowed on the people's representatives the right of naming by whom they would be governed. Thus the Tories were in truth radical reformers; and, in truth, quite as serious, both parties being equally insincere, fighting only for place, and caring little for aught beyond.

The whole country, upon this, became Tory in spirit —as Toryism had now developed itself. Fox in vain explained that he meant that the administration of the government belonged to the Prince of Wales, only if Parliament sanctioned it. In vain the Prince of Wales, through his brother the Duke of York, proclaimed in the House of Lords that he made no claim whatever, but was, in fact, the very humble and obedient servant of the people.

It was precisely because he did assert this claim that the Queen and her friends were alarmed. Should the Prince be endowed with the powers of regent, without restriction, the Queen would be reduced to a cypher, Pitt would lose his place, the ministry would be overthrown with him, and, should the King recover, difficulties might arise in the way of the recovery also of his authority.

Party spirit ran high on this matter, but there was little patriotism to give it dignity. Among the ministry, even, waverers were to be found, who were on the

Prince's side when the King's case seemed desperate, and who veered round to the Sovereign's party as soon as there appeared a hope of his recovery.

A restricted regency the Prince of Wales affected to look upon with ineffable scorn. His royal brothers manifested more fraternal sympathy than filial affection, by pretending to think their brother's scorn well-founded. They all changed their minds as soon as they saw, by Pitt's parliamentary majorities, that they could not help themselves. Ultimately, the Prince consented, with a very ill grace, to the terms which Pitt and the Parliament were disposed to force upon him. Never did man submit to terms which he loathed with such bitterness of disappointed spirit as the Prince did to the following conditions; namely:—

That the King's person was to be entrusted to the Queen; her Majesty was to be also invested with the control of the royal household, and with the consequent patronage of the four hundred places connected therewith, including the appointments of lord-steward, lord-chamberlain, and master of the horse. The Prince, as regent, was further to be debarred from granting any office, reversion, or pension, except during the King's pleasure; and the privilege of conferring the peerage was not to be allowed to him at all.

With a fiercely savage heart did he accept these terms; and when the Irish Parliament, in its eagerness to encourage dissension in England, invited him to take upon himself the unrestricted administration of the Irish government during the royal incapacity, the warmth and ardent gratitude expressed by the Prince in his reply, showed how willingly he would have accepted the invitation if he had only dared.

And now the day was appointed for bringing the Regency Bill regularly before Parliament—the 3rd of February—and the clauses were already under discussion when, a fortnight later, the lord chancellor (Thurlow) announced to the house that the King was declared by his medical attendants to be in a state of convalescence.

When Prince Henry was detected in taking the crown from the head of his invalid and slumbering father, he met the reproof which ensued with tender expressions of sorrow and respect. There was little of similar depth of feeling when the Prince of Wales, with the Duke of York, saw his father for the first time after his recovery. Queen Charlotte alone was present with her husband and sons. The last entered the King's room, and issued therefrom, without a trace of emotion upon their faces or in their bearing. The chagrin with which they saw the power which they had coveted slip from them, might have taught them wisdom, but it only drove them to wine, cards, masquerades, and the profligacy which goes in company therewith. They were not as men rejoicing that Heaven had been merciful to their father and King, but as men striving to forget, amid a hurricane of vicious pleasures, that their sire had really been the object of such mercy. The Prince had indeed some misgivings as to what George III. might think of his conduct during the King's malady; but he affected to assert that it would meet with approbation, while that of Mr. Pitt, he thought, would receive from the monarch a strong reproof. The Duke of York was far less careful as to the paternal, and as little to the public, opinion. He ran up scores in open tennis-courts with well-known black-legs, and promised payment as soon as he had received from his father certain arrears of revenue due to him as Bishop of Osnaburg.

These princely sons were among the last to acquiesce in the opinion that their father was sane, and competent again to exercise his constitutional authority. Lord Grenville thus graphically describes a family scene at Kew :—' The two Princes were at Kew yesterday, and saw the King in the Queen's apartment. She was present the whole time, a precaution for which, God knows, there was but too much reason. They kept him waiting a considerable time before they arrived, and after they left him drove immediately to Mrs. Armistead's in Park Street, in hopes of finding Fox there, to give him an account of what had passed. He not being in town, they amused themselves yesterday evening with spreading about a report that the King was still out of his mind, and with quoting phrases of his to which they gave that turn. It is certainly a decent and becoming thing, that when all the King's physicians, all his attendants, and his two principal ministers agree in pronouncing him well, his two sons should deny it! And the reflection that the Prince of Wales was to have had the government, and the Duke of York the command of the army, during his illness, makes this representation of his actual state, when coming from them, more peculiarly proper and edifying! I bless God that it is some time before these matured and ripened virtues will be visited upon us in the form of a government.'[1]

In the meantime the monarch got so undeniably well and competent to govern, that even his nearest and most expectant heirs could no longer deny the, to them, most unwelcome truth. A ball was given by White's Club to celebrate this event, and the Princes of course were present to show how they were gratified by it! The ball was announced to take place at the Pantheon, and the Prince of Wales, who had engaged to attend, previously did his wretched utmost to render the attendance of others as thin as possible, by canvassing all his friends and admirers to keep away. The club had transmitted to the Prince and the Duke of York a large number of tickets for the accommodation of themselves and the acquaintances to whom, it was presumed, they might be

[1] 'Memoirs,' &c., by the Duke of Buckingham.

desirous to pay the compliment of presenting them with admissions. The brothers sent the whole of these tickets to Hookham's in Bond Street for sale! The club, on hearing of this insulting proceeding, and to prevent the admission of improper persons at a *fête* which had a private and exclusive character, intimated by advertisement that no ticket would entitle its holder to admittance which did not bear on it the signature of a subscriber to the ball, or of the person to whom the committee had sent such ticket. This did not teach the Duke decency. He affixed his princely title to the tickets, to make them saleable and valid; and he himself attended a ball given expressly in his honour, at the Horse Guards.

The first, and graceful, feeling of the Monarch, that he was bound to make a public expression of his thanks to Heaven for his recovery, caused his ministers and friends, and particularly the Queen, much embarrassment. They were afraid of the excitement and its probable consequences. But George III. was now in the condition once noticed by Hunter, the surgeon, in himself. 'My mind,' said the latter, 'is still inclined to odd thoughts, and I am tempted to talk foolishly; but I can govern myself.' The King was in better health than is here indicated, and he bore himself throughout the day—the 25th of June, 1789—as became a grateful man, abounding in piety, and not dispossessed of wisdom. The disgraceful rivalry of his eldest son had almost marred the day. The followers of the latter were posted along the first part of the route between the palace and St. Paul's, and their cheers, associated with his name, put him in high good humour, which was however converted into as high displeasure when the running fire of cheers between Charing Cross and the cathedral was raised only in honour of his father. His conduct, and indeed that of his brothers York and Cumberland, as also of their cousin the Duke of Gloucester, in the cathedral, during service, disgusted all who witnessed it. They talked aloud to one another during the whole otherwise solemn proceeding; and it is only to be regretted that no man was present, with courage equal to his authority, to sternly reprove, or summarily remove, them.

The scene at St. Paul's, as regarded the King himself, was at once magnificent and touching. The internal arrangements were excellent, and the King was composed and devout throughout the service; attentive to the latter, and especially to the anthem, which he had himself selected. His air of sincerity and gratitude was most marked. The Queen was much affected at the solemnity of their first entrance; and the King, who looked reduced, scarcely less so. Lady Uxbridge, who was in attendance on the Queen, nearly fainted away. 'As the King went out of the church,' writes Mr. Bernard to the Marquis of Rockingham, 'he seemed to be in good spirits, and talked much to the persons about him; but he stared and laughed less than I ever knew him on a public occasion.' Mr. Fox and most of the Opposition party were there; and while the Queen returned thanks for the King's recovery, as she looked upon the sons near her, who interrupted the solemnity of the scene by their talking, she might have felt that she had other things to be thankful for also. She must have known, by the conduct of the Prince of Wales, that, had the King's illness lasted much longer, he would have accepted the invitation of the Irish Parliament, and assumed a regency in Ireland, with sovereign power. He would have accomplished then what O'Connell, so long after, failed in achieving—a government altogether independent of, and in antagonism with, England.

After the return of the procession the Prince of Wales and Duke of York entered Carlton House, where, having put on regimentals, they proceeded to the ground in front of Buckingham House, at the windows of which the royal family had stationed themselves, the King and Queen being most prominent; and there, heading the whole brigade of guards, fired a *feu-de-joie* in honour of the occasion. The grave Lord Bulkeley, a spectator of the scene, thus describes the remainder of the proceedings: 'The Prince, before the King got into his carriage—which the whole line waited for before they filed off—went off on a sudden with one hundred of the common people, with Mr. Weltje in the middle of them, huzzaing him; and this was done evidently to lead if possible a greater number and to make it penetrate into Buckingham House. The breach,' adds Lord Bulkeley, 'is so very wide between the King and Prince, that it seems to me to be a great weakness to allow him any communication with him whatever; for, under the mask of attention to their father and mother, the Prince and Duke of York commit every possible outrage, and show every insult they can devise to them. . . . I believe the King's mind is torn to pieces by his sons,' adds the noble lord. And then, in allusion to the King's expressed desire to visit Hanover, the writer remarks thereon : 'He expects to relieve himself by a new scene, and by getting out of the way and hearing of the Prince of Wales, with the hope of being able to detach the Duke of York, whom he fondly and doatingly loves, and prevailing on him to marry on the Continent; of which there is no chance, for in my opinion he is just as bad as the Prince, and gives no hopes of any change or amendment whatever in thought, word, or deed.'

A very short time after the King's recovery the first remark made by the sufferer, on growing convalescent, to Lord Thurlow, was—' What *has* happened may happen again. For God's sake ! make some permanent and immediate provision for such a regency as may prevent the country from being involved in disputes and difficulties similar to those just over.' Thurlow and Pitt agreed on the expediency of the measure, but were at issue relative to the details. When the measure *did* come before Parliament, Queen Charlotte was equally indignant against the Prince of Wales and against those who advocated his claims. It may be added here that the conduct of her three eldest sons continued to be of the most insulting nature to the Queen. They could not forgive her for allegedly standing between them and the power which they coveted. From congratulatory balls, at which she had announced her intention to be present, they kept away all persons over whom they had any influence; and at a ball given by the French ambassador on the 30th of May the Prince of Wales and the Dukes of York and Clarence would neither dance nor remain to supper, lest they should have the appearance of paying the smallest attention to her Majesty, who was present.

The assertion of the Prince of Wales that his royal father would approve of what he had done, and censure Pitt, proved to be totally unfounded. The King conveyed to the Parliament, through the lord chancellor, his approval of the measures taken by ministers, and expressed his gratitude that so much zeal had been manifested by them and Parliament for the public good and for the honour and interest of the crown. Following this came a sweep of all who held removeable offices under the crown, and who had opposed the Queen's interests and the King's cause by supporting the views of the Prince. Among the ejected were the Duke of Queensberry, the Marquis of Lothian, Lord Carteret, and Lord Malmesbury.

Mr. Wright, in his 'History of England under the House of Hanover, illustrated from the caricatures and satires of the day,' states that the popularity of the ministers did not increase in the same proportion as that of the

King; for the reason that though the people approved of the constitutional measures they had adopted at the late crisis, the same people very well knew that they were as little impelled by patriotism as their adversaries. Mr. Wright notices ' a rather celebrated caricature,' by Gillray, entitled ' Minions of the Moon,' published a little later. It is dated the 23rd of December 1791, but is generally understood to refer to this affair. It is a parody on Fuseli's picture of 'The Weird Sisters,' who are represented with the features of Dundas, Pitt, and Thurlow. They are contemplating the disk of the moon, which represents, on the bright side, the face of the Queen, and on the shrouded side that of the King, now overcast with mental darkness. The three minions are evidently directing their devotions to the brighter side.

CHAPTER IX.

ROYALTY UNDER VARIOUS PHASES.

Bishop Watson a partisan of the Prince—The bishop's reception by the Queen—The Prince's patronage of the bishop—Bishop Watson's views on the Regency—Laid on the shelf—The Prince and the bishop's 'Apology'—Ball given on the King's recovery by Brookes's Club; Mrs. Siddons, as Britannia—The Queen's Drawing-room on the occasion— Mrs. Siddons's readings at Buckingham House—Gay life of the Duke of York—Popularity of the Duke of Clarence—His boundless hospitality at the Admiralty—Duel between the Duke of York and Colonel Lennox —Littleness of spirit of the Princes—Royal visit to Lulworth Castle— Assault on the King—Caricatures of the day—Marriage of the Duke of York—Ceremonious royal visit to the young couple—Caricatures of the Duchess of York—Unhappy in her marriage—The Duchess and Monk Lewis—Alleged avarice of the King and Queen—Dr. Johnson's opinion of the King—Etiquette at Court—The Sailor Prince 'too far gone' for a minuet—The Royal family at Cheltenham—The mayor and the master of the ceremonies—Questionable taste of the Queen in regard to the drama—Moral degradation of England during the reign of the first two Georges—Mrs. Hannah More's ideas on morality; and Rev. Sydney Smith's witty remark on it—A delicate hint by the Queen to Lady Charlotte Campbell—The Prince's pecuniary difficulties—The Prince and affairs of the heart—*Mésalliance* of the Duke of Sussex.

AMONG the few bishops who took the 'unrestricted' side on the Regency Bill, Bishop Watson of Llandaff was the most active. No doubt his activity was founded on conscientiousness, for many able men of the period were to be found who were by no means violent partisans, yet who were ready to maintain that, according to the constitutional law, the right of exercising the power of regent in the case of incapacity on the part of the reigning sovereign rested in the next heir, the Prince of Wales.

There is as little doubt as to the Queen's having looked with considerable disfavour on all who held such sentiments. Among those who did was this Bishop of Llandaff. If Queen Charlotte felt towards the prelate as Queen Caroline used to do towards those who stood between her and her wishes, the fault, if fault there were, was not attributable to *her*, but to the minister. *He*, right or wrong—and most persons who knew what the conduct of the elder son of Charlotte was will agree that he was at least morally right—*he*, the minister, represented to her that all who supported the Prince and opposed the ministerial measure which gave great power to the Queen were enemies of the sovereign. Charlotte believed this, and perhaps the Whig bishop is not wrong who says that the Queen lost, in the opinion of many, the character she had hitherto maintained in this country by falling in with the designs of the minister. These many were, however, only the Whigs. It is nevertheless unfortunately true that the Queen distinguished by different degrees of courtesy on the one hand, and by meditated affronts on the other, those who had voted with and those who had voted against the ministers, 'inasmuch,' says Bishop Watson, ' that the Duke of Northumberland one day said to me, "So, my lord, you and I also are become traitors."'

At the drawing-room held on the King's recovery the Queen received Bishop Watson with a degree of coldness which, he says, ' would have appeared to herself ridiculous and ill-placed could she have imagined how little a mind such as mine regarded in its honourable proceedings the displeasure of a woman, though that woman happened to be a Queen.' But it must not be forgotten that if the Queen had, as it were, two faces for the two parties into which society at Court was divided, her eldest son exhibited the same characteristic, and he was accordingly eminently cordial with the prelate of Llandaff. When, at the drawing-room above-named, the Queen looked displeased as the bishop stood before her, the Prince of Wales, who was standing by her side, immediately asked him to come and dine with him. A more unseemly proceeding cannot well be imagined. 'On my making some objection,' says the bishop, ' to dining at Carlton House, the Prince turned to Sir Thomas Dundas and asked him to give us a dinner at his house on the following Saturday.' The party was arranged, the guests met, and, while they were waiting for dinner, the Prince took the bishop by the button-hole, and, says the prelate, ' he explained to me the principle on which he had acted during the whole of the King's illness, and spoke to me with an afflicted feeling of the manner in which the Queen had treated himself. I must do him the justice to say that he spoke, *in this conference*, in as sensible a manner as could possibly have been expected from an heir-apparent to the throne and from a son of the best principles towards both his parents.'

The especial words 'in this conference' would seem to imply that the son of Charlotte did not always speak in so sensible a manner as could have been expected from a royal heir-apparent. It would have been as well, too, if the bishop had told his readers what the principle was on which the Prince had grounded his conduct throughout the King's illness. When he simply talks of the Prince as a son imbued with the best principles towards both his parents, he would have done well if he had added whether he was considering that son politically or morally. It must have been politically, for the right reverend prelate did not impress upon his younger friend that a mother's faults should be invisible to the eyes of her children; but, on the other hand, he rather emphatically charged her with ill-humour by advising the Prince 'to persevere in dutifully bearing with his mother's ill-humour till time and her own good sense should disentangle her from the web which ministerial cunning had thrown around her.' Now to *persevere* in a line of conduct is to continue in that already entered upon, and the line followed by the Prince was one of continual insult and provocation against the Queen. The bishop confesses an inclination to think well of her. 'I was willing,' he writes, ' to attribute her conduct during the agitation of the regency question to her apprehensions of the King's safety, to the misrepresentations of the King's minister, to anything rather than a fondness for power.' There is something inexpressibly ingenuous in the paragraph which follows:—' Before we rose from table at Sir Thomas Dundas's, where the Duke of York and a large company were assembled, the conversation turning on parties, I happened to say I was sick of parties, and should retire from all public concerns. " No," said the Prince, " and mind *who it is that tells you so*, you shall never retire—a man of your talents shall never be lost to the public." ' This testimony of himself was recorded by the bishop in 1814, and was published by his son in the Queen's lifetime in 1817. Like the passage touching the Queen, it gave offence to the principal person concerned in it. The aged Queen was not pleased to have her ' illhumour ' registered before the world, nor was her son flattered by the innuendo which was conveyed in the paragraph which chronicled his promise of conferring preferment on the Bishop of Llandaff. Dr. Watson died prelate of that small diocese.

The clergy of the diocese of Llandaff presented congratulatory addresses to both their Majesties upon the King's recovery. These addresses were written by Bishop Watson; and in that which he presented to Queen Charlotte he inserted a paragraph which he avows, in his memoirs, that he knew would be disagreeable to her. The address in question, after expressing that the sympathy of every family had been extended to the Queen in her late distress, complimenting her on the sincerity of her piety, the amiableness and purity of her manners as Queen, wife, and mother, and referring, in laudatory terms to the concern which she had exhibited for the Monarch during his late unhappy situation, thus proceeds:—'We observed in the deliberations of Parliament a great diversity of opinions as to the *constitutional mode* of protecting the rights of the Sovereign during the continuance of his indisposition; but we observed no diversity whatever as to the *necessity* of protecting them in the most effectual manner. This circumstance cannot fail of giving solid satisfaction to your Majesty; for, next to the consolation of believing that in his recovery he has been the especial object of God's mercy, must be that of knowing that during his illness he was the peculiar object of his people's love; that he rules over a free, a great, and an enlightened nation, not more by the laws of the land than by the wishes of the people.'

Upon this text of his own constructing, the bishop makes the following comment in his 'Autobiography':—
'The first part of this last paragraph I *knew* would be disagreeable to the Queen, as it contradicted the principle she wished to be generally believed, and the truth of which alone could justify her conduct—that the opposition to the minister was an opposition to the King. Now, as there was not a word of disaffection to the King in any of the debates in either House of Parliament during the transaction of the regency, and as I verily believe the hearts of the Opposition were as warm with the King, and warmer with the constitution, than those of their competitors, I thought fit to say what was, in my judgment, the plain truth.' The bishop, however, loses sight of the fact that Queen, ministers, and a great majority of the people desired a restricted regency, in order that the rights of the Sovereign should suffer nothing, in case of

recovery ; and that Queen, ministers, and a great majority of the people felt that the Prince of Wales had no divine right to the regency, but had by his public and private conduct shown that he was entirely unworthy of holding any powers but under constitutional limitation.

Previous to the King's recovery, the Bishop of Llandaff had expressed himself as having been miserably neglected by Mr. Pitt, and 'I feel the indignity as I ought.' The bishop declares that he was overlooked, for want of political pliancy. However, we have seen that, in the allegedly offended Queen's presence, the Prince of Wales ostentatiously patronised the prelate, and subsequently made a post-prandial promise touching preferment, which he never fulfilled. The bishop strongly suspected that the Queen stood in his way. In 1805, the Duke of Grafton wrote to him, to give him early intimation that the Archbishop of Canterbury was not expected to live ; but ' I had no expectation of an archbishopric,' says Dr. Watson, ' for the Duke of Clarence had once said to me, (speaking in conversation no doubt the language of the court), ' they will never make *you* an archbishop ; they are afraid of you.' In the following year, the bishopric of St. Asaph became vacant, and Dr. Watson applied for it to Lord Grenville, stating that it ' would be peculiarly acceptable to himself.' ' It was given to the Bishop of Bangor; and the bishopric of Bangor was given to the Bishop of Oxford.' Hereupon, the diocesan of Llandaff, suspecting that the Queen's influence was exercised against him over the King, addressed a letter to the Duke of Clarence, begging him to lay the same, which contained a statement of the writer's wishes, before the Prince of Wales, whom the bishop 'most earnestly entreated to take some opportunity of doing him justice with the King.' Years, however, passed on ; and, in 1810, we find the right reverend prelate expressing himself in doubt 'whether it is by her or by his Majesty that I am laid on the shelf.' In fact, he was by far worse treated at the hands of the Prince of Wales, whose cause he had supported against Queen, ministers, and a great majority of the people, than he ever was by the Queen herself. The Prince had intimated that such a champion should not go without his reward; and that the Prince would not forget the prelate. His Highness did, however, completely forget the right reverend father. We do him wrong: he remembered him on one occasion. On the 3rd of May 1812 there was a dinner party at Carlton House. At these parties it was no uncommon thing for the Regent to tell stories which sent the Queen's fan up to her face, with a remonstrating 'George! George!' to induce him to have some respect for decency. On the occasion in question, however, the conversation turned on immorality and irreligion. Mr. Tyrrwhitt thereupon told a story how he had been in society with a Sussex baronet, who gave utterance to such profligate and atheistic opinions that Mr. Tyrrwhitt was obliged to leave the room, after recommending the blasphemer and libertine to look into Bishop Watson's 'Apology' for that Bible which the baronet so scoffed at. At the royal table 'the baronet's answer was produced and read, expressive of the greatest thankfulness for having had it put into his hands, as it not only had decided and clearly proved the error and fallacy of every opinion he had before entertained, but had afforded him a degree of secret comfort and tranquillity that his mind had previously been a stranger to.' The Regent thereupon bethought himself of his old friend of Llandaff, and ordered Mr. Braddyll to communicate to him the highly gratifying anecdote. Dr. Watson returned his best thanks for 'this instance of a Prince's remembrance of a retired bishop;' and therewith ended the patronage of the Regent, which was not more profitable to the prelate than the alleged opposition or indifference of the Queen.

The Prince's party were somewhat ashamed, it would seem, at what had taken place in connection with White's Club ball; and the Club at Brookes's resolved to render themselves blameless in the eyes of the Queen, who was supposed to be more indignant than her consort at the measures of their elder sons and their followers. The club at Brookes's hired the Opera-house, and gave a festival to the ladies, consisting of a concert, recitations, a ball, and a supper. At this festival Mrs. Siddons was engaged to appear as Britannia, and recite some silly verses, by silly Merry, in which laudation of the King was qualified by political instructions to the people. 'Long may he rule a *willing* land!' was declaimed by the actress with solemn and melodious dignity; and this line was followed by the hint to the people that 'Oh, for ever may that land be free!' A long roll of 'infinite deal of nothings' followed, in which scant courtesy was paid to ths Queen; and Mrs. Siddons, having got to the end of her 'lines,' astonished the spectators by an exhibition of the 'pose plastique,' assuming the 'exact attitude of Britannia, as impressed upon our copper coin.'

Having noticed what took place at the King's drawing-room, omission must not be made of the Queen's, held by her in March, especially to receive congratulations upon the happy recovery of her consort. More than usual splendour did honour to the occasion. The Queen sat on a chair of state, under a canopy, and surrounded by the great officers of her household. Eye-witnesses declare that the blaze of diamonds which covered her Majesty was something more than the ordinary glory. Around the Queen's neck, too, was a double row of gold chain, supporting a medallion. 'Across her shoulders was another chain of pearls, in three rows; but the portrait of the

King was suspended from five rows of diamonds, fastened loose upon the dress behind, and streaming over the person with the most gorgeous effect. The tippet was of fine lace, fastened with the letter G, in brilliants of immense value. In front of her Majesty's hair, in letters formed of diamonds, were easily legible the words, " God save the King." The Princesses were splendidly, but not equally, adorned. The female nobility wore emblematical designs, beautifully painted on the satin of their caps, and fancy teemed with the inventions of loyalty and joy. At half-an-hour after six o'clock, her Majesty quitted the drawing-room for duties still more interesting.'

What these duties were, after the long drawing-room, Mr. Boaden, from whose 'Life of Kemble' the details are borrowed, does not inform us; but he adds, in a burst of eloquence not unlike the tone of some of the dramas of which he discourses so pleasantly, that he cannot forbear from expressing the full conviction of his understanding and his heart, that no more glorious being than the consort of George III. ever existed. 'I have lived,' he says, ' to see a miserable delusion withdraw some part of the affection of the multitude for a time; but she was in truth the idol of the people, and they paid to her that sort of homage as if in her person they were reverencing the form of VIRTUE itself.'

The same unreserved panegyrist, describing her Majesty's visit to Covent Garden Theatre on the 15th of April 1789, states that she was accompanied by three of the Princesses—the Princess Royal, most unassuming of all Charlotte's daughters; the Princess Augusta, so careless as to what she was dressed in, provided only that she were dressed; and the Princess Elizabeth, who was always anxious to be doing little services for people about the court, as if she wished to forget that she was burdened by being great, and by the formalities which she must observe, to give greatness dignity. Mr. Boaden strikingly describes the scene. ' The Queen entered the royal box alone ; the Princesses not being, for a few minutes, ready. On the appearance of the Queen, a shout arose, of transport, from the spectators ; the curtain ran up, and displayed a transparency which had the words, in striking letters, *Long live the King !* and *May the King live for ever !*' For all this no preparation could be sufficient ; and tears fortunately came to her relief. In this state she paid her compliments to her people. On the entrance of the Princesses, the emotion somewhat subsided—

> It seemed she was a Queen
> Over her passion, which, most rebel-like,
> Sought to be king o'er her.

The entertainments of the evening had no allusion whatever to the event. They consisted of 'He would be a Soldier,' and 'Aladdin.' The simple introduction, by Edwin, of giving the King's health, was the only allusion made to passing events. But the house cheered, and the Queen smiled and nodded her gratification.

Whilst on the subject of theatricals, it may be noticed that the King and Queen not only patronised Mrs. Siddons, but that the patronage which they showed to this lady was not confined to witnessing and applauding her performances on the stage. She was a frequent visitor at Buckingham House and Windsor ; and she was among the first to discover that the King's mind was affected. On occasion of one of her visits, after her task was done of reading a play, at a high desk, before which she stood, the King went up to her, and presented her with a blank paper—blank, with the exception that his signature was at the bottom of it. Such a gift intimated that the giver bound himself to make any amount of pecuniary provision which the will of the actress might choose to name, above the royal signature. The paper was doubtless received with a graceful and grateful dignity, but with equal propriety it was, on the earliest opportunity, presented blank, as it was received, to the Queen. Her Majesty was very pointed in the expression of her approbation at conduct so delicate and dignified; but the virtue of Mrs. Siddons was left to be its own reward.

While the Duke of York was leading a 'gay' life, running in debt, and falling asleep over his cards (his constant habit), to find himself a great loser when he awoke, his next brother, Clarence, with some lively propensities, too, contrived to maintain considerable popularity. He was of a popular profession. At the age of thirteen the King sent him as midshipman on board a man-of-war, and told him to fight his way. He obeyed the injunction by having a *set-to* with another 'middy,' soon after he was afloat, and secured, in this way, the respect of his fellow-officers. He served under Keith, Hood, and Nelson. His sole remark on first seeing the last-named gallant 'shadow,' was, that his tail seemed more than he had strength to carry. The little Duke was present in several actions, and shared in several victories. When the Spanish commander, Don Juan de Langera, was brought prisoner on board the 'Prince George,' and was told that the smart and active midshipman whom he had observed on duty at the gangway was a prince of the blood, and son of the reigning King, the brave but unlucky captain exclaimed, 'Well may England be queen of the seas, when the son of her sovereign is engaged in such a duty!' The companions of the young Prince were not the most suitable for a youth of his condition and prospects, as far as refinement is concerned; they were rude, but I question if their principles of conduct were not as good as any by which modern middies and lieutenants are influenced. In some respects they were better, for I do not imagine that if any one of the lieutenants of

Keith, Hood, or Nelson, had fallen into such a scrape as befel Lieutenant Royer of the 'Tiger,' he would have expressed 'satisfaction' at being permitted, at the theatre, to use the identical glass through which a hostile commander had watched the destruction of a British ship. The rough and ready manner of old days is better than the refinement which takes such form and expression as this; and William Henry was little the worse for the former, although Beau Brummell *did* say of him that he was never good for anything but to walk about a quarter-deck and cry 'luff.'

Walpole writes of him, in 1789: 'The Duke of Clarence, no wonder, at his age, is already weary of a house in the middle of a village, with nothing but a green short apron to the river, a situation only fit for an old gentlewoman, who has put out her knee-pans and loves cards.' The writer adds, that were the Duke a commoner and a candidate, Richmond, if it were a borough, would return him unanimously. 'He pays his bills regularly himself, locks up his doors that his servants may not stay out late, and never drinks but a few glasses of wine.' Miss Burney's report would lead us to a different conclusion. Walpole adds: 'Though the value of crowns is mightily fallen of late at market, it looks as if his Royal Highness thought they were still worth waiting for. Nay, it is said, he tells his brothers he shall be King before either. This is fair, at least.'

William Henry was not always so blameless in his economy as Queen Charlotte loved to see him. His hospitality at the Admiralty was unbounded; but when it is remembered that the exercise of it during fifteen months ran him in debt to the amount of not less than three-and-twenty thousand pounds, such hospitality is rather to be censured than eulogised. He was as profuse when King, until his treasurer, Sir F. Watson, confessed his inability to go on.

The second son of Queen Charlotte delivered his maiden speech in the House of Lords at the close of 1788. A few months after he made another speech, in private society, which might have had a very fatal issue. He stated that Colonel Lennox (afterwards Duke of Richmond) had been addressed at Daubigny's club in language to which no gentleman would have quietly listened as the colonel had done. The latter, on parade, asked for an explanation. The Duke refused, ordered him to his post, and offered him 'satisfaction' if he felt himself aggrieved. The colonel appealed to the club as to whether the members adopted the Duke's statement. They remained silent; and the result was a duel on Wimbledon Common, on the 26th of May 1789. Lord Rawdon accompanied the Duke, and the Earl of Winchilsea attended on the colonel. The duel ended with no bloodier finale than the loss of a curl on the part of the Duke. The latter, it was found, had not fired; he refused to fire, bade the colonel fire again if he were not satisfied, and rejected every inducement held out to him to make some explanation. On this the parties separated.

Some littleness of spirit was exhibited in what followed. The colonel was present at a court ball, at which the Queen presided, and formed part in a country dance of which the Prince of Wales and other members of the royal family were also a portion. The Prince, who was remarkable for his gallantry, did not exhibit that quality on the present occasion. He passed over the colonel, and the lady his partner, without 'turning' the latter, as the laws of *contre-danse* required. The Prince's conduct was imitated by both his brothers and sisters, and the colonel's partner was thus subjected to most unwarrantable insult. The Queen, who had marked her opinion of the colonel's conduct by graciously speaking to him, remarking the chafed look of her son, and addressing some inquiry to him, was answered that he was heated, because he disliked the company. Upon this hint the Queen rose, and the festive scene was brought to a disturbed and sudden conclusion.

The fall of the year was passed in the south of England, with Weymouth for head-quarters. The King and Queen were not without peculiar annoyances here, chiefly in the threats of assassination conveyed in private letters. The Queen indeed, like the King, disregarded them, but she feared the evil effect they might have on his excitable mind. Among the visits paid by them to private individuals was one to the Roman Catholic proprietor of Lulworth Castle, Mr. Weld, a relation, by her first marriage, of Mrs. Fitzherbert. They were present in the chapel attached to the castle during the celebration of divine service, and remained while the anthem was sung,—without any ill effects resulting to Protestantism.

In January 1790 the fears of the Queen were again excited for her consort, at whom a stone was thrown by a mad Lieutenant Frick, as his Majesty was on his way to the House of Lords. The muse was hardly more sane or loyal than the lieutenant, for Peter Pindar wrote of this incident:

> Folks say it was lucky the stone missed the head,
> When lately at Cæsar 'twas thrown;
> I think, very different from thousands indeed,
> 'Twas a lucky escape for the stone.

The Queen, at the time of the King's illness, was assailed with unmeasured vituperation by the Opposition papers. Even her interviews with Pitt were made base account of, in order to raise the public odium against her. In the present year the 'Hopes of the Party,' a caricature so named, by Gillray, served to show the supposed wishes of the Opposition. The caricature represents many revolutionary horrors. Among them is what is termed 'a pair of pendants,' showing the Queen and prime minister each hanging from a lamp iron. 'It is commonly believed,' says Mr. Wright, in the History from which a passage has been already quoted, 'that Pitt and Queen Charlotte were closely leagued together to pillage and oppress the nation; and she was far less popular than the King, whose infirmity produced general sympathy, and who had many good qualities that endeared him to those with whom he came in contact. In another part of Gillray's picture the King is brought to the block, held down by Sheridan, while Fox, masked, acts as executioner. Priestley, with pious exhortations, is encouraging the fallen monarch to submit to his hard fate.' Later in the year, in September, the Queen's second son, Frederick Duke of York, married Frederica, eldest daughter of the King of Prussia. The marriage was solemnised on Michaelmas Day, at Berlin. The bride was then in her twenty-fourth year, her husband in his twenty-eighth. She was fair, virtuous, accomplished, and kindly-hearted,—by far too good a wife for the profligate Prince to whom she was allied. The newly-married pair travelled to England through France, where they met with but rough treatment from the republican mob, some of whom very unceremoniously scratched the royal arms off their carriages. The ceremony of marriage was re-performed in England on the 23rd of November by the Archbishop of Canterbury, in presence of the entire royal family. By an addition of 18,000*l.* to the Duke's income, his revenue amounted to 35,000*l.* a year; and an annual 30,000*l.* was settled on the Duchess, in case of her surviving him.

The Queen, accompanied by the King and the elder branches of her family, paid a visit of welcome to the young couple, which was the most formal and ceremonious matter that can well be conceived. The visit took the form of a tea-party; it ought, therefore, to have been social and chatty, but it was as stiff and silent as much ceremony and formal etiquette could make it. The King's tea was solemnly handed to him by the Prince of Wales, while the Duchess of York, receiving a cup from the Duke, presented it, with much reverence, to the Queen. But in the cups which cheer and not inebriate, ceremony *was* soon dissolved; and the King getting loquacious, the family party, before the night was far gone, became as mirthful and pleasant as if it had been made up of more mirthful and pleasant materials.

Despite the great popularity of the excellent Duchess, the caricaturists spared neither her nor her royal father and mother-in-law. In one of the satirical prints by Gillray, the King and Queen—the latter most outrageously caricatured—are represented in ridiculous attitudes of joy: the King is fairly 'kicking up his heels' in ecstasy, offering eager welcome to the Duchess. The Queen is holding out her apron to receive some of the wealth and jewels which her daughter-in-law was popularly supposed to have brought with her. The latter has *her* apron full of money, and the Duke is introducing her to his parents.

The poor Duchess was soon one of the unhappiest of wives. The profligacy and shameless infidelity of her husband, to whom she had been fondly attached, disgusted her. His extravagance involved him in a ruin from which he could never relieve himself, and which his creditors never forgot. It made many a hearth cold, and it brought misery to that of the Duchess. For six years she bore with treatment from the 'commander-in-chief' such as no trooper under him would have inflicted on a wife equally deserving. At the end of that time the ill-matched pair separated, and the Duchess withdrew from the world; but in her retirement she forgot none of the duties which it could fairly demand of her. She was beloved by all, and was popularly and affectionately mentioned by the popular voice as 'the poor soldier's friend.'

She was indeed the friend of all who needed her service, and did not refuse even to give to poor 'Monk' Lewis the meed of admiration which his little vanity required. He was once met coming in tears from the Duchess's drawing-room; and on intimating to his questioner that they had their source in the very kind and flattering things the Duchess had said to him, the weeper was roughly consoled by his acquaintance, with the soothing advice, to 'Never mind, as perhaps she did not mean it!'

Never was the alleged avarice of the King and Queen more bitterly satirised than during this year (1791). The King, however, was a cheerful giver, and the amount of property which the Queen left at her death proves that she was no hoarder. The caricaturists, nevertheless, smote them mercilessly. Peter Pindar assailed them in coarse and witless lines, that had in them a certain rough humour, but as ill-natured as rough. Gillray exhibited them as cheapening wares in the streets of Windsor. In another print, the King, in the commonest of garbs, was seen toasting his own muffins; and the Queen, with a hideous twist given to her now plain features, and with pockets bursting with the national money, was depicted busily engaged in frying sprats for supper. In another, the Queen is sourly commanding her highly-disgusted daughters to take their tea without sugar, as a saving to papa. There were many of a similar cast, and not a few which exposed the vices to which the Princes of the family —young men of great hopes and with much kindliness of feeling, but with little principle—had unfortunately surrendered themselves.

The King himself was ever depicted as slovenly both in dress and gait—the Queen as mean in attire and sharply sour of visage. The latter always wears a far more acute, but a less inquiring, air than her husband. This was a true reflection. After Dr. Johnson had his celebrated interview with the monarch at Buckingham Palace, he is said to have declared that 'His Majesty seems to be possessed of some good nature and much curiosity; as for his *nous*, it is not contemptible. His Majesty, indeed, was multifarious in his questions; but, thank God, he answered them all himself.'

The public discontent and the general distress increased greatly at this time, and had their effect in throwing a gloom over the court circle. The old formality and not a very diminished festivity were still, however, maintained there, and the republican fashions of France were held in abhorrence at Windsor.

The sons of Queen Charlotte were not so formal in their behaviour towards her, before witnesses, as the daughters were. The Duke of York was now the most observant of ceremony, but he exhibited therewith a show, perhaps a reality, of very tender feeling. Even on common occasions the household of the Queen was encumbered by much stiffness of observance of etiquette. It was not an uncommon occurrence for the Duke of York to attend at his mother's toilette, conversing with her during its closing progress. When this was the case, and the dresser's task was done, that lady could not leave the room if the Duke happened to stand between her and the door; to cross the Duke would have been a terrible breach of good manners. Nor could the Queen help the dresser; all that the illustrious lady could do was to watch till the Duke changed his position, and then with a smile, and a '*Now*, I will let you go,' give freedom to the dresser, longing for liberty.

The Prince William (Duke of Clarence) was the least courteous of the sons of Charlotte. But it must be remembered that he not only went early to sea, but it was at a time when roughness of manner was considered as more becoming to a naval officer than refinement; to support the character, the young Prince probably assumed more coarseness of style and speech than was really natural to him. The Queen's birth-day drawing-room, in 1791, was followed by a ball, at which the pretty Princess Mary was to dance her first minuet in public, and her brother, the sailor Prince, had promised to be her partner. But previous to the ball there was a dinner, and at a birth-day dinner more champagne was drunk by the Prince than on ordinary days. Under its inspiration, the Duke found his way to the table of some of the ladies and gentlemen in waiting. There he ruled as king, insisted upon more champagne, compelled the not-unwilling gentlemen to drink with him glass after glass, laughed at its effects upon them and himself, smacked the servants on the shoulder, abused them good humouredly, praised his sister Mary, had more champagne, kissed the hand of old Madam Schwellenberg with infinite mock heroics, was always going and never went, and ended all he said with the common oath of gentlemen, a loudly-uttered 'By G—!' With a morning so spent, he was not likely to be steady enough for the minuet at night. In fact, he was incapable of appearing at the ball at all; much to the chagrin of the Queen; still more to that of the Princess Mary, to whom, however, the offender made less apology the next morning than confession, that on the Queen's birth-day he had been 'too far gone' to think of dancing.

The Prince of Wales was not more temperate even on

ordinary occasions ; and he was less heartily courteous to
ladies than his brothers, while perhaps he was more formally polite. Miss Burney describes him as staring at her
when she was in attendance upon the Queen, not haughtily
or impertinently, she says, but in an 'extremely curious
manner'—probably as Don Juan may have looked upon
Zerlina.

With all the Queen's respect for the formality of court,
she enjoyed herself most when she was least observant of
it. Reading the letters of Johnson and Mrs. Thrale, she
liked to talk them over with Miss Burney, who could explain so many circumstances connected with them which
would, otherwise, have been incomprehensible to the
Queen. She loved to hear her dresser's graphic account
of Warren Hastings' trial, whither she had sent her with
a reticule stuffed full of cakes from the Queen's own table.
At Cheltenham, when she accompanied the King thither
previous to his late illness, the royal residence was of such
contracted dimensions, and so scant of accommodation,
that her Majesty dressed and undressed in the drawing-
room. Many of her ladies would not have submitted half
so cheerfully as *she* did to such an arrangement. In the
rural expeditions of the royal pair, there was indeed a
comic sort of mixture of formality and fun. At Weymouth, for instance, when the King went to take his
'dip,' the royal machine was followed by another full
of fiddlers and other musical persons, who, as the monarch plunged into the ocean, saluted him and the bold
deed with 'God save the King,' horribly out of tune!

It was when the royal pair were at Weymouth that,
on one occasion, the mayor of the borough, after presenting an address, and receiving the stereotyped answer,
boldly walked up to the Queen to kiss her hand. 'You
must kneel,' whispered the master of the ceremonies.
Mr. Mayor, not heeding the court guide, continued stand-

ing, and in that position kissed the royal hand. As he retired, the highly offended master of the ceremonies remarked, angrily, 'Sir, you ought to have knelt.' 'Sir,' said the Mayor, 'I can't; don't you see I have got a wooden leg?'

It is upon record that the Queen *once* attempted to write some verses; and having got to the third line gave the matter up in despair—leaving her 'reader' to finish and perfect the rhymes. The occasion was on presenting a pair of old-fashioned gloves to Lord Harcourt, who had an affection for ancient gear, and cared more for old gloves than new verses. Miss Burney acquitted herself, however, very well with her *impromptu*; indeed, she may be said to have been the Queen's laureate during the five years she served that Sovereign. Her royal mistress employed her to compose some congratulatory verses on the King's recovery from his serious indisposition; and of these it may be said that if Warton, over whom paralysis was then pending, might have written better, Henry James Pye, the succeeding laureate, could hardly have written worse.

The taste of the Queen was itself not unimpeachable. With regard to the drama, she would rather have seen little Quick in Tony Lumpkin, than Mrs. Siddons in Lady Macbeth. So her 'reader' was not called upon to exert her powers upon any great works. The first book she was required to read aloud was Colman's broad farce of 'Polly Honeycomb.' The young lady must have had a difficult task with the novel-reading Polly, whose heart beat for Mr. Scribble, and into whose head her sire could not beat a favourable opinion for 'the rich Jew's wife's nephew,' Mr. Ledger. The young Princesses were listeners, and it could hardly have been edifying for them to hear the rollicking Polly say of her father, 'Lord, lord! my stupid papa has no taste; he has no notion of humour and character and the sensibility of delicate feeling.' 'A novel,' says Miss Honeycomb, 'is the only thing to teach a girl life;' and she adds, 'Every girl elopes when her parents are obstinate and ill-natured about marrying her.' Her ridicule of the long-lived affection of her parents is expressed in the coarsest manner; and she thinks it a good joke that her father recommends her to read the 'Practice of Piety;' she runs away with a scamp, and her honest lover, rightly disenamoured, declares of her that 'he would not underwrite her for ninety per cent.' What Miss Pope made of Polly and King of Scribble, when this farce was first produced, in 1760, it is not worth inquiring. Miss Pope was considered great in it; but it is worth noticing that when Miss Burney was reading the piece to the Queen and her daughters, an actress whose name can never be separated from that of the Queen's third son was then turning half the heads in town with her Polly. Mrs. Jordan was well supported by Palmer in Scribble, and the piece seems to have found its way to court, as the 'Dragon of Wantley' did in the preceding reign, on the strength of its popularity.

The reader to the royal audience performed her vocation under great disadvantages. She read on in mortal silence on the part of those who listened; neither comment, applause, nor feeling of any sort was ever exhibited; and when Miss Burney had to read other of the elder Colman's plays, and once ventured to relieve the voice, long fatigued by reading, by making some remark on the construction of the piece, the innovation was submitted to without being commended.

This scene of a Queen whose high moral character and purity of taste have been long matters of eulogy, seated amid her daughters, listening to a farce which would hardly now be tolerated, is not pleasant. But society had not yet freed itself from the uncleanness with which it had been overwhelmed during the two preceding reigns.

The unspeakable degradation into which the first two Georges dragged the country must not be forgotten, though it may not be detailed. While detesting the restrictions with which monarchy had been loaded in the great revolution, they indulged unrestrainedly in the worst coarseness of vice. Kept back from pressing despotically upon the people, they yielded unbridled sway to their own passions, and their infamous example corrupted three-fourths of society. Caroline herself would listen to stories told her by Sir Robert Walpole, upon which the eye of the student of history cannot rest without a blush of indignation mantling in his cheek. If the Stuarts were vicious, they were, in a certain degree, gentlemanlike in their vices. The first two Georges were as vicious, but they had none of the refinement of the Stuarts, and would have been to the full as tyrannical had the men of England left them the power. Their conduct was enough to render monarchy detested, and the name of Brunswick execrable. The domestic virtues of George III. and Queen Charlotte insured respect for the first, and surrounded the latter name with something like a halo of love. If there be any yet among us who sing 'Hail, Star of Brunswick!' with any mental reservation, the reason may probably be traced to impressions received from the records of the first Georges. The tone of society had not yet recovered itself fully when Queen Charlotte caused 'Polly Honeycomb' to be read aloud to herself and daughters. It is true that her Majesty also listened in like company to the teaching of Mrs. Hannah More; but even that high moralist hardly as yet understood how the work of morality might best be sped. Even ten years later than the time when Colman's farces were deemed not unfitting to be read to an audience of mother and children, Mrs. More, in 'Cœlebs,' was recommending the observance of modesty on the part of ladies on very selfish grounds. In allusion to the 'naked style' of dress which was then the fashion with women, Mrs. More admonitorily and significantly exclaims: 'Oh, if women in general knew what was their real interest; if they could guess with what a charm even the appearance of modesty invests its possessor, they would dress decorously from mere self-love, if not from principle. The designing would assume modesty as an artifice; the coquet would adopt it as an allurement; the pure as her appropriate attraction; and the voluptuous as the most infallible art of seduction.' When the Reverend Sydney Smith read this passage, he remarked that if there were any truth in it, 'nudity becomes a virtue, and no decent woman for the future can be seen in garments.' This is, perhaps, more smartly than truly said. Queen Charlotte certainly abhorred the style of dress which is censured in 'Cœlebs.' When the Lady Charlotte Campbell, famous for her beauty and for her subsequent connection with Queen Caroline, first went to court, she was attired in the scant costume of the period. She was, in fact, in the very highest of the fashion, and as she was passing before Queen Charlotte, the latter recommended her to 'let out a tuck in her petticoat!'

While on the subject of fashion, it may here be noticed that when the marriage of the Princess Royal with the head of the House of Wurtemburg had been determined on, her Majesty made the bridal dress, and helped to deck her daughter with it. As a King's eldest daughter, she had a right to be attired in a dress of white and silver. The Princess, however, was about to marry a widower, and it appears that custom, consequently, required the bride to wear white and gold. And so the robe was fashioned accordingly, and the preference of the Princess was made to yield to etiquette. This marriage, however, did not take place till 1797.

In 1792, the Prince's pecuniary affairs were in a worse condition than ever. Several executions had been in his house, from one of which he had been saved by the benevolence of Lord Rawdon. His debts now amounted to 400,000l. The Queen advised him to press the King, through the lord chancellor, to apply for an increase of income. What the Prince required was 100,000l. yearly, and if that were granted he proposed to set aside 35,000l. per annum for the liquidation of his debts. He had now abandoned racing, a silly pursuit which had cost him yearly not less than 30,000l.; and having done that, he feigned to be shocked at his equally embarrassed brother, York, remaining on the turf. He added, that if his request were not acceded to, he should shut up Carlton House, go abroad, and live upon 10,000l. a year. It was very properly suggested to him that he would do much better, if the Queen's wishes and his own could not be carried out, by staying in England and showing the people that he could adapt his circumstances to his revenue. This was a course, however, which he had never seriously determined to follow. He was made up of contradictions; and although he was at this period more than ever attached to Mrs. Fitzherbert, it did not prevent him from maintaining the well-known actress, Mrs. Crouch, in the post of 'favourite.' Mrs. Fitzherbert met this course by ridiculing it, and by coquetting on her side. This hurt the Prince's vanity, and brought him again under her influence. What his homage was worth may be judged of by the fact that it was paid to many deities, and while he was maintaining Mrs. Crouch, forgetting poor Perdita Robinson, making love to the beautiful Duchess of Devonshire (who was separated from her husband, but did not on that account in the slightest degree regard the Prince), he had also opened an intercourse with Lady Jersey, who was not half such a prude as the Duchess, and who was the most shameless of those to whom the heartless Prince had pretended to surrender his heart. With many loves, or what were called such, Mrs. Fitzherbert continued the married sultana. He built for her a residence at Brighton, where she kept up the establishment of a queen—really looked like one, for she was a superb woman—had as brilliant diamonds as Queen Charlotte herself, and was greeted by all the bathing women with the respectful appellation of 'Mrs. Prince.'

But the Queen had soon to deplore another *mésalliance*. Her son Prince Augustus (Sussex), when travelling in Italy, had become attached to the Lady Augusta Murray, daughter of the Earl of Dunmore; and, after a courtship during which the Prince wrote love-letters to the lady that, with respect to style were neither sublime nor beautiful, and with regard to grammar were calculated to make Lindley Murray die of despair, the parties were married privately by an English clergyman, and were re-married, at St. George's, Hanover Square, on their return to England. Of this union two children were born, of whom the daughter (once known as Mademoiselle d'Este) became the wife of Lord Truro, who, when Mr. Serjeant Wilde, endeavoured to establish the validity of her father's marriage, and acquired the lady's hand by way of *honorarium*. The moment the marriage of the Duke with Lady Augusta Murray was first declared invalid by the ecclesiastical court, Lady Augusta separated from her husband. The latter appears to have borne the separation very philosophically, but he did not marry again during Lady Augusta's life. In his later days, when his brother, William IV., was King, he married the lady who long survived him under the title of Duchess of Inverness. But a marriage of more importance remains to be noticed.

CHAPTER X.

LENGTHENING SHADOWS.

The Prince of Wales's marriage to the Princess Caroline of Brunswick—Her character—The Prince's behaviour at the marriage ceremony—Lord Holland's two accounts of the Princess irreconcileable—The Prince's hatred of the Princess—Propriety of the Queen's Court—Unpopularity of the King—Pelted by the mob—Birth of the Princess Charlotte—Strict observance of Court etiquette—Marriage of the Princess Royal to the Prince of Wurtemburg—First book stereotyped in England—The volunteer mania—Attempted assassination of the King—Archbishop Cornwallis's drums, and Lady Huntingdon's efforts to induce him to discontinue—Her hot reception by Mrs. Cornwallis—Lady Huntingdon induces the King to aid her—The King's letter to the archbishop—Conduct of the clergy—Incident of the Drawing-room—The Prince a Radical—The King's illness—His excitement—Feeling exhibited by the Duke of York—The Prince of Wales incredulous of the recovery of the King—Conversation between the King and Dr. Willis—The Queen's anxiety—Particulars of the King's illness—Recovery of the King—Home scene at Windsor Castle.

THE subject of the marriage of the Prince of Wales will come more fully under our notice in the Life of Caroline of Brunswick. Here it may be mentioned that the period at which the question of the marriage of the Prince was first moved, is not known with certainty. It was soon, however, publicly ascertained that whenever that much-desired event should take place the Prince's debts were to be paid, on the condition that after such settlement and the fixing of his establishment as a married man, he was never to incur such liabilities again. The agreeing to this condition debarred him from ever again applying to Parliament for pecuniary relief.

There is little doubt as to the wish of Queen Charlotte

that her son should marry a Princess of Mecklenburg. It was sufficient for the Prince that his mother had such desire that he should oppose it. According to Lord Liverpool, the intimation of the Prince's wish to marry was abruptly made to the King, who received the information with a cheerful complacency, and simply required that the lady chosen should be a Protestant and a Princess. Mrs. Fitzherbert was neither.

The King offered to send a commissioner to the German courts on the pleasant mission of reviewing the daughters of the sovereign dukes there, and reporting on their eligibility. The Prince's choice, however, appears to have been made, if that can be called choice which fixes on an object utterly unknown. He named his cousin, the daughter of the Duke and Duchess of Brunswick. Her mother was Augusta, sister of the King, whose birth had taken place at St. James's Palace under circumstances which gave such offence to Caroline and George II. The King made no objection: and yet he must have known that if the object selected was pretty, she was far less fair than the lady of Mecklenburg whom Charlotte would fain have had for a daughter-in-law; and that her reputation, even in Germany, where the best people then construed liberally of female conduct, was none of the best. She was known as a bold, dashing, careless girl, whose tongue was ever in advance of reflection; who called the coarsest things by the coarsest names, and who only needed temptation and opportunity to fall into any sin which had a pleasant side to it. She was not worse than many of her contemporaries with whose doings fame was less busy. Her great defect was a want of self-control, if that be a great defect compared with a want of cleanliness. But in this latter respect Caroline's neglect was not singular. In *her* young days dirtiness had not yet quite gone out of fashion.

It is credibly asserted that the Prince's favourite, Lady Jersey, led him to select the Princess of Brunswick for his wife. It was Lady Jersey's object that he should have a legal consort who must draw him away from his (illegal) wife, Mrs. Fitzherbert; but it was also Lady Jersey's object that the wife should not possess attractions that should prove more powerful than her own.

It will suffice to record here that the marriage took place on the 8th of April, 1795, under unseemly auspices. The behaviour of the Prince at the ceremony undoubtedly may be received as confirming the accounts of his aversion to the bride. He confessed to the Duke of Bedford (one of the two unmarried dukes who supported him at the marriage) that he had taken several glasses of brandy before proceeding to it. He must have taken many, for he was so drunk that the two dukes could scarcely keep him from falling. The conduct of the Prince was, of course, the subject of much remark, and it was set down, at the time, not to brandy but remorse—remorse at the idea of that other marriage which he had contracted with the woman whom he undoubtedly did love, if he ever entertained for woman at all a sentiment worthy of that name. Very few days passed after the solemnisation of the ceremony before 'many coarse and indelicate strictures on the bride's person and behaviour were currently reported as coming directly from the Prince in every society in London.' So says Lord Holland; and that noble writer, who pronounces to be a bad and worthless woman —mad, at least, if not bad—a princess whom his party, if not he himself, held up, in the days of her persecution, as a martyr of virtue, goes on to say, that the ill-usage to which the Princess of Wales was exposed at Brighton and elsewhere from the Prince and his mistress, Lady Jersey, was notorious, unpardonable, and so utterly disgraceful, 'that persons of rank (afterwards indebted to him for advancement in it) have plumed themselves upon refusing to meet him at dinner at my house [Holland House, Kensington], observing that he was not fit company for gentlemen.'

The marriage began miserably, continued miserably, and ended miserably. As Lord Holland observes, neither the Prince's reconciliation with Mrs. Fitzherbert nor his subsequent intimacies with Lady Hertford and others (although such returns and changes of love were usually accompanied by similar changes and returns of a train of favourites, friends, and dependents), ever softened his hatred to the Princess. When, in 1820, on the death of Napoleon, some officious courtier ran up to him to apprise him of the news which he supposed would be welcome to him, in these words, 'Sir, your greatest enemy is dead!'— 'Is *she*, by G—?' was the royal husband's dignified and pious ejaculation.

'Many seeds of discontent,' says Lord Holland, 'were imperceptibly sown during the year 1795, among the supporters of the ministry, which time brought to maturity. Among these may be reckoned the influence of Carlton House. The Prince of Wales thought himself duped by Mr. Pitt about the payment of his debts at the time of his marriage. He had been treated superciliously, more than once, by Mr. Pitt, and he had never liked him, though his own dread of revolutionary principles, quickened by a recent quarrel with the Duke of Orleans, had rendered him eager, and even vociferous, for the war. The last injury, real or supposed, which he had received from Mr. Pitt, by the latter's acquiescing in devoting, on his marriage, the whole increase of his revenue to the payment of his debts, sank into his weak and fretful mind deeper than usual, because he was continually reminded of it by his connection with a woman whom he loathed.'

Meanwhile, the Queen maintained the long-standing reputation of her court with undiminished strictness. 'The Queen's public receptions,' says Sir Jonah Barrington, 'were the most gracious in the world. There could not be a more engaging, kind, and condescending address than that of the Queen of England. An illustration of her strictness is afforded us by an anecdote told of her Majesty and an English duchess, who was aunt to a niece of rather blemished reputation, but to which it was hoped some lustre might be restored if she could only be made to pass through a court atmosphere. The duchess, on asking the Queen to receive her niece at the drawing-room, of course insisted that the young lady's fame had been unfairly atacked, and that she trusted to her Majesty's clemency and generosity to set it fair again with the world. The Queen remained silent; whereupon the duchess, previous to retiring, beseechingly inquired what she might be permitted to say to her niece. 'Tell her,' said Queen Charlotte, 'that you did not dare to make such a request to the Queen.' The duchess, who held some post in the royal household, felt that such a speech involved her own dismissal.

Never was the court so unpopular as at this time. In October 1795 the King, on proceeding to the House of Lords, was not only assailed by seditious cries, but was fired at by some assassin among the mob. On his return from the House he was pelted with stones, and, later in the day, when driving to the Queen's House, in a private carriage, without guards, the excited mob, with cries of 'Bread—cheap bread!' 'No war!' and 'No king!' made an attempt to force open the door of the vehicle in which he was riding. The same spirit was shown in 1796. On the 1st of February the King and Queen went to Drury Lane to see 'The Fugitive.' On their return a stone was thrown at the carriage, which passed through one of the glass panels and struck the Queen in the face. Soon after a female maniac was discovered in the palace, making no secret of sanguinary designs against 'Mrs. Guelph,' her alleged 'mother.' Added to these private vexations, the negotiation entered into, at the King's express desire, to establish a peace with France, entirely failed, and the difficulties of the situation were further increased by Spain uniting with our other enemies against us in war.

In the month previous to that last mentioned the birth of the Princess Charlotte, daughter of the Prince and Princess of Wales, was speedily followed by the separation of the parents. We may cite here an incident of the christening, as the Queen Charlotte is rather the heroine thereof than the infant Princess.

Lady Townshend held the little Princess at the font. Some time elapsed before the officiating prelate took her from Lady Townshend, whose state of health at the time was such as to make her incapable of standing long without some peril to her own future hopes. The Princess of Wales pitied her, and asked the Queen, in a low voice, if she would not command poor Lady Townshend to be seated. But Queen Charlotte liked nothing so little as an interruption of established ceremony; and, blowing the snuff from her fingers, she exclaimed, 'No, no! she may stand—she may stand!' The Queen was nearly as strict in public with her own children. They, on such occasions, never sat down in her presence unless commanded; never spoke, unless first spoken to; and once, it is said, when the Queen was playing at whist, one of the Princesses, standing behind her chair, fell fast asleep from sheer fatigue.

The domestic troubles of the Queen were now in great part connected with the affairs of her eldest son and her daughter-in-law. They will be found alluded to in the

Life of the latter. Another marriage, scarcely more promising, soon occupied her attention. The widowed Prince of Wurtemburg proposed for the hand of the Princess Royal. His first wife was the daughter of Augusta, and sister of the Caroline of Brunswick for whom the Queen, her mother-in-law, had such small measure of affection. This first marriage had been an unhappy one. The Prince had taken his wife to Russia, where she is said to have become so thoroughly corrupted as to have shocked the unclean Czarina, Catherine, herself. From Russia she never returned; but how, when, or where she died, no writer seems to be able to state with certainty. That she died there in confinement cannot be doubted; and yet her sister Caroline used to express her belief that she had been seen in Italy long after the reported period of her death. Queen Charlotte had an especial dislike to the projected match of this Prince with her daughter, nor would the King consent until he had been satisfied that the Prince had not been a cruel husband to his first wife, and that he had not become a widower by unfair means. What the nature of this satisfaction was no one knows. The marriage took place on the 18th of May. After a thirty years' residence in Wurtemburg, during which time that locality was raised to the rank of a kingdom, and the daughter of our own Charlotte was visited more than once by the first Napoleon, of whom her husband was a very active ally, Charlotte Augusta, the 'good Queen-dowager,' and a childless widow, visited England once more, in order to obtain medical relief for a dropsical complaint. On her voyage back, in worse health than when she came hither, the vessel had nearly perished in a storm. To her terrified attendants she calmly remarked, 'We are as surely under the protection of God here as upon the dry land—be not afraid!' She survived her mother ten years, dying in October, 1828. Her letters addressed to the lady who superintended the education of the Princess Charlotte of Wales are creditable alike to her head and her heart.

The Princess Royal was married in 1797. Soon after she had set out from St. James's, early on a morning in June, in tears, and without a relation to bid her adieu, all having gone through that ceremony the night before, in order to be saved the trouble of early rising, the mutiny in the navy broke out—a circumstance which hardly annoyed the King more than the agitation for Parliamentary reform; for it was more easily suppressed. There was some compensation for these vexations in the visit to Duncan's victorious North Sea fleet, and in the triumphs of our other naval squadrons. The year ended appropriately with the royal procession to St. Paul's to render fervent thanksgiving for the success of the arms of England.

It was early in 1798 that the first book was stereotyped in England, and the Queen was the origin of this innovation—not that she had any idea of innovation. The facts are simply these:—The press had been teeming with productions offensive alike to virtue and religion. To protect both was an anxious object with the Queen. According to contemporary report, she procured from a German Lutheran divine (Freylighausen) his 'Abstract of the whole Doctrine of the Christian Religion,' and this she submitted to the judgment of Dr. Porteus, Bishop of London. The prelate, well pleased to see the State thus submissive or suggestive to the Church, read the pamphlet —not only read it, but approved of, and (as it was said, erroneously) translated it into English. He caused it to be printed in stereotype, and this translated book was the first volume that was ever so printed in England. With stereotyping, the name of Queen Charlotte should always be mentioned in honourable connection.

The year 1798 was marked by the Irish rebellion, the national subscription for the exigencies of the state, and for the uneasiness felt at court at the standing toast of the Whigs—'The sovereignty of the people!' That and the following year were *the* years of the Volunteer mania. The King and Queen were too happy to encourage this sort of enthusiasm; and, even in their retirement at Weymouth, the Volunteer reviews were among the most cherished of their amusements. They hoped they had reconquered the love of a people on whom the burden of war pressed heavily. They were at least not safe from popular fanaticism. On the 15th of May, 1800, the royal family attended Drury Lane Theatre, after a review in the morning. As the King entered the box, and was in the act of bowing to the audience, he was fired at from the pit. The Queen and her daughters were entering as the shot was fired; and the King kept them back with his hand, lest, as he said, 'there might be another.' After Hatfield, the assassin, had been secured and carried off, the King and his family sat calmly down, and witnessed the whole representation. This coolness was deservedly admired. On the return to the palace the King replied to a sympathising observation of the Queen, 'I am going to bed with a confidence that I shall sleep soundly; and my prayer is that the poor unhappy prisoner who aimed at my life may rest as quietly as I shall.'

The other domestic incidents in the life of the Queen or King are not of sufficient interest to be worth the detail. We may make exception of one, however, which introduces us once more to the earnest and indefatigable Lady Huntingdon.

Early in the present century we again meet with this lady, busy at, with, and in defiance of courts. In her zeal as a reformer of manners and morals, she was bold without being indiscreet; and she was never more bold that when she attacked, courteously and courageously, no less a person than Dr. Cornwallis, Archbishop of Canterbury. This right reverend lord primate had given several grand routs at his palace. The archbishop was an old-fashioned man; and what had been tolerated in his father and mother must also be permitted to himself and wife, the magnificent Mrs. Cornwallis—leader and slave of *ton*. Let the world have justice done to it, the majority therein were sorely scandalised at these irreverend proceedings. But Lady Huntingdon was the only one bold enough to give expression to what she felt. With the energy and tact natural to such a woman she contrived to obtain the grant of an audience with the primate and his lady, and thither she went, accompanied by the Marquis of Townshend.

The priests of the sacred cities of Anahuac were not more horror-stricken when Cortez asked them to burn their gods, than the primate of all England was when the good lady pressed upon him sacrifices which would entail the necessity of spending very dull evenings. As for Mrs. Cornwallis, she tarred and feathered Lady Huntingdon, metaphorically, by flinging missiles which soiled her who flung them, and by scattering light ridicule which was blown back upon the face and reputation of the scatterer. Lady Huntingdon again and again assaulted the archiepiscopal fortress, but she was driven back by repeated discharges of 'Methodist!' and 'Hypocrite!'

She could do nothing at Lambeth, and accordingly she turned her face towards Kew. Nor had she long to wait before Queen Charlotte and her royal consort admitted her to an interview, to which she was conducted by Lord Dartmouth and the Duchess of Ancaster.

The sovereigns listened to the simple yet earnest story. The King was especially warm in expressing his indignation, and the Queen took her full share in such expression.

'I had heard something of this before,' said George III., 'but I knew not if all was as bad as Lady Huntingdon has detailed it. The archbishop has behaved very ill to the lady. I will see if he dare refuse to listen to a King.' The gay and orthodox courtiers present began to think that the world was at an end. Here was the State placing itself above the Church! Mentally, they no doubt denied the royal supremacy.

In an after-conversation the honest King confessed that Lady Huntingdon herself had been painted to him in very odd colours, and, in admitting her to an interview, he was partly influenced by his curiosity to see whether she was so strange a creature as she had been described by her enemies. To his expressions of admiration for herself and her work the Queen added similar assurances; and could the archbishop have seen two sovereigns thus complimenting a 'Methodist' and a 'Hypocrite,' no doubt the primate, zealous for nightly 'drums,' would have burst into tears, and have declared that the sun of England was set for ever!.

'His Majesty,' said Queen Charlotte, 'had complaints made against yourself, in part, Lady Huntingdon, but chiefly against your students and ministers, whose preaching annoys one or two of our bishops who are careless.' The King nodded assent, adding, it was a pity that these students and ministers could not be made bishops of, as then they would cease to annoy anyone by preaching. It was objected that even the Lady Huntingdon could not be made a bishop of, and so the evil would be as rife as ever. 'I wish we could make her one,' said the Queen, with a smile at the idea; 'I am sure her ladyship would shame more than one upon the bench!'

The King then conversed with Lady Huntingdon, chiefly upon old times and persons of his father's court, at which she had for a while been a frequent visitor.. 'We discussed a great many subjects,' says the lady herself, in her account of the interview, 'for the conversation lasted upwards of an hour, without intermission. The Queen,' she adds, ' spoke a good deal, asked many questions, and, before I retired, insisted on my taking some refreshments. On parting, I was permitted to kiss their Majesties' hands; and when I returned my humble and most grateful acknowledgments for their very great condescension, their Majesties immediately assured me they both felt gratified and pleased with the interview, which they were so obliging as to wish might be renewed.'

The Queen repeatedly expressed her admiration of Lady Huntingdon's conduct on this occasion, one result of which was a stringent letter addressed by the King to the primate. In this royal remonstrance and reproof, the writer told the archbishop that he ' held such levities and vain dissipations as utterly inexpedient, if not unlawful, to pass in a residence for many centuries devoted to divine studies, religious retirement, and the extensive exercise of charity and benevolence . . . where so many have led their lives in such sanctity as has thrown lustre on the pure religion they professed and adorned. From the dissatisfaction,' adds the King, 'with which you must perceive I hold these improprieties, not to speak in harsher terms, and on still more pious principles, I trust that you will suppress them immediately, so that I may not have occasion to show any further marks of my displeasure, or to interpose in a different manner.'

When it was necessary to administer such a reproof as this to an archbishop, we may readily believe that only a sorry sort of reputation attached itself to the clergy generally. This had been the case for many years. Speaking of the Queen's drawing-room, held in January, 1777, Cumberland, who was present, says: ' Sir George Warren had his order snatched off his ribbon, encircled with diamonds to the value of 700*l*. Foote was there and lays it upon the parsons, having secured, as he says, his gold snuff-box in his waistcoat pocket upon seeing so many black gowns in the room.'

Foote's remark was only in jest, but it shows the estimation in which the clergy were held. They were for the most part, and yet with some noble exceptions, but wretched teachers both by precept and example. Where clerical instruction was thus doubly defective, lay practice was not of a very pure character. Only two or three years before Lady Huntingdon waited on Queen Charlotte and the King at Kew, an incident illustrative of my remark occurred at one of her Majesty's drawing-rooms. A great crowd had assembled, and amid the throng—while the Prince of Wales was conversing with the King—he felt a sudden pull made at the hilt of his sword. He looked down and perceived that the diamond guard of the weapon was broken off, but it remained suspended by a small piece of wire, the elasticity of which had prevented it from breaking, and so preserved the diamond-studded guard. No discovery was made as to the author of this felonious attempt, and the Prince did wisely in refusing to fix on the gentleman who stood nearest to his side as the offender.

In 1801 the Prince of Wales was in full opposition against the crown and Pitt. The opposition had a Jacobinical character, and affected Jacobinical opinion without any reserve. Lord Malmesbury remarks of the Prince that even ' his language in the streets is such as would better become a member of Opposition than the heir to these kingdoms.' This conduct was followed at a time when the state of the King's health began again to cause some anxiety. He had contracted a chill and severe cramps by remaining too long in a cold church, on the 13th of February. We find Lord Malmesbury recording on the 17th of February: 'King got a bad cold. Takes James's powders. God forbid he should be ill!' And the next day he writes: 'King-better. Lord Radnor saw him yesterday morning, and he clearly had *only* a bad cold.' One day later, on occasion of an audience of the King being sought by Mr. Pelham, the same writer says: 'Pelham came back to me from court; he had seen and consulted the Duke of Portland, who approved his seeing the King, but said it would not be *to-day*, as the King was unwell, and on such occasions it was not usual to disturb him but on great public business.' On the 21st matters appeared worse. 'Bad accounts from Queen's House; the answer at the door is, the King is better: but it is not so. He took a strong emetic on Thursday, and was requested to take another to-day, which he resisted.' It would seem that the progressive seriousness of the symptoms produced no corresponding effects in the heir-apparent. On Sunday, the 22nd of February, the diarist writes: 'His Majesty still bilious; not getting better; apprehensions of getting worse. Fatal consequence of Pitt's hasty resignation. Princess Amelia unwell. Queen not well. At Carlton House they dance and sing.' As the King grew worse, the intrigues of the husband of Caroline became more active. The regency was the object of these intrigues. In the meantime the condition of the Sovereign grew daily more unsatisfactory. On the 29th of February the King's pulse was at 130 during the night. 'This makes,' says Lord Malmesbury, 'in favour of the mental derangement, and proves it to be only the effect of delirium in consequence of fever, but it puts his life in very great danger.'

His mind had been extraordinarily excited at this period by an agitation which was being carried on against the Church, and in favour of the emancipation of the Romanists. The King had strong views of what he was bound to by the coronation oath, and the idea became the rooted torment of his mind. 'The King, on Monday,' writes Lord Malmesbury, 'after having remained many hours without speaking, at last, towards the evening, came to himself, and said, "I am better now, but will remain true to the Church." This leaves little doubt as to the idea uppermost in his mind. And the physicians do not scruple to say that, although his Majesty certainly had a bad cold, and would under all circumstances have been ill, yet that the hurry and vexation of all that has past was the cause of his mental illness, which, if it had shown itself at all, would certainly not have declared itself so violently, or been of a nature to cause any alarm, had not these events taken place.' They were events which were weighing on the mind of George III., just as the loss of the American colonies had done in the preceding century.

The Duke of York at this juncture is said to have behaved with great propriety towards Queen Charlotte and the Princesses. How his elder brother behaved is thus recorded: 'The Prince of Wales, on Sunday, the 22nd of February, the second day of the King's illness, and when he was at his worst, went in the evening to a concert at Lady Hamilton's, and there told Calonne, the rascally French ex-minister, "Savez vous, M. de Calonne, que mon père est aussi fou que jamais?"' Later we have it recorded, that 'the King at Windsor, about 6th or 7th instant (March), read his coronation oath to his family ;— asked them whether they understood it? and added, If I violate it I am no longer legal sovereign of this country, but it falls to the house of Savoy.' Subsequently, Lord Malmesbury writes : 'Lady Salisbury said the King was quite well enough to have the Queen and Princesses at dinner. *Qui prouve trop ne prouve rien.* Any degree of fever could render this improper in anybody, and if you take away the fever, you have the intellectual derangement without a cause or hopes of recovery. I fear there is so much fever that his life is in imminent peril. The Duke of York deeply affected, and worn out with his assiduous attentions at the Queen's House.'

Lord Vincent, the first lord of the admiralty, declared on the 2nd of March that not only was his Majesty much better, but that, throughout the present attack, he had never been so ill as he was at the moment when, in his previous illness, he had been pronounced by Warren to be convalescent. The King's fever increased alarmingly that very night. On Tuesday, the 3rd of March, Lord Malmesbury thus graphically describes the crisis: 'King so much worse last night that his life was despaired of. About ten he fell into a profound sleep; and awoke in about six hours quite refreshed and quite himself. His Majesty said he was thirsty, and, on being asked what he wished to drink, said, "if *allowed*, a glass of cold water." This was given him. It put him into a perspiration. He fell asleep again, and awoke in the morning with the fever abated, and better in every respect. The crisis of his disorder. Crowds of people round Queen's House, and their expressions of joy very great.'

The cure, however, was not yet complete. Much care was required. The King was disposed to talk on that very subject which had temporarily threatened to overthrow his intellect. And his anxiety for the Church, joined to seeing and conversing with two of his daughters before he was strong enough to argue the question connected with one, or to bear the pleasant excitement of intercourse with his family, produced a disagreeable, although not an enduring, relapse.

The Prince of Wales was the most reluctant of his family to believe in the recovery of his father, whom he openly declared as being more deranged than ever, although he might possibly be improving in bodily health. He affected to complain of being kept in ignorance of what was going on at the Queen's House; but his ignorance arose from the little care he gave himself to become wiser.

The recovery, however, was considered genuine. The illness itself had been marked by one circumstance which distinguishes it from that under which the King suffered so severely in 1788. In the earlier attack sleep never relieved him. Not that he did not sleep well, but that it did not compose his nervous system. He would sleep indeed, soundly, but awake from it, like a giant refreshed by wine, more turbulent than ever. In the illness from which he had just recovered his sleep was healthy and refreshing, and he invariably woke from it quiet and composed.

The first persons whom he saw after his recovery were the Queen and Princesses and the Dukes of Kent and Cumberland. To the Duke of York, whom he saw alone on the 7th of March, he said, after thanking him for his kindness to his mother and sisters, 'I saw them yesterday, because I could send *them* away at any time; but I wish to see you *alone*, and for a long time, and therefore I put it off till to-day.' In inquiring about the Queen's health of the Duke of York, the King expressed great solicitude for them; and the Duke acknowledged that they had suffered greatly, but added, that their chief anxiety was lest now, in getting well, he should be less careful about his health than prudence would warrant. The King confessed to having presumed too much on the strength of his constitution, but promised to be less neglectful for the future. And the conversation turned to political affairs, to the ministry, to what had been done during his malady, and at last to that question of Romanist emancipation which had so shaken his mind, as being connected with that ruin of the Church of England which he thought must follow, and which church he had sworn he would protect. Some weeks before his illness he had said to the Duke of Portland that, 'were he to agree to it, he should betray his trust and forfeit his crown, that it might bring the framers of it the gibbet.' He was beginning to use language almost as strong to the Duke of York, at the first introduction between father and son, after the recovery of the former. The Duke of York, however, very judiciously stopped him, with the assurance that Pitt had abandoned all idea of pressing the Catholic question, that therefore it were wise to let the discussion of it drop also; and that all political parties, who had behaved with great propriety during his illness, had now but one common anxiety—that to see him well again. 'I am now *quite* well; QUITE recovered from my illness,' remarked the King to Mr. Willis, on the occasion of directing him to write to Pitt, 'but what has *he* not to answer for who has been the cause of my having been ill at all?' Pitt was much affected by this reproach, and it is said to have influenced him to surrender the question rather than press it to the peril of the King's health. Indeed, the King had so determinedly expressed himself on the subject that the Duke of Portland had declared that his Majesty had rather suffer martyrdom than submit to this measure.

The interview between the King and the Duke of York was followed by one between the Sovereign and the Prince of Wales. Lord Malmesbury says of the latter, that 'his behaviour was right and proper. How unfortunate that it is not sincere, or rather that he has so effeminate a mind as to counteract all his own good qualities by having no control over his weaknesses!'

The Queen continued in a great state of anxiety touching the King's health, notwithstanding his complete recovery having been declared. He was at times very nervous and depressed—at others, still more nervous and excited. There was less a fear of mental derangement than that his faculties might never recover their former tone. He occasionally behaved strangely in public; was too familiar with the members of the cabinet which succeeded that of which Pitt had been at the head; and, again, was too readily and profoundly affected—too soon elated or cast down—by trifles. On Thursday, the 26th of March, 1801, Lord Malmesbury writes: 'Drawing-room to-day very crowded. Queen looking pale. Princesses as if they had been weeping. They insinuate that the King is too ill for the Queen to appear in public, and to censure her for it. Dukes of York and Cumberland there. The Prince of Wales *was* at the drawing-room, but behaved very rudely to the Queen.' And yet just previously he had made an ostentatious manifestation of his delicacy. Lords Carlisle, Lansdowne, and Fitzwilliam, with Mr. Fox, informed his royal highness that they had formed a coalition, offered him their services, and proposed to hold a conference at Carlton House. The Prince is said to have pleaded, in excuse for declining all they offered, the state of the King's health; but out of respect to his sire, he said that he should consider it his duty to inform Mr. Addington, the minister, of the nature of their proposals. This he did; and it was perhaps because he regretted the step he had taken that he behaved rudely to his royal mother in her own public drawing-room!

The King's condition still required care and watchfulness. Thus, on the 25th of May, Dr. Thomas Willis writes to Lord Eldon:—' The general impression yesterday, from the King's composure and quietness, was that he was very well. There was an exception to this in the Duke of Clarence, who dined here. "He pitied the family, for he saw something in the King that convinced him he must soon be confined again."

'This morning I walked with his Majesty, who was in a perfectly composed and quiet state. He told me, with great seeming satisfaction, that he had had a most charming night, " he could sleep from eleven to half after four," when, alas! he had but three hours' sleep in the night, which upon the whole was passed in restlessness— in getting out of bed, opening the shutters, in praying violently, and in making such remarks as betray a consciousness of his own situation, but which are evidently made for the purpose of concealing it from the Queen. He frequently called out, " I am now perfectly well, and my Queen--my Queen has saved me!" While I write these particulars to your lordship I must beg to remind you how much afraid the Queen is lest she should be committed to him ; for the King has sworn he will never forgive her if she relates anything that passes in the night.'

The Princess Elizabeth subsequently addressed a letter to Dr. Thomas Willis, in which she states that she has the Queen's commands to inform him that 'the subject of the Princess of Wales is still in the King's mind, to a degree that is distressing, from the unfortunate situation of the family.' The writer adds : ' The Queen commands me to say, that if you could see her heart, you would see that she is guided by every principle of justice, and with a most fervent wish that the dear King may do nothing to form a breach between him and the Prince. For she really lives in dread of it; for, from the moment my brother comes into the room till the instant he quits it, there is nothing that is not kind that the King does not do by him. This is so different to his manner when *well*, and his ideas concerning the child (the Princess Charlotte) so extraordinary, that I am not astonished at mamma's uneasiness. She took courage, and told the King that now my brother was quiet he had better leave him, as he (the Prince) had never forbid the Princess seeing the child when she pleased. To which he answered, " That doesn't signify. The Princess shall have her child; and I will speak to Mr. Wyatt about the building of the wing to her present house." You know full well how speedily every thing *is now ordered* and done.'

'The Princess spoke to me on the conversation the King had had with her—expressed her distress; and I told her how right she was in not answering, as I feared the King's intentions, though most rightly meant, might serve to hurt and injure her in the world.' For a few days the symptoms ameliorated; then, on the 12th of June, Dr. Thomas Willis wrote to Lord Chancellor Eldon: 'His Majesty still talks much of his prudence, but shows none. His body, mind, and tongue are all upon the stretch every minute; and the manner in which he is now expending money in various ways, which is so unlike him when well, all evince that he is not so right as he should be.' The Queen, to use her own words, built her faith upon the Chancellor, and doubted not of his succeeding in everything with his Majesty. 'He failed in some nevertheless. He urgently requested the King to allow Dr. Robert Willis to remain in attendance on him. The King hated all the Willises, and Dr. Robert not less than any of them. He concludes a note to Lord Eldon on the 21st of June by saying: 'No person that has ever had a nervous disease can bear to continue the physician employed on the occasion. This holds much more so in the calamitous one which has so long confined the King, but of which he is now completely recovered.'

The health of the Sovereign prevented him from attending the concerts and other entertainments which he was accustomed to honour with his patronage. He was, however, sufficiently recovered to enjoy a sojourn at Weymouth, and, on his return to Kew, to ride over occasionally to visit the Princess of Wales at Blackheath. The daughter of the latter, the Princess Charlotte, was now four years of age, and the question of her separation from her mother was a frequent subject of discussion. In the meantime, the little Princess was very often a visitor at St. James's or Windsor, by command of the Queen, and, of course, unaccompanied by her mother.

On the 29th of October, the King opened Parliament in person. The pleasant announcement was made in the royal speech that the eight years' war had come to a conclusion. The gratification of the public was, however, somewhat marred by finding that the cost of carrying it on had doubled the national debt, and that the supplies required for the year amounted to forty millions.

The royal family now repaired to Windsor; and for the description of a home scene there we will again have recourse to one who describes what he saw and of which he was a part. Lord Malmesbury was a guest at the castle during the 26th, 27th, and 28th of November. 'I went there,' he says, 'to present to the King and Queen copies of the new edition of my father's works. I saw them both alone on the evening of the 26th, and was with them that and the next evening at their card party at the Lodge. Each evening the Queen named me of her party, and played at cribbage with me. I was with the King alone near two hours. I had not seen him since the end of October, 1800—of course, not since his last illness. He appeared rather more of an old man, but not older than men of his age commonly appear. He stoops rather more, and was apparently less firm on his legs; but he did not look thinner, nor were there any marks of sickness or decline in his countenance or manner. These last were much as usual—somewhat less hurried and more conversable: that is to say, allowing the person to whom he addressed himself more time to answer and talk than he used to do when discussing on common subjects, on public and grave ones. I at all times, for thirty years, have found him very attentive, and full as ready to hear as to give an opinion, though perhaps not always disposed to adopt it and forsake his own. He was gracious even to kindness. He asked how I continued to keep well; and on my saying, amongst other reasons, that I endeavoured to *keep my mind quiet*, and dismiss all unpleasant subjects from intruding themselves upon it, the King said, " 'Tis a very wise maxim, and one I am determined to follow ; but how, at this particular moment, can you avoid it ? " And without waiting he went on, saying, " Do you know what I call the peace ? *An experimental peace*, for it is nothing else. I am sure you think so, and perhaps do not give it so *gentle* a name ; but it was *unavoidable*. I was abandoned by everybody —allies and all. I have done, I conscientiously believe, for the best, because I could not do otherwise : but had I found more opinions like mine, better might have been done." '

His Majesty continued, at greater length than it is necessary to follow, to give his opinions upon the men and questions of the day ; and this he did with great calmness, discrimination, and foresight. He was not one that believed Jacobinism was dead merely because it was quiet ; and he spoke of the policy of Prussia of that day, and of the King who adopted it, as men speak of both in the present day—a mixture of atrocity, treachery, and meanness. Lord Malmesbury says little of the Queen, but enough to give an idea of her manner. 'The Queen,' he says, ' kept me only a quarter of an hour. She said she should see me again in the evening, as I must be tired of standing so long with the King. Spoke kindly of my father and my dear children. Princess Mary was all goodhumour and pleasantness : her manners are perfect, and I never saw or conversed with any princess so exactly what she ought to be.'

CHAPTER XI.

THE END OF GREATNESS.

Queen as an author—Domestic life of the Royal Family—Return of the King's illness—His continual agitation—Dr. Symonds not the medical officer for the King—Capricious changes made by the King in his household—His humorous eccentricities—Contest between the King and the Prince—The Queen's conduct—Scant courtesy to the royal invalid—Errors committed by the King—Wellesley and Nelson—Gradual decay of the King—His eccentricity at the installation of Knights of the Garter—Picture of the daily life of the Royal Family—Position of the Queen—The King's resignation on his blindness—Distress of his mind—Renewal of the Regency question—Extraordinary assertion by Lord Eldon—The King's person confided to the Queen—The Queen's letters to Lord Eldon—Her merry letter to him—A touching incident—The Queen's unpopularity—Marriage of the Princess Charlotte—Decline of the Queen's health—Disgraceful reception of her by the City—Her death—Considered as a parent—Her political influence—The debts of Prince of Strelitz—The Court on George III.'s ceasing to exercise authority—Regal retinue about the old King dismissed—The Queen's funeral—Her will—Her diamonds—Death of the Duke of Kent—Death of the King—Visit of the Emperor of the French to the Duchess of Gloucester.

In the year 1804 Queen Charlotte became entitled to be enrolled among royal and noble authors or translators. It was now discovered that she, and not Bishop Porteus, had translated Freylighausen's 'Abstract of the whole Doctrine of the Christian Religion.' The Queen translated it, for the use of her daughters, from a German manuscript in her library. This book was the first that was stereotyped in England according to the Stanhope process. It was familiarly known as 'the Queen's book.' 'The Queen's book has come out, with an introduction by the Bishop of London;' thus writes the Rev. Thomas Belsham to Mr. Aspland, in September, 1804. The letter is printed in the 'Memoirs of the Rev. Thomas Aspland.' The writer adds: 'I have just dipped into it. I presume it was the Catechism which she learned when she was a child, and which she still faithfully adheres to. I have just glanced over it as it lies in Johnson's shop. It is a mass of absurdity.' This testimony, it must be remembered, is given by a disciple of the eminent Dr. Priestley and by an Unitarian minister—the most illustrious of the church which claimed to be Christian as well as Unitarian.

The utmost regularity marked the course of the royal life during the short time which elapsed between the King's last illness and that of 1804. It was the period when anecdotes were being constantly told, and perhaps sometimes made, of his simplicity and gentle nature. The Queen, with a great love for display, could readily adapt herself to the circumstances required by the exigencies of the time; and she as much enjoyed the quietness of their domestic life as she had done the most brilliant days and episodes of her reign. Her eldest son, who, in spite of his conduct, loved his mother as well as he could love anybody, caused her continual anxiety; but this was little compared with the trials which awaited her from another source.

The mental maladies of the King usually occurred after taking cold; but this fact did not seem to render him in any way cautious and prudent. Thus, early in the present year he caught a violent cold, followed by gout, in consequence of remaining in wet clothes after returning from a walk in the rain. The malady speedily assumed the appearance of something more formidable than a mere attack on his bodily health. At the evening assembly at the Queen's House, held in celebration of her Majesty's birthday, the King was unusually incoherent in his style of speaking. The Queen played at cards, as was her custom; but her anxiety was very manifest, and she never kept her eyes off the King during the entire time the assembly lasted.

In the course of a few weeks the King grew worse; and, in addition to his ordinary physicians, the attendance was required of persons accustomed to these peculiar cases. The royal dislike to the Willises (father and son) was the cause of Dr. Symonds being called in. The august patient was in extreme danger during the 12th and 13th of January. He partially recovered; but the mania, in a modified form, still continued. He remained in this condition till May—fanciful, suspicious, and unsteady in his manners and conversation, particularly with the Queen and royal family and his usual society. 'He was apparently quite himself,' says Lord Malmesbury, 'when talking on business and to his ministers. He then collected and re-collected himself.' Dr. Symonds was by no means so efficient a man in these cases as the Willises, against whom the monarch had taken a rooted antipathy. In the King's first illness, as Willis, the clergyman, once entered the room to visit the patient, the latter asked him if he, a clergyman, was not ashamed of himself for exercising such a profession. Willis gently hinted that the Saviour himself went about healing the sick. 'Ay, ay!' said the King, 'but he hadn't 700*l.* a-year for it.'

The King's illness proved temporary; but he had troubles enough to keep his mind in a continual agitation. On the 26th of May, 1804, Lord Malmesbury thus writes:—

'The King calls the Grenvilles "the brotherhood;" says "they *must* always either govern despotically or oppose government violently." Duke of Portland has little doubts of the King's doing well; quiet will set him right and nothing else; he has been fatigued by being too much talked to on the new arrangements. . . . . Lady

Uxbridge, at half-past two, very uneasy about the King; said his family were quite unhappy, that his temper was altered. He had just dismissed his faithful and favourite page (Brown), who had served him during his illness with the greatest attention. Quiet and repose were the only chance. She said the Chancellor was to go to Windsor with him, which she was glad of. King has stipulated, before he went to Windsor, that he would not go to chapel, nor on the terrace, nor take long rides. Lady Uxbridge thinks Dr. Symonds an unfit man; that the Willises, and particularly the clergyman Willis, was a more proper person to be about the King when he was getting well; so thinks Mrs. Harcourt.'

The next day we find the following entry in the diary: —'Sunday, May 27. Mrs. Harcourt confirms all that Lady Uxbridge had told me; that the King was apparently quite well when speaking to his ministers or those who kept him a little in awe, but that towards his family and dependents his language was incoherent and harsh, quite unlike his usual character. She said that Symonds did not possess in any degree the talents required to lead the mind from wandering to steadiness; that in the King's two former illnesses this had been most ably managed by the Willises, who had this faculty in a wonderful degree, and were men of the world who saw ministers and knew what the King ought to do; that the not suffering them to be called in was an unpardonable proof of folly (not to say worse) in Addington, and that now it was impossible, since the King's aversion was rooted; that Pitt judged ill in leaving the sole disposal of the household to the King; that this sort of power in his present weak (and, of course, suspicious) state of mind had been exercised by him most improperly; he had dismissed and turned away and made capricious changes everywhere, from the lord-chamberlain to the groom and footman; he had turned away the

Queen's favourite coachman, made footmen grooms, and *vice versâ*, and what was still worse, because more notorious, had removed lords of the bedchamber without a shadow of reason ; that all this afflicted the royal family without measure ; that the Queen was ill and *cross* ; the princesses low, depressed, and quite sinking under it ; and that unless means could be found to place some very strong-minded and temperate persons about the King he would either commit some extravagance or he would, by violent carelessness and exercise, injure his health and bring on a deadly illness. I asked where such a man did exist or had existed. She said none she knew of ;. that Smart, when alive, had some authority over him ; that John Willis, the clergyman, also had acquired it, but in a very different way ; the first obtained it from regard and high opinion, the other from fear ; that, as was always the case, cunning and art kept pace in the King's character with his suspicions and misgivings, and that he was become so very acute that nothing escaped him. Mrs. Harcourt ended her recital by great recommendations of secrecy, and submitting it to me whether I would or would not state it to Mr. Pitt. I asked her if the Chancellor knew it. She said *all:* he is the only person who can in any degree control the King : he is the best man possible, and when he is near, things go on well. I said in that case Mr. Pitt *must* know it ; and if he knew it, would, if he could, apply a remedy ; and that if he did not I must suppose he was at a loss what to do, and that the hearing what he already knew from me would be useless to him and look like a pushing intrusion on my part. After her Lord Pembroke came into my room, and asked me whether I was aware of what was passing at the Queen's House ; and he then repeated, but in a still stronger manner and with additional circumstances, what I had before heard. We then both dwelt on the very serious and dangerous consequences to which it might lead, and in vain sought about for a remedy.'

And again, on the 1st of June, we find Lord Malmesbury recording as follows :—' General Harcourt, who came to me in the evening from the Queen's House, gave me a most comfortable account of the King. He had seen him often and for a long time, and that he was, in looks, manner, conduct, and conversation, quite different from what he had been since his illness—very different indeed from what he was at Windsor; and General Harcourt, who is not a sanguine man, really seemed to think most favourably of the King.'

Some of the King's acts smacked rather of a humorous eccentricity than anything worse. Thus, early in this month, when Lord Pelham carried his seals of office to the Queen's House to deliver them up to the King, the latter said, ' Before I can allow you to empty *your* hands you must empty mine;' and therewith he thrust upon him the *stick* of captain of the yeomen of the guard. Lord Pelham looked as much horrified as if his Majesty had offered to knight him, and the poor sovereign, remarking this, observed to him encouragingly, ' It will be less a sinecure than formerly, as I intend living more with my great officers.' The noble lord was too awkwardly placed and had too much respect for the King to return the unwelcome stick. There was something additionally comical in the circumstance in this: Pitt was hurt at his Majesty thinking of conferring an office without previous communication with *him*; and Pelham was hurt at Pitt's having entrapped him, as he supposed, into the not very exalted office of captain of the yeomen.

The poor monarch had in reality enough provocation at home, to say nothing of the anxieties caused him by the aspect of foreign affairs, to render irritable, if not to throw off its balance, a mind so unhinged and ill at ease as his own. It was at this period that a contest was going on between him and the Prince of Wales relative to the residence and education of the Princess Charlotte. The Monarch, with much reason, wished her to reside at Windsor, there to be educated in the character of ' a queen that is to be.' The Prince opposed the proposition for the opposition's sake, being also moved thereto by advisers who belonged to the party in Parliament adverse to the crown. It was very much feared that if his wishes were really disregarded the consequences to his health would be serious. The Prince himself hardly knew his own mind, and perhaps had no well-grounded opinion upon the matter at all.

'The two factions,' says Lord Malmesbury, 'pulled different ways. Ladies Moira, Hutchinson, and Mrs. Fitzherbert were for his ceding the child to the King; the Duke of Clarence and Devonshire House most violent against it, and the Prince was inclined to the faction he saw last. In the Devonshire House cabal Lady Melbourne and Mrs. Fox act conspicuous parts, so that the alternative for our future Queen seems to be whether *Mrs. Fox* or *Mrs. Fitzherbert* shall have the ascendancy.'

Father and son had an interview. After a whole year's estrangement, for *one day* child and parent agreed tolerably well; but they did not long continue to be of one mind. The conduct of the Prince was insulting to the authority of the King and to his office as father. To some extremely sensible remarks on the educational plan best calculated to promote the welfare and happiness of the Princess, her father, the Prince of Wales, returned an answer so improperly worded that the Chancellor declined to present it to the King. The latter was made irritable and ill at no answer having reached him from the Prince, and he was only beguiled into patience by being misinformed that the Prince had misconceived the King's letter, and that it was necessary to set him right on the misconceived points before a reply could be expected.

The Queen was rendered more anxious than any other member of the royal family, of whom Lord Malmesbury simply records that 'the sons behave tolerably, the princesses most perfectly.' At this time the Queen, with all her natural anxiety, exhibited some strangeness of conduct. 'She will never receive the King,' says the noble diarist just quoted, 'without one of the princesses being present; piques herself on this discreet silence, and, when in London, locks the door of her *white room* (her *boudoir*) against him. The behaviour of the Queen alarms me more than all the other of Mrs. Harcourt's stories; for if the Queen did not think the King likely to relapse she would not alter in her manners towards him, and her having altered her manners proves that she thinks he *may* relapse.'

If the royal invalid thus met with scant courtesy at the hands even of his consort, whose fears made her unkind, he received still less at the hands of some of his servants. For instance, when Addington, Lord Sidmouth, broke with Pitt, and repaired to the King to surrender the key of the council-box (he had been president of the council), the King told him, somewhat angrily, 'You must not give it to me, but to Lord Hawkesbury.' The retiring statesman excused himself on the ground that he and Lord Hawkesbury were not on speaking terms; to which George wisely enough rejoined that *that* was no affair of *his*. He would thereupon have ended the audience, but Addington remained talking to and at him for an hour, and so fatigued and displeased him, that when the King returned to his family (the scene passed at Windsor), he said, 'That —— has been plaguing me to death!' It was soon after this occurrence that Pitt's administration was broken up by the death of the great statesman, and Lord Grenville and Fox came in as chiefs of the cabinet of 'All the Talents.' The Prince of Wales is recorded as having gone most heartily and unbecomingly with them; lowering his dignity by soliciting offices and places for his dependents, and by degrading himself to the 'size of a common party-leader.'

The King himself occasionally committed errors that must have considerably annoyed those of his family and cabinet who entertained more correct views and opinions. Thus, it is pretty well known that George III. was very reluctant to admit Sir Arthur Wellesley to act as commander-in-chief. It is mentioned by Lord Holland, in his 'Memoirs of the Whig Party,' that Nelson himself was looked coldly upon at court, even when he made his first appearance there after the glorious victory of the Nile. Incompetent and unsuccessful officers were there conversed with, while scarcely a word of recognition was vouchsafed to the diminutive conqueror. He had doubly offended. His connection with Lady Hamilton was an offence to both King and Queen. He had besides accepted an 'order' from the King of Naples, without first asking permission. He had been told not to wear it *above* the order of the Bath, but his reply was that the latter order was in its right place; and as the King of Naples had affixed his own on the spot which it then occupied on the admiral's coat, he would let it remain where the Neapolitan king had graciously condescended to put it. This independent line of conduct was not likely to gain favour either with the King or Queen; and though they submitted to have victories gained for them by his head and hand, they had very little esteem for him who won their battles. The King is known to have been very averse to the public funeral with which honour, poor enough, was done to the remains of the hero. He was nevertheless sensitive touching the honour of the country, and fierce in his remarks against the public men who seemed to disregard it.

The remaining years of the King's life were years of gradual decay on his part, and of watchfulness over him on the part of the Queen. Apart from state occasions, the royal couple lived in a retired manner, but with all the elegancies of refinement around them. The most marked incident of 1805 was the visit of the Princess of Wales, with the Princess Charlotte, to Windsor Castle, where the Queen paid her daughter-in-law less attention than the King, who treated her with a distinction that was offensive alike to Queen and Prince. With something of like distaste the Queen acquiesced in the King's wish to make a permanent residence of Windsor, for which purpose nearly the whole of the splendid library was removed from the Queen's House to the castle.

Queen Charlotte preserved her quiet dignity and self-possession on all public occasions. Her bearing, according to Sir Jonah Barrington, 'was not that of a heroine of romance, but she was the best bred and most graceful lady of her age and figure I ever saw; so kind and conciliating that one could scarcely believe her capable of anything but benevolence. She appeared plain, old, and of dark complexion; but she was unaffected, and commanded that respect which private virtues ever will obtain for public character.'

The King, too, still enjoyed all occasions on which he could display any magnificence. The retirement was rather a sanitary than a voluntarily adopted measure; and exciting scenes injured himself and alarmed his consort. Thus, at the gorgeous installation of the Knights of the Order of the Garter, on St. George's day, 1805, his conduct was marked by the petulant vivacity of a boy rather than by the gravity of a monarch who had occupied the throne for nearly half a century. The Queen witnessed it with amazement. He was ostentatiously patronising with the Princess of Wales, joking with some of the lords, solemnly trifling with others; and he spoke of the spectacle with the sentiment of a stage-manager who had 'got up' a showy piece with unqualified success.

The following picture of the 'economy of the royal family at Windsor,' at this time, is quoted as interesting from its faithfulness, showing the position of the Queen in her household, and being generally 'germane to the matter.'

'Our Sovereign's sight is so much improved since last spring that he can now clearly distinguish objects at the extent of twenty yards. The King, in consequence of this favourable change, has discontinued the use of the large flapped hat which he usually wore, and likewise the silk shade.

'His Majesty's mode of living is now not quite so abstemious. He now sleeps on the north side of the castle, next the terrace, in a roomy apartment not carpeted, on the ground floor. The room is neatly furnished, partly in a modern style, under the tasteful direction of the Princess Elizabeth. The King's private dining-room, and the apartments *en suite* appropriated to his Majesty's use, are all on the same side of the castle.

'The Queen and the princesses occupy the eastern wing. When the King rises, which is generally about half-past seven o'clock, he proceeds immediately to the Queen's saloon, where his Majesty is met by one of the princesses—generally either Augusta, Sophia, or Amelia; for each in turn attend their revered parent. From thence, the Sovereign and his daughter, attended by the lady in waiting, proceed to the chapel in the castle, where divine service is performed by the dean or sub-dean; the ceremony occupies about an hour. Thus the time passes until nine o'clock, when the King, instead of proceeding to his own apartment and breakfasting alone, now takes that meal with the Queen and the five princesses. The table is always set out in the Queen's noble breakfast-room, which has been recently decorated with very elegant modern hangings; and, since the late improvement by Mr. Wyatt, commands a most delightful and extensive prospect of the Little Park. The breakfast does not occupy half-an-hour. The King and Queen sit at the head of the table, and the princesses according to seniority. Etiquette in every other respect is strictly adhered to. On entering the room the usual forms are observed agreeably to rank.

'After breakfast the King generally rides out, attended by his equerries; three of the princesses, namely, Augusta, Sophia, and Amelia, are usually of the party. Instead of only walking his horse, his Majesty now generally proceeds at a good round trot. When the weather is unfavourable, the King retires to his favourite sitting-room, and sends for Generals Fitzroy or Manners, to play at chess with him. His Majesty, who knows the game well, is highly pleased when he beats the former, that gentleman being an excellent player. The King dines regularly at two o'clock; the Queen and princesses at four. His Majesty visits and takes a glass of wine and water with them at five. After this period, public business is frequently transacted by the King in his own study, where he is attended by his private secretary, Colonel Taylor. The evening is, as usual, passed at cards in the King's drawing-room, where three tables are set out. To these parties many of the principal nobility residing in the neighbourhood are invited. When the castle clock strikes ten the visitors retire. The supper is set out, but that is merely a matter of form, and of which none of the family partake. These illustrious personages retire to rest for the night at eleven o'clock. The journal of one day is the history of a whole year.' The history is not a lively one, perhaps, but it shows agreeably the domestic simplicity of the court. He who was at the head of the latter did not want for a certain religious heroism under affliction. On his growing blindness being compassionately alluded to by some one in his hearing the King remarked: 'I am quite resigned, for what have we in this world to do but to suffer and perform the will of the Almighty!' He was resigned, however, partly because he was not yet deprived of hope. In 1809, the jubilee year of his reign, he was unable to attend the grand *fête* given by Queen Charlotte at Frogmore in honour of the event; and though he rode out, his horse was now led by a servant. On foot, he felt his way along the terrace by the help of a stick. Stricken with such an infliction as rapidly advancing blindness, his predilection for the 'Total Eclipse' of Handel was, at least, singular. It affected him to tears, and the Queen could not listen to the performance of this composition without being similarly affected. And yet the King himself seemed mournfully attached to both the music and the words. One morning, we are told, the Queen, or the Prince of Wales—for each has been mentioned—but probably the former, on entering the King's apartment, found him pathetically reciting the well-known lines from Milton—

> Oh dark! dark! dark! amid the blaze of noon
> Irrevocably dark! Total eclipse
> Without all hope of day!
> Oh first created beam, and thou great word,
> Let there be light, and light was over all;
> Why am I thus deprived thy prime decree!

Indeed, although a royal, it was a troubled household. Circumstances in the lives of two of the sons of the King —York and Cumberland—caused him great anxiety; but the death of his youngest, and perhaps best-loved daughter, Amelia, in 1810, finished the ravage which care and other causes had inflicted on his intellect. Walcheren and Amelia were said to be ever in his thoughts, as long, at least, as he had the power to think and the privilege to weep. The idea of the loss of his royal authority, too, pressed heavily upon him. The time came, in 1811, when such deprivation was necessary, and that year commenced the unbroken period of what may be termed his gentle insanity.

When the unquestionable presence of this calamity necessarily introduced into Parliament the Regency question, 'Scott (Eldon) made one of the most extraordinary assertions that Parliament was ever called upon to listen to.' He affirmed that, when the King was incapable, the sovereignty, for the time being, resided in the Great Seal. He added that Parliament had a right to elect the Regent, the principle of hereditary right not being here applicable. The right of the Queen was spoken of; but it was intimated, as if from authority, that the Queen was not likely to oppose the government of her son.

That government was established; but the care of the King's person remained with the Queen, who was assisted by a council. This rendered an almost constant attendance at Windsor necessary; but the restraint was compensated for by an additional ten thousand a-year.

The Queen's letters to Lord Chancellor Eldon are all expressive of the utmost gratitude for services rendered. and of suggestions touching offices expected. She is anxious that at ' *her* council ' the great officers of state should be present, to receive the reports of his Majesty's health made by the physicians who are in daily attendance upon him. When a gleam of improvement manifests itself in the King's gloomy condition, she is anxious that too much should not be made of nor expected from it. Of these promises of amelioration no one was more readily sensible than the King himself; and his inclination to believe that he was well, or on the point of becoming perfectly so, was an inclination which she thought was by no means to be encouraged. Her urgency on this point is remarkable, and is singularly at variance with common sense; for a quiet acquiescence in the King's often-expressed conviction that he was convalescent would seem to have been less likely to agitate him than as often a repeated assurance that he was entirely mistaken. The Queen's letters on this melancholy matter do not exhibit much dignity, either of sentiment or expression; nor, indeed, was she a woman to affect either. She cared as little for sentiment as she did for grammar, and she is said at this time to have exhibited a disregard for a consistent use of pronouns. In 'Lord Eldon's Life,' by Horace Twiss, is a note of hers, addressed to the Lord Chancellor, which commences with 'The *Queen* feels,' passes into an allusion touching how severe '*our*' trials have been, and ends with an '*I* hope Providence will bring *us* through.'

But she could write merry little notes too, and to the same august person. With the establishment of the Regency it seemed as if a great burthen had been taken from her, and her sprightliness at and about her son's festivals was quite remarkable in an aged and so naturally 'staid' a lady. On occasion of the Regent's birthday, in 1812, she despatched a letter to the Lord Chancellor, in court. It commences merrily with a sort of written laugh at the surprise the grand dignitary will doubtless feel at seeing a lady's letter penetrate into his solemn court; and thus sportively it runs on with a gay invitation to come down to Frogmore, to spend the Regent's birthday. 'You will not be *learnedly* occupied, perhaps,' suggests the mirthful old lady, 'but you will be, at least, legally engaged, in the lawful occupation of dining.' In 1814, the old monarch's first love, Lady Sarah Lennox, afterwards Lady Sarah Bunbury, and, lastly, Lady Sarah Napier, had become a charming old lady; but she had not passed through life without affliction. In the above year, the Dean of Canterbury preached at St. James's Church, for the benefit of the infirmary for the cure of diseases of the eye. The Dean alluded to the miserable condition of the monarch. George Tierney was present, and he wrote in a letter now extant: 'On the seat immediately before me was an elderly lady, who appeared to be deeply affected by the whole of this part of the discourse. She wept much, and I observed that she herself was quite helpless from the entire loss of sight, and was obliged to be led out of church. The tears which I saw thus shed in commiseration to the sufferings of the King fell from the eyes of ——', the once young and beautiful Lady Sarah Lennox, the innocent rival of Queen Charlotte herself.

The office held by the Queen was not a pleasant one, but she contrived to reconcile it with a considerable amount of enjoyment. The events of her life, which brought her in collision with her daughter-in-law, will be found detailed in the story of the latter. Those of her office as guardian of the King sometimes brought her in connection with touching incidents. Thus, she one day found him singing a hymn to the accompaniment of a harpsichord, played by himself. On concluding it, he knelt down, prayed for his family, the nation, and finally that God would restore to him the reason which he felt he had lost! At other times he might be heard invoking death, and he even imagined himself dead, and asked for a suit of black that he might go into mourning for the old King! These incidents were great trials to the Queen, who witnessed them, or had them reported to her. But she had trials also from another source.

In 1816, the public distress was very great, and those in high places were unpopular, often for no better reason than that they *were* in high places, and were supposed to be indifferent to the sufferings of the more lowly and harder tried. The Queen came in for some share of the popular ill-will, but she met the first expression of it with uncommon spirit; a spirit indeed which gained for her the silent respect of the mob, who had begun by insulting her. As her Majesty was proceeding to hold her last drawing-room, in the year 1815, she was sharply hissed, loudly reviled, and insultingly asked what she had done with the Princess Charlotte. She was so poorly protected that the mob actually stopped her chair. Whereupon, it is reported, she quietly let down the glass, and calmly said to those nearest to her: 'I am above seventy years of age; I have been more than half a century Queen of England; and I never was hissed by a mob before.' The mob admired the spirit of the undaunted old lady, and they allowed her to pass on without further molestation.

Her son, the Prince Regent, sent several aides-de-camp to escort his mother from St. James's to Buckingham House, but she declined their attendance. They told her that, having had the orders of the Regent to escort her safely to her residence, they felt bound to perform the office entrusted to them by the Prince. 'You have left Carlton House by his Royal Highness's orders,' said Queen Charlotte; 'return there by mine, or I will leave my chair and go home on foot.' She was, of course, carefully watched, in spite of her commands, but the cool magnanimity she displayed was quite sufficient to procure respect for her from the crowd.

Although the King had some lucid intervals, he never again became perfectly conscious of the bearing of public events, and if he was deprived of some enjoyment thereby, he was also spared much pain. He was as little aware of what passed in his own family; and although he could make pertinent questions, and sometimes argue correctly enough from wrong premises, he was unable to comprehend the meaning of much that was told to him. Thus the marriage of his grand-daughter, a circumstance to which he used to allude playfully, was now to him a perfect blank. This ceremony took place on the 2nd of May 1816. It will be more fully alluded to hereafter. In this place it may, however, be stated that the drawing-room in honour of the marriage of the Princess Charlotte to Prince Leopold was held at Buckingham House. It was brilliant, the Queen was gracious, and only the Regent exhibited a want of his usual urbanity, by turning his back on a lady who was about to enter the service of the Princess of Wales. The bride did not look her best on this public occasion. She stood apart from the royal circle, in a recess formed by a window, with her back to the light, and was 'deadly pale.' There was an expression of pleasure on her countenance, but it was thought to be forced. 'Prince Leopold,' says a contemporary writer, 'was looking about him with a keen glance of inquiry, as if he would like to know in what light people regarded him.' The Queen either was, or pretended to be, in the highest possible spirits, and was very gracious to everybody. All the time I was in this courtly scene, and especially as I looked at the Princess Charlotte, I could not help thinking of the Princess of Wales, and feeling very sorry and very angry at her cruel fate. . . . I dare say the Princess Charlotte was thinking of the Princess of Wales when she stood in the gay scene of to-day's drawing-room, and that the remembrance of her mother, excluded from all her rights and privileges in a foreign country, and left almost without any attendants, made her feel very melancholy. I never can understand how Queen Charlotte could dare refuse to receive the Princess of Wales at the public drawing-room, any more than she would any other lady of whom nothing has been publicly proved against her character. Of one thing there can be no doubt—the Queen is the slave of the Regent.'

Of this assertion, however, very grave doubt may be entertained. The Regent, at this time, certainly loved the 'old Queen,' as she was familiarly called, if a service of tender respect, deference, courtesy, and apparent goodwill may be taken as proofs of such a love existing.

Her own health was now beginning to give way, and she sought to restore it by trying the efficacy of the Bath waters; but with only temporary relief. She was at Bath when the news of the death of the Princess Charlotte reached her, in November 1817, and her health grew visibly worse under the shock. Her absence from the side of the young Princess at this period, which was followed by such fatal consequences, was at the request of the Princess herself, who knew that the Queen's good-will in this case was stronger than her ability. The popular voice, however, blamed her, and it was unmistakably expressed on her return to London.

The last visit paid by the Queen to the City differed in every respect from that which she had paid it when a bride. Her first visit had been one of form and ceremony; mingled, however, with a hearty lack of formality in some of the occurrences of the day. She went amid the citizens surrounded by guards; and this attendance was not as doubting the loyalty of the Londoners, but that royalty might look respectable in their eyes. On the occasion of the last visit her Majesty intimated to the Lord Mayor, Alderman Christopher Smith, that she wished to be received without ceremony; and this wish the corporate magnates construed as meaning without protection; there was as little of that as of civil politeness. The High Constable of Westminster attended near her Majesty's carriage as far as Temple Bar, the eastward limit of his jurisdiction. On arriving there, however, he found no one in authority to receive the Queen, and accordingly he continued to ride by the side of the royal carriage until it reached the Mansion House. The mob was a-foot, active, numerous, and rudely-tongued that day. As the Queen passed through she was assailed by the most hideous yells, and many of the populace thrust their heads into the carriage, and gave expression to the most diabolical menaces. If it be true, as has been reported, that the Queen minutely detailed in writing the memoirs of her own life, the events of this day must have been penned by a trembling but indignant hand. At the Mansion House, so little protection was afforded her that the foremost of the people were almost thrust upon her, their violence of speech shocked her ears, and they attempted, but unsuccessfully, to disarm one of her footmen of his sword. In the evening of this melancholy last visit she dined with the Duke of York, and it was there that she first suffered from a violent spasmodic attack, from the effects of which she never perfectly recovered. The Lord Mayor stoutly maintained that the visit had very much improved her Majesty's health. He thought, perhaps, that excitement was a tonic to age and infirmity. The Queen's health really suffered materially from the excitement; and it was not with her wonted calmness that she could even listen, on the following Sunday, to the usual weekly sermon, always read aloud to her by one of the princesses.

It is certain that from the early part of the year 1818 the aged Queen may be said to have been in a rapidly declining state. Her condition, however, was not highly dangerous till the autumn, when her spasmodic attacks became more frequent and the progress of dropsical symptoms more alarming. Her sufferings were very great, and if she experienced temporary ease the slightest variation of position renewed her pain. She continued in this condition until the 14th of November, when, by a slight rupture in the skin of both ankles, from which there took place a considerable effusion of water, the venerable lady experienced some relief. Her condition, however, was not bettered thereby, for mortification soon set in, and that portion of her family which was in attendance upon her soon learned that all hope was abandoned; after an interval of more than eighty years England was again about to lose a Queen-consort; but no Queen-consort had for so long a period shared the throne of the empire as Charlotte. For fifty-seven years she had occupied the high place from which she was now about to descend. On Tuesday, the 16th of November 1818, at one o'clock P.M., the Queen calmly departed, at her suburban palace at Kew. Her last breath was drawn in a low arm-chair, that cannot be called an *easy* chair, and which is still preserved at Kew. The Regent, the Duke of York, the Princess Augusta, and the Duchess of Gloucester were present. The Princess Elizabeth of Hesse Homburg was said to have been absent, on account of some difference between herself and her royal mother, but it was afterwards ascertained that a reconciliation had taken place between mother and child before the Princess left the kingdom for her own home. How far the Queen had acquitted herself as a parent towards her children was made a 'vexed question' at the time of her death; and an endeavour was made to connect the fact of the dispersion of several of the princes and princesses in foreign countries with the mother as an irritating cause thereof. The 'Times,' at the period of which we are treating, entered largely upon this subject; and that organ was evidently inclined to conclude that her Majesty had not succeeded in attaching to her the hearts of her children. 'The Duke of Cumberland,' said the 'Times,' 'is out of the question. The inflexible, but well-meant determination of the

Queen to stigmatise her niece, by shutting the doors of the royal palace against her, may excuse strong feelings of estrangement or resentment on the part of the Duchess and her kindred. But that the Dukes of Clarence, Kent, and Cambridge at the same time should have quitted, as if by signal, their parent's death-bed, is a circumstance which, in lower life, would have at least astonished the community.' The 'Times' adds, that 'the departure of the Princess Elizabeth, the Queen's favourite daughter, who married and took leave of her in the midst of that illness which was pronounced must shortly bring her to the grave, may, perhaps, have been owing to the express injunctions of her Majesty. The Duke of Gloucester stands in a more remote degree of relationship; Prince Leopold more distant still; but they all quitted the scene of suffering at a period when its fatal termination could not be doubted; and, as these have departed, it is no less apparent to common observers that the Queen of Wurtemburg might have approached the bed of a dying mother, from whom, by the usual lot of princes, she has been so long separated, as that her royal parent has not accepted from her the performance of that painful duty.' The same authority, however, confesses that the leading members of the royal family who remained in England were unwearied in their attendance on their dying parent, and so far set an example to the people of England, over whom they had been placed by Providence.

The influence of Queen Charlotte in political affairs, even had she been as much inclined to exercise it as her enemies charged her with, was but small. It could not be otherwise in a country with such a constitution as ours—a limited monarchy, the ministers of which are sure to be made responsible for grave consequences arising from the surrender of their authority to a power unrecognised by the constitution. That the influence, however, was not quite dormant was seen in the fact of the government paying the debts of her Majesty's brother, the Prince of Strelitz, with 30,000l. of the public money; and the same influence was suspected when the Queen's friend, the Earl of Suffolk, who had undertaken to arrange the embarrassed affairs of the Prince of Strelitz, was appointed to the office of Secretary of State.

If the Queen was not always a liberal recompenser, she, at least, was a punctual payer. In this respect she excelled the King himself. On the other hand, when the latter was at issue with his brothers or children, because of objectionable marriages entered into by them, the Queen did not aggravate the quarrel, although she felt keenly on the subject. She was in many respects a 'homely' woman, but in matters of homeliness the King set the example. He watched incessantly over the mental and physical education of his children; 'and the daily discipline of the nursery itself did not escape his paternal solicitudes.' But, says the 'Times,' 'that her Majesty's voluntary tastes were not exactly those which had been inferred from the habits of her matrimonial life, may be conjectured from the revolution which they seemed to undergo soon after the period when her royal husband ceased to exercise the supreme authority in this realm. At that period a transition was observed " from grave to gay." The sober dignity, the chastened grandeur, the national character of the English court seemed to vanish with the afflicted sovereign. A new species of grandeur now succeeded, in which there was more of the exterior of royalty and less of its becoming spirit. A long series of what was meant to be festivities—crowded balls and elaborate suppers, glittering pomp, gaudy and gorgeous, yet fluttering decoration—reckless, capricious, yet never-ending profusion—all the apparatus of commonplace magnificence were introduced with the Regency and countenanced, or apparently not discountenanced, by the Queen.' It must be remembered, however, that in these matters she had no control over the Regent; indeed we have, in a former page, seen her called his 'slave.' During her life she, at all events, had influence enough to maintain a regal retinue about the person of her afflicted husband. She had no sooner expired, however, when her son dismissed immediately nearly the whole of this retinue, on the ground of its uselessness to the unconscious King, and the very great expense it was to the country. The country was not unwilling to see a few thousands a-year economised by stripping the fine old monarch of some of the superfluous grandeur by which he was surrounded. The country, nevertheless, was sorely perplexed and bitterly indignant when it saw that the thousands which had been paid to numerous officers in daily service on the King were now to be paid to the Duke of York, who, for ten thousand a-year, constrained his filial affection to the severe labour of inquiring after his sick sire once a week.

The Queen's funeral took place on the 2nd of December, at Windsor. It was a public funeral, in the accepted sense of that term, but the arrangements were inappropriate. The procession mainly consisted of military, horse and foot, as if they had been escorting a warrior, and not a woman, to the tomb. The members of the peerage did scant honour to the Queen whom they had professed to reverence when alive. Few, and those not of note, were present. The absence of peeresses was especially noted. Indeed the public funeral of Charlotte was more private than the private funeral of her predecessor Caroline.

The will of Queen Charlotte was that of a woman of foresight and good memory rather than of feeling and affection. The document was proved by Lord Arden and General Taylor, the executors. It was in the General's handwriting, and was witnessed by Sir Francis Millman and Sir Henry Halford. The personal property was sworn to as being under 140,000*l*.

The substance of the will was as follows :—The royal testatrix directed that her debts and the legacies and annuities noticed in her will should be paid out of the personalty, or sale of personals, if there should not be wherewith in her Majesty's treasury to provide for those payments. The personal property was of various descriptions; part of it comprised the real estate in New Windsor, which she had purchased of the Duke of St. Albans, and which was known as the Lower Lodge (left to the Princess Sophia); but the personalty of the greatest value may be said to have been those splendid jewels which she cherished so dearly, and for which she affected to have such little care. These the systematic Sovereign divided into three parts—those presented to her by the King on her marriage, worth 50,000*l*.; those presented to her by the Nabob of Arcot, for the acquisition of which she paid by a temporary forfeiture of what she very little regarded—popular favour; and those purchased by herself, or which she had received as presents on birthday occasions. Such *souvenirs* were to her the most welcome gifts that could be made to her on that or any other anniversary. Of these jewels she made the following disposal: She directed that the diamonds given to her by the King on her marriage should revert to him only on condition that with survivorship there should be recovery of his mental faculties. If he were not restored to reason, she then directed—what he never would have consented to had his reason been restored to him—that they should be made over to the Crown of Hanover, as an heir-loom. Such a disposal of property which should have remained in England transferred the diamonds to Hanover whenever that kingdom should be divided from England by the accession, in the latter country, of a Queen—who, according to the law of Hanover, could not reign in that continental kingdom.

The splendid tribute which the Nabob of Arcot had deposited at her feet she divided among four of her daughters. The excepted daughter was the Queen of Wurtemburg, whom she looked upon as exceedingly well provided for. To the remaining four the careful mother did not bequeath the glittering gems, but the value of them after they were sold, and after certain debts were discharged from the produce of the sale. The four princesses divided between them what remained. The jewels which she had bought, or had received as birthday presents, were also to be divided among the same four daughters, according to a valuation to be made of them. The diamonds were valued at nearly a million. In ready money the Queen left behind her only 4,000*l*.

Frogmore was bequeathed to the Princess Augusta; and the plate, linen, pictures, china, books, furniture, &c., were left to the four princesses already named. Of her sons the testatrix made no mention, nor to them left any legacy. There were other persons mentioned, but who came off as badly as though they had never been named. Her Majesty directed that certain bequests as set down in certain lists annexed to her will, and to which due reference was made, should be paid to them; but not only were no such lists so annexed, but it was ascertained that her Majesty had never drawn any out herself nor directed any to be drawn by others.

There *was*, however, another list, touching which the aged Queen had been by no means so forgetful. This list contained a detail of property which the testatrix declared she had brought with her, more than half a century before, from Mecklenburgh Strelitz. Thither she ordered it to be sent back—to the senior branch of her illustrious house. After millions received from this country during her residence in it, she would not testify her gratitude for such munificence by permitting it or her family in England to profit by the handful of small valuables she had brought with her from Strelitz. To the head of the house of Mecklenburgh Strelitz reverted the few old-fashioned things brought over here in the trunks of the bride; and, if they have been worth preserving, the old-world finery of Sophia Charlotte of Strelitz and England is now possessed by the Grand Duchess of Mecklenburgh, the daughter of Charlotte's son, Adolphus of Cambridge.

The will was dated only the day previous to her Majesty's demise. It had been put together at various periods since the 2nd of the previous May, by an officer of her Majesty's establishment—General Taylor. About a fortnight previous to her Majesty's decease she was for the first time made acquainted with her dangerous condition by a communication delicately conveyed to her by order of the Prince Regent, and to the effect, 'that if her Majesty had any affairs to settle it would be advisable to do so while she had health and spirits to bear the fatigue.' The royal sufferer well comprehended what was meant by such a message, and was very seriously affected by it. She had entertained strong hopes, amounting almost to confidence, that by the skill of her medical attendants she would be again restored to health. This recommendation to set her 'house in order' was an announcement that her case was hopeless. Affected as she was, she did not lose her dignity or self-possession, but resigned herself to death, even while regretting she was about to depart from life. This was natural; and as there had never been any false sentiment about Queen Charlotte, so was she above exhibiting any in her last moments. Her patience was extreme, and in the acutest of her agony she never once suffered a murmur of complaint to escape her.

It has been said that the Queen left no diamonds to her daughter, the Dowager Queen of Wurtemburg. She left her, however, a superb set of *garnets*. The reason assigned was, that garnets were the only precious stones that could be worn with mourning, which the Dowager Queen had announced her intention of wearing for life. Queen Charlotte had, as ladies averred who spoke with *connaissance du fait*, the finest wardrobe in Europe, the highly-consoled legatee of which was Madame Beckendorff, the Queen's chief-dresser. It may be noticed here that the Queen's debts—chiefly contracted, it was said, by allowing her contributions to charitable objects to exceed her available income, which is no excuse whatever for any one incurring debt—amounted to 9,000*l*. The debt was acquitted out of the produce of the sale of the diamonds.

While on the subject of the will and the jewels, it may not be amiss to mention that the Queen, after wearing her diamonds and other gems on public occasions invariably consigned them to the care of Messrs. Rundell, Bridge & Co., the well-known goldsmiths of Ludgate Hill. The Queen herself put her diamonds into the hands of one of the partners of that house, by whom they were conveyed to the Bank. The only exception to this rule was after the last drawing-room was held by her, when her Majesty was too ill to make her usual consignment, and retired rather hurriedly to Kew. A few days subsequently, the diamonds were placed in the ordinary London guardianship by the Princess Augusta, who carried them up expressly from Kew. The Queen, however, held in her own keeping the 'George' and the diamond-hilted sword worn on public occasions by her consort. These were kept in a cabinet at Windsor Castle. Immediately after the Queen's death this cabinet was examined by the Prince Regent, but neither 'George' nor diamond-hilted sword was to be found therein; and the heir was not more astonished than perplexed, for the Queen had left no intimation as to where the valuables were deposited.

The inquiry set on foot was not at first encouraging. Suggestions could only be made that the coveted property might have been deposited by the late Queen in some of the cabinets, which would remain locked until after the royal funeral. Some surmised that George III. himself had stowed them away, and that his heirs might be extremely puzzled to discover the place of deposit. This was considered the more likely, as her Majesty had, on one occasion, missed from her room a gold ewer and basin of exquisite workmanship, enriched with gems. They were missed previous to the last mental indisposition of the King, who professed that he knew nothing whatever about them, but greatly feared that they had been stolen by a confidential servant. His Majesty was strongly suspected of having been himself the thief. Many months after his malady had set in, the ewer and basin were discovered behind some books in his study, to which he alone had access. It is supposed that, having concealed them by excess of caution, he totally forgot the circumstance, through growing infirmity of intellect.

In a few days it was announced that all that was 'now missing of the late King's jewels were his star and garter,' valued at about seven thousand pounds. How the diamond-hilted sword was discovered is not stated in the current news of the day; but while that was recovered the garter appears to have been lost, for no mention of such loss had been previously made.

The consort of Queen Charlotte survived until January 1820. Her son, Edward Duke of Kent, died a week previously. During the last years of the old King—who seemed to grow in majesty as his end approached—he lived in a world of his own, conversed with imaginary individuals, ran his fingers ramblingly over his harpsichord, and was in every other respect dead to all around him. He passed out of the world calmly and unconsciously after a long reign—and perhaps a more troubled reign than that of any other King of England. Of the children of Charlotte four ascended thrones. George and William became successive Kings of England, Ernest King of Hanover, and Charlotte Augusta Queen of Wurtemburg. The married daughters, Charlotte, Elizabeth, and Mary, died childless. Of her married sons only the King of Hanover and the Dukes of Kent and Cambridge left heirs behind them—the first a son, the second a daughter, our present Queen, the last a son and two daughters.

With the old royal family Kew is inseparably connected. Mr. Jesse, in his 'Memoirs of the Life and Reign of George III.,' says that when, many years since, 'he wandered through the forsaken apartments at the old palace at Kew, he found it apparently in precisely the same condition as when George III. had made it his summer residence, and when Queen Charlotte had expired within its walls. There were still to be seen, distinguished by their simple furniture and bed-curtains of white dimity, the different sleeping-rooms of the unmarried princesses, with their several names inscribed on the doors of each. There were still pointed out to him the easy chair in which Queen Charlotte had breathed her last; the old harpsichord which had once belonged to Handel, and on which George III. occasionally amused himself with playing; his walking-stick, his accustomed chair, the backgammon board on which he used to play with his equerries; and, lastly, the small apartment in which the pious monarch used to offer up his prayers and thanksgivings. In that apartment was formerly to be seen a relic of no small interest, the private prayer-book of George III. In the prayer which is used during the session of Parliament the King, with his own hand, had obliterated the words "our most religious and gracious King," and had substituted for them "a most miserable sinner."' The old 'palace' still retains many interesting memorials of King George, Queen Charlotte, and the princes and princesses during their happy days at Kew.

CAROLINE OF BRUNSWICK,

WIFE OF GEORGE IV.

CHAPTER I.

MOTHER AND DAUGHTER.

Marriage of Princess Augusta to the Prince of Brunswick—His reception at Harwich—Wedding performed with maimed rites—The Prince at the opera—A scene—Odd mode of travelling of the bride and bridegroom— Issue of this marriage—Dashing replies of Princess Caroline—Her mother the Duchess a weak and coarse-minded woman—Education of German princesses—Infamous conduct of the Duke of York—Lord Malmesbury sent to demand Princess Caroline in marriage for the Prince of Wales— His account of the Princess—Eloquence of the Duchess on the virtues of the Princess—The Duke's mistress, and picture of the Court of Brunswick—The Duchess's stories of bygone times—The marriage by proxy —Celebration of the wedding-day—The marriage treaty—Eccentricity of the Duke—Education of the Princess neglected—The courtesan champion of morality—The Duke's fears for the Princess—Lady Jersey and the Queen—Lord Malmesbury's advice to the Princess—Madame de Hertzfeldt's portraits of the Princess—The Princess's exuberant spirits at a court masquerade—More admonitions by Lord Malmesbury— Madame de Waggenheim's taunt, and Lord Malmesbury's thrust *en carte*.

ON the 12th of January 1764, Charles William Frederick, the hereditary Prince of Brunswick, landed at Harwich (then the portal by which royal brides and bridegrooms had ingress to and egress from England), to take the hand which had been already asked and not over-graciously granted of the Princess Augusta, the sister of George III. This half-reluctance was on the part of the King and Queen, but especially of the latter. There was none on the part of the bride.

The young Prince was a knightly man, lacking a

knightly aspect. His manner was better than his looks.
His reputation as a hero was, however, so great that the
people of Harwich, expecting to see an Adonis, nearly
pulled down the house in which he temporarily sojourned,
in order to obtain a better view of the illustrious stranger.
When the Prince did show himself they were rather
disappointed. His renown for courage, however, made
amends for all shortcomings, and even the Quakers of
Harwich warmed into enthusiasm. One, more eager
than the rest, not only forced his way into the Prince's
apartment, but took off his hat to him, called him 'Noble
friend!' kissed his hand, and protested that, though not
a fighting man himself, he loved those who *could* fight
well. .' Thou art a valiant Prince,' said he, ' and art to
be married to a lovely Princess. Love her, make her a
good husband, and the Lord bless you both!'

The bridegroom got no such warm greeting from any
other quarter as he did from the Quaker, and it is to be
regretted that he did not follow the counsel which was
offered him by his humble and hearty friend. He loved
his wife and made her such a husband as heroes are too
wont to do—who are accustomed to love their neighbours' wives better than their own.

The marriage took place on the 16th with something,
if not of maimed rites, at least of diminished ceremony.
The 'Lady Augusta' was wedded with as little formality
as was observed—under the same roof too—at her birth.
The latter vexed Queen Caroline because so little etiquette was followed at it. The wedding troubled Queen
Charlotte lest there should be too much and of too costly
a sort. Not a gun was fired by way of congratulatory
salute, as had been done when Anne, the daughter of
Caroline, married the Prince of Orange. More trifling
testimonies of respect were denied on this occasion, even
when the bride had petitioned for them, on the ground
that there was no precedent for them in the 'Orange

marriage.' The bride, fairly enough, complained at quotation of precedent in one case which had been followed in no other.

The servants of the King and Queen were not even permitted to put on their new attire, either for the wedding ceremony or the drawing-room next day. They were ordered to keep their new suits for the Queen's birthday. The ceremony performed, the bridal pair betook themselves to Leicester House, where they presided at a right royal supper; and this was the last time that Kings, Queens, Princes, Princesses, and half the peerage met together in Leicester Square to hold high festival.

Political party spirit ran very high in the early years of King George's reign; and such especial care was taken to keep the Prince from encountering any of the Opposition that, as Walpole remarks, he did nothing but take notice of them. He wrote to fidgety Newcastle, and called on fiery Pitt, and dined twice with '*the* Duke'— of Cumberland. On the evening of the second dinner he was engaged to attend a concert given in honour of himself and wife by the Queen. As he did not appear inclined to leave the table when the hour was growing late, Fironce, his secretary, pulled out his watch. The ducal host took the hint, and expressed a fear, which sounded like a hope, that the hour had come when his guest must leave him. '*N'importe!*' said the Prince; and he sat on, sipped his coffee, and did not get to the Queen's concert until after eight o'clock, at which hour, in those days, concerts were half concluded.

Fironce, the Duke's secretary, who sought to influence his master thus early, long continued to aim at exercising the same power. In 1794 Fironce was the Duke of Brunswick's prime minister, when the command of the Austrian army against France was offered to the Duke. The latter was inclined to accept, and Fironce had nothing to say against it; but Fironce's wife (who was a democrat) had, and she forbade her husband furthering the object of Austria.

During the short sojourn between the bridal and the departure, the whole of the royal family went to Covent Garden Theatre to see Murphy's decidedly dull and deservedly damned comedy, 'No One's Enemy but his Own'—a comedy which even Woodward could not make endurable. The feature of the night, however, was the difference which the public made between their reception of the King and Queen and that given to the newly-married pair. For the latter there was an ebullition of enthusiasm; for the former, who were suspected of being more cold to the bridegroom than his deserts warranted, little fervour was shown; and the then young Queen Charlotte was not a woman to love either bride or bridegroom the better for *that*.

On the following night the same august party appeared at the Opera House. The multitude which endeavoured to gain access to the interior would have filled three such houses as that in the Haymarket. Ladies, hopeless of reaching the doors in their carriages, left them in Piccadilly, and, gathering up their hoops, attempted to make their way on foot or in sedans. So great were the concourse and confusion in the Haymarket that the gentlemen, to force a passage for these adventurous ladies and themselves, drew their swords and threatened direful things to all who stood between them and their boxes!

In the meantime the house was overflowing; and Horace Walpole, who has faithfully painted the scene—except, perhaps, where he presumes to construe the politeness of the Prince into contempt for his royal brother and sister-in-law—tells us: 'The crowd could not be described. The Duchess of Leeds, Lady Denbigh, Lady Scarborough, and others, sat in chairs between the scenes; the doors of the front boxes were thrown open, and the passages were all filled to the back of the stoves. Nay, women of fashion stood in the very stairs till eight at night. In the middle of the second act, the hereditary Prince, who sat with his wife and her brothers in their box, got up, *turned his back* to King and Queen, pretending to offer his place to Lady Tankerville, and then to Lady Susan. You know enough of Germans and their stiffness to etiquette to be sure this could not be done inadvertently, especially as he repeated this, only without standing up, with one of his own gentlemen in the third act.'

After a brief sojourn, the slender young Prince, who looked older than his years (twenty-nine), left town with his bride for Harwich. Bride and bridegroom travelled in different coaches, with three or four silent and solemn attendants in each. Never did newly-married couple travel so sillily unsociable. The farewell speech, too, of the bridegroom, before he went on board, rang more of war than of love. He had already, he said, bled in the cause of England, and would again. In this he kept his word, for *he* was the Duke of Brunswick who fell gloriously at Jena, at the age of threescore years and eleven, subsidised by Great Britain, and unthanked by ever-ungrateful Prussia, so deservedly punished for her habitual double-dealing on that terrible day.

As bride and bridegroom travelled from the court to the coast in two coaches, so now did they traverse the seas in two separate yachts. No wonder they were storm-tost. Their passage from Holland, where they landed, to their home in Brunswick was quite an ovation. The little courts in their route did them ample honour; there were splendid receptions, and showy reviews, and monster *battues* at which ten thousand hares, and winged game in proportion, were slaughtered in one morning; after which, in the evening, the slayers all appeared at the opera in their hunting-dresses! Finally, the 'happy couple' arrived at Brunswick, where the various members of the ducal family greeted their arrival, and—no less a person than the Countess of Yarmouth, the Walmoden of George II., the mistress of the bride's grandfather, bade them welcome!

Of this marriage were born two most unhappy women; Charlotte, in December 1764, and Caroline, in May 1768. There were also four sons: Charles, born in 1767; George in 1769; William in 1771; and Leopold in the following year. Of these, two died gloriously; the first fell in battle at the head of the Black Brunswickers, on the bloody field of Quatre Bras; the last perished not less gloriously in an attempt to save the lives of several persons, when the river Oder burst its banks, in 1785. Of this family we have only especially to do with the second daughter, Caroline Amelia Elizabeth, ultimately Queen-consort of our George IV.

'In what country is the lion to be found?' asked her governess, after a lesson in natural history. 'Well,' answered the little Princess Caroline, 'I should say, you may find him in the heart of a Brunswicker!' In these sort of dashing replies the girl delighted. She was as much charmed with dashing games. In the sport of the 'ring,' in which the aimers at that small object are mounted on wooden horses fixed on a circular frame, she was remarkably expert. On one occasion, when she was flying round with something more than common rapidity, one of her attendants expressed fear of the possible consequences. 'A Brunswicker dares do anything,' exclaimed the undaunted Caroline; adding, 'A Brunswicker does not know that thing fear.'

Accustomed to enjoy a place, even when very young, at her father's table, she early acquired a habit of self-possession, became as pert as young Cyrus, and as forward as the juvenile Wharton. 'How would you define time and space?' said her father once to Mirabeau. The Princess Caroline, then twelve years old, anticipated the witty Frenchman's answer, by replying, 'Space is in the mouth of Madame von L——, and time is in her face.' When told that it was not fitting for so young a lady to have an opinion of her own, she observed, correctly enough, 'People without opinions of their own are like barren tracts which will not bear grass.' As her mother seldom asked any other question than 'What is the news?' and loved the small gossip which arises out of such a query, the Princess was more frequently engaged in serious discussions with her instructress than with the Duchess. The Countess von Bade having remarked that she herself was wicked because an evil spirit impelled her, and that she was by nature too feeble to resist, 'If that be the case,' observed the young lady, ' you are simply a piece of clay moulded by another's will.' The orthodox Lutheran lady was about to explain, but the daughter of a mother who had brought ' her girls ' up to membership with no church in particular cut short the controversy with an infallible air which would have done credit to Pope Joan, ' My dear, we are all bad—very bad; but we were all created so, and it's no fault of ours.' The utterer of this speech was doubly unfortunate: her intellect was fine, but it was ill-trained; she was the daughter of a kind-hearted woman, incapable of fulfilling with propriety the duty of a mother; and she became the wife of a prince who was, as Sheridan remarked, 'too much a lady's man ever to become the man of one lady.'

The Princess, at a very early period, discovered how to be mistress of her weak mother. Therewith, however, she had a heart that readily felt for the poor. She was terribly self-willed, and played the harpsichord like St. Cecilia.

Her thoughtlessness was on a par with her sensibility;

and it is said that a very early seclusion from court, to which she was condemned by parental command, was caused by a double want of discretion. She was too fond, it was reported, of relieving young peasants in distress, and of listening to young aides-de-camp who affected to be miserable. She was taught that princesses were never their own almoners, and that it did not become them to converse with officers of low degree. On her return to court, an aged lady, whose years were warrant for her boldness, recommended an exercise, in future, of more judgment than had marked the past. 'Gone is gone and will never return,' was the remark of the pretty, sententious, young lady; 'and what is to come will come of itself.' It was the remark of a girl brought up like that very Polly Honeycomb whose story Colman wrote and Miss Burney read to Queen Charlotte. Like that heroine, the Princess Caroline had not the wisest of parents. Like her, she was addicted to romance, and was too ready to put in practice all that romances teach, and to enter into correspondence at once pleasant and dangerous. Again and again was forced seclusion adopted as the parental remedy to cure a wayward daughter of too much warmth of heart and too little gravity of head.

Her heart, however, would not beat warmly at the bidding of every new suitor. An offer was made to her, when very young, by a scion of the house of Mecklenburgh, whose offer was supported by both the parents of Caroline. That Princess ridiculed her lover, and flatly refused the honour presented for her acceptance. She similarly declined the offers of the Prince of Orange and the Prince George of Darmstadt. Her father was now reigning Duke of Brunswick, burning with desire to destroy the French Republic, and eager to obtain a consort for his daughter. He cannot be said to have succeeded much more happily in the latter than in the former. As for this daughter, she would herself have been happier, in those days when her education—or no education—was scrambled through, had she possessed any religious principles. But she was like other German princesses, who, as it was not known into what royal families they might have the good-luck to marry—Russo-Greek, Roman Catholic, or Protestant—were taught morality (and that but indifferently) in place of faith and a reason for holding it. One consequence was, that they deferred believing anything convincedly until they were espoused—and then they joined their husband's church, and remained precisely what they were before.

The Princess was in something like this state of suspense, and her sire was in a state not very dissimilar with regard to the part he should take in the war of Germany against France, when the Duke of York, commander of the English force in Holland, destined to act bravely inefficient against the French, visited the ducal court of Brunswick. He is said to have been very favourably impressed with the person and attainments of the Princess Caroline; and it has been supposed that his favourable report of her first led the King, his father, to think of the daughter of 'the Lady Augusta' as a wife for his son George.

If, however, Mrs. M. A. Clarke may be believed, the Princess had been thought of as a wife for the Duke of York, who, on seeing her, did not like her. In one respect he behaved infamously to her. The King had entrusted to the Duke a splendid set of diamonds, intended as a present for the Princess. The Duke, meanwhile, lent them to his favourite, Mrs. Clarke, who appeared in them at the opera, and enjoyed the splendid infamy.

The King was more than ordinarily anxious for the marriage of his son, and the latter was made to perceive that, however his affections may have been engaged, it was his interest to marry in obedience to the King's wishes. He was overwhelmed with debts, and the payment of these was promised as the price of his consent. The wildest stories have been told with regard to the share which the Prince took in furthering his own marriage. Some say that he especially selected the Princess Caroline of Brunswick as the lady he had resolved to marry; others affirm that, while coldly consenting to espouse her, he wrote her a letter expressive of his real feelings, and not at all flattering to those of his proposed wife. The latter is said to have replied to this apocryphal letter with spirit, and to have declared her readiness to incur all risks, and her resolution to win the heart which now affected to be careless of her. Due notice was given to Parliament of the coming event, and a dutiful and congratulatory reply was made by that august assembly.

The King knew nothing of his niece but by report; but he was resolved that the union, upon which he had now determined, and to which he was engaged by his message to Parliament, should take place, be the Princess of what quality she might. He had himself married under similar circumstances, and nothing had come of it but considerable felicity and a very numerous family.

The able and renowned diplomatist, Lord Malmesbury, having received the instructions of the King to demand the hand of the Princess Caroline of Brunswick for the Prince of Wales, proceeded to the duchy—a lover by proxy—to perform his mission. He had no discretionary powers allowed him. That is, although little was known of the Princess at the English court, he was not commissioned to give any information to that court which might have ultimately saved two persons from being supremely miserable. He was commissioned to fetch the Princess. The fitness of the Princess was the last thing thought of. The bride herself used often to say, in after life, to the attendants—who, while they served, sneered at her—that, had she only been allowed to have paid a visit to England, to have first made the acquaintance of the Prince, what a world of misery they might both have been spared ! The fact was, no time was to be lost. All the marriageable princesses in Germany were learning English, for the express purpose of bettering their chances of becoming Princess of Wales. They all waited for an offer ; and that offer, after all, was made to a Princess who had not made the English language her particular study.

The hymeneal envoy reached Brunswick on the 28th of November 1794. Nine years before, namely, on the 21st of December 1785, the Prince whom he represented was married to Mrs. Fitzherbert (a Roman Catholic, and twice a widow) in her own drawing-room, by a Protestant clergyman, and in presence of two of her relatives. The court of Brunswick thought nothing of this matter. Lord Malmesbury was received with as hilarious a welcome as that which was given to the Earl of Macclesfield at Hanover, when he appeared there with the Act of Settlement which opened the throne of England to the Electoral Family. There was the same hospitality, the same offer of service ; and the business was opened, as so much earthly business is, with a grand banquet at court, on the same night, at which Lord Malmesbury saw the future Queen of England for the first time. She was embarrassed on being presented to him, but the experienced diplomatist was not so. He looked at and studied the appearance of the Princess, and saw ' a pretty face—not expressive of softness ; her figure not graceful ; fine eyes ; good hair ; tolerable teeth, but going ; fair hair, and light eyebrows ; good bust ; short ; with what the French call " des épaules impertinentes." *Vastly happy with her future expectations.*' She had got over an omission on the part of the Prince which had for a moment pained her. With the offer or demand in marriage there came no greeting from the suitor. The Princess naturally felt disappointed, and she said in a plaintive little voice: 'le Prince n'a donc rien écrit!' She was at the time a pretty woman; she had delicately-formed features, and her complexion was good. Those who can only remember her as she appeared when on her last visit to England, in the House of Peers, at Alderman Wood's window, or at the balcony of Brandenburgh House, with features swollen and disfigured by sorrow and an irregular life, can have no idea of how she looked in her youth. Her eyes were described then as being quick, penetrating, and glancing; they were shaped *en amande*; and they were, moreover, not merely beautiful, but expressive. Her mouth was delicately formed; she could be noble and dignified when she chose, or occasion required it. It might be said that her only defect, personally, consisted in her head being rather too large and her neck too short. But, setting this aside, there was a greater defect still, though it was one not uncommon to the ladies of the time. There was, in fact, to use a Turkish phrase, 'garlic amid the flowers.' The pretty creature was not superfluously clean. To say that she was so superficially would, perhaps, be even more than truth would warrant. As for her mother, that Princess Augusta at whose birth, at St. James's Palace, such confusion occurred, and who had been in her time so 'parlous' a child, Lord Malmesbury found her full of nothing but her daughter's marriage, and talking incessantly. Her talk was not of the wisest, particularly if she indulged in it in presence of her daughter, for part of it consisted in abuse of Queen Charlotte, the future mother-in-law of Augusta's child. The Duchess spoke of Queen Charlotte as an envious and intriguing spirit; alleged that she had exhibited that spirit as soon as she arrived in England, and that she was an enemy of her mother, the Princess of Wales, as well as of herself, Augusta. She added that the Queen had so little feeling that while the Princess of Wales was dying her Majesty took advantage of the moment to alter the rank of her Highness's ladies of the bedchamber. The Duchess's judgment of King George, her brother, was, that he was more kind-hearted than wise-headed, which was not far from the truth.

But the Duchess was most eloquent upon the projected marriage, the virtues of her daughter, and the care which had been taken, by precept and example, to establish such virtues in Caroline. The Duchess had very excellent ideas as to the duties of a mother-in-law, as appears from her expressed resolution never to interfere in the household of the newly-married royal couple. Indeed the idea of visiting England at all was odious to her. If she were to repair thither, she was sure, she said, that her visit would result in discomfort to herself, and a jealousy and vexation excited against her in the hearts of others. Poor lady, she did not foresee that a dozen years later she would be a fugitive from Brunswick, seeking an asylum in England, after forty years' absence.

The Duchess affected to treat the marriage of her daughter with the Prince of Wales as perfectly unexpected by her, but as she added that 'she never could give the idea to Caroline' we may fairly suppose that the thought of such a thing being possible had really entered for a moment into her own mind. George III., however, had been accustomed to speak disapprovingly of the marriage of cousins-german, and with good reason. It is only to be regretted that he did not act in accordance with his own expressed opinions on this point. It may be noted as a strange fact that the prelate who performed the marriage ceremony which made of the two cousins, so closely akin by blood, man and wife, would have been very much shocked had he been asked to do the same office for a man about to marry the sister of his deceased wife, and with whom he had not the slightest blood relationship.

The Duchess, as has already been remarked, spoke of her brother, George III., as having more amiability than intellect. If amiability mean the power of loving others, she very much qualified the remark by observing that 'he loved her very much, *as well as he could love anybody;*' an equivocal phrase, which is made clear enough by the context; for the Duchess added, that her long absence, and his thirty years of intercourse with Queen Charlotte, had caused him to forget the sister whom he loved as much as he could love anybody.

The court of this Duchess, who had been so anxious to make of virtue a fixed possession for her daughter, was not a court where virtue itself was a fixed resident. The mistress of the Duke was quite as important a lady there as the Duchess; and yet the lady herself, or one of those who held the post which was shared by many, had the sense to be a trifle ashamed of her position. Her name was Hertzfeldt. She had ennobled the name by putting a *de* before it, but she had not dared upon the prefix of the Teutonic *von*. Lord Malmesbury thus notices her. 'In the evening with Mademoiselle de Hertzfeldt—old Berlin acquaintance, Duke's mistress—much altered, but still clear and agreeable; full of lamentations and fears; her apartments elegantly furnished, and she herself with all the *appareil* of her situation; she was at first rather ashamed to see me, but she soon got over it.'

Mademoiselle de Hertzfeldt, too, was among those who were anxious that the Princess Caroline should be worthy of the position now open to her. This was a strange *entourage* for the bride; and there were both strange people and strange things at this ducal court. Some of the names of the officials and residents call up memories of the past. There was a Count von Schulemberg among the former. We hear also of a Herr von Walmoden, the son of that 'Master Louis' whose mother was the 'Walmoden' of whom George II. made a Countess of Yarmouth, and whose father was that royal sovereign himself. There was also an exemplary couple in the court circle, Herr and Frau von Waggenheim, of whom indeed little is said, save that the gentleman drank, and that the lady thought the example worth following. This was but an indifferent place from which to select a future Queen of England; but, depraved as the court was, there were others more so, from which, nevertheless, princesses had gone to be honoured wives and virtuous matrons in other circles.

The ducal family were never so well pleased as when they could get the envoy from the bridegroom in one of their own little *coteries*, and there it was the delight of the Duchess to make much of him, and inundate him with stories of bygone times. She was particularly pleased to tell anything disparaging of Queen Charlotte. That her brother, King George, had, on her marriage, presented her with a handsome diamond ring as a wedding gift. This generosity rendered the Queen peevish and jealous, and her Majesty is said to have actually wished that the gift should be recalled and conferred upon herself. In such tales the Duchess delighted, and she had an attentive listener.

To him she further told that the King had proposed to marry one of his daughters to her favourite son, Charles; requiring only that he should first pay a visit to England, a course to which she strongly objected, and apparently for very efficient reasons—'she was quite sure, if he was to show himself, none of the Princesses would have him.'

On the 3rd of December these very small matters were varied by the arrival of Major Hislop, who brought with him the portrait of the royal bridegroom, and a private letter to Lord Malmesbury, urging him 'most *vehemently* to set out with the Princess Caroline *immediately*.'

And thereupon, on the 8th of December 1794, followed the marriage, whereat the vehement lover appeared only by proxy. All parties behaved with due decorum. The paternal and warrior Duke, a man infirm of purpose, was rather embarrassed, but performed his office with dignity. The Duchess was of course overcome, and shed tears. The bride herself was affected, as maiden well might be, at a rite which took her from a home where she had, latterly, enjoyed the highest freedom, and which flung her on the bosom of a husband whose arms were scarcely opened to receive than they were raised to reject her.

The wedding-day was spent in a remarkably comfortable style of celebration. First, after the ceremony, there was an early and an 'immense' dinner. Then a grand court was held, at which felicitations were made to the new Princess of Wales. This was followed by grave whist for the older aristocrats, and gayer games for the younger people, addicted to more liveliness. Last of all came a great supper, but how the terrible meal was got through the court historians do not say. We only learn that during the progress of the banquet Lord Malmesbury informed the Duke of Brunswick of the nature of the contents of the Prince's letter, and the wish therein expressed so vehemently for his instant departure with the impatiently-expected bride. He of course supposed that the Duke would at once appoint a day for the solemn departure. But the sovereign of Brunswick was not a man who liked to compromise himself. He accordingly answered oracularly: 'We depend entirely on you, my lord; you cannot possibly decide in a wrong way.' It was leaving Lord Malmesbury ample powers, of which he was anxious to avail himself; but he had much to do with and for the bride before he led her safely to the asylum of her husband's cold hearth.

The bride was, meantime, herself anxious to depart to her new home; her mother, fussy, fond, and agitated, was desirous to accompany her a part of the way; and Lord Malmesbury, who had been honoured with the gift of a 'snuff-box' from the Duke and a diamond watch from the Princess, was quite as willing to get to the end of his mission. There was the impatient Prince, too, in London; but the diplomatist held his powers from the King, and rather obeyed the precise and deliberate order of the monarch than the urgently gallant appeals of his princely son.

In due form, therefore, the marriage treaty, drawn up in English and Latin—French was prohibited, by royal order—was signed by all the high contracting parties on the 4th of December. After the pleasant labour a sumptuous banquet followed, and the envoy and Duchess announced to the bridegroom at home that his bride would set out on the 11th, provided by that time intelligence was received of the sailing from England of the fleet which was to serve for a wedding escort across the sea.

The Duke of Brunswick was a man who, whenever he asserted that he was going to speak to you with perfect frankness, was really about to treat you with anything but candour. Even in his breast, however, the feelings of the father were not always dormant; and occasionally he manifested considerable perception with regard to the true nature of his daughter's position. 'He was perfectly aware,' says Lord Malmesbury, ' of the character of the Prince, and of the inconveniences that would result with almost equal ill effect either from his liking the Princess too much or too little.' The Duke was as thoroughly cognisant of the peculiar disposition of Queen Charlotte, and, curiously enough, 'he never mentioned the King.' The paternal comment on his own daughter was thoroughly impartial: 'She is not a fool,' said he, 'but she has no judgment; and she has been severely brought up, as was very necessary with her.' He knew well where peril lay, and, to do him justice, he did his little best to save his daughter from the danger.

The severity of the education of the Princess was only imaginary, or, if it had existed, it had been entirely ineffective. We may judge of this by remarking what the Duke begged of the envoy—to recommend to the Princess discretion; to pray of her not to be curious, nor free in giving her opinions aloud upon individuals and things— a fault which this severely-trained young lady inherited from her mother, who, throughout her life, had been given to 'appeler un chat, *un chat!*' and who was excessively free, easy, and loud-tongued in her dissertations upon both men and manners. The poor Duke probably thought of the mother, too, when he asked Lord Malmesbury to advise his daughter never to be jealous of her husband, and 'if he had any *gouts*, not to notice them.' The Duke added that he had written all this down *in German* for his daughter's benefit, but he thought it would be none the worse for being repeated orally by Lord Malmesbury. These audiences and consultations of the morning were succeeded by dinners and operas in the evening, and the Princess Caroline was of course the heroine of every festival.

A cynic might have laughed, a more religious philosopher would have sighed, at the further illustration of the severity of manners at the ducal court, and the 'serene' anxiety for the proper conduct of the newly-married Princess. The Duke actually sent his mistress to engage Lord Malmesbury to set the bride in a right path. Mademoiselle de Hertzfeldt represented to the envoy the necessity of being very *strict* with the Princess. The courtesan champion of morality represented the Duke's daughter as not clever, neither was she ill-disposed, 'but of a temper easily wrought on, and had no *tact.*' The good lady thought that the envoy's advice would have more effect than the paternal counsel, as, 'although the Princess respected him, she also feared him as a severe rather than an affectionate father; that she had no respect for her mother, and was inattentive to her when she dared.' No more terrible testimony could be rendered against a daughter than this. For if a girl love not her mother, whom shall she ever love? and if she hide not her disregard from the mother whom she cannot in her heart honour, whom will she ever truly regard? The Princess was as anxious in imploring guidance and direction from Lord Malmesbury as any of her relatives, and she was probably quite as sincere in asking for counsel.

At dinner and supper, concert and opera, there was the same diet and the same song. For hours of a morning the paternal admonitions were poured into the bride's ear, and for hours of an evening Lord Malmesbury had to listen to what the Princess had been told. The advice was good of its sort, but its constant repetition shows that the Duke had great fears touching his daughter's character. The Duke wished to make her feel 'that the high situation in which she was going to be placed was not simply one of amusement and enjoyment; that it had its duties, and those perhaps hard and difficult to fulfil.' Lord Malmesbury was especially invoked not to desert the Princess in England. The Duke was quite right in foreseeing that future peril, and *what* future peril for his daughter, lay in that direction. 'He dreaded the Prince's habits.' Well he might. They were not dissimilar from his own. On the very evening that the Duke told the envoy that he dreaded the Prince's habits, Lady Eden, who had just arrived at Brunswick from London, told Lord Malmesbury that 'Lady ———,' meaning, doubtless, Lady Jersey, 'was very well with the Queen; that she went frequently to Windsor, and appeared as a sort of favourite.' 'This, if true,' says Lord Malmesbury, 'is most strange, and bodes no good.' The intelligence seems to have strongly impressed the envoy; and when, in the evening, he sat next the Princess Caroline at supper, he counselled her 'to avoid familiarity, to have no *confidants*, to avoid giving any opinion, to approve but not to admire excessively, to be perfectly silent on politics and party, to be very attentive and respectful to the Queen—to endeavour, at all events, to be well with her.' He was evidently thinking of the rival that was already well with the Queen, and still better with the Prince. This condition of things boded no good. The Princess, whose eyes were red with tears—the consequence of taking leave of some of the dear young friends of her heart—had good cause to weep on. Never was bridal attended by prospect more forlorn. The bride, however, was as variable as an April day. On the evening following that just noticed, Lord Malmesbury records that he sat 'next to Princess Caroline at table; she improves very much on closer acquaintance—cheerful, and loves laughing.'

The penalty of her new position came before her, too, in another shape. She was beset with applications for her patronage, and she was induced to seek for Lord Malmesbury's aid to realise the expectations of the petitioners. He at once counselled her to have nothing to do with such matters, and to check or stop solicitation at once, by intimating that she could not interfere in any way in England by asking political or personal favours for others. Lord Malmesbury added that, if she were sincerely desirous to further the fortunes of a really deserving person, he would find means to enable her to accomplish what she wished. But even then it were far better, he said, not to engage herself by any promise. He added much more of excellent admonitory advice, in all of which the Princess readily acquiesced. He especially counselled her to be discreet in all her questions. She promised solemnly that she would, and forthwith she began to put some queries to him touching the Prince's 'favourite.' Not that she knew Lady Jersey to be the occupier of so bad an eminence. Still the question was indiscreet. 'She appeared to suppose her an *intriguante*, but not to know of any partiality or connection between her and the Prince. I said that, with regard to Lady ——, she and all her other ladies would frame their conduct towards her by hers towards them; that I humbly advised her this should not be too familiar or too easy; and that it might be affable without forgetting she was Princess of Wales; that she should never listen to them when they attempted anything like a *commerage*, and never allow them to appear to influence her opinion by theirs. She said she wished to be popular, and was afraid I recommended her too much reserve; that probably I thought her too *proné à se livrer*. I said I did; that it was an amiable quality, but one that in her situation could not be given way to without great risk; that, as to popularity, it never was retained by *familiarity;* that it could only belong to respect, and was only to be acquired by a just mixture of dignity and affability. I quoted the Queen as a model in this respect.'[1]

Lord Malmesbury thoroughly understood the characters both of the Princess Caroline and the Queen Charlotte. Of the latter the Princess expressed great fear, and

[1] Lord Malmesbury's Diary.

added a conviction that the Queen would be jealous of her and do her harm. On that very account she was advised to be scrupulously attentive in rendering to this terrible mother-in-law, as she seemed, every mark of respect due to her; and the Princess was further counselled to set a guard upon her too prompt tongue in the Queen's presence, and to be especially careful not to drop any light remarks. The bride promised all she was asked, and then observed, by way of illustration of her watchfulness, that she was quite aware that the Prince was *leger;* that she had been prepared on that point, and was determined never to appear jealous, however much she might be provoked. Her monitor commended the wisdom of a resolution which he said he believed (but it must have been in a diplomatic sense) she would never be called upon to put in force. Still more diplomatically, he added that if she ever *did* 'see any symptoms of a *gout* in the Prince, or if any of the women about her should, under the love of fishing in troubled waters, endeavour to excite a jealousy in her mind,' he entreated her, ' on no account to allow it to manifest itself.' Sourness and reproaches on the part of even a young neglected wife, it was suggested, not only would not reclaim a husband whose ' tottering affections' might be won back by patient endurance and softness, but reproof and vexation would only survive to give additional value to her rival and that rival's charms. In short, my Lord as good as intimated that, if she would only re-enact the part of Griselda, she would please her husband; whereas, if she ran counter to his wishes, ' it would probably make him disagreeable and peevish, and certainly force him to be false and dissembling.'

. But if the English envoy enlightened the bride upon the character of the Prince, her father's mistress, Mdlle. de Hertzfeldt, was not less liberal in affording to Lord Malmesbury portraits of the Princess, drawn in all lights and with no lack of shadow. One lecture from the 'favourite,' which the envoy set down in French, deserves to be quoted, in spite of its length. 'I conjure you'—thus began the anxious lady—'I conjure you to induce the Prince, from the very commencement, to make the Princess lead a retired life. She has always been kept in much constraint and narrowly watched, and not without cause. If she suddenly finds herself in the world, unchecked by any restraint, she will not walk steadily. She has not a depraved heart—has never done anything wrong —but her words are ever preceding her thoughts. She gives herself up unreservedly to whomsoever she happens to be speaking with; and thence it follows, even in this little court, that a meaning and an intention are given to her words which never belonged to them. How then will it be in England, where she will be surrounded, so it is said, by cunning and intriguing women, to whom she will deliver herself body and soul, if the Prince allows her to lead a dissipated life in London, and who will make her say just what they please, and that the more easily as she will speak of her own accord, without being conscious of what she has uttered? Besides, she has much vanity, and, though not void of wit, she has but little principle. Her very head will be turned if she be too much flattered or caressed, or if the Prince spoil her; and it is quite as essential that she should fear as that she should love him. It is of the utmost importance that he should keep her closely curbed; that he should also compel her respect for him. Without this, she will assuredly go astray! I know,' added she to the noble envoy, who wrote down her speech in his Diary as soon as it was delivered, 'I know that you will not compromise me, for I speak as to an old friend. I am attached heart and soul to the Duke. I have devoted myself to and lost myself for him. I have the welfare of his family at heart. He will be the most wretched of men if his daughter does not succeed better than her elder sister. I repeat, she has never done anything that is bad; but she is without judgment, and she has been judged of accordingly. I fear the Queen. The Duchess here, who passes her entire life in thinking aloud or in never thinking at all, does not like the Queen; and she has talked too much about her to her daughter. Nevertheless, the happiness of the Princess depends upon being well with the Queen; and for God's sake,' exclaimed the Duke's devoted mistress, who so airily satirised the Duke's lawful wife, 'say as much to her as indeed you have done already. She heeds you; she finds that you speak reason cheerfully; and you will make more impression on her than her father, of whom she is too much afraid, or than her mother, of whom she is not afraid at all.'

That night there was a masquerade at the court opera-house. Amid the gay and festive throng the envoy never left the side of the bride, over whom it was his mission to watch. He talked with her in a strain which became so gay a scene, but on every jest hung counsel. *She* was for giving way to the temper of the entertainment; but as the Princess grew more hilarious and 'more mixing,' he checked the rising spirit of fun, and prevented its becoming 'fast and furious,' by treating her with a vast outlay of increased seriousness and respect.

If there was something strange in this scene, what followed was stranger still. Mentor and maiden retired to a box on the *Balcon*, and there they discussed anew the chances of domestic happiness, and the rules by which it might be accomplished. As minuets were being statelily walked below, the envoy categorically laid down the regulations observation of which might purchase connubial felicity. He gave expression to an urgent wish that she would never miss going to church on Sundays, as the King and Queen never failed being present—although it must be added that, severe as Queen Charlotte was in strictly and formally attending divine worship on the Sabbath, the service itself was no sooner over than (at *that* period of her life) she proceeded to hold a drawing-room. It was one generally more brilliantly attended than that held on the Thursdays.

The prospect of being compelled to attend church every Sunday was but a gloomy view, it would seem, thus presented at the very gayest portion of the masquerade. The Princess probably thought she saw a way of escape, for she inquired if the Prince was thus strict in his weekly attendance. Lord Malmesbury dexterously replied that if he were not she would bring him to it; and if he would not go with her, she would do well to set a good example and go without him. 'You must, in such case,' added the bride-trainer, 'tell him that the fulfilling regularly and exactly this duty can alone enable you to perform exactly and regularly those you owe him. This cannot but please him, and will in the end induce him also to go to church.'

The Princess evidently liked this part of her prospect less and less. We may fairly judge so by her observation, that my Lord had 'made a very serious remark for a masquerade.'

The envoy defended himself from the attack made under cover of this insinuation, and he defended himself with gaiety and success. The Princess herself acknowledged as much, and Lord Malmesbury rather naïvely observes that, after descanting to the bride upon the necessity of regular church-going when she got to England, he was glad he had set her thinking on the *drawbacks* as well as of the *agrémens* of her situation. The attendance at church was, in *his* eyes, a rather severe discipline; but, as he so forcibly impressed on the mind of his charge, 'in the order of society, those of a very high rank have a price to pay for it. The life of a Princess of Wales is not to be one of pleasure, dissipation, and enjoyment. The great and conspicuous advantages belonging to it must necessarily be purchased by considerable sacrifices, and can only be preserved and kept up by a continual repetition of those sacrifices.' The Princess probably sighed as she weighed the pomp of her position against the piety by which she was to formally illustrate it.

Lord Malmesbury could not play the mentor without the godless wits of the court treating him to a little raillery. On the evening when he had been expatiating on the uses of attendance at church, during the noise and revelry of a masquerade, he encountered Madame de Waggenheim She was the lady who 'drank,' and whom the noble diarist sets down upon his tablets as 'absurd, ridiculous, ill-mannered, and *méchante*.' 'How did you find the little one?' said she, alluding thereby to the Princess. 'Rather old as she is, her education is not yet *finished*.' Lord Malmesbury felt the taunt, but parried it with the remark that 'at an age far beyond that of her Royal Highness persons might be found in whom the education of which she spoke had not even begun.'

CHAPTER II.

THE NEW HOME.

The Princess desires to have Lord Malmesbury for her lord chamberlain—
The Duchess a coarse-minded woman—The Duke of Clarence her bitter
enemy—The Duke and Duchess's caution to Lord Malmesbury, and his
dignified reply—The Abbess of Gandersheim's opinion of mankind—
Difficult question proposed by the Princess, and Lord Malmesbury's
gallant reply—The Abbess without human sympathy—A state dinner,
and a mischievous anonymous letter—The Princess's departure for England—Her indifference to money—Instances—Ignorance of the Duchess
—Difficulties of the journey—The Princess's design to reform the Prince
of Wales—Indefatigable care of Lord Malmesbury—Story of the Princess at Hanover—Care as to her toilette recommended—Presents given
by the Princess—Her arrival in England—Ridiculed by Lady Jersey—
Reproof administered to her ladyship by Lord Malmesbury—The first
interview of the Prince and Princess—Cold reception of the bride—Flippant conduct of the Princess—Lord Malmesbury reproached by the
Prince of Wales.

IT is to the credit of the Princess Caroline that she took in such good part all that Lord Malmesbury told her, and that she was desirous of having him appointed her lord chamberlain ; a prematurely expressed desire which did her honour, gratified the object of it, and was never realised. She, no doubt, respected him, for the advice he gave her was not only parental, but much of it might have come from a tender and affectionate mother. But *her* mother was a coarse-minded, weak-hearted woman, who had little regard for propriety, was not affected by the disregard of it in her husband, and who told stories at table, in her daughter's presence, that would have called up a blush of shame, if not of indignation, on the cheek of a dragoon.

It was after such stories that Lord Malmesbury particularly enjoined the Princess, if she cared to please, to commune much with herself, and to think deeply before she spoke. Her family was a strange one, but not stranger, in many respects, than that into which she was going. Her admission there, indeed, at all, was perhaps a consequence of hate rather than love. Prince William, Duke of Clarence, had been among the first to speak of the Princess Caroline of Brunswick as a wife for the Prince of Wales. He had been led to do this because he hated the Duchess of York, knew that the Princess and Duchess hated each other, and felt sure that the marriage of the former with the heir to the throne would be wormwood to the Duchess. The Duke of Clarence was, ultimately, one of the bitterest and the most unreasonable of the enemies of this very Princess whom he had helped to drag up to greatness.

With regard to the feelings of the Princess against the excellent Duchess of York, the envoy endeavoured to turn them into a sentiment of respect for one who was worthy of such homage. Indeed, he was so indefatigable with his counsel that the ducal parents became fearful lest there might be even too much of it for his own profit, if not for their daughter's good. It was suggested to him that the Princess, in a moment of fondness, might communicate to the Prince all he had said to her, and so he 'would run the risk of getting into a scrape' with his Royal Highness on his return. Lord Malmesbury, who was the envoy of the King and not of the Prince, replied with readiness, dignity, and effect. 'I replied,' he said, 'that luckily I was in a situation not to want the Prince's favour; that it was of infinitely more consequence to the public, and even to me (in the rank I filled in its service), that the Princess of Wales should honour and become her high situation, recover the dignity and respect due to our princes and royal family, which had, of late, been so much and so dangerously let down by their mixing so indiscriminately with their inferiors, than that I should have the emoluments and advantages of a favourite at Carlton House; and that idea was so impressed on my mind that I should certainly say to the Prince everything I had said to the Princess Caroline.' He had a difficult pupil in the latter lady. After a whole page of record touching how important it was that she should practise reserve and dignity, we remark the condemnatory entry: 'Concert in the evening; the Princess Caroline talks very much—quite at her ease— too much so.'

In another chapter of the family romance we find the aunt of the Princess—the Abbess of Gandersheim— exhorting her niece to put no trust in men at all; assuring her that her husband would deceive her, that she would not be happy, 'and all the nonsense of an envious and a desiring old maid.' The gaiety of the Princess was eclipsed, for a moment, by the chill cloud thrown across it by the remarks of her aunt. The envoy, however, restored the ordinary sunshine by requesting the Princess, the next time the Abbess held similar discourse, to ask her whether, if she proposed to give up the Prince to her aunt, and take the Abbey of Gandersheim in place thereof, she would then 'think men to be such monsters, and whether she would not expose herself to all the dangers and misfortunes of such a marriage?' This sally, with good counsel to garnish it, not only restored the good-humour of the Princess, but made her more desirous than ever to attach the envoy personally to her service as soon as her household as Princess of Wales should be established. Lord Malmesbury avoided an explicit answer, but entreated her not to solicit anything in his behalf. 'I had,' he says, ' the Duke of Suffolk and Queen Margaret in my thoughts.' He, further, was more anxious than ever with reference to the results of this marriage. With a *steady* man, he thought, the impulsive bride might have a chance of bliss; but with one that was not so he saw that her risks were many and great indeed. In the meanwhile he poured counsel into her mind—as Mr. Gradgrind used to pour facts into the juvenile intellect at Coketown—by the imperial gallon. The Princess continued to take it all well, but the giver of it was shrewd enough to see that 'in the long run it must displease.' He was right in his conclusion, for the night after he expressed the conviction the Princess remarked, on some grave monition of his, that she should never learn it all, and that she was too light-minded ever to do so.

Ward and guardian had been running a parallel between the former and her sister-in-law, younger than herself, the hereditary Princess of Brunswick. The Princess Caroline had asked Lord Malmesbury which he thought would make the better Princess of Wales, herself or her sister-in-law? To this difficult question the envoy replied gallantly that he knew which would be the Prince's choice; that she possessed by nature what the hereditary Princess neither had or could ever acquire —beauty and grace. He added, in his character of mentor, 'that all the essential qualities the hereditary Princess has *she* might attain—prudence, discretion, attention, and tact.' 'Do I want them?' 'You cannot have too much of them.' 'How comes my sister-in-law, who is younger than myself, to have them more than I?' 'Because, at a very early period of her life, her family was in danger; she was brought up to exertion of the mind, and now she derives the benefit *d'avoir mangé son pain bis le premier!*' 'I shall never learn this,' was the remark of the Princess, with some confession of her defects. Lord Malmesbury encouraged her by saying that when she found herself in a different situation she would be prepared for its exigencies if she questioned and communed deeply with herself now. In short, he gave excellent advice, and if counsel could have cured the radical defects of a vicious education, Caroline would have crossed the seas to her new home peerless among brides.

At length the hour approached for the departure of the bride, but before it struck there had well-nigh been an angry scene. Lord Malmesbury had faithfully narrated to the Prince all that his commission allowed him to narrate touching his doings. His opinion of the bride he of course kept to himself. The Prince wrote back a complete approval of all he had done, but added a prohibition of the Princess being accompanied to England by a Mademoiselle Rosenzweit, who, as his Royal Highness understood, had been named as 'a sort of reader.' The Prince, for what reason is not known, would not have her in that or in any other character. The Duke and Duchess of Brunswick were exceedingly annoyed by this exercise of authority on the part of the royal husband, but they were, of course, compelled to submit. The motive for the nomination of this lady deserves to be noticed, particularly as the Duke, who kept a 'favourite' at the table where his wife presided, and the Duchess, who told coarse and indelicate stories there which disgusted the 'favourite,' had been particularly boastful concerning the very severe education of the Princess.

When it was agreed that Mademoiselle Rosenzweit should not accompany the Princess as 'a sort of reader,' the Duke of Brunswick took Lord Malmesbury aside, and stated that the reason why he wished her to be with the Princess was, that his daughter wrote very ill and spelt ill, and he was desirous that this should not appear. The noble diarist adds, 'that his Serene Highness was not at all so serenely indifferent on the matter as he pretended to be. He affected to be so, '" but at the bottom was hurt and angry."'

The last day the unhappy bride ever spent in a home which, considering all things, had been a happy home to *her*, was one of mingled sighs, tears, dignity, and meanness. The Duke rose into something like dignity also, and exhibited a momentary touch of paternal feeling as the hour of departure drew near, and his glory, as well as his paternal affection, was concerned in the conduct and bearing of his daughter.

There was a dinner, which would have been cordial enough but for the arrival of an anonymous letter, warning the Duchess and the Princess of the dangers the latter would run from a profligate 'Lady ——,' the blank of which may be filled up with the name of Jersey. The letter had been addressed to the Duchess, but that extremely prudent lady had informed her poor daughter of its contents, and discussed the letter openly with all those who cared to take part in the discussion. Lord Malmesbury suspected the epistle to come from the party of the disappointed Mademoiselle de Rosenzweit. It was a vulgar epistle, the chief point in which was the assertion that the 'Lady ——' would certainly do her utmost to lead the Princess into some act of injury to her own husband's honour. The Princess was not herself much terrified on this point, and for *that* reason Lord Malmesbury told her very gravely that it was *death* for a man to approach the Princess of Wales with any idea of winning her affections from her husband, and that no man would be daring enough to think of it. The poor bride, something startled, inquired if *that* were really the law. Lord Malmesbury answered, 'that such was the law; that anybody who presumed to *love* her would be guilty of *high* treason, and punished with *death*, if she were weak enough to listen to him; so also would *she*.' This startled her. Naturally so; between advice, evil prophecy, menace, dark innuendoes, the necessity of going to church, and the possibility of ending on a scaffold, the bride might well be startled.

Nor was the letter above alluded to the only one which was a source of uneasiness to the Princess. George III. had written to the Duchess, expressing his 'hope that his niece would not indulge in too much vivacity, but would lead a sedentary and retired life.' This letter also was exhibited by the injudicious mother to her daughter; and while the latter was wondering what the conclusion of all this turmoil might be, Mademoiselle de Hertzfeldt reiterated that the only way for the Prince to manage her would be by fear. 'Ay,' said the virtuous lady, 'even by terror; she will emancipate herself if care be not taken of her. Watched narrowly and severely, she may conduct herself well!'

Amid such a confusion of scenes, incidents, things, and persons, the Princess Caroline was variously affected. Her last banquet in her father's halls was an epitome of the sorrows, cares, mock-splendour, and much misery of the time to come.

On Monday, December the 29th, 1795, the bride left Brunswick 'for good.' It was two o'clock in the afternoon when the envoy departed from the palace with his fair companion in his charge. To render her safety less exposed to risk, Major Hislop had gone forward ' to give notice in case of danger from the enemy.' The cannon from the ramparts of the city thundered out to her their last farewell, and the citizens assembled in crowds to see the Princess pass forth on her path—of roses, as they good-naturedly hoped; but, in fact, on her way strewn with thorns.

For three days the travellers pressed forward in something of long file, making, however, short journeys, and not getting very rapidly over them. On the third day the Princess, weary of being alone with two ladies, invited Lord Malmesbury to ride in the same coach with her. He 'resisted it as impossible, from its being improper;' and he continued to discountenance the matter, and she to laugh at him for his inviolable punctilio.

What with the impediments thrown in their way by the war then raging in front of them, between the French on one side and the Dutch and English on the other—and the alternating features of which now enabled them to hurry on, now checked their course—what with the incidents of these stirring times, and the hard frost during which they occurred, cavaliers and ladies made but tardy way, were half-frozen, and not inconsiderably dispirited. For a time they tarried at Osnaburg, where Lord Malmesbury narrates an anecdote for the purpose of showing the character of the Princess, and which is to this effect.

Many distressed French *émigrés* were to be found at Osnaburg, some of them 'dying of hunger, and through want.' The rest, the gallant leader of our escort shall tell in his own words: 'I persuaded the Princess Caroline to be munificent towards them—she disposed to be, but not knowing *how* to set about it, I tell her liberality and generosity is an enjoyment, not a sworn virtue. She gives a *louis* for some lottery tickets. *I* give *ten*, and say the Princess ordered me—she surprised. I said I was sure she did not mean to give for the ticket its *prime* value, and that I forestalled her intention. Next day a French *émigré* with a pretty child draws near the table. The Princess Caroline immediately, of her own accord, puts the louis in a paper and gives them to the child. The Duchess of Brunswick observes it, and inquires of me (I was dining between them) what it was. I tell her *a demand on her purse.* She embarrassed: "Je n'ai que mes beaux doubles louis de Brunswick." I answer: "Qu'ils deviendront plus beaux dans les mains de cet enfant que dans sa poche." She ashamed, and gives three of them. In the evening the Princess Caroline, to whom this sort of virtue was never preached, on my praising the coin of the money at Brunswick, offers *me very seriously eight or ten double louis*, saying : " Cela ne me fait rien—je ne m'en soucie pas—je vous prie de les prendre." I mention these facts to show her character: it could not distinguish between giving as a benevolence and flinging away the money like a child. She thought that the art of getting rid of the money, and not seeming to care about it, constituted the merit. I took an opportunity at supper of defining to her what real benevolence was, and I recommended it to her as a quality that would, if rightly employed, make her more admirers and give her more true satisfaction than any that human nature could possess. The idea was, I am sorry to see, new to her, but she felt the truth of it ; and she certainly is not fond of money, which both her parents are.'

This indifference to money was amply manifested throughout the course of her after life. At a period of that life when she was most distressed she might have earned a right royal revenue, had she cared to sacrifice to it—her reputation. With all her faults, she had none of the avarice of her mother especially. She had more of the ignorance of the latter, but even she would not have been led into betraying it as her mother did when looking at the Dusseldorff collection of pictures, which at this time had been removed to Osnaburg, to save it from the calamities of war. Her Serene Highness was shown a Gerard Dow. 'And who is Gerard Dow?' said she; 'was he of Dusseldorff?' The severity of this lady's education must have been something like that given to the Princess. The mother had never heard of Dow!

The daughter wrote ill and spelt worse. She, some years subsequent to the journey upon which we are now accompanying her, described the Princess Charlotte in a letter as her 'deer angle.' She was indeed ever profuse with epithets of endearment. The ladies whom she saw for the first time during this her bridal progress to her husband's house were addressed by her as 'Mon cœur, ma chère, ma petite.' Lord Malmesbury again played the monitor when these freedoms were indulged in, and his pupil began to care less for both advice and adviser. The bride's mother, too, got weary of her journey—afraid of being taken prisoner by the enemy, and was anxious to leave her daughter and return home. The envoy resisted this as improper, until the moment she had placed the Princess in the hands of her proper attendants. Lord Malmesbury not only made 'her lady mother' continue at her post, but, on leaving Osnaburg, he induced her to give fifty louis to the servants—very much indeed against her will. She neither loved to give money away herself, nor to have the virtue of liberality impressed upon her daughter as one worth observing. In most respects, however, the daughter was superior to the mother. Thus, when at Benthem, they were waited on and complimented by President Fonk and Count Benthem de Steinfort—two odd figures, and still more oddly dressed—the Duchess burst into a fit of laughter at beholding them. The Princess had the inclination to do as much, but she contrived to enjoy her hilarity without hurting the feelings of the two accomplished and oddly-dressed gentlemen who had come to do her honour.

The Princess was less delicate with regard to odd women. Thus, she met Madame la Présidente Walmoden at Osnaburg, whom she asked to play at cards at her table, and made giggling remarks about her, in half-whispers, to the younger ladies of the party. The Princess disliked the Présidente; the Duchess, on the other hand, had pleasure in her society. Présidente and Duchess vied with each other in telling stories, and the latter was comically indelicate to her heart's content.

Great difficulties had still to be encountered in the way of their progress towards the sea-coast, and more than one wide wave from far-off battles drove them back, again and again, to cities of which they had before taken, as they believed, a final farewell. In the midst of it all there was much 'fun,' some frowning, a little bickering, advice without end, and amendment always beginning. Still, as the party proceeded, half-frozen to death on their way by the rigour of a winter such as Lord Malmesbury had not felt since he was in Russia, the Princess especially loved to talk of her future prospects and intentions. Perhaps the most singular dream in which she indulged was that of undertaking and accomplishing—for she had no doubt as to the result—the reformation of the Prince. She felt, she said, that she was to fill the *vide* in the situation in which he stood, caused by his isolation from the King and Queen. She would domesticate him, she said, and give him a taste for all the private and home virtues. His happiness would then be of a higher quality than it ever had been before, and he would owe it all to her. This was the pleasant dream of a young bride full of good intentions, and who was strangely called upon to project the reformation of her husband, even before she had seen him, or could have taken that interest in him which could only arise from esteem founded on personal intercourse. This result, she declared, the nation expected at her hands; and she would realise it, for she felt herself capable of effecting it.

To all this agreeable devising Lord Malmesbury replied in encouraging speeches, mingled with gravest counsel and solemn admonition as to her bearing. This the

Princess generally took in excellent part, while the Duchess, her mother, was grumbling at the intense cold or slumbering uneasily under it; and the servants outside the carriages were as nearly frozen as people could be, but were kept from that absolute catastrophe by generous liquor and the warmth of their indignation.

The bride ought to have been perfect in her character, for her mentor lost no opportunity in endeavouring to so prepare her that she might make a favourable impression upon the King and Queen. It must, too, be said for her, that her amiability under this reiterated didactic process was really very great. She felt nothing but respect for her teacher, and that says much for the instruction given, as also for the way in which it was conveyed. On one occasion, we are told, she ended, on retiring for the night, by saying that she hoped the Prince would let her see Lord Malmesbury, since she never could expect that any one would 'give her such good and such free advice as myself;' and she added, 'I confess I could not bear it from any one but you.'

On Saturday, the 24th of January 1795, the travellers entered Hanover blue with cold, of which the benumbed Duchess complained in no very elegant terms. Lord Malmesbury was exceedingly anxious that the Princess should be popular here, as according to the impression of her reported hence to England would probably be that of the King and Queen on her arrival. Lord Malmesbury told her that she was Zémire and Hanover Azor; and that, if she behaved rightly, the monster would be metamorphosed into a beauty; that Beulwitz (at the head of the regency, the most ugly and most disagreeable man possible) would change into the Prince of Wales; that the habit of proper princely behaviour was *natural to her* —an assertion which was not true, as even the diplomatist showed, by adding 'that it would come of itself;

that *acquired* by this (in that respect) fortunate delay in our journey, it would belong to her, and become familiar to her on her coming to England, where it would be of infinite advantage.'

And yet Hanover was not a very particular place; that is, it was not inhabited—the court end of it, at least —by very particular, strict, or strait-laced people. The Princess was particularly careful of her conduct before persons, some of whom appear to have generally got intoxicated before dinner was over. Nevertheless, Lord Malmesbury did effect a very notable change for the better in the Princess's habits. He had been before addressing himself to the improvement of principle; he now came to a personal matter, and, if one might be pardoned for laughing at any incident in the life of a poor woman whose life was anything rather than a matter to be laughed at, this is the time when one might do so with least reproach.

The party had been three weeks at Hanover, and, during that time, Lord Malmesbury had held frequent discussions with the Princess upon the very delicate matter of the toilette. She prided, or to use the noble lord's own term, 'she piqued herself on dressing quick.' He disapproved of this; for a quick dresser is a slovenly and unclean dresser. On this point, however, she would not be convinced: probably she was the less inclined to be so as the weather continued intensely cold, and the next luxury to lying in bed was being quickly dressed when she got out of it. He could not come to details with a young bride who despised perfect ablutions; but he found a court lady, Madame Busche, through whom he poured the necessary amount of information that should induce the Princess to be more liberal towards her skin in the dispensation of water. He desired Madame Busche to explain to her that the Prince was very delicate, and that he expected a long and very careful *toilette de propreté*, of which she had no idea. 'On the contrary,' he says, 'she neglects it sadly, and is offensive from this neglect. Madame Busche executes her commission well, and the Princess came out, the next day, *well washed all over!*'

But still the envoy's trouble in connection with his charge in no way diminished. Now, he was gently reproving her for calling strange ladies by very familiar terms; anon, he had to censure her for unasked-for confidences touching past loves; and then, more seriously than all, to reprimand her even, and with strong license of phrase, for her undutiful and sneering conduct towards her mother, who, although silly and undignified, yet deserved the respect of her own child. On all these occasions there was some pouting, followed by acquiescence in the reproof, and ardent promises of improvement, that were still long a-coming. In the meantime, that delicate article of personal cleanliness remained, upon which the Princess became as indifferent as ever. We must again have recourse to the envoy's own description of what passed between him and the pretty, wayward girl he was endeavouring to persuade out of dirtiness. On the 6th of March he says: 'I had two conversations with the Princess Caroline. One on the toilette, on cleanliness, and on delicacy of speaking. On these points I endeavoured, as far as it was possible for a *man*, to inculcate the necessity of great and nice attention to every part of dress, as well as to what was hid as what was seen. I knew she wore coarse petticoats, coarse shifts, and thread stockings, and these never well washed or changed often enough. I observed that a long toilette was necessary, and gave her no credit for boasting that hers was a *short* one. What I could not say myself on this point I got said through women: through Madame Busche, and afterwards through Mrs. Harcourt. It is remarkable how amazingly on this point her education has been neglected, and how much her mother, although an Englishwoman, was inattentive to it. My other conversation was on the Princess's speaking slightingly of the Duchess, being peevish to her, and often laughing at her or about her. On that point I talked *very seriously* indeed; said that nothing was so extremely improper, so *radically* wrong; that it was impossible, if she reflected for a moment, that she should not be sorry for everything of the kind which escaped; and I assured her it was the more improper from the tender affection the Duchess had for her. The Princess felt all this, and it made a temporary impression. But on this, as on all other subjects, I have had too many opportunities to observe that her heart is very, *very* light, unsusceptible of strong or lasting feelings. In some respects this may make her happier, but certainly not better. I must, however, say that on the idea being suggested to her by her father that I should remain on business in Germany, and not be allowed to attend her to England, she was most extremely affected, even to tears, and spoke to me with a kindness and feeling I was highly gratified to find in her.'

On the 24th of March the travelling bridal party quitted Hanover. The bride made presents to the amount of 800 golden Fredericks—a generosity which cost her little, for the money was supplied by Lord Malmesbury, who took a receipt for it, like a man of business. It was now that the mother and daughter parted—not again to meet till the former was without a duchy and the latter without a spouse. The Duchess was considerably affected. The Princess kept up her spirits, and behaved with grace and propriety. After passing through Rottenberg and Klosterseven, where they 'slept at the curate's,' the wayfarers reached Stade on Friday, the 27th of March. Early on the following morning they embarked in

Hanoverian boats upon the Schwinde; by nine they reached the 'Fly' cutter, and in that, when the wind served, or in boats when it slackened, they proceeded down the river, and at seven o'clock were taken on board the ' Jupiter,' fifty-gun ship, amid all the dreadful noise, confusion, and smoke which go towards doing welcome to an illustrious traveller. As she was stepping on board a young midshipman, named Doyle, handed her a rope, in order to assist her. He was the first to help her, as it were, into England. Something more than a quarter of a century later he who thus aided the bride was charged with the mission of taking back her body. The fleet re-echoed the thundering salute which burst from the sides of the 'Jupiter,' yards were manned, streamers flung out their silky lengths to the wind, and as the Princess passed on to Cuxhaven all went as merrily as became a marriage party.

The next day they cleared the Elbe, and on the following were off the Texel. The Princess was cheerful, affable, good-humoured, not alarmed by the terrors of the sea or the sight of French privateers, and a favourite with both officers and seamen. She only made one 'slip' on the passage, from a repetition of which the jealous Lord Malmesbury guarded her by giving her a lesson in English, and counselling her not to use a nasty word to express a nasty thing. While the royal bride was conning her lesson her guardian was conferring with 'Jack Payne,' from whom he learned that the bridegroom at home was not behaving in the most prudish way possible, and that his favourite was comporting herself with the impudence natural to favourites before they fall.

On Good Friday morning, the 3rd of April, the 'Jupiter' passed Harwich, and in the evening anchored at the Nore. On the following day the bride ascended the Thames to Gravesend, whence, in a barge, on Easter Sunday, and amidst thousands of welcoming spectators, she proceeded to Greenwich, where she arrived at twelve, and found —not a soul from St. James's to receive her. She waited a full hour before the royal carriages arrived, and the delay was attributed to the contrivance of the Prince's favourite. In the meantime the officers at the Hospital did their honest best to welcome the poor stranger. At length the carriages arrived, but with them no eager bridegroom. To represent him came his mistress, with a bevy of lords and ladies. Lady Jersey no sooner beheld the embarrassed Princess than she began to ridicule her dress; and having done that till she was sharply reproved for her effrontery by Lord Malmesbury, she made a sort of claim to be placed by the side of the Princess in the carriage, on the ground that riding backwards always made her sick. But Lord Malmesbury would listen to no such claim, told her that she was unfit to be a lady of the bedchamber if she were unable to ride with her back to the horses, and although the favourite would have been glad now to ride even in that fashion in the same carriage with the bride, the envoy would not permit it. He placed there two ladies who were not addicted to qualms in such a situation; and with the Princess occupying a seat alone, and sitting forward, so as to be more easily seen, the *cortège* set out for the metropolis. The bride was but coldly received by the few spectators on the road, and when she alighted at the Duke of Cumberland's apartments, in Cleveland Row, St. James's, at half-past two, she must have half wished herself back again in Brunswick.

On due notice of the arrival being made to the royal family the Prince of Wales went immediately to visit his cousin and bride. What occurred at the interview, of which Lord Malmesbury was the sole witness, he has the best right to tell. 'I, according to the established etiquette, introduced (no one else being in the room) the Princess Caroline to him. She very properly, in consequence of my saying to her it was the right mode of proceeding, attempted to kneel to him. He raised her (gracefully enough) and embraced her, said barely one word, turned round, retired to a distant part of the apartment, and, calling me to him, said: "Harris, I am not well; pray get me a glass of brandy." I said: "Sir, had you not better have a glass of water?" Upon which he, much out of humour, said with an oath: "*No*; I will go directly to the Queen." . And away he went. The Princess, left during this short moment alone, was in a state of astonishment, and on my joining her said: "Mon Dieu, est-ce que le Prince est toujours comme cela? Je le trouve très gros et nullement aussi beau que son portrait."'

What could the bringer of the bride say to comfort her? He stammered out that his Royal Highness was naturally much affected and fluttered—poor bashful man and susceptible creature—at the interview; but he would be better by dinner time!

The Princess, however, was not herself blameless. She had already entirely forgotten, or entirely disregarded, the good advice given to her by Lord Malmesbury, and, short as the time had been which she had spent at Greenwich with Lady Jersey, she had been foolish enough to communicate to that person the alleged fact of her heart having been already preoccupied by a young German. The interesting intelligence was speedily communicated to the Prince, and the knowledge so acquired—although the fact itself may have been at first doubted—certainly had great influence on the conduct observed by the bridegroom to the bride.

Lord Malmesbury was exceedingly perplexed. He had been so careful of his charge that when the chances of war had obstructed the progress of their journey, sooner than take her back to a court, the ladies of which, never expecting to see her raised to a more exalted station than that in which she was born, had treated her with great familiarity, he had conducted her to dull and decorous Hanover. So tender had he been of her that he would not allow her to remain at Osnaburg, for the simple reason that Count d'Artois was in the vicinity; and although Lord Malmesbury was, as he says, very far from attributing, either to him or to those who attended him, all those vices and dangerous follies which it was said belonged to them in the days of prosperity, yet he felt it highly improper that the Princess of Wales and a fugitive French prince should remain in the same place. His charge could not have had a colder welcome had such a meeting taken place, and all the inconveniences resulted from it which the noble lord foresaw and dreaded. The poor deserted lady was now upon the point of indulging in some sharp criticism upon her welcome, when her troubled conductor, feigning necessity to attend upon the King, left the room, and her alone in it, or with no better company than her meditations.

The usual Sunday drawing-room had just come to a close, and Lord Malmesbury found his Majesty at leisure to converse. The last thing, however, thought about by the King was the subject of the Princess. His whole conversation turned upon home and foreign politics. That ended, he inquired if the Princess were good-humoured. Lord Malmesbury reported favourably of her in this respect, and the King expressed his gratification in such a tone as to induce his lordship to believe that his Majesty had seen the Queen since she had seen the Prince, and heard from him an unfavourable report of the Princess.

The after-conduct of the latter was not calculated to create a favourable impression. At the dinner which took place that day the Princess was ' flippant, rattling, affecting raillery and wit,' and throwing out coarse, vulgar hints about Lady Jersey, who was present, silent, and biding her time. The disgust of the bridegroom was now permanently fixed; and the disgust raised by lightness of bearing and language passed into hatred when the Princess began to indulge in coarse sarcasm.

The Prince, heartily weary of his bargain, asked Lord Malmesbury, after one of these dinners, what he thought of the manners exhibited at them by the Princess. The envoy could not defend them; on the contrary, he expressed his unqualified censure, and informed the Prince of the paternal injunctions of the Duke of Brunswick, whereby he recommended that a strict curb should be kept upon the Princess, or she would certainly emancipate herself. The Prince declared that he saw it too plainly, and half reproachfully asked 'Harris' why he had not told him as much before. The envoy, thus appealed to, pleaded the strictness of his commission, which was not discretionary, but which directed him to ask for the hand of the Princess Caroline in marriage, and nothing more; and that, had he presumed to give any opinion of his own upon the lady, he would have been guilty of an impertinent disregard of his instructions, which were at once limited and imperative. Lord Malmesbury endeavoured to put the gentlest construction upon the sentiments expressed by the Duke of Brunswick concerning his daughter, and added that, for his own part, he had seen nothing but slight defects of character, which he hoped might be amended; and that, had he observed anything more serious, he should have considered it his duty to communicate it, but only confidentially, to the King himself. The Prince sighed, appeared to acquiesce, but was neither consoled nor convinced.

The ceremonial of the unhappy marriage was celebrated on Wednesday, the 8th of April, in the Chapel Royal, St. James's. The whole of the royal family previously dined together at the Queen's Palace, Buckingham House, after which they proceeded to their several apartments at St. James's to dress. As the Princess passed through the hall of Buckingham House the King saluted her in the heartiest fashion, and then shook as heartily, by both hands, the Prince of Wales who had in vain sought to raise his spirits by the adventitious aid of wine. The bridal party assembled in the Queen's apartment, and walked from thence to the state drawing-rooms, which were not rendered less gloomy than usual by any addition of festive light. They were 'very dark,' says Lord Malmesbury, who walked in the procession, by command of his Majesty. The chapel was very crowded. There is a picture of the interesting scene, which is said to have been painted, at the King's command, by Hugh Douglas Hamilton, an Irish artist, whom both King and Queen had, formerly, much patronised. All the royal sons and daughters—a beautiful family group they were —are present in the Chapel Royal, St. James's. The bride is dressed in a white satin dress, worked down the front with pearls. She wears a small crown, and from her shoulders falls a robe of rich red crimson velvet, lined with ermine. The Prince of Wales wears a court costume, knee breeches and buckles with pointed shoes. His coat, of blue velvet, is richly ornamented somewhat after the fashion of the ornaments on the dress of his bride. The ladies wear enormous hoops, except the bride, who has no hoop. Their hair is powdered, and their arms project from their bodies in rather a stiff attitude, rendered necessary by the projection of the hoops. They all wear long, white kid gloves, which extend nearly up to the elbow. Ostrich feathers bend or bow on the ladies' heads, rising from the forehead, and curling gracefully at a considerable height. Near the bride are her 'maids,' Lady Mary Osborne, Lady Charlotte Legge, Lady Caroline Villiers, Lady Charlotte Spencer, Lady Caroline Waldegrave. When Queen Charlotte heard of this picture (she appears not to have sat for it) she is said to have declared that if it was brought into Windsor Castle she would go out of it. The King paid for but declined to receive this work, which ultimately was disposed of by lottery, and is now in the Tussaud Gallery, in Baker Street.

The ceremony which it represents was performed by the Archbishop of Canterbury, Dr. Moore. The 'Prince of Wales gave his hat, with a rich diamond button and loop, to Lord Harcourt to hold, and made him a present of it. After the marriage we returned to the Queen's apartment. The Prince very civil and gracious, but I thought I could perceive he was not quite sincere, and certainly unhappy, and as a proof of it he had manifestly had recourse to wine or spirits.'

Upon this point Lord Holland has afforded ample corroborative evidence. The noble baron has stated that the Prince of Wales had had such recourse to brandy that he with difficulty could be kept upright between two dukes. The wedding was as melancholy a one as was ever celebrated. The only hearty actor in it was the King, who advanced to give the bride away with an eager alacrity. As for the bridegroom, after having been got upon his knees, he rose, unconsciously, but restlessly, before the proper time. The Archbishop paused, the service was interrupted, and the Prince looked very much as if he were inclined to run away. The King, however, had presence of mind for all. He rose from his seat, crossed to where his son was standing with a bewildered air, whispered to him, got him once more upon his knees, and so happily, or unhappily, brought the ceremony to a conclusion.

The usual legal formalities followed; these were succeeded by a supper at Buckingham House, and at midnight the luckless pair retired to their own residence at Carlton House, quarrelling with each other, it is said, by the way. Meanwhile the metropolis around them was rejoicing and exhibiting its gladness by the usual manifestations of much drunkenness and increased illumination to show it by. Asmodeus might have startled the Spanish student that night with an exhibition such as he had never seen beneath any of the unroofed houses of Madrid!

It sounds singular to hear that the young husband's first serious occupation, on thus beginning life, was the settlement of his debts. These were enormous, and their amount only proved the reckless dishonesty of him who had incurred them. Mr. Pitt proposed that the income of the Prince should be 125,000l. a-year, exclusive of the revenue of the Duchy of Cornwall, some 13,000l. more. This was eventually agreed to. In addition, Parliament fixed the jointure of the Princess of Wales at 50,000l. per annum; and the smaller but pleasant items of 20,000l. for jewels and 26,000l. for furnishing Carlton House were also agreed upon. Out of the above-named revenue, however, a yearly deduction was to be made, in order that the debts of the Prince should be discharged within nine years. This deduction he denounced, and his brothers joined him in the denunciation, as a breach of contract, he having married solely upon the promise that his debts should be paid off at once. He immediately claimed the amount of the accumulation of the receipts of the Duchy of Cornwall during his minority. He was answered, on the part of the King, that the receipts had been expended on his education and establishment. The consequent debates were a scandal to the nation, a disgrace to royalty in the person of the Prince, and cruelly insulting to the Princess, as they betrayed to her the fact that the heir-apparent had accepted her as a consort solely on condition that his debts should be paid off. When the Romans made a bargain they confirmed it by breaking a bit of straw between them. This straw was called 'stipula,' and the Princess Caroline was the bit of straw that was broken—the stipulation, in fact, whereby it was agreed that if the Prince married the woman whom he already detested his creditors should have satisfaction in full of all demands!

Some of these were found heavy. There was a bill of 40,000*l.* to his farrier! Bills like these were allowed. Not so an annuity of 1,400*l.* to Mrs. Crouch, the actress. The Parliament took a commercial view of the matter and disallowed the claim, on the ground that no valuable consideration had been given for the liability which the Prince had voluntarily incurred. For the allowed debts, debentures payable with interest were given, and the Prince immediately withdrew into comparative retirement, in order, as Lord Moira stated in the House of Lords, that he might be able to save enough to discharge certain claims upon his honour. These claims were supposed to exist on the part of the Landgrave of Hesse Cassel and the Duke of Orleans, from whom the Prince had borrowed money. Perhaps they included the 10,000*l.* per annum which he had engaged himself to pay to Mrs. Fitzherbert, whom he had settled in a superb mansion in Park Lane, and comforted with assurances that his attentions to her would be as devoted now as before his marriage! All this was an outrage on the poor bride, whom the Prince took down to Windsor on a visit to the King and Queen. That persons might not suppose this was a commencement of positive domestic and virtuous life, the husband took with him his mistress, Lady Jersey.

The usual formality, which George III. loved, of visiting the public at the theatre, was observed on this occasion, and a short time after the royal marriage the wedded couple were accompanied to Covent Garden by the whole of the royal family. They were very dully entertained with the very worst of O'Keefe's comedies, 'Life's Vagaries,' in which two cousins fall in love and marry; and so perhaps the piece was thought appropriate. It was followed by 'Windsor Castle,' a *pièce d'occasion* by Pearce, who brought together in it Edward III., Peleus, the Prince of Wales, Minerva, Thetis, and the Countess of Kent. The last lady is represented as expected at the castle; she is detained on her way by an overflow of the Thames which threatens to drown her, and from which she is rescued by the Prince of Wales; whereupon all the heathen gods and goddesses are as much delighted as if they formed an Olympian Royal Humane Society, and exhibit their ecstasy by dancing and singing. In such wise were our rulers entertained when George III. was king.

Queen Charlotte had looked grimly cold upon the Princess, but she gave an entertainment in honour of the event which made Caroline of Brunswick a Princess of Wales. The locality was Frogmore, and the scene was brilliant, except that the hostess looked, as Lord Malmesbury once described her, 'civil, but stiff,' and her daughter-in-law superbly dressed, and black as midnight.

Meanwhile, the Prince's first wife, Mrs. Fitzherbert, was in sorrow. Their honeymoon had not lasted long. The Prince had met Lady Jersey at Brighton, and a letter from him, which was put into Mrs. Fitzherbert's hands at a dinner at the Duke of Clarence's, where she had expected to meet the Prince, satisfied her that all intimacy between them had come to an end. From that time, according to what appears to be an erroneous statement in the 'Memoirs of Mrs. Fitzherbert,' 'she never saw the Prince;' and this interruption of their intimacy was followed by his marriage with the Queen (Princess) Caroline, brought about, as Mrs. Fitzherbert conceived, under the twofold influence of the pressure of his debts on the mind of the Prince, and a wish on the part of Lady Jersey to enlarge the royal establishment, in which she was to have an important situation!

CHAPTER III.

THE FIRST YEAR OF MARRIED LIFE.

The Princess's letters to her family intercepted—Unkindness exhibited to her—The Prince seeks a separation—Acceded to by the Princess—She removes to Blackheath—Her income settled—Merry hours spent by the Princess at Blackheath—Intercourse between the Princess and her daughter—The Princess's unfortunate acquaintance with Lady Douglas—The boy Austin—Lady Douglas's communication to the Prince attacking the Princess—The *delicate investigation*—Witnesses examined—The Princess hardly dealt with—Her memorial to the King—Delay in doing her justice—The Monarch's decision—Exculpated from the grave charges—Comparison of Caroline Queen of George II. and Caroline of Brunswick—The Prince and Lady Hertford—Miss Seymour, and the Prince's subornation of witnesses—Persecution of the Princess by her husband—Her appeal to the King—Menace of publishing *The Book*—The Princess received at the Queen's drawing-room—Meeting of the Prince and Princess—Death of the Duke of Brunswick at the battle of Jena—The Duchess a fugitive—The Princess's debts.

THE Princess had cause then, and stronger reason soon after, for her melancholy. She had written a number of letters to her family and friends in Germany. These she intrusted to the Rev. Dr. Randolph, who was about to proceed to Brunswick, for delivery. The illness of Mrs. Randolph kept the doctor in England, and he returned the letters to the Princess of Wales, under a cover addressed to Lady Jersey. The letters fell into the Queen's hands. This, however, was only discovered later; and the discovery accounted for the cold reserve of Queen Charlotte towards the Princess, for the letters contained some sarcastic remarks upon the Queen's appearance and manners. In the meantime, on the packet failing to reach its proper owner, due inquiry was made, but nothing further was discovered, except that the reverend doctor declared that he had transmitted it to Lady Jersey, and that individual solemnly protested she had never received it. That it reached Queen Charlotte, was opened, and the contents read, was only ascertained at a later period.

In whatever rudeness of expression the Princess may have indulged, her fault was a venial one compared with those of her handsome and worthless husband. While she was in almost solitary confinement at Brighton he was in London, the most honoured guest at many a brilliant party, with Mrs. Fitzherbert for a companion. On several occasions these two were together, even when the Princess was present. The latter, by this time, knew of the private marriage of her husband with the lady, and that he had denied, through Fox, who was made the mouthpiece of the lie, that his 'friendship' with Mrs. Fitzherbert had ever gone to the extent of marriage. If we have to censure the after-conduct of the Princess, let us not forget this abominable provocation.

Except from the kindly-natured old King, Caroline experienced little kindness, even during the time immediately previous to the birth of her only child, the Princess Charlotte. This event took place at ten in the morning of the 7th of January 1796, amid the usual solemn formalities and the ordinary witnesses. Addresses of congratulation were not lacking. Among them the city of London prepared one for the Prince, but the conventionally 'happy father,' who had looked down upon his legitimate child with the critical remark that 'it was a fine girl,' declined to receive the congratulations of the City, unless in private. The pretext given was that a public reception was too expensive a matter in the Prince's reduced condition; and the pretext was so insulting to the common sense of the corporation that the members very properly refused to 'go up' at all.

The truth was that the Prince shrunk from being congratulated upon his prospects as a husband, seeing that he was about to separate himself for ever from the society of his wife. The latter had caused the removal of Lady Jersey from her household. This was effected by the hearty intervention of him whom the Scottish papers not inaptly called that 'decent man, the King.'

The intimation of the Prince's desire for a separation was conveyed to the Princess of Wales by Lady Cholmondeley. Her Royal Highness made only two remarks—first, that her husband's desire should be conveyed to her directly from himself in writing; and that, if a separation were now insisted on, the former intimacy should never under any circumstances be resumed.

If his Royal Highness had acceded to all his consort's wishes with the alacrity with which he fulfilled this one in particular, there would have been more happiness at their hearth. In his letter to her he said : ' Our inclinations are not in our power, nor should either of us be answerable to the other, because nature has not made us suitable to each other. Tranquillity and comfortable society are, however, in our power; let our intercourse, therefore, be restricted to that.' It is what Froissart might call 'sadly amusing' to find him offering tranquillity when he was predisposed to persecute, and recommending that their intercourse should take the character of a 'comfortable society,' when he was about to turn her out of her home, and without any greater fault laid to her charge than that she had outlived his liking. With regard to the Princess's expressed determination that, if there were a separation now, it must be 'once and for ever,' he agreed to it with alacrity; 'even in the event,' he said, ' of any accident happening to my daughter, which I trust Providence in its mercy will avert, I will not infringe the terms of the restriction by proposing, at any period, a connection of a more particular nature.'

Her Royal Highness, in her reply, acknowledged that his conduct during the year of their married life saved her from being surprised by the communication addressed to her. She does not complain, desires it only to be publicly understood that the arrangement is not of her seeking, and that 'the honour of it belongs to you alone;' and appeals to the King, as her protector, whose approbation, if he can award as much to her conduct, would in some degree console her. 'I retain,' she thus concludes, 'every sentiment of gratitude for the situation in which I find myself enabled, as Princess of Wales, by your means, to surrender myself unconstrainedly to the exercise of a virtue dear to my heart—I mean charity. It will be my duty, also, to be influenced by another motive—desire to give an example of patience and resignation under every trial.'

In October 1804 Mr. George Rose entered in his diary that the Princess of Wales had recently said to Mr. George Villiers: 'I cannot say I positively hate the Prince of Wales, but I certainly have a positive horror of him.' 'They lived,' adds Mr. Rose of the ill-matched pair, 'in different houses, dined at different hours, and were never alone together. The Princess said: "Nothing shall shake the determination I have taken to live in no other way than the state of separation we are now in."'

Exactly after a year's experience of married life the luckless pair finally separated. The Princess's allowance was at first fixed at 20,000*l.* per annum, but after some undignified haggling on both sides touching money, the Princess declined the allowance proposed and, throwing herself on the generosity of the Prince, rendered him liable for any debts she might possibly contract. 'It was settled that the Princess should retain her apartments at Carlton House, with free access to her child, who had a nursery establishment of her own, under the superintendence of Lady Elgin. This lady did not live in Carlton House, but was in attendance on the child at meals, ordered everything, and was the medium of communication between her parents respecting her. The Princess Caroline, naturally fond of children, doted on the baby; the Prince cared little about her, though he jealously asserted his authority, and was always on the watch to restrain interference on the part of the mother. In the summer of 1797, a sub-governess was appointed to reside in Carlton House, and act under the orders of Lady Elgin. The office was confided to Miss Hayman, who seems by her correspondence to have been a warm-hearted, devoted person. The Princess took a great fancy to her, and drew her into an intimacy which the Prince probably disapproved, for he dismissed her at the end of three months.'[1] With a few ladies the Princess subsequently retired to a small residence at Charlton, near Woolwich; but on being appointed Ranger of Greenwich Park she removed to Montague House, on Blackheath, where she had the care of her daughter, was very frequently visited by the King, and never on any occasion by her Majesty. At this period her income was settled. It was partly derived from the Prince, who contributed to her, as 'Princess of Wales,' 12,000*l*. per annum. The exchequer supplied another 5,000*l*.; the *droits* of the admiralty added occasionally a few pecuniary grants; and altogether her revenue amounted to about the same which she had previously declined to accept. With it she appeared content, lived quietly, cultivated her garden, looked after the poor, taught or superintended the teaching of several poor children, and, without a court, had a

[1] 'Brief Memoir of the Princess Charlotte of Wales.'

very pleasant society about her, with whom, however, she was alternately mirthful and melancholy.

If her residence at Blackheath was in many respects a sad one, it was not without its sunny side. There were joyous parties there occasionally, and the friends of the Princess, in spite of their sorrows and indignation, contrived, with their illustrious *protégée*, to pass a merry time of it between the lulls of the storm. The merriest hours there were those passed in playing at blind-man's buff, where the Princess herself, that grave judge, Sir William Scott, and that equally grave senator, George Canning, were the sprightliest at the game. The company the Princess received there included some of the foremost people, for rank and for intellect, from all quarters of the world. Here is one of several entries relating to this subject, taken from William Windham's Diary, October the 20th, 1805 :—' Dined at Princess's : present Monsieur the Comte d'Artois (afterwards Charles X.), Duc de Berri, Prince de Condé, Duc de Bourbon, M. de Rulhière, Count de Escars, Lady Sheffield, Miss Cholmondeley, Mr. W. Lock, and Mr. J. Angerstein. When the Prince left, the Princess made a sign for us to stay, when a small supper was brought, which kept us till twelve.' The *petits soupers* were hilarious and unceremonious. The Princess of Wales had not been long a resident at Montague House before her daughter, the Princess Charlotte, was removed to a mansion in the vicinity, where, under the superintendence of Lady Elgin, her early education was commenced with favourable auspices. It may, however, be questioned whether that be a proper term to apply in a case where a mother is deprived of the right to superintend the education of her own child. But it must be allowed that, though the Princess of Wales had a little taste, about the same amount of knowledge, and could stick natural flowers on ground glass so as to deceive the most minutely examining or the most courtly of Germans, she was as little capable of being governess to her own daughter as her mother had of being instructress to the Princess Caroline. The interviews between the latter and the Princess Charlotte now occurred but once a-week; and, under the circumstances, that was as frequent as interviews could be permitted. The little Princess, meanwhile, did not fare badly, nor did she lack wit, or lose opportunity of showing it. She delighted Dr. Porteus, Bishop of London, who, during a visit, had told her that when she repaired, as was intended, to Southend, for sea-bathing, she would then be in his diocese, by at once going down on her knees and asking his blessing.

Her poor mother was always as ready to make friends, but she wanted judgment to balance her tenderness. She never had such cause to repent at leisure for over-hastiness of action as when she made the acquaintance of Sir John and Lady Douglas. The former was an officer lately returned from Egypt; the latter was the mother of an infant whose reported beauty inspired the Princess with a desire to see it. Without any previous intimation to Lady Douglas, with whom she was totally unacquainted, the Princess, one winter morning, the snow lying deep upon the ground, crossed the heath, 'in a lilac-satin pelisse, primrose-coloured half-boots, and a small lilac travelling-cap, furred with sable,' and presented herself at the gate of Lady Douglas's house. She was invited to enter, under the supposition that she wished to rest. She did not see the infant; but there was an old Lady Stuart there, quite as childish, and of her the lady in attendance upon the Princess (during the hour the visit lasted) made some 'fun;' the same old lady 'being a singular character, and talking all kind of nonsense.'

It was in all respects an evil hour when this acquaintance was first formed. It ripened, for a time, into intimacy; and when the mutual intercourse was at its highest, in 1802, the Princess, who had a strong inclination to patronise infants, and had several placed out at nurse, at her charge, in a house upon the heath, 'took a liking' for the infant son of a poor couple named Austin. The boy was born in Brownlow-street Lying-in Hospital, and Mrs. Austin was his mother. These two important facts were established beyond all doubt. Why the Princess should have resolved to take personal charge of so young an infant, only a few months old, defies conjecture. It may, perhaps, be accounted for by the fact that she knew she was narrowly watched by enemies who felt an interest in accomplishing her ruin, and she was elated with the idea of mystifying them by the presence of an infant at Montague House.

However this may have been, the intercourse with the Douglases continued with some degree of warmth on both sides. It was ultimately broken off by the Princess, who had been warned to be on her guard against Lady Douglas, as a dangerous and not very irreproachable character; and thereon the Princess of Wales declined to receive any more visits from her. The baronet and his lady, with Sir Sidney Smith, a very intimate friend of both parties, so incessantly besieged the Princess for some explanation of her conduct that she at length called into her council her brother-in-law, the Duke of Kent.

The Duke consented to see Sir Sidney Smith upon the subject, and from him his Royal Highness learned that Sir John was not so much aggrieved at the refusal of the Princess to receive Lady Douglas as he was at an anonymous letter accompanying a coarse drawing representing Sir Sidney and Lady Douglas, which had been forwarded to him, and of which he believed the Princess to be the author.

The Duke of Kent was a little too credulous, but he did not act unwisely. Apparently afraid that there was ground for the charge implied by Sir John, he was still more fearful of the effect the knowledge of it would have upon the King, then in a highly nervous condition, and he was more than all afraid of the evil consequences it might have, if divulged, of exasperating the existing fierce quarrel between the Prince of Wales and the King, whose visit to the Princess excited the utmost wrath in the bosom of the Prince. Taking all these circumstances into consideration, he succeeded in advising the parties to 'let the matter drop.' Sir John consented to do so if he were left unmolested. It must be added that Lord Cholmondeley, who was perfectly acquainted with the Princess's handwriting, pronounced the letter as certainly not having been written by her. Of the drawing he could form no opinion, except one not at all flattering to the artist.

It was not likely that the matter would rest as the Duke of Kent desired. Sir John himself was not as quiescent as he had promised to be, and the details already mentioned came to the ears of the Duke of Sussex. The latter considered it his duty to make report thereof to the Prince of Wales, and the heir-apparent, of course, called upon Lady Douglas for a statement. His request was complied with, and a deposition was taken down from the lady's own lips. It is a document of too great length to be inserted here, but its chief points may be stated. It professed great admiration of the Prince of Wales, and the exact reverse of his consort. It detailed the circumstances of the origin of the acquaintance between the Princess and Lady Douglas, and of the latter becoming one of the ladies-in-waiting to the former. The Princess was described as coarse in character, loose in conversation, and impure in action. Circumstances were detailed of her alleged intrigues, of her attempt to corrupt the virtue of

Lady Douglas herself, of trying to seduce her into the commission of very serious sin, and of her laughing at her for not yielding to the seduction.

The lady went on to describe the common talk of the Princess as being such as to disgust the men, and to cause mothers to send away their daughters if the latter happened to be listeners. The Queen was said to be the especial object of the ridicule of the Princess, and she hinted at an improper intercourse existing between her Majesty and Mr. Addington! The whole royal family, it was further alleged, were the objects of her satire; but all the statements in the deposition fade into nothing before one respecting the Princess, in which the latter is represented as confessing to Lady Douglas that she was about to become a mother, laughing heartily at the confession itself, hinting that it would not be difficult to fix the paternity on the Prince, and ending by declaring that the matter would be settled satisfactorily by making the world believe that she had adopted an infant belonging to some other person. The deponent then says that she saw the Princess a short time previous to her alleged adoption of the child (subsequently proved to be the son of the Austins); that then her condition of health was not to be mistaken; and that some time subsequently she saw the child and Princess together, and that the latter laughingly acknowledged it to be her own. The immediately succeeding details will not bear telling; and this is the less necessary as they are excessively improbable, and were proved to be untrue. They are followed by others regarding the coolness which sprung up between the Princess and lady, with consequent squabbles, and final separation at the end of 1803. In conclusion, we hear of the return of the Douglases from Devonshire, the refusal of the Princess to receive her former lady-in-waiting, the receipt of the anonymous letters and drawings, the appeal to the

Duke of Kent, the temporary suspension of hostilities, and lastly, the communication made to the Duke of Sussex, which the latter conveyed to the Prince of Wales, and which was followed by the deposition of which I have endeavoured, however imperfectly, to furnish a *resumé* that may be comprehended without giving offence. Those who are acquainted with the original document will allow that this is no very easy task.

Upon this statement, made in 1805, a commission was formed, under which various witnesses were examined. On the 11th of January 1806, William Cole, page to the Princess (a discarded servant), averred that he had been dismissed by the Princess of Wales, for no worse offence than looking indignant at conduct between his mistress and Sir Sidney Smith which shocked him, the page. He described various immoral proceedings as having gone on during his residence, that he had heard of worse after his departure from other servants, particularly from Fanny Lloyd, who had kindly informed him of the very improper conduct of her Royal Highness and Captain Manby of the Royal Navy, during the sojourn of the Princess at Southend, in the year 1804; and Cole added that he himself had witnessed conduct as infamous between the Princess and 'Lawrence the painter' as early as 1801.

Another witness, Bidgood, who, after being in the service of the Prince of Wales near a quarter of a century, was transferred to that of the Princess in 1798, went further than his predecessors. The least offensive part of his deposition was that in which he swore that he had seen Captain Manby kiss the Princess, who was in tears at his leaving. This witness spoke to alleged facts equally startling respecting her Royal Highness and Captain Hood. The depositions of the female servants were even more strong in their coarseness and weight of testimony against the Princess. All these persons, it must be remembered, were appointed to serve her, she herself having had no voice in the selection. When they became witnesses against her she was not allowed to know the nature of their evidence.

It was in consequence of their allegations having been submitted to his Majesty that the King issued his warrant in May 1806 to Lords Erskine, Grenville, Spencer, and Ellenborough, whereby they were directed to inquire into the truth or falsehood of these allegations and report accordingly.

The witnesses were all examined on oath; and it is due to Sir John Douglas to say that he seemed to wish to make of his evidence a simple account of hearsay communications from his wife. He knew nothing of what had taken place between his wife and the Princess but what the former had told him of long after the period of its occurrence. He swore, however, to having been convinced that the Princess was about to become a mother. The depositions of most of these witnesses varied considerably from those previously made by them, and fresh witnesses, called to prove the case against the Princess, did more harm than good to their own side. Others, who were servants of the Princess, distinctly denied that the allegations made against her were true. The proof that young Austin was simply an adopted child was complete. The commissioners were unanimous on this point, and therewith was established the falsehood of the depositions made by the Douglases with respect to it. The commissioners, however, did not feel so certain upon the other items of evidence; and they gave it as their opinion, not that the Princess should be held innocent until she could be proved guilty, but that the allegations should be credited until they could be satisfactorily disproved!

Never was accused woman more hardly used than the

Princess in this matter. For a long time she knew nothing of the nature of the evidence tendered against her, and every obstacle was put in her way to rendering the satisfactory answer, wanting which the commissioners, though they acquitted her of high treason, thought she must be held *quasi* convicted of immorality. She was equal, however, to every difficulty, and she did not lack assistance. Mr. Perceval wrote, in her name, a memorial to the King, which is a masterpiece of ability, so searchingly does it sift the evidence, crush what was unfavourable to her, point out where she had a triumph, even without a witness, indignantly deny the charges laid against her, and which she had not hitherto been permitted to disprove, and touchingly appeal to her only protector, the King himself, for a continuance of his favour to one not unworthy of that for which she so ardently petitions. The memorial would almost occupy this volume entirely; it is only possible, therefore, thus to describe and refer to it. A passage or two from the conclusion will give, however, some idea of its spirit :—

'In happier days of my life, before my spirit had been yet at all lowered by my misfortunes, I should have been disposed to have met such a charge with the contempt which, I trust by this time, your Majesty thinks due to it. I should have been disposed to have defied my enemies to the utmost, and to have scorned to answer to anything but a legal charge before a competent tribunal. But in my present misfortunes such force of mind is gone. I ought, perhaps, so far to be thankful to them for their wholesome lessons of humility. I have therefore entered into this long detail to endeavour to remove at the first possible opportunity any unfavourable impressions, to rescue myself from the dangers which the continuance of these suspicions might occasion, and to preserve to me your Majesty's good opinion, in whose kindness, hitherto,

I have found infinite consolation, and to whose justice, under all circumstances, I can confidently appeal.'

The memorial, however, would have been of very little worth but for the depositions by which it was accompanied. These were sworn to, not by discarded servants, but by men of character—men, that is, of reputation. Thus Captain Manby, on oath, replies to the allegation of Bidgood that he had seen the Captain kiss the Princess of Wales:—'It is a vile and wicked invention, wholly and absolutely false; it is impossible that he could ever have seen any such thing, as I never upon any occasion, or in any situation, had the presumption to salute her Royal Highness in any such manner, or to take any such liberty as to offer any such insult to her person.' To Bidgood's allegation that the Captain's frequent sleeping in the house was a subject of constant conversation with the servants, Captain Manby again declares upon oath that he never in his life slept in any house anywhere that had ever been occupied by her Royal Highness. 'Never,' he adds, 'did anything pass between her Royal Highness and myself that I should be in any degree unwilling that all the world should have seen.'

This was conclusive; the deposition of Lawrence, the great artist, was not less crushing. In answer to a strongly-worded deposition of Cole, the page, Lawrence declares on oath that during the time he was painting the portrait of the Princess at Montague House he never was alone with her but upon one occasion, and then simply to answer a question put to him at a moment he was about to retire with the rest of the company. Like Captain Manby, he solemnly swears that nothing ever passed between her Royal Highness and himself which he would have the least objection that all the world should see and hear.

One of the female servants had accused Mr. Edmondes,

the surgeon to her Royal Highness's household, of having acknowledged circumstances touching the Princess which, if true, would have proved her to have been the very basest of women. Mr. Edmondes was said to have made this statement to a menial servant, after having bled her Royal Highness. That gentleman, however, denied on oath that he had ever made such a statement as the one in question; and perhaps the animus of the inquisitors was betrayed, on the reiterated denial of Mr. Edmondes, by a remark to him of Lord Moira. 'Lord Moira,' says the surgeon, 'with his hands behind him, his head over his shoulder, his eye directed towards me, with a sort of smile, observed, "that he could not help thinking there must be *something* in the servant's deposition," as if he did not give perfect credence to what I said.'

Mr. Mills, another medical man attached to the Princess's household, and also accused by a female servant of having intimated, in 1802, that her Royal Highness was in a fair way of becoming a mother, proved that he had not been in the house since 1801, and declared the accusation to be a most infamous falsehood. Finally, two of the menservants at Montague House swore to having seen Lady Douglas and Bidgood in communication with each other, that is, meeting and conversing together—a short time previous to the commission of inquiry being opened.

With respect to the alleged familiarities said to have taken place between the Princess and Sir Sidney Smith, the Princess herself remarks upon them, in the memorial addressed by her to the King, to the effect that 'if his visiting frequently at Montague House, both with Sir John and Lady Douglas, and without them; at luncheon, dinner, and supper; and staying with the rest of the company till twelve or one o'clock, or even later; if these were some of the facts which must give occasion to unfavourable interpretations, they were facts which she could never contradict, for they were perfectly true.' She further admits that Sir Sidney had paid her morning visits, and that they had frequently on such occasions been alone. 'But,' said the memorial, 'if suffering a man to be so alone is evidence of guilt from whence the commissioners can draw any unfavourable inference, I must leave them to draw it, for I cannot deny that it has happened frequently, not only with Sir Sidney Smith, but with many others— gentlemen who have visited me—tradesmen who have come for orders—masters whom I have had to instruct me in painting, music, and English—that I have received them without any one being by. I never had any idea that it was wrong thus to receive men of a morning. There can have been nothing immoral in the thing itself, and I have understood that it was quite usual for ladies of rank and character to receive the visits of gentlemen in the morning, though they might be themselves alone at the time. But if this is thought improper in England, I hope every candid mind will make allowance for the different notions which my foreign education and habits may have given me.'

Nine weeks elapsed since the Princess had addressed the above memorial and depositions to the King, and still no reply reached her, except an intimation through the Lord Chancellor that his Majesty had read the documents in question, and had ordered them to be submitted to the commissioners. She complained, justly enough, at being left nine weeks without knowledge as to what judgment the commissioners had formed of the report drawn up in reply to their sentence, which acquitted her of gross guilt, yet left her under the weight of an accusation of having acted in a manner unbecoming her high station, or, indeed, unbecoming a woman in any station. From such delay, she said, the world began to infer her guilt, in total ignorance, as they were, of the real state of the facts. 'I feel myself,' she then said, 'sinking in the estimation of your Majesty's subjects, as well as what remains to me of my own family, into (a state intolerable to a mind conscious of its own purity and innocence) a state in which my honour appears at least equivocal, and my virtue is suspected. From this state I humbly entreat your Majesty to perceive that I can have no hope of being restored until either your Majesty's favourable opinion shall be graciously notified to the world, by receiving me again into the royal presence, or until the false disclosures of the facts shall expose the malice of my accusers, and do away every possible ground for unfavourable inference and conjecture.'

The Princess then alluded to the fact that the occasion of assembling the royal family and the King's subjects 'in dutiful and happy commemoration of her Majesty's birthday' was then at hand; and she intimated that if the commissioners were prevented from presenting their final report before that time, and that consequently, at such a period, she should be without any knowledge of the King's pleasure, the world would inevitably conclude that her answers to the charges must have proved altogether unsatisfactory, and the really infamous charges would be accounted of as too true.

Some months longer, notwithstanding this urgent appeal, was the Princess kept in suspense. There seemed a determination existing somewhere that, if her accusers could not prove her guilt, she should at least not be permitted to substantiate her innocence. At length, on the 25th of January 1807, the King having referred the entire matter, with her Royal Highness's letters, to the cabinet ministers, the latter delivered themselves of their lengthily gestated resolution.

The ministers modestly declared themselves an incompetent tribunal to pronounce judicially a verdict of *guilty* or *not guilty* upon any person, of whatever rank. Their office was, indeed, more that of grand jurymen called upon to pronounce whether a charge is based upon such grounds, however slight, as to justify further proceedings against the person accused. They acquitted the Princess by their judgment that further proceedings were not called for, but, having been requested by the King to counsel him as to the reply he should render to his daughter-in-law, the nature of such counsel may be seen in the royal answer to the Princess's memorial. The King exculpated her from the most infamous portion of the charge brought against her by Lady Douglas, and declared that no further legal proceedings would be taken except with a view of punishing that appalling slanderer. Of the other allegations stated in the preliminary examinations, the King declared that none of them would be considered as legally or conclusively established. *But*, said the King, and severely imperative as was this sovereign *but*, it was not uncalled for—' In these examinations, and even in the answer drawn in the name of the Princess by her legal advisers, there have appeared circumstances of conduct on the part of the Princess which his Majesty never could regard but with serious concern. The elevated rank which the Princess holds in this country, and the relation in which she stands to his Majesty and the royal family, must always deeply involve both the interests of the state and the personal feelings of his Majesty in the propriety and correctness of her conduct. And his Majesty cannot, therefore, forbear to express, in the conclusion of the business, his desire and expectation that, in future, such a conduct may be observed by the Princess as may fully justify those marks of paternal regard and affection which the King always wishes to show to every part of the royal family.'

There is no doubt that this admonition was seriously called for. The conduct of the Princess had been that of an indiscreet, rash, and over-bold woman. At the court of the two preceding Georges such conduct would only have been called lively; but the example of Charlotte had put an end to such vivacity. The Queen Caroline of the former reign had, in her conversations with Sir Robert Walpole especially, gone far beyond the gaiety of the dialogues maintained by the Princess Caroline and Sir Sidney Smith under George III. But the Princess was as yet 'without blemish,' only in the degree that Queen Caroline was. She was not delicately minded, and was defiant of the Court-world when she had been cast out from it unjustly. The two Carolines were wronged in much the same degree, but the husband of the one respected the virtue of the wife whom he insulted; the husband of the other had no respect for either virtue or wife; nay, he would have been glad to prove that there had been a divorce between the two. He had failed to do so, and the King's intimation to the Princess that ' his Majesty was convinced that it was no longer necessary for him to decline receiving the Princess into the royal presence,' while it was the triumphant justification of the wife, was the unqualified condemnation of the husband, beneath whose roof the slander was first uttered by Sir John Douglas to the Duke of Sussex. And so ended the 'delicate investigation.' A history of it was actually printed, but the copies were bought up and suppressed. A writer in ' Notes and Queries ' (No. 128, 1852), says:—

'Several years ago I was present when the sum of 500*l*. was paid for a copy of " The Delicate Investigation " by an officer high in the service of the then government. —H. B.'

The husband of Caroline was at this time suffering from a double anguish. He was snubbed by his political friends, and he was what is called deeply in love with Lady Hertford. The 'passion' for this lady was contracted during some negotiations with her family, entered upon for the purpose of placing Miss Seymour (a niece of Lady Hertford's) under the care of Mrs. Fitzherbert. When this passion was in progress the Prince aimed at bringing it to a successful issue by the strangest of love-processes. He was accustomed, if not actually ill, to make himself so, in order that he might appear interesting, and have a claim upon the compassion of the 'fair,' who might otherwise have proved obdurate. With this end in view he would submit to be bled several times in the night, and by several operators, when in fact ' there was so little necessity for it that different surgeons were introduced for the purpose unknown to each other, lest they should object to so unusual a loss of blood.'[1] It was reported that, after the rupture with his second wife, the Prince sought to renew his intimacy with his first, but that Mrs. Fitzherbert would not consent till a brief arrived from Rome assuring her, in answer to a statement of her case expressly laid before the Court, that the wishes of the Prince were quite legitimate. This is intended to imply that the Papal Court actually looked upon a marriage ceremony performed by a Protestant minister, and uniting a Roman Catholic with a Protestant, as a valid ceremony! The assurance was enough for the lady. The old intimacy was renewed, and inaugurated by a public breakfast, at her own house, to all the fashionable world, with the Prince at the head of it! The 'next eight years' of her connections with the Prince she described as supremely happy years. They were extremely poor, she said, but 'as merry as crickets,' and 'joyously proud, on once returning to Brighton from London, that they could not raise 5*l*. between them.' So runs this Idyll.

If he was ridiculous in this, he was criminal in other respects. The pretty child, Miss Seymour, was placed

[1] Lord Holland.

with Mrs. Fitzherbert, and the Prince became greatly attached to her. The guardians of the young lady, rightly or wrongly, thought that a person in the position which Mrs. Fitzherbert occupied was not exactly a fitting guide for a motherless girl. The law was had recourse to in order to obtain the removal of the latter, and ultimately the matter was brought before the supreme tribunal of the peers. It is a well-known fact that when this was the case the Prince, in whose heart there had been lit up a flame of genuine affection warmer than anything he had ever felt for his own daughter, became alarmed at the idea of losing Miss Seymour. He therefore actually stooped to canvass for the votes of peers in this, a purely judicial question, which they were called upon to decide according to law and their consciences. An heir-apparent to a throne, and so engaged, presented no edifying spectacle. And it must be remembered that at the time he was thus suborning witnesses (for to canvass the vote of a judicial peer was subornation of those whose office it was to enforce the due administration of the law) he had set his small affections upon a child, and was living in open disregard of the seventh commandment, and of that portion of the tenth which relates to our neighbour's wife. He was accusing, through suborned testimony, his own wife of crimes and sentiments of a similar nature, and with no better result than to make patent his own infamy, and to establish nothing worse than thoughtless indiscretion on the part of the consort whom he had abandoned.

The Princess, who was still suffering from debility consequent upon an attack of measles, was naturally elated at the result of the protracted inquiry, and respectfully requested to be permitted to 'throw herself at his Majesty's feet on the following Monday.' The monarch reminded her of her debility, bade her take patience, and promised to name a day for receiving her, when he was assured of her being fully restored to health. She waited patiently for the expression of the King's pleasure upon the matter, and was preparing once more for the enjoyment of again being received by him, when all her hopes were suddenly annihilated by an intimation from the King that—the Prince of Wales having stated that he was not satisfied with the result of the late inquiry—the Prince had placed the matter in the hands of his legal advisers, and had requested his Majesty to refrain from taking further steps in the business for the present; the King consequently 'considered it incumbent on him to defer naming a day to the Princess of Wales until the further result of the Prince's intention shall have been made known to him.' This note was dated 'Windsor Castle, the 10th of February, 1807.' From that day the Princess looked upon her husband as assuming the office of public accuser against her. The Blackheath plot had failed, and the Prince was now appealing against the decision of judges to whose arbitrament he had committed the responsible duty of examination and sentence. What he required was a judgment unfavourable to his wife; not having succeeded, he sought for another tribunal, and virtually requested the monarch and the nation to hold his consort guilty until he might have the luck or leisure to prove her to be so. Had she been twice the imprudent woman she was, such conduct as this on the part of the Prince was sure to make a popular favourite of the Princess.

 The courage of the latter rose, however, as persecution waxed hotter; and the advisers who now stood by her, of whom Mr. Perceval was the chief, were doubly stimulated by political as well as personal feelings. The Princess continued to address vigorous appeals to the King, whose intellect was beginning to be too weak to comprehend, and his eyesight too feeble for him to be able to read them. Their cry was still for justice; they claimed for her a public reception at court, and apartments in some one of the royal palaces, as more befitting her condition. Intimation, too, was made that if the justice demanded were not awarded her, a full detail of the whole affair, taken from the view held of it by the advisers of the Princess, would be forthwith published. It is said that the menace touched even Queen Charlotte herself, who had a dread of 'THE BOOK,' as it was emphatically called, upon which Mr. Perceval was known to be busily engaged, and which it was feared he was about to publish. But the temporary triumph of the Princess was at hand. In March 1807 the Grenville administration, the members of which were known to be favourites with the Queen and enemies of the Princess of Wales, retired from office, and within a month the new ministry advised the King that the complete innocence of the Princess had been established, and that it would be well for him to receive her at court in a manner suitable to her rank and station. The ministers present at the meeting of council when this advice was rendered were Lord Chancellor Eldon, Lord President Camden, Lord Privy Seal Westmoreland, the Duke of Portland, the Earl of Chatham, the Earl of Bathurst, Viscount Castlereagh, Lord Mulgrave, Mr. Canning, and Lord Hawkesbury.

In May 1807 the Princess was accordingly received at court, at a drawing-room held by Queen Charlotte. The latter illustrious lady exhibited no demeanour by which it could be construed that she was happy to see her daughter-in-law. The utmost honour paid her was a cold and rigid courtesy. The Queen was again 'civil, but stiff.' The nobility and gentry present were more expansive in the warmth of their welcome. From them the Princess received a homage of apparently cordial respect. Sir Jonah Barrington, in his 'Personal Sketches of his own Times,' gives a rather different description of the scene, at which he was present. From this account we collect that the Princess, leaning on the arm of the Duke of Cumberland, appeared in deep mourning—for her father. She 'tottered' up to the Queen, as if fearing a repulsive welcome. The reception of her was ' kind ' on the Queen's part, ' and a paroxysm of spirits seemed to succeed, and mark a strange contrast to the manner of her entry. I thought it was too sudden and too decisive. She spoke much and loud, and rather bold. Her circle was crowded, the presentations numerous, but on the whole she lost ground in my estimation.'

On the occasion of the King's birthday on the following month the Princess again repaired to court. The welcome resembled that which she had received at her last visit, but there was an incident at this which rendered it more interesting, at all events to lookers-on. It was at this drawing-room that the Prince and Princess of Wales encountered each other for the last time. They met in the very centre of the apartment—they bowed, stood face to face for a moment, exchanged a few words which no one heard, and then passed on ; *he*, stately as an iceberg, and as cold—*she*, with a smile, half mirthful, half melancholy, as though she rejoiced that she was there in spite of him, and yet regretted that her visit was not under happier auspices. The triumph, however, was complete as far as it went, for she assuredly was present that day contrary to the inclination of both her husband and her mother-in-law.

There was one being upon earth whom this Princess unreservedly loved, and of whom she was deprived this year—her father, the Duke of Brunswick. He had been but an indifferent husband and father, but his wife did not complain, and his daughter Caroline feared and adored him.

The father of the Princess of Wales, at the age of seventy-one, perished on the fatal field of Jena, on that day on which Prussia was made to pay the penalty of mingled treachery and imbecility. It had been her policy, throughout the troubles of the time, to save herself at any other nation's cost. Such a policy caused her to fall into the ruin which overcame her at Jena, without securing the sympathy even of those nations which then fought against the then common enemy. In this battle the father of Caroline had done his utmost to win victory for Prussia, but in vain, and he lost his own life in the attempt. His ability and courage were all cast away. He had with him in the camp a very unseemly companion, in the person of a French actress, who was the friend of his aide-de-camp, Montjoy. This officer was close to him when, in the midst of his staff, and at a distance altogether from where the battle was raging, the old Duke was shot by a man on foot, 'who presented his carabine so close that the ball went in under the left eye (the Duke was on horseback) and came out above the right, quite through the upper part of the nose.' It is Lord Malmesbury who suggests, without pretending to assert, that 'Montjoy's brother, the Grand Veneur to Prince Max, the pretended King of Bavaria, and who was with Bonaparte, knew exactly where the Duke of Brunswick was to be found, and by a connivance with Montjoy produced the event.'

After the death of the Duke, the Duchess became a fugitive, for the Duchy of Brunswick was in the possession of the French. And accordingly the poor Augusta, at whose birth in St. James's Palace there had been such scant ceremony and excess of commotion, came now in her old age, and after an absence of forty years, to ask a home at the hearth of the brother who loved her, as she used to say equivocally, as warmly as he *could* love anything, and of the sister-in-law who, as the poor Duchess knew, regarded her with some dislike, and who was met with the same amount and quality of affection on the part of Augusta of Brunswick.

She had, however, little cause to complain, as far as these relatives were concerned. They received her cordially; and, though they gave her no home in the palace in which she was born, they helped her to an humbler home elsewhere, and occasionally lent it cheerfulness by paying her a visit. In the meantime the widowed mother sat at the hearth of her deserted daughter, and though neither of them had sufficient depth of sentiment to bring her affliction touchingly home to the other, each was sufficiently stricken by severity of real sorrow to render her eloquent upon her own misery, if not attentive to the twice-told tale of her companion.

Meanwhile, there was pressure of another sort upon the Princess—a pressure of debt, incurred principally by the uncertainty with which she had hitherto been supplied with pecuniary means, and also the want of a controlling treasurer to give warning when expenditure was exceeding probable income. Prudent people find such an officer in themselves; but then the Princess was not a prudent person, and among the things she least understood was the management or the worth of money. She was, however, in 1809, in so embarrassed a situation as to render an application to the King's ministers necessary, when it was found that her debts exceeded 50,000*l*. A final arrangement was then come to. The Prince and Princess signed a deed of separation. The former consented to pay the debts to the amount of 49,000*l*. on condition of being held non-responsible for any future liabilities incurred by his consort. Her fixed income was settled at 22,000*l*. per annum, under the control of a treasurer, who was to discharge the remaining liabilities out of the present year's income, and to guard against any other occurring in years to come, if he could.

As wide a separation as possible was made between mother and child. They were happy Saturday afternoons that the Princess Charlotte was allowed to spend at Blackheath, where she met the Hon. Miss Wellesley (afterwards Countess of Westmoreland) and other children, and partook of childish delights. Under her grandmother the Queen, at Windsor, she was stiffly disciplined. Once expressing a wish to be allowed to go and say 'good-bye' to a young friend who was about to leave England, Queen Charlotte remarked 'it was contrary to princely dignity to seek after any one.' Some young girls who had been allowed to come to Windsor, and were the companions of the Princess for an occasional day, were not allowed to grow into familiarity or intimacy. The old Queen's sour notice of them to her grand-daughter was: 'I cannot *taste* these young ladies!' In this cruel way were all the warm sympathies of a warm-hearted child set at naught.

The relations into which the Prince entered with Lady Hertford, while the question of the guardianship of Miss Seymour was pending, led to the ascendency of that lady, and brought to a final close the intimacy which had existed between the Prince and Mrs. Fitzherbert. At a dinner given to Louis XVIII., to which she was invited, the Prince replied to her inquiry as to where she was to sit, 'You know, Madam, you have no place.' 'None, sir,' she rejoined, 'but what you are pleased to give me.' He assigned none, and she kept away. The last morning she ever saw the Prince was at a soirée at Devonshire House. The Duchess was conducting her to the Duke's apartments, where he was confined with the gout, but where he received a few old friends. As the two ladies passed through one of the rooms, Mrs. Fitzherbert saw the Prince and Lady Hertford in a tête-à-tête conversation, and nearly fainted under all the impressions which then rushed upon her mind, but, taking a glass of water, she recovered and passed on.[1]

[1] 'Memoirs of Mrs. Fitzherbert.

CHAPTER IV.

MOTHERS AND DAUGHTERS.

Imbecility finally settled on the mind of George III.—Intercourse between the Princess and her daughter obstructed—The Whigs betrayed by the Prince—Sketch of the Duchess of Brunswick—The Princess's Court at Kensington diminished—Her pleasant dinners there—Lively outbreaks of the Princess—Her sketches of character—Her indiscretion—An adventure—Description of the Princess Charlotte—The Princess of Wales's demeanour to her mother—Thoughtlessness of the Duchess of Brunswick—Popularity of the Princess on the wane—Her determination to bring her wrongs before the public—She becomes more melancholy—An incident—Continued agitation of the Princess—She becomes querulous—The poet Campbell presented to her—A humorous fault of orthography—The Prince and John Kemble.

By the exertions chiefly of Mr. Perceval the Princess had been declared innocent of the charges brought against her, had been received at court, and had apartments assigned her in Kensington Palace, which she occupied conjointly with her house at Blackheath. The clever friend of the Princess was high in the popular esteem for these things, and the public awaited at his hands that banquet of scandal which he had promised them in the volume to be called 'The Book.' When, however, they found the work suppressed by its author, and that he was soon after made Chancellor of the Exchequer, the public professed to discern here both cause and effect. They looked upon the elevation of Perceval as the reward of his literary self-denial. The honourable gentleman cared little for what the public thought, nor can it be said that, either as friend of the Princess or servant of the Prince, he served either of these illustrious persons, or even the public, unfaithfully.

In 1810, when imbecility settled upon the mind of George III., Perceval proposed a restricted regency, but there was less cause for restriction now than there had been before, and the restriction was only maintained during one year. It was a period of great distress at home, and abroad of such costly triumphs as made victory itself a glory not to be glad over. At this juncture the Regent acquired some degree of public esteem, and it was not ill-earned, by declining to receive an increase of revenue when the people were taxed to an extent such as no nation had ever before experienced. The public, however, would fain have seen the Princess of Wales raised also in a corresponding degree with the Regent, by some distinctive mark to show that she was the Regent's wife.

It was rather an unreasonable expectation, and Mr. Perceval was rather unreasonably censured for not realising it. The deed of separation was, if not a cause, at least an apology or authority, for keeping the Princess in the condition of a private person. She could claim no higher title till the period that should make her husband a king. But this was no reason that she should be irritated by obstructions thrown in the way of her seeing her daughter. These obstructions were unworthy of their author, and failed in their object. They were excused on the ground that the manners of the mother were not edifying to the child, but when the two did meet there was ample evidence of an affection existing between them stronger than might have been expected at the hands of a daughter who had certainly not been educated in the holy faith that her mother was worthy of all the filial reverence that child could pay her.

In the meantime the Regent had his difficulties. He

who betrayed the Whigs, by whose advice he had been
guided during the time of his father's sanity, but who had
cast them off after the death of Fox in 1806, now sought
to strengthen his government by the accession of some of
his old friends. The Whigs, however, would not act with
Perceval, and after the assassination of that minister in
1812 they lost, by their arrogance, the opportunity of
forming an independent administration. The boast of
Grey and Grenville that they would ride rough-shod
through Carlton Palace led to the formation of the Liverpool Tory Ministry, which began its long tenure of office
in June 1812.

During these changes and negotiations the Princess of
Wales remained at Kensington or Blackheath, while her
mother was very indifferently lodged in New Street,
Spring Gardens, in half-furnished, dirty, and comfortless
apartments. Amid filthy lamps on a sideboard, and common chairs ranged along dingy walls, sat the aged Duchess,
'a melancholy spectacle of decayed royalty.' She is
described as having good-nature impressed upon her
features, frankness in her manners, with a rough, abrupt
style of conversation, that rendered her remarkable. She
loved to dwell upon the past, though it was full of melancholy remembrances; and she is said to have been charitable to the frailties of the period of her own early days,
but a strict censurer of those of the contemporaries of her
old age.

Up to the period of the King's illness the Princess of
Wales did not want for friends to attend her dinners and
evening parties. When the only advocate she had among
the royal family virtually died, and the Prince of Wales
became really King, under the title of Regent, the number of her allies seriously diminished. They had to choose,
as in the days of the first and second George, between
two courts. They declared for that which was most likely

to bring them most profit in galas and gaieties. Still the diminished court at Kensington was not so dull as that made up of a few venerable dowagers at the Duchess of Brunswick's. The Princess called her mother's court a 'Dullification,' and yawned when she attended it, with more sincerity than good manners. But freedom from restraint was ever a delight to her, and she has been known on a birthday, kept at Kensington, to receive her congratulating visitors wrapped up in a pink dressing-gown. It was at a birthday reception that her brother, the Duke of Brunswick, who afterwards fell at Quatre Bras, presented her with a splendid compliment and a worthless ring. It was as much as duchyless duke could afford. On the other hand, on the same natal day, Queen Charlotte showed a good-natured memory of the festival by sending the Princess a very handsome aigrette. The young Princess Charlotte was with her mother on that day, and she observed, rather flippantly, that the present was 'really pretty well, considering who sent it!'[1] The Princess was at this time a fine girl, somewhat given to romping, but with the power of assuming a fine air of dignity when occasion required.

At the pleasant dinners at Kensington, when the servants were out of the room, and a dumb waiter (all the better, as Sir Sidney Smith used to say, for being a deaf waiter also) was at the elbow of every guest, the Princess would seem to take delight in going over the history of the past. What little there was good in her, she once remarked to Count Munster, was owing to the count's mother, who had been her governess. She acknowledged that the natural petulance of her character was rather active at the period of her marriage. 'One of the civil things his Highness said just at first was to find fault with my shoes; and as I was very young and lively in those

[1] 'Diary illustrative of the Times of George IV.'

days, I told him to make me a better pair and send them to me. I brought letters from all the princes and princesses to him from all the petty courts, and I tossed them to him and said : " There ——, that's to prove I'm not an impostor." ' She married, she said, entirely to please her father, for whom she would have made any sacrifice. She regretted that the union was determined on before the parties had been introduced to each other. 'Had I come over here as a Princess, with my father, on a visit, as Mr. Pitt once wanted my father to have done, things might have been very different; but what is done cannot be undone.'[1] Her own condition at home, however, was, at the time, but melancholy. She had there but a sorry life, between her father's mistress and her own mother. Civility to the one always procured her a scolding from the other. No wonder that she was, as she asserted, ' tired of it.'

Her spirit, depressed as it often was during her presence at Kensington, except on the few occasions when her daughter was permitted to see her, sometimes experienced the very liveliest of outbreaks. She thought nothing, for instance, of slipping through the gardens, with a single lady-in-waiting, both of them attired, perhaps, in evening costume, and, crossing Bayswater, stroll through the fields, and along by the Paddington Canal, at the great risk of being insulted, or followed by a mob, if recognised. She thought as little of entering houses that were to let, and inquiring about the terms. These are but small, yet they are significant, traits. One of more importance is her study and perception of character. At Kensington she kept a book, in which she wrote down, in indifferent English, but with great boldness and spirit, the characters of many of the leading persons in England. It is doubtful whether this book was destroyed, as the writer, when

[1] 'Diary illustrative of the Times of George IV.'

dying, ordered it to be. If it could be recovered, with the diary of Queen Charlotte and that kept by poor Sophia Dorothea, something from them might be culled of more interest than anything that is yet to be found in the histories of these three Queens.

The indiscretions of the Princess of Wales were attributed by her mother to a touch of insanity. On an occasion when Lord and Lady Redesdale were invited to meet the Duchess of Brunswick at dinner at the Princess's house at Blackheath, they found themselves there long before any of the rest of the company. For half an hour the Duchess was alone with them. She had known Lord Redesdale from her childhood, and she talked with him unreservedly. Alluding to the eccentricity and imprudence of her daughter, she added: 'But her excuse is, poor thing, that she is not right here,' putting her hand to her forehead. Lord Redesdale told this story to Miss Wynn in 1828, and that lady has recorded it in her 'Diaries of a Lady of Quality.'

The indiscretion of the Princess was very strongly marked by her selecting Sundays as the days for her greatest dinner-parties and her evening concerts. Queen Charlotte, before her, used to hold drawing-rooms on Sundays, without any idea of wrong. Since her time, too, the Countess St. Antonio, and indeed other English ladies, were accustomed to hold highest festival on this holiest day. In the case of the Princess, no doubt much prejudice was excited against her, in consequence of such proceedings. Yet she was not insensible to public opinion; and she not only wished to know what was said of her, but wished to hear it from the lips of the people.

'One day,' says the author of the 'Diary of the Court and Times of George IV.,' 'the Princess set out to walk, accompanied by myself and one of her ladies, round Kensington Gardens. At last, being wearied, her Royal Highness sat down on a bench occupied by two old persons, and she conversed with them, to my infinite amusement, they being perfectly ignorant who she was. She asked them all manner of questions about herself, to which they replied favourably. Her lady, I observed, was considerably alarmed, and was obliged to draw her veil over her face to prevent her betraying herself, and every moment I was myself afraid that something not so favourable might be expressed by these good people. Fortunately, this was not the case, and her Royal Highness walked away undiscovered, having informed them that if they would be at such a door, at such an hour, at the palace, on any day, they would meet with the Princess of Wales, to see whom they expressed the strongest desire.' These off-hand adventures she delighted in, as she did in offhand expressions. One day, when the Princess was ready to set out on a visit to the British Museum, and three of her gentlemen, Keppel Craven, Gell, and Mercer, stood awaiting her orders, ' Now,' said she, as she stepped into her carriage, ' toss up a guinea to know which shall be the happy two to come with me!' The trio had not a guinea amongst them, and the Princess named Mercer and Keppel Craven.

Except in reading aloud, the Princess does not appear to have had any intellectual pursuits at Kensington. Her health too was at times indifferent, but her constitution was not undermined, mentally and physically, as the Regent's was at this period; and she had one joy, which, however, she seemed to appreciate less than at its true worth, in the occasional society of the Princess Charlotte. The daughter is described as having been at this time ' extremely spread for her age; her bosom full, but finely shaped; her shoulders large, and her whole person voluptuous.' There was thus early a prospect of that obese development which so soon despoiled the attractions of her mother, and which very early marred the grace and beauty of the Princess Charlotte.

'Her skin is white,' says Lady Charlotte Campbell, 'but not a transparent white; there is little or no shade in her face, but her features are very fine. Their expression, like that of her general demeanour, is noble. Her feet are rather small, and her hands and arms are finely moulded. She has a hesitation in her speech, amounting almost to a stammer—an additional proof, if any were wanting, of her being her father's own child; but in everything she is his own image. Her voice is flexible and her tones dulcet, except when she laughs; then it becomes too loud, but is never unmusical.' Her Royal Highness exhibited to this observer traits of disposition which seemed to certify to an existence in her character of self-will, some caprice, and also obstinacy; but in a person so kind-hearted, clever, and enthusiastic as this young Princess these symptoms were susceptible of being converted into positive virtues; for a sensible, kindly-natured, and ardent character can sooner be taught to bend its own will to the liking of others—caprice becomes fixedness of principle, and obstinacy gives way to resolution, which is only determinedly maintained on conviction of its being rightly grounded. The young heiress to the throne was more gentle in her demeanour to her mother than the latter was to *her* parent, the old Duchess of Brunswick. To *her* the Princess of Wales was harder in her demeanour than she was to others. The Duchess was certainly a mother who had never won her daughter's respect, and who did not now know how to properly estimate her daughter's sorrows. The Duchess was not only visited by Queen Charlotte, but she was invited to dinner by the Regent; and of this last honour she triumphantly boasted in the presence of that daughter who was ejected from the Regent's house. But the poor

'Lady Augusta' was as awkward in her remarks in her old days as she had been in the days of her youth. When the dismayed circle amid which the invitation was boasted of observed a silence, which a sensible old lady would have taken for as severe a comment as could be passed, she broke the silence by abruptly asking the daughter, 'Do you think I shall be carried up stairs on my cushion?' To which the Princess coolly replied: 'There is no upstairs, I believe : the apartments are all on one floor.' 'Oh charming! that is delightful!' rejoined the Duchess; and with a few more queries, to which the Princess always replied with the greatest self-possession and *sang-froid*, as though she were not in the least hurt, this strange royal farce ended.

The brother of the Princess of Wales, if he had not an unbounded regard for his sister, at least knew what was due to her and propriety better than his mother. By his directions the Princess represented to the Duchess that if she accepted the Prince's invitation she would tacitly acknowledge that he was justified in his treatment of his wife. The old lady, as obstinate as her own grandfather, George II., was not to be moved. She saw the matter, she said, in quite another light. She loved her daughter, would do anything in the world for her, but certainly she would not give up going to Carlton House. And in this determination she remained fixed, till, meditating upon the matter, and conceiving that the invitation *may* have been less out of compliment to herself than intended to draw her into a tacit condemnation of her daughter, she suddenly declined to go, and with mingled womanly and especially matronly feeling she invited the Princess to dine with her, instead.

The Princess of Wales was, undoubtedly, fast losing the small remnant of popularity among the higher classes which had hitherto sustained her. As her more noble friends silently cast her off she filled the void left by them with persons of inferior birth, and sometimes of indifferent reputation. Her own immediate attendants laughed at her, her ways, her pronunciation, and her opinions. She was indeed a puzzle to them. Sometimes they found in her a tone of exalted sentiment; at others she was coarse or frivolous: the 'tissue of her character' was made up of the most variegated web that ever went to the dressing of a woman. Perhaps one of the most foolish, if not the most unnecessary, of her acts, was an attempt which she made to sell a portion of her jewels. It was doubtless intended by way of proof that an application to parliament for an increased allowance was a necessity on her part.

She was, however, most intent on bringing forward the story of her wrongs before the public; and she was doubtless encouraged in this by a party, some members of which, without any of the sympathy which they affected to feel, looked upon her as an admirable tool wherewith to shape their particular and political ends. In the meantime the dinner parties at Kensington were of a joyous and unrestrained character. The Princess had poets and philosophers at her table when the royal fugitives from France invented maladies as an excuse for not visiting her, and she gained by the exchange; but, strange to say, with a very liberal income, irregularly paid, perhaps, she was as poor as the poets, and had not the consolation of philosophy. The house of Drummond and Co. declined to advance her the poor sum of 500*l.*, although she is said to have offered to pay *cent. per cent.* for the loan. Probably the stupendous liberality promised by the would-be borrower rendered the bankers suspicious.

As she failed to acquire all the public sympathy which she thought herself entitled to by her condition, she became at once more melancholy and more recklessly mirthful. The dinner-parties, beginning late, continued to sit till dawn. On one of these heavily entertaining occasions, one of the guests, weary of his amusement, ventured to hint that morning was at hand. 'Oh!' exclaimed the Princess, ' God, he knows when we may meet again.' And then, using her favourite expression, she added, ' *To tell you God's truth*, when I am happy and comfortable I would sit on for ever.' The describer of this scene says: ' There was heaviness in the mirth, and every one seemed to feel it; so they sat on. At last one rose from the table, many of the guests went away, some few lingered in the drawing-room, amongst whom I was one. I was left the last of all. Scarcely had Sir H. Englefield, Sir William Gell, and Mr. Craven reached the drawing-room, when a long and protracted roll of thunder echoed all around, and shook the palace to the very foundations; a bright light shone into the room, brighter than the beams of the sun ; a violent hissing noise followed, and some ball of electric fluid, very like that which is represented on the stage, seemed to fall close to the window where we were standing. Scarcely had we recovered the shock, when all the gentlemen, who had gone out, returned, and Sir H. Englefield informed us that the sentinel at the door was knocked down, a great portion of the gravel walk torn up, and every servant and soldier was terrified. " Oh !" said the Princess, undismayed, but solemnly, " this forbodes my downfall," and she shook her head ; then rallying, she desired Sir H. Englefield to take especial notice of this meteoric phenomenon, and give an account of it in the " Philosophical Transactions ; " which he did.' [1]

So passed away her life up to the period when restrictions were taken off the Regency, and the Prince of Wales

---

[1] 'Diary illustrative of the Times of George IV.'

became virtually King. The friends of the Princess in the House of Commons served her cause with some dexterity, and seldom made a statement in reference to her without temporarily reviving some of the half-extinct sympathy of the general public. Others of her 'faction,' as her friends were called, kept her in a state of irritability and excitement by speaking of publishing her memoirs in full detail. Some persons, with less pretence to the name of friends, injured her extremely by statements affectedly put forward in her behalf. Her agitated condition of life was still further aggravated by the obstacles put in her way so as to prevent her seeing her daughter as often as she desired. She was even bold enough, and justifiably bold enough under the circumstances, to go down to Windsor to see the Princess. This audacious step, as it was considered, was met by a message from the Regent, through Lord Liverpool, requesting her never to repeat so uncalled-for an expedition. She promised obedience, on condition that she should be permitted to see the Princess once a-week; but otherwise she threatened a repetition of the visit. Such menaces gratified those who provoked them. The more they could goad the Princess of Wales into demonstrations of violent and vulgar indignation, the more, as they well knew, would she lose the public esteem. Her nature was too prone thus to lose sight of dignity and self-possession on being provoked. The grandeur of endurance was a flight beyond her ken. She mourned the loss of a wise friend in Perceval, who was partly lost to her, however, before his death, as soon as he became minister. There were reports, too, at this time, probably ill-founded, that she was to be removed to Hampton Court, the apartments at Kensington Palace being required for the Princess Charlotte. This, and the abandonment of her by some of her old partisans among the nobility, rendered her naturally querulous. 'No, no!' she said, 'there is no more society for me in England; for do you think, if Lady Harrowby and the Duchess of Beaufort, and all of that set, were to come round to me now, that I would invite them to my intimacy? Never! They left me without a reason, as time-servers, and I never can wish for them back again.'[1] She felt that she could hold no court in presence of that of the Regent, and that as long as he lived she must be patient, and ' nothing.' Could she only have been the former, she perhaps would not have come to be of such small esteem as that which she ultimately experienced.

The Princess, however, still had some good taste. She patronised poets in other fashion than that followed by Sophia Dorothea, who gave them rings; or by Caroline, who made poor parsons out of poetic ploughmen, like Duck; or by Charlotte, who gave to the sons of the Muses little beyond empty praises and smiles that would not nourish. The Princess of Wales was a great admirer of Campbell, and in 1812 he was presented to her by his own 'chieftain's fair daughter,' Lady Charlotte Campbell —a lady who has etched the doings of her royal mistress in aqua fortis. The Princess showed her esteem for the Scottish poet by dancing reels with him in her drawing-room at Blackheath. Campbell has left his opinion of her at this time in a letter addressed to a friend. ' To say what I think of her, without being bribed by the smiles of royalty—she is certainly what you would call in Scotch a fine body; not *fine* in the English sense of the word, but she is good-humoured, appears to be very kind-hearted, is very acute, naïve, and entertaining; the accent makes her, perhaps, comic. . . . I heard that she was coarse and indelicate. I have spent many hours with her and Lady Charlotte alone, and I can safely say she showed us no symptoms of that vulgarity attributed to

[1] 'Diary illustrative of the Times of George IV.'

her.' An instance of the mistakes, rather than the peculiarity of pronunciation, which distinguished her, is given by Dr. Wm. Beattie. He relates that, one day, the Princess was showing her pleasantly-arranged house to a noble peer of great celebrity. They were both in the gallery, where the Princess had recently hung some new pictures, and to one of these she directed the attention of her guest. It was his own portrait, and he acknowledged the honour by a very profound bow. The Princess, to enhance the value of the compliment, said, ' You see, my lord, that I do consider you one of my great household dogs.' She meant ' gods,' poor lady ; but she did terribly abuse the divinities, and her daughter was ever her very dear ' angle.' These faults of orthography and errors in pronunciation bring less blame upon her than upon her mother. That the child of an Englishwoman born should have been so ignorant was the fault of the Englishwoman, and not of her child. The sister-in-law of Queen Charlotte was incapable of instructing her children as that Queen did, but she might have taught her daughter English by conversing with her in that language. The latter knew, however, less of it than she did of French and German ; and when she conversed in these, it was not upon subjects that were edifying to the future Queen of England or creditable to herself. Queen Charlotte was far more particular on the question of correct delivery. In the case of her husband, Quin had 'taught the boy to speak ;' and it was the exact propriety of the utterance of Mrs. Siddons that led to her appointment as reading preceptress of Queen Charlotte's daughters.

CHAPTER V.

HARSH TRIALS AND PETTY TRIUMPHS.

The Princess again in public—Restricted intercourse between the Princess and her daughter—Sealed letter addressed by the Princess to the Prince—Published—The Princess's appeal to Parliament—Bitterness on both sides—Meeting of the Princess and her daughter—The Princess at Vauxhall—Death of the Duchess of Brunswick—Last interview between the Duke of Brunswick and the Princess—Her depressed spirits—Unnoticed during the festivities of 1814—Sacrifice made by the Princess—Unnoticed by the Emperor of Russia and the King of Prussia—The Princess at the opera—A scene—Not invited to the great city banquet—Mr. Whitbread's advice to the Princess—A freak—Reception of the Regent in the city—The Princess excluded from the drawing-rooms—Correspondence between the Queen and the Princess—Her letter to the Regent—Discussed in the House of Commons.

FROM the comparative retirement in which the Princess had lived for a few years she was now, in 1813, again to issue and appear before the public more like an athlete on the arena than a suppliant with wrongs to be redressed.

Her retirement had given, however, much subject for comment on the part of the public, for censure on the part of her enemies. The latter still pointed to her habits of life as forming apology enough for the restrictions set upon her intercourse with her daughter. The fashion of opening *all* her apartments to her visitors at Kensington was considered indecorous; and the popular tongue dealt unmeasuredly with her cottage at Bayswater, at which she was *said* to have presided at scenes of at least consummate folly—and folly in such a woman was but next to serious guilt, and almost as sure to accomplish her utter ruin.

It is difficult to say positively in what light the Princess Charlotte looked upon the restrictions which kept her mother and herself apart. Report accredited her with being a thorn in the side of Queen Charlotte, and a continual trouble to the Regent. She is said to have paid to neither an over-heaped measure of respect, and she seriously offended both by marring the splendour of her first 'drawing-room,' at which she was to be presented by the Duchess of York, and which was postponed because she insisted upon being presented by her mother.

Early in January a sealed letter was addressed to the Prince Regent by the Princess of Wales, and forwarded by Lady Charlotte Campbell, through Lord Liverpool and Lord Eldon. It was immediately returned unopened. The letter was sent back as before. It was again returned, with an intimation that the Prince would not depart from his determination not to enter into any correspondence. Under legal advice, it was once more transmitted, with a demand that the ministers should submit it to the Prince. Finally, intimation was conveyed to the Princess that the Regent had become acquainted with the contents of the letter, but had no reply to make to it. Upon this the letter was published in a morning paper. Though addressed to the Regent, it was evidently intended for the public solely; and its appearance in the papers excited a wrath in the Prince which brought upon the Princess much of her subsequent persecution, and exposed her to considerable present animadversion, even at the hands of many of her friends.

The letter was long, but it may be substantially described as containing a protest of the supposed writer's innocence; a remonstrance against the restrictions, now more stringent than ever, which kept her apart from her daughter; an assertion that such restrictions were injurious to the latter, and a fatal blow against the honour of the mother; and finally a stinging criticism upon the secluded system of education by which her daughter was *not* educated, and which was not calculated to develop the character of the future Queen of Great Britain.

A bomb in the palace could not have created more excitement than was caused by the appearance of this letter in the papers. It was met by a refusal to allow any meeting at all, for the present, between the Princess Charlotte and her mother, and by an assembling of the Privy Council, the members of which speedily showed why they had been called together, by making a report to the Regent, in which it was stated that the lords of the council, having read the letter of the Princess, and having examined the documents connected with the investigation into the conduct of the Princess in 1806, were decidedly of opinion that any intercourse between the mother and daughter should continue to be subject to regulations and restraint. This report, which was tantamount to a mortal stab to the reputation of the Princess of Wales, and not altogether unprovoked by her, was signed by the two archbishops and all the ministers. The stab was dealt back as fiercely as it could be by an appeal to the people through parliament. To this body the Princess, in March, addressed a letter asserting her innocence, denouncing the system which pronounced her guilty without letting her know on what evidence the verdict was founded, and without allowing her to produce testimony to rebut it; and, finally, requiring that parliament would authorise a full and strict investigation, from which she felt that her honour would issue pre-eminently triumphant. This request brought on an animated debate upon a motion for the production of papers connected with the inquiry of

1806, and the evidence adduced thereon. The motion was lost; but ministers were compelled to acknowledge that the Princess stood fully acquitted of the charges then and there brought against her. The assertion made by Lord Castlereagh, that government had not proceeded against the degraded and infamous Sir John and Lady Douglas, because they were reluctant to trouble the world with the indelicate matters that must be raked up again, excited shouts of derision. Mr. Whitbread stoutly asserted that never had woman been so falsely accused or so fully triumphant; and Mr. Wortley, despite all his respect for the house of Brunswick, could not help lamenting that the royal family was the only one in the kingdom that seemed careless about its own welfare and respectability.

The subject was frequently brought before parliament, but with no other effect than to show that there was much exaggerated bitterness of feeling on both sides, and that the best friends of the Princess were those who were of no party. Parliament was, at last, but too happy to let the matter drop. Meanwhile, the publication of the 'Spirit of THE BOOK' did the Princess no good, and was, perhaps, not intended to have that result. The daughter was now established at Warwick House, and the Duchess of Leeds had succeeded as governess to Lady de Clifford, much to the dissatisfaction of the Princess Charlotte herself, who asserted that she was old enough to live without such superintendence. She could not be frightened into a conviction of the contrary by rude remarks from Lord Eldon, who also sought to terrify the Princess of Wales into absolute silence, on the ground that such a course would more entirely conduce to her own safety; to which that spirited lady replied that she was under the safeguard of the British constitution, and had no fears for her own safety whatever.

That she saw her daughter ' in spite of them ' was to

her a matter of legitimate triumph. She had been forbidden to call at Warwick House, but she could not fail to encounter the Princess Charlotte on the public highways. This meeting first occurred early in the spring; the mother espied the daughter's carriage at a distance, and ordered her own to be driven rapidly after it. She was then on Constitution Hill—the Princess was near Hyde Park—and the pursuer came up with the pursued near the Serpentine. Each leaned forward from her own carriage to kiss the other and for several minutes they remained in deep and, apparently, affectionate conversation—a crowd the while surrounding them with ever-ready sympathy.

It was said, however, that in the rarely-permitted meetings which subsequently took place between the mother and daughter the former occasionally complained of the coldness of manner of the latter. The Princess of Wales was, in fact, not satisfied with an ordinary demonstration of attachment from any one. She required enthusiasm—sought and bid for it. When the Regent was rising into something like popularity by the splendid entertainments which he gave—partly for the benefit of trade, and partly because he was pleased to the very top of his bent when playing the magnificent Amphitryon—the Princess appeared in public at a *fête* at Vauxhall, whither she was escorted by the Duke of Gloucester, on whose arm she leaned as she passed along, soliciting, as it were, signs of sympathy at a festival patronised and presided over by the Duke of York.

In these public scenes she assumed a dignity which well became her, but which she was as well pleased to lay aside as soon as the occasion which called for it had passed. Nothing gave her more gratification, for instance, after receiving congratulatory addresses from corporations and other similar bodies, which she did with mingled stateliness and courtesy, than to not only change her dress of ceremony for a more ordinary one, but to take off her stays! The latter odd fashion was not favourable to a figure which was now far removed from the grace which had distinguished the Princess in her earlier years.

It can be scarcely said that in this year she lost one friend more by the death of her mother. The declining years of the aged Duchess of Brunswick had been years of sorrow. She had long been a sufferer from confirmed asthma, and in March 1813 she was attacked by an epidemic which was fatally prevalent throughout the metropolis. It was attended by, or rather consisted of, cough and difficulty of breathing. This attack aggravated her other sufferings; but, though confined to her bed, she was not considered in danger when her daughter saw her for the last time, on the 22nd of March 1813. The Princess remained with the Duchess several hours, and took leave without suspecting that she was never again to see her mother alive. At nine that night the Duchess was seized with violent spasmodic attacks, under which she rapidly sunk; and, at seventy-six years of age, the 'Lady Augusta,' who was born in St. James's Palace, died in a modest lodging-house, and was quietly interred in Westminster Abbey.

It is due to the Prince Regent to say that on the occasion of the death of the Duchess of Brunswick he exhibited becoming and courteous feeling, by suggesting to the Princess Charlotte that she should pay a visit to her mother, to condole with her on this bereavement. It was suggested that after the funeral would be the most appropriate season for such a visit; but the Princess, with quicker wit or more ready sympathy, repaired at once to her mother's residence, and thus afforded her a gratification which was probably the more appreciated as it was the less expected. This was more sympathy than she received at the hands of some persons, who probably conceived that by behaving rudely to her they should be paying court to a higher power. Thus, in the course of the summer the Princess went to sup at Mr. Angerstein's. Lord and Lady Buckinghamshire were there. 'The latter behaved very rudely, and went away immediately after the Princess arrived. Whatever her principles, political or moral, may be, I think,' says Lady Charlotte Campbell, who tells the anecdote, 'that making a curtsy to the person invested with the rank of Princess of Wales would be much better taste and more like a lady than turning her back and hurrying out of the room.'

In addition to her mother, the Princess may be said to have also lost her brother this year; for though the gallant Duke of Brunswick did not fall at Quatre Bras till 1815, she never saw him again but for a brief moment on his departure from this country, two years previously. The Duke was simply a soldier and nothing more, except that he was a gallant one. He had a few relics with him in this country of the treasures of Brunswick, such as old books and antique gems, the value of neither of which did he in the least understand. His habits were of the simplest, except in the fashionable dissipation of the times; but if he was the slave of some pleasures, he was by no means the servant of luxury. He slept on a thin mattress placed on an iron frame, and covered by a single sheet. He had enjoyed sweeter sleep on it, he used to say, than many who lay upon the softest down.

When he went to take leave of his sister he was in the highest spirits, from having at last the prospect of an active career in arms. The actor and the scene are well-described by the author of 'The Diary:'—'There never was a man so altered by the hope of glory. His stature

seemed to dilate, and his eyes were animated with a fire
and an expression of grandeur and delight which
astonished me. I could not help thinking the Princess
did not receive him with the warmth she ought to have
done. He detailed to her the whole of the conversation
he had with the ministers, the Prince Regent, &c. He
mimicked them all admirably, particularly Lord Castlereagh—so well as to make us all laugh; and he gave the
substance of what had passed between himself and those
persons with admirable precision, in a kind of question
and answer colloquy that was quite dramatic. I was
astonished, for I had never seen any person so changed
by circumstance. He really looked a hero. The
Princess heard all that he said in a kind of sullen silence,
while the tears were in several of the bystanders'
eyes. At length the Duke of Brunswick said: "The
ministers refused me all assistance; they would promise
me neither money nor arms. But I care not. I will go
to Hamburg. I hear that there are some brave young
men there, who await my coming, and if I have only my
orders from the Prince Regent to act, I will go without
either money or arms, and gain both." "Perfectly
right!" replied the Princess, with something like enthusiasm in her voice and manners. "How did Bonaparte conquer the greater part of Europe?" the Duke
continued: "he had neither money nor arms, but he
took them; and if *he* did that, why should not *I*, who
have so much more just a cause to defend?" The Duke
then proceeded to state how the Regent and the ministers
were all at variance, and how he had obtained from the
former an order he could not obtain from the ministers.
After some further conversation, he took leave of his
sister. She did not embrace him. He held out his hand
to me kindly, and named me familiarly. I felt a wish to
express something of the kindly feeling I felt towards

him : but, I know not why, in her presence, who ought to have felt so much more and who seemed to feel so little, I felt chilled, and remained silent. I have often thought of that moment since with regret. When the Duke was fairly gone, however, she shed a few tears, and said emphatically, " I shall never see him more ! " '

The early part of 1814 was spent by the Princess in lowness of spirit and littleness of pursuits. Miss Berry speaks of the mournful ' house-warming ' by which the Princess inaugurated her tenancy some time before :— On the 1st of December she writes, ' We both of us (the two sisters) dined with the Princess in Connaught Place, the first time she had given a dinner in her new home, which is still all upside down. The company consisted only of Gell and Craven, who arrived in town to-day, Lady C. Campbell and Lady C. Lindsay in waiting. The Princess was particularly melancholy; wept when speaking to me of herself, confessed herself entirely overwhelmed with her situation and her prospects for the future. On the 30th the aspect was not gay. Dined at the Princess's. There were only Mr. Craven, Little Willy (Austin) and a young playfellow of his, and Lady Orme. These dinners become insupportable. The dulness makes me almost ill in the course of a long evening, only interrupted by the Princess's singing with Mr. Craven, which is a screeching of which no idea can be formed without hearing it.' The Princess was now established in Connaught Place, near the Edgeware Road ; the mansion is that now numbered ' 7' Connaught Place. She seldom saw her daughter, and did not consult her own dignity by taking ' strolls ' across the fields in the direction of the canal, or by ridiculing the Regent at her own dinner-table. It was this sort of conduct which made people account of her as being worse than she really was. For London, it was a year of triumphs and congratulations, but she shared in neither; it was the year of sovereigns, when European potentates crowded our streets, and passed by the house of the Princess without inquiring for her. In June, mortification was heaped upon her. She had an undoubted right to be present at the drawing-rooms held by the Queen; but her Majesty, who had announced her intention to hold two in honour of the foreign monarchs then in England, announced to the Princess that she would not be permitted to be present at either. No other ground for this expulsion was alleged than the Regent's will. His Royal Highness had declared that never again would he meet her, either in public or in private, and consequently her appearance on the occasions in question could not be permitted for a moment. She had prepared a letter of indignant remonstrance, but Mr. Whitbread counselled her not to forward it, but rather to write one in a submissive tone, accepting with humility the ill-treatment to which she was thus subjected. This counsel is said to have given considerable discontent to Mr. Brougham, who was inclined to make assertion of her right to be present, and to go even further, if that were necessary.

She made, however, greater sacrifices than that of refraining from appearing at court on a gala day. Her finances had become embarrassed, in spite of the presence of a controlling treasurer, and her friends made application to parliament on her behalf. The Regent had caused it to be understood that he did not wish to curtail her personal comforts or cause her any pecuniary embarrassment, and Lord Castlereagh came down to the house with a proposition of settling on her 50,000*l*. per annum. Of her own will she surrendered 15,000*l*. of this sum, and it was agreed that the revenue of 35,000*l*. per annum should be awarded to the 'Princess of Wales.' The sacrifice made by the Princess was gracefully noticed in the House by Mr. Whitbread, at whose suggestion it is said to have been cordially entered into, the Princess having, as he said, a full sense of the burthens that lay heavy on the nation. Such conduct ought to have won for her a little regard, and a visit from that King of Prussia in defence of whose dominions her father had not long before laid down his life, a stout old soldier, dying in his harness, like a knight of the olden time.

She sent her chamberlain to welcome the King of Prussia on his arrival in this country, and the King acknowledged the courtesy by sending *his* chamberlain to return thanks for it. The same stiff intercourse passed with the other sovereigns and princes; but it is said that Sir Thomas Tyrwhitt was especially charged by the Prince to request the Russian Emperor Alexander to abstain from visiting the Princess of Wales! They saw each other, nevertheless, though under different circumstances from those which the Princess herself could have desired. The incidents of this eventful evening are thus described by one of the ladies-in-waiting on the Princess:—' There came a note from Mr. Whitbread advising her at *what* hour she should go to the opera, and telling her that the Emperor was to be at eleven o'clock at the Institution, which was to be lighted up for him to see the pictures. All this advice tormented the Princess, and I do not wonder that she sometimes loses patience. No child was ever more thwarted and controlled than she is; and yet she often contrives to do herself mischief, in spite of all the care that is taken of her. When we arrived at the opera, to the Princess's and all her attendants' infinite surprise, we saw the Regent placed between the Emperor and the King of Prussia, and all the minor princes in a box to the right. 'God save the King' was performing when the Princess entered; and, consequently, she did not sit down. I was behind, and of course I could not see the house very distinctly, but I saw the Regent was at that time standing, applauding the Grassini. As soon as the air was over, the whole pit turned round to the Princess's box and applauded *her*. We who were in attendance on her Royal Highness entreated her to rise and make a curtsy, but she sat *immoveable;* and, at last, turning round, she said to Lady ——: "My dear, Punch's wife is nobody when Punch is present." We all laughed, but still thought it wrong not to acknowledge the compliment paid her; but she was right, as the sequel will prove. "We shall be hissed," said Sir W. Gell. "No, no," again replied the Princess, with infinite good humour; "I know my business better than to take the morsel out of my husband's mouth. I am not to seem to know that the applause is meant for me till they call my name." The Prince seemed to verify her words, for he got up and bowed to the audience. This was construed into a bow to the Princess, most unfortunately; I say most unfortunately, because she has been blamed for not returning it. But I, who was an eye-witness of the circumstance, knew that the Princess acted just as she ought to have done. The fact was that the Prince took the applause to himself, and his friends, to save him from the imputation of this ridiculous vanity, chose to say that he did the most beautiful and elegant thing in the world, and bowed to his wife! When the opera was finished, the Prince and his supporters were applauded, but not enthusiastically, and scarcely had his Royal Highness left the box when the people called for the Princess, and gave her a very warm applause. She then went forward and made three curtsies, and hastily withdrew."[1] The semi-ovation in the house was followed by a demonstration something more noisy in the streets. The Princess's charioteer was unable to drive through the

[1] 'Diary illustrative of the Times of George IV.'

crowd of vehicles in Charles Street. The carriage was therefore, 'backed' and driven round by Carlton House. In front of this royal residence the mob surrounded her Royal Highness, saluting her with loud and reiterated shouts. The ladies who were accompanying her were more alarmed at the popular demonstration than *she* was. The people opened the carriage door, insisted on shaking hands with her, and asked if they should burn Carlton House. ' No, my good people,' was her reply ; ' be quite quiet, let me pass, and go home to your beds.' They then allowed the carriage to pass on its way, as she desired, but they continued following it as long as they had strength, swiftness, and breath enough, shouting the while the favourite cry, 'The Princess of Wales for ever!' She was pleased, says the original narrator of this scene, at this demonstration of feeling in her favour, and she never showed so much dignity or looked so well, we are told, as she did under this excitement. She was depressed in spirits, however, the next day, for the same people crowded the parks, and flung those strong salutes which so offended the delicate Casca, at the company of foreign sovereigns and princes who were riding in the ring, and who refused to pay her the scant courtesy of a visit in the house from which she could hear the loud huzzas that greeted them as they passed by it.

She lived on, feverishly, and in continually disappointed hope that the Emperor of Russia would yet offer her the poor homage of a morning call. In this hope she was encouraged by some of her ladies-in-waiting, who told her that they had heard, from good authority, it was the imperial intention to pay a formal visit to Kensington on a day named. With no better official authority than this to trust to she sat up dressed, ready for the reception of the potentate whose presence, she hoped, would lend her some of the prestige of respectability which she fancied herself losing by his prolonged absence. And still he came not. On the other hand, she met with disappointment even more bitter. Her city friends did not even render her the courtesy of forwarding an invitation to the grand banquet at which they were about to regale the sovereigns and the retinue of princes in their train. Not that they entirely forgot her, but then their remembrance of her was rather insulting than flattering. Alderman Wood, for instance, was absurd enough to offer her a window in Cheapside, from which she might view the procession of monarchs and minor potentates on their way to dine with the city king! This vexed her sorely, as so emphatically 'rude' a proceeding was likely to do. The Princess would have less felt her exclusion from an entertainment in the city where her friends abounded had it been a festival from which ladies were altogether excluded. Her 'sensibility' was wounded at hearing that the Duchess of Oldenburg, the sister of the Emperor Alexander, was to be present, with four other ladies. 'This was galling,' says Lady Charlotte Campbell in her 'Diary,' and the Princess felt her own particular exclusion from this *fête* given by the city very hard to bear, as she had considered the city folks her friends. They, however, were not to blame, as these royal ladies were self-invited or invited by the Regent, and the Princess's friends had not time to call a council and discuss the matter. Immediately after this bitter pill came another from Mr. Whitbread, recommending her, *upon no account*, to go to Drury Lane on Thursday evening, after having, a few days before, desired her to go. 'You see,' said the Princess to one of her ladies; 'you see, my dear, how I am plagued;' and, although she mastered her resentment, the tears came into her eyes. 'It is not,' she said, 'the loss of the amusement which I regret, but being treated like a child and made the puppet of a party. What does it signify whether I come in before or after the Regent, or whether I am applauded in his hearing or not; that is all for the gratification of *the party*, not for *my* gratification; 'tis of no consequence to the Princess, but to Mr. Whitbread; and that's the way things go, and always will till I can leave this vile country.'

Wonderfully elastic, however, were the spirits of the Princess, and at dinner, on the day when her disappointment drew tears from her eyes, she entertained a large party with some grace and more gaiety. The question of her being present at the theatre on the following Thursday was discussed, and a baronet present, whom the authoress of the ' Diary ' partially veils under the initials of Sir J— B—, insisted that, unless Mr. Whitbread gave some very strong reasons to the contrary, the Princess would do right in going. 'But I fancy,' said Sir John, ' he has some good reasons, and then she must yield. Gad!' he added to a neighbour at table, ' if I were she, and Whitbread didn't please me, I would send for Castlereagh, and every one of them, till I found one that did. To tell you the truth, I am sorry the Princess ever threw herself into the hands of Whitbread—it is not the staff on which the royalties should lean.'—' Ah!' replied the baronet's neighbour, ' but at the moment he stepped forth her champion and deliverer, who was there that would have done as much?'

The sequel is too characteristic and singular to be passed over. The Princess was sometimes more vigorous than refined in her expressions, and this less from coarseness than ignorance of the value and sound of English terms. Thus, when a letter arrived from Mr. Whitbread, during this very dinner, intimating to her that there was a box reserved for her if she strongly desired to be present at the theatre when the foreign potentates were to appear there, but at the same time strongly urging her to refrain from being present, she exclaimed, after despatching a lady to request Mr. Whitbread to come to her immediately, 'If he gives me good reasons I will submit; but if he does not, *d—n me, den I go!*' 'Those were her words, at which I could not help smiling,' says the authoress of the 'Diary,' 'but she was in no mind to smile, so I concealed the impulse I felt to laugh.'

When Mr. Whitbread waited on the Princess she received him rather coolly, and listened silently to his enumeration of the persons whose opinion it was that she should not appear at Drury Lane. He said that Mr. Tierney, Mr. Brougham, and Lord Sefton were of opinion that, however much the Princess might be applauded, the public would say it was at the instigation of Mr. Whitbread, and was not the spontaneous feeling of the people; that the more she was applauded, the more they would say so, and that if, on the contrary, a strong party of the Prince Regent's friends and paid hirelings were there, and that one voice of disapprobation were heard, it might do her considerable harm. 'Besides,' continued Mr. Whitbread, 'as the great question about an establishment for your Royal Highness comes on to-morrow, I think it is of the utmost importance that no one should be able to cast any invidious observation about your forcing yourself on the public, or seeming to defy your Royal Highness's husband.' In fine, the Princess was overruled.

In the midst of her disappointments she was enlivened by renewed hopes of a visit from the Emperor of Russia, whose expressed intention to that effect was said to have given considerable uneasiness to the Regent. Meanwhile, the Princess found solace in various ways—and not always in the most commendable, if we are to put implicit truth in the following account of a freak, which seems more like a 'freedom' of the ladies at the Court of Charles II.

than a frolic of more modern and less lively times. Such a story is best told in the words of a witness—Lady Charlotte Campbell.

'To amuse herself is as necessary to her Royal Highness as meat and drink, and she made Mr. Craven and Sir W. Gell and myself promise to go with her to the masquerade. She is to go out at her back door, on the Uxbridge (Bayswater) road, of which " no person *under Heaven*" (her curious phraseology) has a key but her royal self, and we are to be in readiness to escort her Royal Highness in a hackney-coach to the Albany, where we are to dress. What a mad scheme at such a moment, and without any strong motive either to run the risk! I looked grave when she proposed this amusement; but I knew I had only to obey. I thought of it all night with fear and trembling.' In the supplementary matter to the 'Diary' we have the following detail as the 'curious story respecting this masquerade':—'The Princess,' says the editor, apparently, 'it was related to me by undoubted authority, would go to the masquerade, and, with a kind of girlish folly, she enjoyed the idea of making a grand mystery about it, which was quite unnecessary. The Duchess of York frequently went to similar amusements *incognita*, attended only by a friend or two, and nobody found fault with her Royal Highness. The Princess might have done the same; but no!—the fun, in her estimation, consisted in doing the thing in the most ridiculous way possible. So she made two of the ladies privy to her schemes; and the programme of the revel was that her Royal Highness should go down her back staircase with one of her ladies, while the cavaliers waited at a private door which led into the street, and then the *partie quarée* was to proceed on foot to the Albany, where more ladies met her Royal Highness, and where the change of dress was to be made. All of this actually took place; and Lady —— told me she never was so frightened in her life as when she found herself at the bottom of Oxford Street, at twelve at night, on her cavalier's arm, and seeing her Royal Highness rolling on before her. It was a sensation, she told me, betwixt laughing and crying, that she should never forget. The idea that the Princess might be recognised, and of course mobbed, and then the subsequent consequences, which would have been so fatal to her Royal Highness, were all so distressing that the party of pleasure was one of real pain to her. This mad prank, Lady —— told me, passed off without discovery, and certainly without any impropriety whatever, except that which existed in the folly of the thing itself. It was similar imprudences to this which were so fatal to the Princess's reputation.' And no wonder, if indeed these stories, as alleged, are true in their details, or are founded on truth.

It was a time when the mob was accustomed to speak pretty plainly. What a contrast is this pedestrian ramble by night, to dress for Mrs. Chichester's masquerade, to the state procession of the Regent into the city, where he twice dined—once at an entertainment given by the merchants, and once at a banquet given by the lord mayor and corporation! On the latter occasion especially his passage from Temple Bar nearly to the dinner-table itself was assailed by most uncomplimentary vociferations on the part of the populace. Their most general cry was, ' Where's your wife ?'—and that portion of the mob which apparently consisted of women was loudest in its unsavoury exclamations against the Vicegerent of the kingdom. He dined with what appetite he might, and he made the Lord Mayor (Domville), according to ancient custom when kings sat at the board of a first magistrate, a baronet; but he registered a vow, which he never broke, that never again would he condescend to be a guest among citizens to whose table he could not pass without running the gauntlet through the scourge of vile tongues that attacked him on his way. His mother, Queen Charlotte, did subsequently honour a lord mayor with her presence; but at her, too, the loud popular tongue wagged so insolently that the royal lady, although she courageously concealed her alarm, became indisposed on her return home, where she was first seized with those cruel spasmodic attacks which ultimately overcame her strength and surrendered her to death.

But the way in which the populace resented on the head of the Prince his conduct to his wife was but small consolation to the latter for the disappointment and insults which she experienced at the hands of her persecutors. She may be said to have been literally ejected from court. She was not allowed to present her own daughter, although that daughter had declared she would be presented by her mother or by nobody. It was not enough either that the foreign sovereigns and great captains for or with whom her father had fought and shed his blood—it was not enough that these should be induced to turn away from the house where dwelt a lady who, through her father, at all events, had some claims upon such small courtesy— but the determination that she should not meet them at court was more insulting still. The Queen thought she had skilfully provided against every possible emergency, when the *two* drawing-rooms were announced as about to be held in 1814. It was doubtless intended, at first, not to exclude the Princess from both, but simply to prevent her from being present at the one to be graced by the Regent and his imperial and royal guests. But the Regent himself was determined that his consort should not be permitted to appear at either. He addressed a letter to his mother, in which he modestly intimated that her court would be no court without him; that he should attend both drawing-rooms to lend them greater lustre (almost as much was expressed in words); and that, as he had resolved never to encounter his wife, it was of course necessary that she should stay away. The Queen accepted the conclusion as logically arrived at ; and to the dignified letters addressed to her by the Princess—letters which would have been as touching as they were dignified had they been of her own inditing, and not the vicarious sentiments of her friends—the Queen addressed now taunting, now contemptuous replies. The spirit of them was, in a bitter insinuation, that though the commission which had examined into her conduct had pronounced her free from guilt, her husband would account of her as still guilty, and the court would hold her as one convicted. In this correspondence 'Caroline P.' shines with more lustre than 'Charlotte R.' The latter appears so to have hated the former as to be glad of the opportunity to insinuate that she was infamous.

But 'Caroline' turned from exchanging sharp notes with 'Charlotte' to addressing her husband. He might, she said, possibly refuse to read the letter, but the world must know that she had written it. In this communication she states she would have exercised her right of appearing at the drawing-room had she not been 'restrained by motives of personal consideration towards her Majesty.' She protests against the insult, appeals to her acquittal, to her restoration thereupon by the King to the full enjoyment of her rank in his court, and she adds: 'Since his Majesty's lamented illness, I have demanded, in the face of parliament and the country, to be proved guilty, or to be treated as innocent. I will not submit to be treated as guilty.' There is something, too, of the taunting style which the Queen could manage with so much effect in the succeeding passage. The Prince had vowed that never again would he meet her, either in public or in private. 'Can your Royal Highness,' she asks, 'have contemplated the full extent of your declaration? .... Occasions may arrive (one, I trust, is far distant) when I must appear in public, and your Royal Highness must be present also. .... Has your Royal Highness forgotten the approaching marriage of our daughter, and the possibility of our coronation.' .... The illustrious heir of the House of Orange had announced himself to her, she said, as her future son-in-law; and then she adds, coupling the presence of the Orange Prince with that of the illustrious strangers in the metropolis: '*This* season your Royal Highness has chosen for treating me with fresh and unprovoked indignity; and of all his Majesty's subjects I alone am prevented, by your Royal Highness, from appearing in my place to partake of the general joy, and am deprived of the indulgence in those feelings of pride and affection permitted to every mother but me.' It was possible, as the writer remarked, that this letter was never read to the exalted individual to whom it was addressed. It is certain that the letter was not thought worthy of notice. But the presumed writer was determined that, escaping the courteous notice of her husband, it should not escape the more general notice of the world. She accordingly sent copies of her correspondence with the Queen and one of the correspondence of the latter with the Prince to the House of Commons, with an expression of her fears that there were 'ultimate objects in view pregnant with danger to the security of the succession and the domestic peace of the realm.'

This communication raised a discussion, and Mr. Methuen proposed an address to the Prince, requesting him to acquaint the house by whose advice he had determined never to meet the Princess. The proposition, however, was withdrawn. Mr. Bathurst, the only government advocate, stated that no imputation was intended against the character of the Princess. 'The charges of guilt,' he admitted, 'had been irresistibly refuted at a former period.' The so-called exclusion from court, he said, simply resolved itself into the non-invitation of the Princess to a court festival—nothing more. But, as Mr. Whitbread subsequently remarked, 'such non-invitation was an infliction worse than loss of life: it is loss of reputation, blasting to her character, fatal to her fame.' The government thought to pacify the Princess by holding out to her the prospect of an increase of income; but her friends in parliament asserted that she would scorn to barter her rights for an increased income, or to allow her silence to be purchased in exchange for an adequate provision.

CHAPTER VI.

A DOUBLE FLIGHT.

The Prince of Orange proposes to the Princess Charlotte—His suit declined—Dr. Parr—A new household appointed for the Princess Charlotte—Her astonishment and immediate flight—Alarm and pursuit—Princess Charlotte removed to Cranbourne Lodge—The Princess of Wales determines to leave England—Her departure from Worthing—The Regent's continued hatred of her.

AMONG the refugees of exalted rank whom revolution and the fortunes of war had driven to seek an asylum in England, the members of the family of the Stadtholder of Holland were the most conspicuous. The eldest son of this noble family became almost an Englishman by education and habit, and Oxford yet reckons him with pride among the honoured of her *alumni*.

As revolution and the fortunes of war had brought the family hither, so a happy turn in the same took them home, and restored them to a country which had now become for them a kingdom. At the peace of 1814 the Prince of Orange once more came to England, not as a refugee, but a visitor and suitor. The heir to a Dutch throne came to sue for the hand of the heiress to the Crown of Great Britain, and his suit was powerfully backed by the sanction of the heiress's father. Her mother gave no such sanction, nor was she, indeed, asked for any. Most important of all, the young lady thus wooed did not at all sanction the proceeding. Of all the episodes of the season there was none more stirring than this.

It was said that the Regent himself had procured the previous admission of the suitor into Warwick House, under the feigned name of the Chevalier de St. George, but that the Princess would not receive him. In this refusal she was supposed to be supported by her mother, and to act under the advice of the Duchess of Oldenburgh, who already had in view a humbler and, as it turned out, a luckier aspirant for the hand of the heiress. Meanwhile, all England agreed to approve of the match, and chose to look upon the union as a thing settled. The ballad-singers made the streets re-echo with singing 'Orange Boven,' and Irish wits accused her Royal Highness of holding an Orange Lodge.

The Regent had hated and thwarted the Princess from her birth. Her death would have been no grief to him, if he could have divorced her mother. The next best thing was to be rid of the daughter. Accordingly her father had this match at heart, and longed to see it concluded. The Princess allowed herself to be handed to her carriage by the princely wooer from the dykes, and granted him more than one interview. It soon became evident that they were not agreed. The Princess pleaded her youth, her love of her country, and her desire to be more intimately acquainted with the latter and with its laws, history, and constitution, before she should surrender herself to the cares and duties of the married state. The Prince of Orange insisted, as far as lover dared, that his wife must necessarily reside with him in Holland. The prospect made the Princess shudder; but it remarkably suited the wishes of her sire, whose most ardent desire was to place as wide a distance as possible between the daughter and her mother. The Prince of Orange had made no secret of his desire that, in the event of his marriage with the Princess, her mother should take up no permanent residence in Holland. This desire—not over mildly expressed—had, perhaps, the most to do with rendering the union impossible. The Princess, indeed, was not inclined towards the Prince, and would not willingly have left the country of her birth ; but to her warm friends, at least, she declared that, in the present critical situation of the Princess of Wales, she would not abandon her mother. The latter was touched ; but it was just the moment when she was most strongly possessed by a desire to go abroad, and she thought that this desire might be more speedily realised if her daughter were married than if she remained single. She was on the whole rather disappointed than otherwise—except that the breaking off of the match was an annoyance to the Regent, and *that* was some consolation, at all events. How the match was broken off is thus told in the 'Brief Memoirs of the Princess Charlotte ' :—

'The Princess Charlotte resented as a great mark of neglect that she was not invited to any of the entertainments given to the Allied Sovereigns, and was the more sore because the Prince of Orange went everywhere and would make no effort to vindicate her claims. The Regent had lost none of his anxiety to keep her out of sight, and the Prince did not choose to provoke the displeasure of the father by fighting the battles of the daughter. The same divergence in their views broke out when she spoke of her mother, and said that on her account it would be inexpedient that she should leave England for some time after her marriage, that when she had a house of her own it must be open equally to both her parents, and that as the child of both she must ignore all differences between them. The Prince of Orange feared the Regent and cared nothing for the Princess of Wales, who had always been hostile to the marriage, and the reasons urged by the Princess Charlotte for stopping in England were arguments to him for getting away from disagreeable complications. He combated her resolution, and said that he had been willing to stand by her in getting the article which secured her freedom inserted in the marriage treaty, but did not suppose that she would refuse altogether to go abroad with him, and that if this was her intention their respective duties were irreconcilable and their marriage impossible. A discussion ensued, and common every-day squabbles occurred to exasperate the dispute. The Princess Charlotte wanted the Prince of Orange to ride with her in the riding-house. He started objections, and she reproached him, till, annoyed at her vehemence and pertinacity, he left her to recover her temper. The climax had come, and in the evening she wrote peremptorily to say that their engagement must cease. Her first note was dashed off in a fit of temper, and a friend who was with her, and whom she asked to light the candle for her to seal it, said, 'I will not hold the candle to any such thing.' The Princess consented to pause before she despatched her note, and the result of her reflection was the following decisive dismissal:—

'*Princess Charlotte to the Prince of Orange.*

'June 16, 1814: Warwick House.

'After reconsidering, according to your wishes, the conversation that passed between us this morning, I am still of opinion the duties and affection that naturally bind us to our respective countries render our marriage incompatible, not only from motives of policy but domestic happiness. From recent circumstances that have occurred, I am fully convinced that my interest is materially connected with that of my mother, and that my residence out of this kingdom would be equally prejudicial to her interest as to my own. As I can never forget the maternal claims she has upon my duty and attachment, I am equally aware of the claims your country has on you. It was this consideration, added to the design I had of complying with your wishes, that induced me some time ago to agree to accompany you to Holland, if I obtained satisfactory securities of having it in my power to return. Since that time the many unforeseen events that have occurred, particularly those regarding the Princess, make me feel it impossible to quit England at present, or to enter into any engagements leading to it at a future time. After what has passed upon this subject this morning between us (which was much too conclusive to require further explanation), I must consider our engagement from this moment to be *totally and for ever at an end*. I leave the explanation of this affair to be made by you to the Prince in whatever manner is most agreeable to you, trusting it entirely to your honour, of which I have never for a moment doubted. I cannot conclude without expressing the sincere concern I feel in being the cause of giving you pain, which feeling is, however, lessened in a degree by the hope I stand acquitted in your eyes of having acted dishonourably by you in the case of this business, or of having ever raised false hopes in your mind with respect to my consenting to a residence abroad. You must recollect in a letter from me, in answer to yours of May 3, that I told you it was impossible for me to give any promise on that subject, as it must totally depend upon circumstances. It only remains for me to entreat you to accept my sincerest and best wishes for your happiness, and to express the kindness and interest I shall always feel towards you.

'CHARLOTTE.'

Meanwhile, the dinners at Connaught House and the little parties at Blackheath continued as usual. If a great deal of frivolity were present at them, it cannot be said that grave wisdom was always lacking; for by the side of a public singer would sometimes be seated no less a person than Dr. Parr. Of personal intercourse between the mother and daughter there was now scarcely any, but their correspondence was still kept up; and it was not the less sincere on the poor mother's side from the circumstance of her occasionally forgetting orthography in the ardour of her affection.

The Regent, soured by his defeat with respect to the union of his daughter and the Prince of Orange, was more than commonly irritated by the knowledge that his wife and child were engaged in a frequent epistolary correspondence, and that he had, hitherto, been unable to prevent it. He was satisfied that such correspondence could not be maintained without the connivance of the ladies of his daughter's household, and he determined to meet the evil by dissolving the establishment.

Before this resolution had been arrived at the Princess Charlotte was subjected to much petty persecution, rendered the more annoying by being continual, and which made up in enduring length what it wanted in intensity. It was said at the time that even the letters in her writing-desk found their way into her father's hands; and there was so much done at this time that was degrading to the doers that the report is recommended at least by its probability. At all events, 'wearied out by a series of acts all proceeding from the spirit of petty tyranny, and each more vexatious than another, though none of them very important in itself,' the Princess was driven to a very extreme measure by the uncalled-for and undignified severity of her irritated sire. Lord Stourton (referring indeed to an earlier time) states, in his 'Memoirs of Mrs. Fitzherbert':—'On one occasion Mrs. Fitzherbert told me she was much affected by the Princess Charlotte throwing her arms round her neck and beseeching her to speak to her father that he would receive her with greater marks of his affection; and she told me that she could not help weeping with this interesting child.'

On the 16th of July, 1814, the Prince Regent, who had previously secured Cranbourne Lodge, in Windsor Forest, as a residence for his daughter, and had even, equally unknown to her, but in concert with Queen Charlotte, nominated the new ladies of the Princess's household, repaired to Warwick House, accompanied by the ladies so named. The party had only to traverse the gardens of Carlton House to arrive at their destination. The ladies were the Duchess-dowager of Rosslyn and the Countess of Ilchester, the two Misses Coates, and Miss Campbell, formerly sub-governess to the Princess. They were placed in an apartment adjacent to that into which the Regent entered, as soon as he knew that it was occupied by the Princess.

Without ceremony he announced to the astonished Princess that her establishment in that house was from that moment dismissed; that she must instantly repair to the seclusion of Cranbourne Lodge; and that the newly-appointed ladies of her household were in the next apartment, ready to wait upon and accompany her.

The Princess was astonished, but she was wonderfully self-possessed, and her presence of mind, helped by her love for a little romantic adventure, admirably served her on this occasion. She requested a few minutes' respite, that she might retire, take leave of her now dismissed ladies, and superintend some preparations for departure. The Prince acquiesced, and leaving the new ladies in charge of the Princess, returned to Carlton House to dress for a dinner *en ville.*

He was hardly gone when the Princess was gone too. Silently and swiftly descending the stairs, she issued from the doors, and in half a minute stood alone upon the pavement of Cockspur Street. Lord Brougham says: 'It was a fine evening in July, about the hour of seven, when' —he adds with a sort of contempt for people of the lower order, and indeed with much inaccuracy to boot—' when the streets were deserted by *all persons of condition.*' From the old stand at the bottom of the Haymarket she called a coach, whose lucky driver (Higgins) obeyed the summons, and having handed the heiress of England into the damp straw of his dirty and rickety vehicle, listened to the order to drive to the Princess of Wales's in Connaught Place—to be quick, and he should not have to regret it. The guileless Higgins concluded that he was taking a lady's lady out to tea, and that the maid of one establishment was going to make an evening of it with the maids of another. Unconscious that he was contributing in his own person to the history of England on that eventful summer's evening, Higgins in due course of time reached Connaught Place, and when he heard, to the inquiry of his 'fare' whether her mother was at home, that the page answered, 'No, your Royal Highness, the Princess of Wales is at Blackheath,' he became proudly sagacious of *largesse* to come, and was convinced that he had been a right royal coachman that night, by token that he received three guineas for his honorarium.

A messenger was despatched to Blackheath with a request to the Princess to return immediately to her. She was met by the bearer of the message on her way, and with ready good sense drove to either house of parliament, in search first of Mr. Whitbread, then of Lord Grey, but without success in either case. Meanwhile, another messenger had been despatched for Mr. Brougham, the law-adviser of the Princess of Wales, and a third for Miss Mercer Elphinstone, the young bosom friend of the Princess Charlotte. Mr. Brougham arrived first, and soon after Miss Elphinstone had reached the house the Princess

of Wales also arrived, accompanied by Lady Charlotte
Lindsey. 'It was found,' said Mr. Brougham, 'that the
Princess Charlotte's fixed resolution was to leave her
father's house and that which he had appointed for her
residence, and thenceforward to live with her mother.'
But Mr. Brougham is understood to have placed himself
under the painful necessity of explaining to her that by
the law, as all the twelve judges but one had laid it
down in George I.'s reign, and as it was now admitted to be settled, the King or the Regent had the
absolute power to dispose of all the royal family while
under age. Another account states that the Princess met
this announcement by the declaration, made amid many
tears and much sobbing, that she would rather toil for her
daily bread at five shillings a week than continue to endure the persecution to which she had of late been subjected. The Princess of Wales was very much affected by
this demonstration of her daughter's affection and confidence, but she united with Mr. Brougham in urging her
to submit to her father's will. The Princess Charlotte
continued to show fixed reluctance to adopt such a course,
and was expressing her determination not to follow it
when the Archbishop of Canterbury arrived; but the page
refused to give him admission, and he remained at the
door seated in a hackney coach. The first great official
from the Regent's side who was admitted into the house
was Lord Eldon. He had been despatched from the Duke
of York's, where the Regent was dining, when the intelligence of his daughter's flight had been conveyed to him
by the ladies to whose care he had committed her. 'The
Lord Chancellor Eldon,' says Lord Brougham, 'first arrived, but not in any particular imposing state, regard
being had to his eminent station, for indeed he came in a
hackney coach. Whether it was that the example of the
Princess Charlotte herself had for the day brought this

simple and economical mode of conveyance into fashion, or that concealment was much studied, or that despatch was deemed more essential than ceremony and pomp, certain it is, that all who came, including the Duke of York, arrived in similar vehicles, and that some remained enclosed in them, without entering the royal mansion.' Lord Eldon appears to have treated the Princess with some roughness, adding threats to the entreaties of others, and menacing her with being closely shut up if she did not obey. In his own account of this evening and its incidents he says that the Princess, in answer to his observations, only 'kicked and bounced,' and protested that she positively would not go back. The chancellor declared as positively that he would not leave the house without her. 'At length,' Lord Brougham concludes his narrative, 'after much pains and many entreaties used by the Duke of Sussex and the Princess of Wales herself, as well as Miss Mercer Elphinstone and Lady Charlotte Lindsey (whom she always honoured with a just regard), to enforce the advice given by Mr. Brougham, that she should return without delay to her own residence and submit to the Regent, the young Princess, accompanied by the Duke of York and her governess, who had now been sent for and arrived in a royal carriage, returned to Warwick House between four and five o'clock in the morning.'

Soon after this occurrence the Princess was removed to Cranbourne Lodge, where she bore the secluded life she was constrained to lead with more of a calm than a cheerful resignation. She was not, however, there forgotten by her friends. The Duke of Sussex rose in his place in parliament to inquire if his royal niece was or was not in a sort of 'durance,' and whether she were permitted to see her friends. Ministers replied to these queries in that official way which answers without enlightening, and further measures were spoken of; but the Duke of Sussex was seized with an attack of asthma, which popular report attributed to a sharp communication made to him by the Regent, and therewith no further mention was made of the royal recluse in Windsor Forest.

But there was another recluse anxious to emancipate herself and fly from the restrictions and conventionalities of English living to the greater liberty allowed on the Continent. There were very few persons who thought the Princess of Wales well advised in this desire except Mr. Canning. Into his hands the wife of the Regent committed a letter, which Lord Liverpool was requested to submit to the Prince. It contained a brief description of her unmerited condition, expressed a wish of being allowed to withdraw to the Continent, chiefly for the purpose of visiting her brother, and finally made offer of resigning the Rangership of Greenwich Park in favour of her daughter, and also to make over to her the residence (Montague House) which her mother had occupied at Blackheath. The principal reason assigned for her wishing to withdraw was that she had nothing now to bind her to England but her daughter, and from *her* society she was now entirely and most unjustly excluded.

Through Lord Liverpool the Regent returned for answer that she was entirely free to go or stay; that no restraint whatever would be put upon her in that respect; that, as regarded the Rangership, on her resignation of that office, the Regent would see to its being filled up by a properly qualified person; with respect to Montague House, the daughter of the Prince Regent could never be permitted by him to reside in a house which had ever been the dwelling-place of the Princess of Wales.

This reply—the Princess's comment on which was ' end well, all well '—reached her at Worthing, whither, after a brief interview with her daughter, she had already repaired. She remained in the neighbourhood but a few days after she received the desired missive, and the 'Jason' frigate, commanded by Captain King, lay in the offing, waiting her pleasure and convenience to embark. She lingered during those few days as if reluctant, after all, to leave the land where she had not known an hour's happiness since she had first set her foot upon its shore. She would linger on the beach at night, regardless of the admonitions of her attendants, sitting dreamily and despondingly, gazing over the waters or at the moon by which they were illumined, and once breaking from her reverie with the ejaculation: 'Well, grief is unavailing when fate impels me.'

On the 9th of August, she for the last time appeared on Worthing beach, with Lady Charlotte Lindsey and Lady Elizabeth Forbes. It was her intention to embark from thence, but fearful of the crowd that was then collecting, she quietly withdrew to South Lancing, about two miles off, whither the captain's barge proceeded to meet her. She was followed, however, by nearly all the persons, in carriages, mounted or on foot, whose curiosity, it may be added, was especially aroused by the appearance of a large tin-case among the luggage, on which was painted in white letters, 'Her Royal Highness the Princess of Wales, to be always with her.' It seemed as if she for ever wished to have some mystery attached to her, or that she desired the mystification of others. Her domestics had gone on board at Worthing. On South Lancing beach she appeared dressed in 'a dark cloth pelisse with large gold clasps, and a cap of velvet and green satin, of the Prussian hussar costume, with a green feather.' She was, with her ladies, driven down to the beach, in a pony chaise, by her own coachman.

On taking her seat in the barge she turned round and

kissed her hand to the assembled people, by way of farewell. To the mute greeting the people returned as mute reply. The ladies waved their handkerchiefs, the men uncovered. She probably construed this silent *adieu* as intended to denote respect and regret, and she was so overcome that she fainted on her way to the ship. On the deck she was received by Captain King, to whom one of the Regent's brothers had previously remarked: 'You are going to convey the Princess of Wales to the Continent. You are a great fool if you don't make love to her.'

Greatly as her spirits were depressed at starting, their natural elasticity soon brought her round again to her ordinary condition of cheerfulness. On the 12th of August, the Regent's birthday, as the ship was passing the Texel, a royal salute was fired, by her order, it is said, in honour of the day. The salute would, probably, have been fired without any such command. What were, without doubt, her own spontaneous acts were the birthday banquet at which she presided; the health of her husband, which she gave with a spirit that might have been taken for sincerity; and the ball at which she danced as joyously as though she had been a youthful bride being borne to the bridegroom she loved, and not a mature and child-deprived matron cast out by her husband, between whom and herself there reigned as bitter a hatred as ever raged in the bosom of any pair of mortal beings. The hatred on his part is illustrated by an anecdote which was in circulation at this unhappy period. According to this story, 'On the evening previous to the Princess of Wales's departure from England, the Regent had a party and made merry on the joyful occasion. It is even said that he proposed a toast: " To the Princess of Wales's d——n, and may she never return to England!" It seems scarcely possible that any one should have allowed his tongue to utter such a horrible imprecation; but it may be believed the Regent did, so great was his aversion to his wife. Besides, he was not, probably, very well aware what he was saying at that moment.'

CHAPTER VII.

THE ERRANT ARIADNE.

The Princess arrives at Hamburgh—Assumes the title of Countess of Wolfenbüttel—Travels in Switzerland—Meeting of the Princess with the ex-Empress Maria Louisa, and the divorced wife of the Grand Duke Constantine—The Princess at Milan—Her English attendants fall off—Her reception by the Pope—At a masked ball at Naples—Her imprudence—Her festivals at Como—The Princess at Palermo—Bergami her chamberlain—The Princess at Genoa—Corresponds with Murat—Personal vanity of Queen Charlotte—The Pope visits the Princess—Surrounded by Italians—Her roving life—Proceeds to Syracuse—At Jericho—Lands at Tunis and visits the Bey—Liberates European slaves—The Princess at Athens—At Troy—At Constantinople—At Ephesus—At Acre—Stopped at Jaffa—Enters Jerusalem—Her reception by the Capuchin Friars—Institutes a new order of chivalry—Life on board the polacca—The Princess and Countess Oldi at Como—Private theatricals a favourite pastime—Agents and spies—Innocent incidents converted into crimes—Bergami divested of his knighthood—The Princess at Carlsruhe—Contemptuously neglected at Vienna—The chamberlain her only attendant—The Princess in public—Deeply affected by the death of Princess Charlotte—As uncircumspect as ever.

THE early period of the travels of the Princess on the Continent calls for nothing more than simple record. She left the 'Jason' under all the customary honours; and when she entered Hamburgh on the 16th she dropped her English to assume a German title, that of the Countess of Wolfenbüttel. Her suite consisted of the two ladies we have already named, with Mr. St. Leger and Sir William Gell. Mr. Keppel Craven subsequently joined her at Brunswick. Dr. Holland accompanied her as physician, and Captain Hesse as equerry. Thus attended she appeared at the theatre at Hamburgh, where she was received with a storm of applause, and entered Brunswick, where she was welcomed by her brother the Duke, and with a loud-tongued cordiality by the inhabitants.

The reception touched her, but not deeply enough to induce her to profit by it. Within a fortnight she brushed the tears from her eyes, left Brunswick behind her, and was on the high-road of Europe, as self-willed and as obstinate a Princess as ever destroyed a reputation and rushed blindfold upon ruin.

She now travelled under the appellation of Countess of Cornwall, and had one English gentleman less in her train, Mr. St Leger having withdrawn from the honour of waiting on her at Brunswick. The time had not yet arrived when the *mot d'ordre* had been given to treat her with disrespect. The governors of German cities were courteous to her as she passed, and the Marshal Duke de Valmy, with all the authorities of Strasburg, offered her the expression of their homage when she traversed that portion of France. After spending the greater portion of September in a tour through Switzerland, she finally sojourned for a while at Geneva, where she met with the ex-Empress of France, Maria Louisa, and became for a time on intimate terms with an imperial lady who, like herself, was separated from her husband. Like her, she was stripped of her old dignity, and, like her, she was accompanied by a young boy. But those boys were not more different in their rank than the two women were in their position, similar as this was in many respects. The boys were Napoleon Francis, ex-King of Rome, and William Austin, son of the Blackheath labourer.

The two women, illustrious by rank rather than character, lived much in each other's society. They dined together, sang together, together listened to the discussions of the philosophers whom they assembled around them, and when together they attended a fancy dress ball one at least astonished the other—the Princess surprising the ex-Empress by appearing in what was called the costume of Venus, and waltzing with a lack of grace that might have won laughter from the goddess of whom the waltzer was the over-fat representative.

Maria Louisa was not the only unhusbanded wife whom the wandering Princess encountered in Switzerland. The divorced wife of the Grand Duke Constantine was of this illustrious society. This lady was the Juliana of Saxe-Coburg who, on marrying the Russian Prince, took for her new appellation the name of Anna Feodorowna, and who was so rejoiced to lay that name down again after she had escaped from the brutalities of her husband. The Countess of Cornwall looked upon her with more than ordinary interest, for she was the sister of that Prince Leopold who ultimately married the Princess Charlotte, and whose aspiring hopes were known to, and sanctioned by, the wandering 'Countess' herself. The presence in one spot of three princesses, all separated from their then living husbands, had something as singular in it as the meeting of Voltaire's unsceptred kings at the *table-d'hôte* at Venice. The ex-Empress was separated from *her* husband because she did not care to share his fallen fortunes; the Grand Duchess was living alone because the Grand Duke did not care for his wife; and the other lady and her husband had the ocean between them because they heartily hated each other—three sufficient reasons to unite the triad of wanderers within the territories of the Swiss republic.

In October, the Countess of Cornwall, or Princess of Wales, as it will be more convenient to call her, had passed into the imperial city of Milan. Her passage had something of a triumphant aspect; she reviewed the troops drawn up in honour of her visit, smiled at the shouts of welcome, mingled with cries for the liberty of Italy, which greeted her, and endured the noisy homage uttered by a dozen *bouches à feu*. She had now but one English lady in her suite, Lady Charlotte Lindsey having resigned her office when in Germany.

It was at Milan that her suite first began to assume a foreign aspect. The Princess was about to enter on a wide course of travel, and it was said that she needed the services of those who had had experience in that way. The first and most celebrated official engaged to help her with his service was a Bartholomew Bergami, a handsome man, of an impoverished family, who had served in the army as private courier to General Count Pino (bearer of his despatches, it is to be presumed), had received the decoration of some 'order,' and—whether by right of an acre or two of land belonging to his family, or because of his merits—bore the high-sounding name, but not very exalted dignity, of 'Il Signor Barone.' He had three sisters, all of whom were respectably married; the eldest and best known was a Countess Oldi, a true Italian lady, who loved and hated with equal intensity.

At Milan, as at Geneva, the Princess, undoubtedly, failed to leave a favourable impression of her character. At the latter place the sight of herself and the great Sismondi, both stout, and the former attired as the Queen of Love, waltzing together, was a spectacle quite sufficient to make the beholders what, it is said, the Princess herself would have called, 'all over shock.' Then she insisted on undue homage from her attendants, and made such confusion in the geographical programme of her travels 'that it was enough,' as she herself used to say on other occasions, 'to die for laugh.'

On the progress of the Princess through Italy her

English attendants fell off, one by one, till she was finally left without a single member of her suite with whom she had originally set out. They probably ventured to give her some good advice, for she complained of their tyranny. They certainly counselled her to return and live quietly in England; but this counsel was always under consideration, yet never followed by the result desired. She was rendered peevish, too, by receiving no letters from her daughter, of whom she had taken but brief and hurried leave previous to her departure from England.

Meanwhile, she traversed Italy from Milan to Naples, and was everywhere received with great distinction. In the little states the minor potentates did their poor but hearty best to exhibit their sympathy. The crownless sovereigns, like those of Spain and Etruria, condoled with her. At Rome the very head of the faithful stooped to imprint a kiss or whisper a word of welcome to the wandering lady. After a week of lionising at Rome she proceeded to Naples, where Murat received her with the splendour and ostentation which marked all his acts. He had a guest who was quite as demonstrative as her host. Court and visitor seemed to vie with each other in extravagance of display. *Fêtes* and festivals succeeded each other with confusing rapidity, and never had Parthenope seen a lady so given to gaiety, or so closely surrounded by spies, so narrowly watched, and so abundantly reported, as this indiscreet Princess. It was at Naples that she appeared at a masked ball attired as the Genius of History, and accompanied, it is said, by Bergami. She changed her dress as often as Mr. Ducrow in one of his 'daring acts;' and, finally, she enacted a sort of *pose plastique*, and crowned the bust of Joachim Murat with laurel.

It seemed as if she wished to bury memory of the

past and to destroy the hopes of the future in the dissipation of the present. To say the least of her conduct, her imprudence and indiscretion were great and gross enough to have destroyed any reputation; and yet she herself described her course of life as *sedentary*, when she often retired to bed 'dead beat' with fatigue from sight-seeing by day and vigorous dancing by night. It was here that she made the longest sojourn, and enjoyed herself, as she understood enjoyment, the most. The purchase of the villa on the Lake of Como was also now effected; and Bergami was soon after raised to the dignity of chamberlain, and to the privilege of a seat at her own table. She claimed a right to bestow honours, and to distinguish those on whom she bestowed them; but her want of judgment in both regards amounted to almost a want of intellect, or a want of respect for herself, or for the opinions of those whose good opinion was worth having.

At one of her festivals at Como she indulged in some freedoms with a guest whom she strongly suspected of being a spy upon her. Her conversation was of a light and thoughtless nature, well calculated to give him abundance of matter to be conveyed to the ears of his employers. A friend present suggested to her that caution, on her part, was not unnecessary, as within a fortnight everything she said or did was known at Carlton House. 'I know it,' was her reply, 'and therefore do I speak and act as you hear and see. The wasp leaves his sting in the wound, and so do I. The Regent will hear it? I hope he will; I love to mortify him.' And to satisfy this peevish love she courted infamy; for even if she did not practise it, her self-imposed conduct made it appear as if she and infamy were exceedingly familiar.

Still errant, she wandered from Como to Palermo, visiting the court there, and receiving a welcome which could not have been more hearty had she been really of as indifferent character as she seemed to be. At this court she presented Bergami, on his appointment of chamberlain, and shortly after she proceeded to Genoa, where she intended to sojourn for a considerable time. She was conveyed thither in the 'Clorinde' frigate, the captain of which spoke to those around him in no measured terms of her conduct and course of life, particularly at Naples. She was well-lodged at Genoa. The scene, and she who figured on it so strangely, are thus described by the writer of a letter in the 'Diary':—'The Princess of Wales's palace is composed of red and white marble. Two large gardens, in the dressed formal style, extend some way on either side of the wings of the building, and conduct to the principal entrance by a rising terrace of grass, ill-kept, indeed, but which in careful hands would be beautiful. The hall and staircase are of fine dimensions, although there is no beauty in the architecture, which is plain even to heaviness; but a look of lavish magnificence dazzles the eyes. The large apartments, decorated with gilding, painted ceilings, and fine, though somewhat faded, furniture, have a very royal appearance. The doors and windows open to a beautiful view of the bay, and the balmy air they admit combines with the scene around to captivate the senses. I should think this palace, the climate, and the customs must suit the Princess, if anything can suit her. Poor woman! she is ill at peace with herself; and when that is the case what can please?' .... Referring more directly to the Princess, the writer says : 'The Princess received me in one of the drawing-rooms opening on the hanging terraces, covered with flowers in full bloom. Her Royal Highness received Lady Charlotte Campbell (who came in soon after me) with open arms and evident pleasure, and without any flurry. She had no rouge on, wore tidy shoes, was grown rather thinner, and looked altogether uncommonly well. The first person who opened the door to me was the one whom it was impossible to mistake, hearing what is reported—six feet high, a magnificent head of black hair, pale complexion, mustachios which reach from *here to London*. Such is *the stork*. But, of course, I only appeared to take him for an under-servant. The Princess immediately took me aside and told me all that was true, and a great deal that was not. . . . . Her Royal Highness said that Gell and Craven had behaved very ill to her, and I am tempted to believe that they did not behave well; but then how did she behave towards them? . . . . It made me tremble to think what anger would induce a woman to do, when she abused three of her best friends for their cavalier manner of treating her. . . . . " Well, when I left Naples, you see, my dear," continued the Princess, " those gentlemen refused to go with me, unless I returned immediately to England. They supposed I should be so miserable without them that I would do anything they desired me, and when they found I was too glad to *get rid of 'em* (as she called it) they wrote the most humble letters, and thought I would take them back again, whereas they were very much mistaken. I had *got rid of them*, and I would remain so." '

The Princess appears to have corresponded with Murat. The soldier-king is said to have addressed to her a very flattering note, beginning ' Madame, ma chere, chere sœur,' as if she had already been a queen, and that he were treating with her on a footing of equality. Her reply is described as clever but flippant, beneath her dignity, and so wild and strange as to be entitled to be considered one of the most extraordinary specimens of royal letter-writing that had ever been seen.

There was yet no inconsiderable number of English

guests who gathered round the table of the Princess, and some of the former ladies of her suite here rejoined her. Among the guests is noticed a 'Lord B——,' who had been a great favourite with the Prince of Wales, and was equally esteemed by the Princess. He had been a witness of the marriage of Mrs. Fitzherbert with the Prince, and was now the most welcome visitor of the Princess. The illustrious pair, it has been often observed, had 'a strange sympathy in their loves and habits.' Alluding to the style of the Princess's conversation with her guests, the 'Diary' affords us another illustration. 'Sometimes Monsieur —— opened his eyes wide at the Princess's declarations, and her Royal Highness enjoys making people stare, so she gave free vent to her tongue, and said a number of odd things, some of which she thinks, and some she does not; but it amuses her to astonish an innocent-minded being, and really such did this old man appear to be. He won her heart, upon the whole, however, by paying a compliment to her fine arm and asking for her glove. Obtaining it, he placed it next his heart; and, declaring it should be found in his tomb, he swore he was of the old school in all things.' The little vanity of being proud of a fine arm was one as strong in Queen Charlotte as in her daughter-in-law. The former had as fine an arm as, and perhaps not a better temper than, the latter, but she could better control that temper, and had the additional advantage of being possessed of a more refined taste. This was not, perhaps, always shown when she sat and listened to rather loose talk from the Regent, with no more of reproof than her gently-uttered 'George, George!' by way of remonstrance. She, however, never erred so grossly as the Princess of Wales, who not only would listen unabashed to conversation coarse in character, but was not at all nice herself in either story or epithet. In Italy such things were then accounted of but as being small foibles ; and when the Pope visited her at Genoa he probably thought none the worse of her, nor bated no jot in his courtesy towards her, because of her reputation in this respect. She certainly loved to mystify people, and took an almost insane pleasure in exciting converse against herself. Her adoption of Victorine, a daughter of Bergami, was a proof that she had acquired no profitable experience from the consequences which followed her adoption of young Austin.

During 1815 the Princess was ever restless and on the move. She was now entirely surrounded by Italians. Mr. St. Leger refused to be of her household, nor would he allow his daughter to be of it. Many others were applied to, but with similar success. Sir Humphrey and Lady Davy also declined the honour offered them. Mr. William Rose, Mr. Davenport, and Mr. Hartup pleaded other engagements. Dr. Holland, Mr. North, and Mrs. Falconet were no longer with her. Lord Malpas begged to be excused, and Lady Charlotte Campbell withdrew, after her Royal Highness's second arrival at Milan. The Princess, however, had no difficulty in forming an Italian Court. Some of her appointments were unexceptionable. Such were those of Dr. Machetti, her physician, and of the Chevalier Chiavini, her first equerry. Many of the Italian nobility now took the place of former English visitors at her 'court,' and two of the brothers of Bergami held respectable offices in her household, while the Countess of Oldi, sister of the chamberlain, was appointed sole lady of honour to the lady, her mistress. On several of the excursions made by her Royal Highness from her villa on the Lake of Como to Milan, Venice, and other parts of Italy, she was accompanied by Mr. Burrell, a son of Lord Gwydyr. This gentleman ultimately took his leave of her in August, to return to England. He was sojourning at Brussels, on his way, when his servant, White, narrated to his fellows some accounts of what he described as the very loose way of life of the Princess at Milan. These stories, all infamous, but few, perhaps, which could not be traced back to some indiscretion of this most unhappy lady, and marvellously amplified and exaggerated, came to the ears of the Duke and Duchess of Cumberland, then sojourning at the same hotel; and it is declared that on the report made by the former to his brother, the Regent, was founded the famous 'Milan Commission,' which was one of investigation, appointed to sit at Milan, to inquire into the conduct of the Princess, and to report accordingly. The commissioners sat and took evidence without making the Princess aware of the fact; and to an indignant remonstrance addressed to the Regent, wherein she demanded to know the object of the commission, no answer was returned. It was soon known, however, that the report was of a most condemnatory character, but no proceedings were immediately instituted. Meanwhile, the Princess continued her roving life, now on sea, now on land; now on board the 'Leviathan,' and sometimes on the backs of horses or mules. Her familiarity on all these occasions with her chamberlain was offensive to persons of strict ideas and good principles, and those were precisely the persons whose prejudices she loved, perhaps out of mere mischief, to startle. He dined with her at her table, and she leant upon his arm in their walks.

Early in January 1816, she again embarked on board the 'Clorinde,' Captain Pechell, with the intention of proceeding to Syracuse. The captain, having previously seen Bergami occupying a menial state about her Royal Highness, declined to admit him to his table, at which he entertained the Princess—who refused such entertainment, however, on the captain persisting on the ejection of the chamberlain. The desired port was reached only with difficulty, and for some months the Princess resided in Sicily, with no one near her but this Italian household. To her chamberlain she certainly was some such a mistress as Queen Guinever to Sir Lancelot. In liberality of sunny smiles and largesses there can be no doubt of this; and perhaps the quality of her favour is best illustrated by the fact of her having bestowed her picture upon him, for which she had sat in the character of a 'Magdalen.' She professed to have procured for him also his elevation to be a Knight of Malta, and she did obtain for him the dignity of Baron de la Francino, to heighten the imaginary grandeur.

The next seven months were spent in continual travelling and change of scene. The limit of her wandering was Jericho, whither she went actually, and also in the popular sense of the word, which describes a person as having gone thither when ruin has overtaken him on his journey through life.

She embarked, with her Italian followers, on the 26th of March, and nine days subsequently, after being beaten about by equinoctial storms till the little 'Royal Charlotte' had scarcely a sound plank about her, she reached Tunis, and struck up a very warm acquaintance with the Bey. He lodged and partially fed her, introduced her to his seraglio, perfumed her with incense till she was nearly suffocated, and then as nearly choked her with laughter by causing to play before her his famous female band, consisting of six women who knew nothing of music, every one of whom laboured under some unsightly defect, and of whom the youngest confessed to an honest threescore years. For this entertainment she made a really noble return, by purchasing the freedom of several European slaves. A greater liberator than she, however, was at hand, in Exmouth and his fleet. It was in obedience to the advice of the Admiral, who expected to have to demolish Tunis, as the Bey seemed disinclined to ransom the Christian slaves he held in durance, that the Princess, after a hasty glance at the sites of Utica and Carthage, re-embarked, after a month's sojourn with the most splendidly hospitable of barbarians, and, passing through the saluting English fleet, directed the prow of her vessel to be turned towards Greece. She went on her way accompanied by storms, which prevented her from landing until, with infinite difficulty, she reached the Piræus, early in May, and proceeded to Athens, where she took up her residence in the house of the gallant French consul. Since the days of Aspasia, Athens had seen no such lively times as marked the period of the residence there of the Princess. Her balls were brilliant festivities. In return for them she was permitted to witness the piously ecstatic dancing of the Dervises (for the city of Minerva was under the Crescent then), who have plagiarised a maxim of St. Augustine, only altering it to suit their purpose, as ecstatic persons will do with sacred texts, and proclaiming *orat qui saltat*. The Princess had some nerve, and was by no means a fastidious woman, but she saw here more than she had reckoned upon, and was glad to escape from the exhibition of uncleanness and ferocity. Athens, however, afforded more interesting spectacles than this; she exhausted them all, according to the guide-books and the cicerones; and she gratefully expressed her pleasure by liberating three hundred captives, whom she found languishing in the debtors' prison. The fame of the deed travelled as swiftly as if it had been a deed disgraceful to the actor, and at Corinth she was subsequently entertained, during two whole days, with a profusion and a gaiety that would have gladdened the heart of Laïs, who was herself so often and so splendidly 'at home' in this ancient city.

From Hellas to the Troad was a natural sequence

She went thither, as before, storm-tost—stood on the plain where infidels assert that Troy had never stood, and, leaning on the arm of the noble and bearded Bergami, twice crossed the Scamander. With the first day of June she was in Constantinople, making her entry with Mdlle. Dumont and another lady, in the springless cart or carriage of the country, drawn by a pair of lusty bulls. She resided in the house belonging to the British embassy. It was the last time in the course of her travels that she found rest and protection beneath our flag. The plague, however, being then in the city, she quitted it for a residence some fifteen miles distant, from which she made excursions into the Black Sea, till, growing weary of the amusement, she once more embarked and spent a week at sea, on a frail boat, tossed by storms and watched by corsairs; and at length reaching Scio, sought repose, and indulged in contemplation, or may be supposed to have done so, in the school of Homer. By the end of the month she was amid the ruins of Ephesus. Beneath the ruined vestibule of an ancient church she pitched her tent. The heat was great even at night, the errant lady was sleepless, and the Baron di Francino, ever assiduous, watched near his mistress till dawn, and performed all faithful service required of him.

From the locality once jealously guarded by chaste Diana she passed to the spot where her old Blackheath friend, Sir Sidney Smith, had gained imperishable fame by gallantly vanquishing a foe ever bravely reluctant to confess that he had met his conqueror. Even this place might have interested the Princess by the association of ideas which it may have furnished her as matter for meditation. She did not, however, lose much time in contrasting the gossiping Sir Sidney, who made Montague House ring with his laughter, with the stern warrior who here turned back Napoleon from his way toward India.

She was longing to find rest within the Holy City, and this she accomplished at last, but not till many an obstacle which lay in her way had been surmounted.

Her progress was suddenly checked at Jaffa. The party, which consisted of more than two dozen persons, had no written permission to pass on to Jerusalem, and the Pacha could give his consent only to five of the number to visit the city. After some negotiations with the governor of St. Jean d'Acre, the difficulty was removed, a large armed escort was provided, with tents, guides, and other necessary appendages. Surrounded by these, the Princess and her attendants had very much the air of a strolling party of equestrians on a summer tour. They had a worn, yet 'rollicking' look. There was a loose air about the men and a rompish aspect about the ladies, while the sorry steeds, mules and donkeys, on which they were mounted, seemed denizens of the circus and saw-dust, with the sun-bronzed Princess as manageress of the concern. The similitude was not lessened by the circumstance that, more than once on the road, the Princess, from sheer fatigue and want of sleep, rolled off her donkey to the ground.

The journey was performed beneath one of the very fiercest of suns, and the travellers, light of heart as they were, groaned beneath the hot infliction and the blisters raised by it. They passed many an interesting spot on the way, but were too listless or weary to heed the objects as they passed. Her Royal Highness bore the perils and minor troubles of the way better than any of her followers, but she too became almost vanquished by fatigue; and when she entered Jerusalem, on the 12th of July, seated on an ass, Mdlle. Dumont impiously contrasted her virtues, sufferings, equipage, and person with those of the Saviour. This lady was subsequently the very first who, with eager alacrity, swore away the reputation of her mistress, and heaping her indiscretions together, gave them the bearing of crimes, and did her unblushing utmost to destroy what she had professed to reverence.

The Capuchin friars gave her Royal Highness a cordial reception, and within their sacred precincts even allowed her and some of her French attendants to sleep. In return for this knightly rather than saintly courtesy, she instituted an order of chivalry, and, after looking about for a saint by way of godmother to the new institution, she fixed upon St. Caroline. In vain was it suggested to her that there was no such saint in the Calendar. She had a precedent by way of authorisation. Napoleon had compelled St. Roch to make way for St. Napoleon, and why should not Caroline have 'Saint' prefixed to it, and shine as the patroness of the new order? She, of course, had her way, created poor young Austin a knight, and solemnly instituted Baron Bergami as grand master. They looked more like strolling players than ever; the Baron none the less so when his royal mistress placed on his breast the insignia of the order of 'St. Sepulchre' by the side of the star of the newly-appointed St. Caroline.

With these new dignitaries the party proceeded to view all the spots where there is nothing to be seen, but where much that is false may be heard if the guides be listened to. For miles round there was not a scene that had been the stage of some great event, or was hallowed by the memory of some solemn deed or saintly man, that the Princess did not visit. Having spent upon them all the emotion she had on hand, she trotted off to Jericho, her panting attendants following her; and, having found the place uninhabitable from the fierce heat which prevailed there, the strolling Princess and her fellow-players rushed back to the sea, and, scarcely pausing at Jaffa, embarked hurriedly on board the polacca there awaiting them, and set sail in hopes of speedily encountering refreshing gales and recovering the vigour they had lost.

Their singing 'Veni Aura' brought not the gale they invoked. The sun darted his rays down upon them with greater intensity than ever, and accordingly the Princess raised a gay tent upon the deck, beneath its folds sat by day, took all needful refreshment, and slept by night; the Grand Master of the Order of St. Caroline fulfilling during all that time the office of chamberlain.

The weary and feverish hours were further enlivened by a grand festival held on board on St. Bartholomew's day, in honour of Bartholomew Bergami and the saint of the former name, who was supposed to be the patron and protector of all who bore it. The Princess drank to the Baron, and the latter drank to the Princess, and mirth and good humour, not to say jollity, abounded; and perhaps by the time the incident is as old as the descent of the Nile by Cleopatra is now it may appear as picturesque and poetical as that does. It certainly lacks the picturesque and poetical elements at present.

It is the maxim of sailors that they who whistle for a breath of air will bring a storm. Our travellers only longed for the former, but they were soon enveloped by the latter, through which they contrived to struggle till, on the 20th of September, they made Syracuse, and were inexorably condemned to a quarantine of the legitimate forty days' duration. At the end of this time an Austrian vessel conveyed them to Rome. After a brief but by no means a dull sojourn in that city, the Princess led the way to her home in the Villa d'Este, on the Lake of Como, where she and the Countess Oldi exhibited the proficiency they had acquired as travellers by cooking their own dinners and performing other little feats of amiable independency.

And now, as if to authorise the simile made with

respect to the illustrious party, and their resemblance to a strolling company of players, private theatricals became the most frequent pastime of the lady of the villa and her friends. If she enacted the heroine, the Baron was sure to be the lover. Marie Antoinette, it was said, used to act in plays on the little stage at Trianon. The case was not to be denied; but then the wife of Louis XVI. did not exchange mock heroics with an ex-courier. On the other hand, the dukes and counts she played with were often less respectable than the loosest of menials.

The agents, whose employers were to be found in England, had not been idle during the Princess's period of travel. They had been helped by none so effectually as by herself. She had courted infamy by her heedless conduct, and, cruelly as she was used, the blame does not rest wholly with her persecutors. Her indiscretions seemed indulged in expressly to give warrant for suspicion that she was more than indiscreet, and therewith even the most innocent incidents were twisted by the ingenuity of spies and their agents into crimes. The Baron d'Ompteda had been the most assiduous and the best paid of the spies who hovered incessantly about her, to misrepresent all he was permitted to see. He was banished from the Austrian territory at the request of the Princess, whose champion, the gallant Lieutenant Hownam, sought in vain to bring him to battle and punish him for his treachery towards a lady. On the other hand, the Austrian authorities commanded Bergami to divest himself of the Cross of Malta, which he was wearing without legal authorisation—a disgrace which his rash and imprudent mistress thought she had effaced by purchasing for the disknighted chevalier an estate, and putting him in full possession of the rights and dignity of lord of the manor.

Early in 1817 the Princess repaired to Carlsruhe, on

a visit to the Grand Duke of Baden. She was received courteously, but not warmly enough to induce her to make a long sojourn. This Duke was not anxious to detain a guest so eccentric. Lord Redesdale told Miss Wynn, who set the story down in her 'Diaries,' that 'when the Princess was at Baden, and the Grand Duke made a *partie de chasse* for her, she appeared on horseback with a half pumpkin on her head. Upon the Grand Duke's expressing astonishment, and recommending a *coiffeur* rather less extraordinary, she only replied that the weather was hot, and that nothing kept the head so cool and comfortable as a pumpkin. Her next point was Vienna, from which city she had frightened Lord Stewart, the British ambassador, by an intimation that she was coming to take up her residence with him, and to demand satisfaction for the insults to which she had been subjected by persons who were spies upon her conduct. She experienced nothing but what she might have expected in Vienna—a contemptuous neglect; and soon quitting that city she repaired to Trieste, and tarried long enough there to compel the least scrupulous to think that, if she possessed the most handsome of chamberlains, she was herself the weakest and least wise of ladies. He was now her constant and almost only attendant in public. English families had long ceased to show her any respect. They could not manifest it for a woman who, by courting an evil reputation, evidently did not respect herself. What was her being innocent, if she always so acted as to make herself appear guilty? She might as well have asserted that her openly attending Mass with Bergami was not to be taken as proof of her being a very indifferent Protestant.

She became in every sense of the word a mere wanderer, apparently without object, save flying from the memories which she could not cast off. She was constantly changing her residence—so constantly as to make her career somewhat difficult to follow; but we know that she was residing at Pescaro when she received intelligence which she least expected, and which deeply affected her. During her absence from England her daughter had married Prince Leopold, and the mother had hoped to find friends at least in this pair, if not now, at some future period. But now she had heard that her child and her child's child were dead. 'I have not only,' she wrote to a friend in England, 'to lament an ever-beloved child, but one most warmly attached friend, and the only one I have had in England; but she is only gone before—I have not lost her, and I now trust we shall soon meet in a much better world than the present one. For ever your truly sincere friend, C. P.'

This calamity, however, had no effect in rendering the writer more circumspect. Her course of life, without being one of the gross guilt it was described, was certainly one not creditable to her. Exaggerated reports, which grew as they were circulated, startled the ears of her friends and gladdened the hearts of her enemies. They were at their very worst when, in 1820, George III. ended his long reign, and Caroline Princess of Wales became Queen-consort of England.

As a sample of the effect produced by the above-named reports the following, from a letter by Lady Charleville to Lady Morgan, in February 1820, may be quoted :—' The report of all travellers who have had any knowledge of the Princess of Wales renders it imperative that such a woman should not preside in Great Britain over its honest and virtuous daughters, and something is to be done to prevent it.' In April of the same year Lady Morgan was in Rome, and she wrote thence to Lady Clarke more favourably: 'We have Queen Caroline here; at first this made a great fuss, whether she was or was not to be visited by her subjects, when, lo! she refused to see any of them, and leads the most perfectly retired life! We met her one day driving out in a state truly royal; I never saw her so splendid. Young Austin followed in an open carriage; he is an interesting-looking young man. She happened to arrive at an inn near Rome when Lord and Lady Leitrim were there. She sent for them, and invited them to tea. Lady Leitrim told me her manner was perfect, and altogether she was a most improved woman. The Baron attended her at tea, but merely as a chamberlain, and was not introduced. Before you receive this; if accounts be true, her Majesty will be in England.'

The Roman authorities treated her with scant courtesy. As soon as the death of almost the only friend she ever had in England, George III., was certified, Cardinal Gonzalvi, refusing to recognise in her person a Queen of Great Britain, sent her passport to her as Princess Caroline of Brunswick.

CHAPTER VIII.

THE RETURN TO ENGLAND.

Report of the Milan Commissioners—The Princess's determination to return to England—Studied neglect of her by Louis XVIII.—Lord Hutchinson's proposal to her to remain abroad—Her indignant refusal—Bergami's anger on the refusal of the proposition—Discourtesy of the French authorities to the Princess—Her reception in England—The Regent's message to Parliament—The green bag—Sympathy for the Queen—Desire for a compromise evinced; meeting for the purpose at Lord Castlereagh's—The contending parties in Parliament—Mr. Wilberforce as Mr. Harmony—Mr. Brougham the Queen's especial advocate—The Queen's name in the Liturgy demanded—Mr. Denman's argument for it—Address of the House of Commons to the Queen—Her reply, and appeal to the nation—A secret inquiry protested against—The Queen at Waithman's shop—Violence of party spirit.

THE report rendered by the gentlemen who formed the Milan Commission to inquire secretly into the conduct of the Princess of Wales was so unfavourable to the latter that the Regent would have taken immediate steps to have procured a divorce, but for the assurance of his legal advisers that, even in the case of the Princess becoming Queen-consort, she would never return to this country, provided only that the income assigned to her by parliament as Princess of Wales were secured to her after she was Queen. There had been some negotiation to this effect in 1819, when it was understood that the title of Queen would never be assumed by the Princess if the payment of the annuity was punctually observed. Her most intimate friends, therefore, did not reckon upon her appearance in this country after the accession of her husband to the throne.

Lord Liverpool addressed a letter to Mr. Brougham, adverting to this arrangement as having been originally proposed by Queen Caroline—a conclusion against which she protested with great indignation. Her first step was to pass through France to St. Omer, where she awaited the arrival of her legal advisers. The then reigning French monarch had in the time of his own adversity received substantial aid and continual courtesy from the Queen's father; but now, in the hour of the distresses of his former benefactor's daughter, he beset her passage through France with difficulties, and commanded her to be treated with studied neglect. However mortified, she was a woman of too much spirit to allow her mortification to be visible, and for the lack of official honours she found consolation in the sympathy of the people. On the first intimation of the omission of her name from the Liturgy, the Queen wrote thus, without consulting any one: 'The Queen of this Relams wishes to be informed, through the medium of Lord Liverpool, First Minister to the King of this Relams, for which reason or motife the Queen name has been left out of the general Prayerbooks in England, and especially to prevent all her subjects to pay her such respect which is due to the Queen. It is equally a great omittance towards the King that his Consort Queen should be obliged to soummit to such great neglect, or rather araisin from a perfect ignorance of the Archbishops of the real existence of the Queen Caroline of England.' It was finely remarked by Mr. Denman, after he became the Solicitor-General (at Brougham's recommendation), that the Queen *was* included in the Liturgy, in the prayer 'for all who are desolate and oppressed.'

At the inn of St. Omer she was met by Mr. Brougham

and Lord Hutchinson. The latter came as the representative of the ministry, with no credentials, however, nor even with the ministerial proposition reduced to writing. The Queen refused to receive it in any other form. Lord Hutchinson obeyed, and made a written proposal to the effect that, as she was now without income by the demise of George III., the King would grant her 50,000*l.* per annum, on the special condition that she remained on the continent, surrendered the title of Queen, adopted no title belonging to the royal family of England, and never even visited the latter country under any pretext. It was further stated that, if she set foot in England, the negotiation would be at an end, the terms violated, and proceedings be commenced against her Majesty forthwith.

It has been said that the Queen's immediate and decided rejection of these proposals, and her resolution to proceed to England at once, were undoubted proofs of her innocence. The truth, however, is, that the acceptance of such terms would have been a tacit confession of her guilt, and, had she been as criminal as her accusers endeavoured to prove her, her safest course would have been that which she so spiritedly adopted. The infamy here was undoubtedly on the part of the ministry. Here was a woman in whom they asserted was to be found the most profligate of her sex, and to her they made an offer of 50,000*l.* per annum, on condition that she laid down the title of Queen of England, of which they said she was entirely unworthy; and this sum was to be paid to her out of the taxes of a people the majority of whom believed that she had been 'more sinned against than sinning.'

It has been believed, or at least has been reported, that the Queen was counselled to the refusal of the compromise annuity of 50,000*l.* by Alderman Wood. The city dignitary, in such case, got little thanks for his advice at the hands of Baron Bergami. The latter individual, on hearing that Queen Caroline had declined to accept the offer, and that the alderman was her adviser on the occasion, declared that if he ever encountered the ex-mayor in Italy he would kill him. The courier-baron's ground of offence was, that, had the Queen received the money, a great portion of it would have fallen to his share, and that he considered himself as robbed by the alderman, whom he would punish accordingly.

Caroline refused the proposals with scorn. In one of her characteristic letters she said: 'The 30th of April I shall be at Calais for certain; my health is good, and my spirit is perfect. I have seen no *personnes* of any kind who could give me any advice different to my feelings and my sentiments of duty relatif of my present situation and rank of life.' Fearful of further obstacle on the part of the French government, she proceeded at once to Calais, dismissed her Italian court, and with Alderman Wood and Lady Anne Hamilton she went on board the 'Leopold' sailing packet, then lying in the mud in the harbour. No facilities were afforded her by the authorities; the English inhabitants of Calais were even menaced with penalties if they infringed the orders which had been given, and no compliment was paid her, except by the master of the packet, who hoisted the royal standard as soon as her Majesty set foot upon the humble deck of his little vessel. She sat there as evening closed in, without an attendant saving the lady already named and the alderman, who not only gave her his escort now but offered her a home. She had solicited from the government that a house might be provided for her, but the application had been received with silent contempt.

Her progress from Dover to London was a perfect ovation. Mr. Brougham had given her good advice at St. Omer. 'If,' he said, 'your Majesty shall determine to go to England before any new offer can be made, I earnestly implore your Majesty to proceed in the most private and secret manner possible. It may be very well for a candidate at an election to be drawn into towns by the population, and they will mean nothing but good in showing this attention to your Majesty; but a Queen of England may well dispense with such marks of popular favour, and my duty to your Majesty binds me to say very plainly that I shall consider any such exhibition as both hurtful to your Majesty's real dignity and full of danger in its probable consequences.' 'That Brougham is afraid,' said the Queen; and so he was—afraid of her, afraid of some scandal, unknown to him then, coming out after her arrival. If he could have had his way he would not have consented to her coming to England at all. The people saw in her a victim of persecution, and for such there is generally a ready sympathy. They were convinced, too, that she was a woman of spirit, and for such there is ever abundant admiration. There was not a town through which she passed upon her way that did not give her a hearty welcome, and wish her well through the fiery ordeal which awaited her. She reached London on the evening of the 7th of June, 1820, and the popular procession of which she was the chief portion passed Carlton House on its route to the residence of Alderman Wood, in South Audley Street. There Alderman Wood used to spread a rug for her Majesty to tread upon, when, to satisfy the loud-tongued mob, she appeared twenty times a day on the little balcony. The Attorney-General would not allow his wife to call on her; and Mrs. Denman received a similar prohibition from Mr. Denman, who, subsequently, regretted the course he had taken.

The Queen had scarcely found refuge beneath the alderman's hospitable roof when Lord Liverpool in the House of Peers, and Lord Castlereagh in the House of

Commons, conveyed a message from the King to the parliament, the subject of which was that, her Majesty having thought proper to come to this country, some information would be laid before them, on which they would have to come to an ulterior decision, of vast importance to the peace and well-being of the United Kingdom. Each minister bore a 'green bag,' which was supposed and perhaps did contain minutes of the report made by the Milan commissioners touching her Majesty's conduct abroad. The ministerial communications were made in the spirit and tone of men who, if not ashamed of the message which they bore, were very uncertain and infinitely afraid as to its ultimate consequences.

Not that they were wanting in an outward show of boldness. The soldiers quartered at the King's Mews, Charing Cross, had been so disorderly some days previous, allegedly because they had not sufficient accommodation, that they were drafted in two divisions to Portsmouth. When the Queen was approaching London a mob assembled in front of the guard-house, and called upon the soldiers still remaining there to join them in a demonstration in favour of the Queen. Lord Sidmouth, who was passing on his way to the House of Lords, seeing what was going on, proceeded to the Horse Guards, called out the troops there, and stood by while they roughly dispersed the people. It was called putting a bold face upon the matter, but less provocation on the part of a government has been followed by revolution.

A desire to compromise the unhappy dispute was no doubt sincerely entertained by ministers, and all hope was not abandoned, even after the arrival of the Queen. Mr. Rush, the United States ambassador to England at this period, permits us to see, in his journal, when this attempt at compromise or amicable arrangement of the affair was first entered upon by the respective parties. On the 15th of June that gentleman dined at Lord Castlereagh's with all the foreign ambassadors. 'A very few minutes,' he says, 'after the last course, Lord Castlereagh, looking to his chief guest for acquiescence, made the signal for rising, and the company all went to the drawing-room. So early a move was unusual: it seemed to cut short, unexpectedly, the time generally given to conversation at English dinners after the dinner ends. It was soon observed that his lordship had left the drawing-room. This was still more unusual; and now it came to be whispered that an extraordinary cause had produced this unusual scene. It was whispered by one or another of the corps that his lordship had retired into one of his own apartments to meet the Duke of Wellington, as his colleague in the administration, and also Mr. Brougham and Mr. Denman, as counsel for the Queen in the disputes pending between the King and Queen.' Mr. Rush, after mentioning that the proceedings in parliament were arrested for the moment by members purporting to be common friends of both King and Queen, proceeds to state that ' the dinner at Lord Castlereagh's was during this state of things, which explains the incident at its close, the disputes having pressed with anxiety on the King's ministers. That his lordship did separate himself from his guests for the purpose of holding a conference in another part of his own house, in which the Duke of Wellington joined him as representing the King, with Mr. Brougham and Mr. Denman as representing the Queen, was known from the former protocol, afterwards published, of what took place on that very evening. It was the first of the conferences held with a view to a compromise between the royal disputants.' On the 28th of June the American ambassador was at the levée at Carlton House, where he learns that ' the sensibilities of the King are intense, and nothing can ever reconcile him.' The same diplomatist then presents to us the following graphic picture: 'The day was hot, excessively so for England. The King seemed to suffer. He remarked upon the heat to me and others. It is possible that other heat may have aggravated in him that of the weather. Before he came into the entrée room, from his closet, —— of the diplomatic corps, taking me gently by the arm, led me a few steps with him, which brought us into the recess of a window. "Look!" said he. I looked, and saw nothing but the velvet lawn covered by trees in the palace gardens. "Look again!" said he. I did; and still my eye only took in another part of the same scene. "*Try once more*," said he, cautiously raising a finger in the right direction. —— had a vein of drollery in him. I now for the first time beheld a peacock displaying his plumage. At one moment he was in full pride, and displayed it gloriously; at another he would halt, letting it drop, as if dejected. "Of what does that remind you?" said ——. "Of nothing," said I; "*Honi soit qui mal y pense!*" for I threw the King's motto at him, and then added that *I* was a republican, *he* a monarchist, and that if he dreamt of unholy comparisons where royalty was concerned I would certainly tell upon him, that it might be reported at his court. He quietly drew off from me, smiling, and I afterwards saw him slyly take another member of the corps to the same spot, to show him the same sight.'

Meanwhile, the contending parties in parliament wore about them the air of men who were called upon to do battle, and who, while resolved to accomplish their best, would have been glad to have effected a compromise which, at least, should save the honour of their principal. As Mr. Wilberforce remarked, there was a mutual desire to 'avoid that fatal green bag.' There were many difficulties in the way. The Queen, naturally enough, insisted on her name being restored in the Liturgy; and none of her friends would have consented for her, nor would she have done so for herself, that she should reside abroad without being introduced by the British ambassador to the court of the country in which she might take up her residence. The government manifested too clearly an intention not to help her in this respect, for they remarked that, though they might request the ambassador to present, they could not compel the court to receive her. They wanted her out of the way, bribed splendidly to endure an indelible disgrace. She was wise enough, at least, to perceive that to consent to such a course would be to strip her of every friend, and to shut against her the door of every court in Europe.

Mr. Wilberforce hoped to act the 'Mr. Harmony' of the crisis, by bringing forward a motion expressive of the regret of parliament that the two illustrious adversaries had not been able to complete an amicable arrangement of their difficulties, and declaring that the Queen would sacrifice nothing of her good name nor of the righteousness of her cause, nor be held as shrinking from inquiry, by consenting to accept the counsel of parliament, and forbearing to press further the adoption of those propositions on which any material difference of opinion is yet remaining. The Queen's especial advocate, Mr. Brougham, felicitously contrasted the eager desire of ministers to get rid of her Majesty, by sending her out of the country with all the pomp, splendour, and ceremonies connected with royalty, with their meanness in allowing her to come over in a common packet, and to seek shelter in the house of a private individual. He added that the only basis on which any satisfactory negotiation could be carried on with her Majesty was the restoration of her name to the Liturgy. Mr. Denman, in alluding to the case of Sophia Dorothea, which had been cited by ministers as precedent wherein they found authority for omitting the Queen's name from the Liturgy, remarked that, ' As to the case of the Queen of George I., to which allusions had been made, it was not at all in point. She had been guilty of certain practices in Hanover which compromised her character, and was never considered Queen of England. On the continent she lived under the designation of Princess of Halle ; and though the Prince of Wales had afterwards called her to this country for the purpose of embarrassing the government of his father, to which he happened to be opposed, still she was never recognised in any other character than Electress of Hanover.' In this statement it will be seen that the speaker calls her Queen whom he denies to have been accounted as such, and he adds that the Prince of Wales called her to this country in his father's lifetime, when he had no power to do so ; whereas he simply expressed to his friends his determination to invite her over if she survived his father as Queen-dowager of England. This invitation he never had the power of making, for his mother's demise preceded the decease of his father. Mr. Denman was far happier in his allusion to a ministerial assertion that the omission of the Queen's name from the Liturgy was the act of the King in his closet. This assertion was at once a meanness and a falsehood, for, as Mr. Denman remarked, no one knew of any such thing in this country as ' the King in his closet.' Indeed the ministers were peculiarly unlucky in all they did ; for while they asserted that the omission was never made out of disrespect towards the Queen, they acknowledged that it never would have been thought of but for the revelations contained in the fatal green bag as to her Majesty's alleged conduct. Finally, the House agreed to Mr. Wilberforce's motion.

The announcement of the resolution to which the House of Commons had come was made to her Majesty, now residing in Portman Street, in an address conveyed to her by Mr. Wilberforce and three other members of the Lower House. On this occasion all the forms of a court were observed. The bearers of the address appeared in full court dress. The Queen, in a dress of black satin, with a wreath of laurel shaded with emeralds around her head, surmounted by a 'plume of feathers,' stood in one portion of the little drawing-room; behind her stood all the ladies of her household, in the person of Lady Anne Hamilton, and on either side of her Mr. Brougham and Mr. Denman, her Majesty's Attorney and Solicitor Generals, in full-bottomed wigs and silk gowns. As the deputation approached, the folding doors which divided the members in the back drawing-room from the Queen and her court in the front apartment were then thrown open, and the four gentlemen from the House of Commons knelt on one knee and kissed her Majesty's hand. Having communicated to her the resolutions of the House, the Queen, through the attorney-general, returned an answer of some length, the substance of which, however, was, that with all her respect for the House of Commons she could not bind herself to be governed by its counsel until she knew the purport of the advice. In short, she yielded nothing, but appealed to the nation. When the assembled crowd learned the character of the royal reply its delight was intense, and certainly public opinion was generally in favour of the Queen and of the course now adopted by her. There was one thing she and the public too supremely hated, and that was the formation of a secret committee, formed principally too of ministerial adherents, and charged with prosecuting the inquiry against her, without letting her know who were her accusers or of what crimes she was accused, and without affording her opportunity to procure evidence to rebut the testimony brought against her.

Against such a proceeding she drew up a petition, which she requested the Lord Chancellor to present. That eminent official, however, asserting that he meant no disrespect, excused himself on the ground that he did not know how to present such a document to the House, and that there was nothing in the journals which could tend to enlighten him.

The petition, however, the chief prayer in which was that the Queen's counsel might be heard at the bar of the House against an inquiry by secret committee, was presented by Lord Dacre, and the prayer in question was agreed to.

The request of Mr. Brougham was for a delay of two months, previous to the inquiry being further prosecuted, in order to leave time for the assembling of witnesses for the defence—witnesses whom the Queen was too poor to purchase, and too powerless to compel to repair to England. Her Majesty's Attorney-General asked this the more earnestly as some of the witnesses on the King's side were of tainted character, and one of them was an ex-domestic of the Queen's, discharged from her service for robbing her of four hundred napoleons. The learned advocate concluded by expressing his confidence that the delay of two months would not be considered too great an indulgence for the purpose of furthering the ends of justice, and providing that a legal murder should not be committed on the character of the first subject of the realm. The best point in Mr. Denman's speech in support of the request made by his leader was in the quotation from a judgment delivered by a former lord chancellor, and which was to this effect—it was delivered with the eyes of the speaker keenly fixed on those of Lord Eldon—' A judge ought to prepare the way to a just sentence, as God useth to prepare His way, by raising valleys and taking down hills, so when there appeareth on either side a high hand, violent prosecutions, cunning advantages taken, combination, power, great counsel, then is the virtue of a judge seen to make inequality equal, that he may plant his judgment as upon an even ground.'

While the Lords were deliberating on the request for postponement, Lord Castlereagh was inveighing in the Commons against the Queen herself, for daring to refuse to yield to the wishes of parliament, and rejecting the advice to be guided by its counsel. Such rejection he interpreted as being a sort of insult which no other member of the House of Brunswick would have ventured to commit. 'That illustrious individual,' he said, 'might repent the step she had taken.' Meanwhile, the Commons suspended proceedings till the course to be decided upon by the Lords was finally taken. In the latter assembly Earl Grey made a last effort to stay the proceedings altogether, by moving that the order for the meeting of the secret committee to consider the papers in the 'green bag' should be discharged. The motion was lost, but an incident in the debate which arose upon it deserves to be noticed. The omission of the Queen's name from the Liturgy had been described as the act of the King in his closet. Lord Holland now charged the Archbishop of Canterbury as the adviser of the act; but Lord Liverpool accepted the responsibility of it for himself and colleagues, as having been adopted by the King in council, at the ministerial suggestion.

The Lords having resolved to commence proceedings by a preliminary secret inquiry, the Queen protested against such a course, but no reply was made to her protest. With the exception of appearing to return answers to the addresses forwarded to her from various parts of the country, she withdrew, as much as possible, from all publicity. Her personal friends, however, were busier than she required in drawing up projects for her which she could not sanction. One of these busy advocates thought that she might fittingly compromise the matter by gaining the restoration of her name in the Liturgy, being crowned, holding one drawing-room, yearly, at Kensington Palace, and having her permanent residence at Hampton Court, with 55,000*l*. a year to uphold her dignity. The terms were not illiberal; but if the Queen rejected them, it was, probably, because she knew they would never be offered. Her own remark upon them is said to have been, that she did not want a victory without a battle, but a victory after showing that she had deserved it.

She was the more eager for battle from the fact that the contents of the green bag were by no means unknown to her. At least, it has been asserted that she had long held duplicates of some of the evidence, if not of the report made by the Milan commissioners, and she was satisfied she could rebut both. She possessed one, and it was her solitary, advantage in this case. The ministers, if not in so many words, yet by their proceedings, had stigmatised her as utterly infamous, and yet they had considered it not beneath them to desire to enter into negotiations with one whom they considered guilty of all the implied infamy. The Queen's rejection of the proposals to compound 'the stupendous felony' raised up for her many a friend in circles where she had been looked upon, if not as guilty, yet, at best, as open to very grave suspicion.

The Queen's health required her not to confine herself within the narrow limits of her residence in Portman Street. She accordingly paid one public visit to Guildhall, and occasionally repaired to Blackheath. It was on her way back from one of these latter excursions that she honoured Alderman Waithman's shop with a visit. The incident is perhaps as well worth noticing as that which tells of the trip made by the young Queen Mary to the shop of Lady Gresham, the lady mayoress, who appears to have dealt in millinery. The city progresses of the Queen did her infinite injury. The very lowest of the populace, who cared little more for her than as giving opportunity for a little excitement, were wont on these occasions to take the horses from her carriage, harness themselves to the vehicle, and literally drag the Queen of England through the mud of the metropolis. She could only suffer degradation and ridicule from such a proceeding, which a little spirit might have prevented. Her enemies bitterly derided her through their organs in the press. They expressed an eagerness to get rid of her, and added their indifference as to whether 'the alien' was finally disposed of as a martyr or as a criminal. On the other hand, her over-zealous partisans gave utterance to their convictions that there was a project on foot to murder the Queen. Party spirit never wore so assassin-like an aspect as it did at this moment. Caroline, it must be added, was not displeased with these popular ovations. 'I have derived,' she remarked in her reply to the City address, 'unspeakable consolations from the zealous and constant attachment of this warm-hearted, just, and generous people, to live at home with and to cherish whom will be the chief happiness of the remainder of my days.' But her chief occupation now was to look to her defence, for the time had arrived when her accusers were to speak openly.

CHAPTER IX.

QUEEN, PEERS, AND PEOPLE.

The secret committee on the Queen's conduct—Encounter between the Queen and Princess Sophia—Bill of Pains and Penalties brought into the House of Lords—The Queen demands to know the charges against her—Her demand refused—The Queen again petitions—Lord Liverpool's speech—The Queen's indignant message to the Lords—Money spent to procure witnesses against her—Public feeling against the Italian witnesses—Dr. Parr's advice to the Queen—His zealous advocacy of her cause—Lord Erskine's efforts in her favour—Her hearty protest against legal oppression—Gross attack on her in a provincial paper—Cruel persecution of her—Her sharp philippic against Ministers—Lord John Russell's letter to Mr. Wilberforce, and petition to the King—The Queen at Brandenburgh House—Death of the Duchess of York—Her eccentricities—Her character—Addresses to the Queen, and her replies.

THE secret committee charged with examining the documents in the sealed bags made their report early in July. This report was to the effect that the documents contained allegations, supported by the concurrent testimony of witnesses of various grades in life, which deeply affected the honour of the Queen, charging her, as they did, with a 'continued series of conduct highly unbecoming her Majesty's rank and station, and of the most licentious character.' The committee reluctantly recommended that the matter should become the subject of solemn inquiry by legislative proceeding.

The ministers postponed any explanation as to the course to be adopted by them upon this report until the following day. The Queen exhibited no symptoms of being daunted by it. She appeared in public on the evening of the day on which the report was delivered, and, if cheers could attest her innocence, the *vox populi* would have done it that night. As the Queen's carriage was passing in the vicinity of Kensington Gate it encountered that bearing the Princess Sophia. The two cousins passed each other without exchanging a sign of recognition, and the doughty livery servants of the Princess showed that they had adopted the prejudices or convictions of *their* portion of the royal family by refusing obedience to the commands of the mob, which had ordered them to uncover as they passed in presence of the Queen.

On Wednesday, the 5th of July, Lord Liverpool brought in the ever-famous Bill of Pains and Penalties, a bill of degradation and divorce. Lord Liverpool had previously protested against a divorce. Why he now turned to a still more dangerous expedient he explains in a letter inserted in his Memoirs. 'In the case of a private individual the question of divorce is a question of personal relief. The law of man, not the law of God, says properly in this case, we will not give you the relief unless by your conduct you are entitled to it. But the King does not, and cannot, apply for relief as an individual; his accusation is a public accusation, resting on public grounds. Adultery in a Queen is a crime against the State. The private offence is merged in the public crime, and must follow the effect of it. How is it possible to entertain a charge of recrimination against a King, who in the eye of the law can do no wrong?'

The Queen demanded, by petition, to be furnished with the specific charges brought against her, and to be heard by her counsel in support of that demand. The House refused, and Lord Liverpool went on with his Bill.

The Queen again interfered by petition, requesting to have the nature of the charges against her distinctly stated, and to be heard in support of her request by counsel. These requests were negatived. Lord Liverpool then, in introducing the bill, did his utmost to save the King from being unfavourably contrasted in his character of complainant with the Queen in that of defendant. He alleged that their Majesties were not before the House as individuals. The parties concerned were the Queen as accused party and the State! The question to be considered was whether, supposing the allegations to be substantiated, impunity was to be extended to guilt, or justice be permitted to triumph. The bill he thus introduced noticed the various acts of indiscretion which have been already recorded. These were the familiarity which existed between herself and her courier, whom she had ennobled, and in honour of whom she had unauthorisedly founded an order of chivalry, of which he had been appointed grand master. The bill further accused her of most scandalous, vicious, and disgraceful conduct 'with the said Bergami,' but was silent as to time and place. The document concluded by proposing that Caroline Amelia Elizabeth should be 'deprived of her rank, rights, and privileges as Queen, and that her marriage with the King be dissolved and disannulled to all intents and purposes.' The bill, in short, pronounced her infamous. It was the penalty which she paid for the exercise of much indiscretion. Earl Grey complained of the want of specification, and asserted her Majesty's right to be furnished with the names of witnesses. Lord Liverpool, however, treated the assertion as folly, and the claim made as unprecedented and inexpedient.

A copy of the bill was delivered to the Queen by Sir Thomas Tyrwhitt. She received it not without emotion, and this was sufficiently great to give a confused tone to her observations on this occasion. Had the bill, she said, been presented to her a quarter of a century earlier, it might have served the King's purpose better. She added that, as she should never meet her husband again in this world, she hoped, at least, to do so in the next, where certainly justice would be rendered her.

To the Lords she sent a message expressive of her indignant surprise that the bill should assume her as guilty simply upon the report of a committee before whom not a single witness had been examined. Her friends continued to harass the government. In the Commons, Sir Ronald Ferguson attempted, though unsuccessfully, to obtain information as to the authority for the organising of the Milan commission for examining spies. That commission, he intimated, originated with the vice-chancellor, Sir John Leach, and had cost the country between thirty and forty thousand pounds, for one half of which sum, he added, Italian witnesses might be procured who would blast the character of every man and woman in England.

The feeling against Italians did not require to be excited. Those who arrived at Dover to furnish evidence against the Queen were very roughly treated; and so fearful were the ministers that something worse might happen to them, that they were, after various changes of residence in London, transferred to Holland, much to the disgust of the Dutch, before they were finally cloistered up in Cotton Garden, at hand to furnish the testimony, for the bringing of which they received very liberal recompense.

Meanwhile, Dr. Parr, in ponderous sermons, exhorted her Majesty not to despise the chastening of the Lord; and the Queen's devout deportment at divine service was cited by zealous advocates as evidence in favour of her general propriety.

Indeed the Queen had no more zealous champion than the almost octogenarian Parr. On the fly-leaf of the Prayer-book in the reading-desk of his parish church at Hatton he entered (and one can hardly say of Dr.

Parr's act on this occasion *dispar sibi*) a stringent protest against the oppression to which she had been subjected; adding a conviction entertained by him of her complete innocence, and expressing a determination, although forbidden to pray for her by name, to add a prayer for her mentally, after uttering the words in the Liturgy, ' *all* the Royal family.' In his heart the stout old man prayed fervently; nor did he confine himself to such service. A friend, knowing his opinions, his admiration of the Queen, and the friendly feelings which had long mutually existed between them, earnestly begged of him not to interfere in her affairs at this conjuncture. Dr. Parr answered the request by immediately ordering his trunk to be packed, and by proceeding to London, where he entered on the office of her Majesty's chaplain, procured the nomination of the Rev. M. Fellowes to the same office, and in conjunction with him, and often alone, wrote those royal replies to popular addresses which are remarkable for their force, and for the ability with which they are made to metaphorically scourge the King, without appearing to treat him with discourtesy.

There was as much zeal, and perhaps more discretion, in those impartial peers who, on occasion of Lord Liverpool moving the second reading of the Bill for the 17th of August, insisted on the undoubted right of the Queen, as an accused party, to be made acquainted with the names of the witnesses who had come over to charge her with infamy. Lord Erskine was particularly urgent and impressive on this point, but all to no purpose, except the extracting an assurance from Lord Chancellor Eldon that the accused should have, at a fitting season, a proper opportunity to sift the character of every witness as far as possible. Lord Erskine repeatedly endeavoured to obtain the full measure of justice for the accused which he demanded. The Queen herself entered a hearty protest against the legal oppression, and further begged by petition that, as the names of the witnesses against her were withheld, she might at least be furnished with a specification of the times and places, when and where she was said to have acted improperly. The request was characterised by Lord Eldon as ' perfectly absurd,' seeing that the Queen could make no use of the information, if she intended, as declared by her, to defend her case at the early period named, of the 17th of August. The reply was harsh, insulting, and illogical.

But to harshness and insult she became inured by daily experience. It may be safely said that, if such a drama had to be enacted in our own days, the press would certainly not distinguish itself now exactly as it did then. Party spirit might be as strong, but there would be more refinement in the expression of it. And assuredly, not even a provincial paper would say of a person before trial as a Western journal said of the Queen—that she was as much given to drunkenness as to other vices, and that it was ridiculous to hold up as an innocent victim a woman who, ' if found on our pavement, would be committed to Bridewell and whipped.'

But ministers themselves were not on a bed of roses. They were exceedingly embarrassed by the Queen's announcement that she intended to be present every day in the House of Lords during the progress of what was now properly called ' The Queen's Trial.' Their anger, too, was excited at the sharp philippics against them inserted in her Majesty's replies to the addresses presented to her. In those replies the passages complained of wounded more than those against whom they were pointed; and the authors of them had, no doubt, some mirth over sentences intended to spoil it in the breasts of ministers charged with rebelliously seeking to dethrone their lawful Queen. The royal replies, too, were equally, but not so directly, severe against those former counsellors and advocates of her Majesty who were now arrayed on the side of her Majesty's enemy. These replies were, of course, not censured by the ministerial opponents in either House of Parliament. The addresses which called them forth, however, did not escape reproach from this quarter. Lord John Russell, in a letter to Mr. Wilberforce, does not indeed go so far as reproach. He says: 'I regret, though I cannot severely blame, the language of many of the addresses that have been presented to the Queen.'

Lord John acknowledged the political nullity of the Whigs at this time, but he held that the Wilberforce party in the Commons were sufficiently powerful to have successfully resisted the scandal which the Government had brought upon the kingdom. 'In your hands, sir,' he says, 'is perhaps the fate of this country. The future historian will ask whether it was right to risk the welfare of England—her boasted constitution, her national power— on the event of an inquiry into the conduct of the Princess of Wales in her villa upon the Lake of Como? From the majority which followed you in the House of Commons, he will conclude you had the power to prevent the die being thrown. He will ask if you wanted the inclination.'

To this letter Lord John Russell appended a form of petition to the King, which may not uncourteously be termed the petition of the powerless Whig statesman. This petition smartly and smartingly complimented his Majesty upon his liberality in offering to allow his Queen fifty thousand a year, and to introduce her to a foreign court, at a time when he pretended to know that she was, allegedly, perfectly worthless, as woman, wife, and mother. With the domestic broils of King and Queen Lord John would not interfere; but, the King having made of them an affair of state, the 'humble petition' informs his

Majesty that he has been exceedingly ill-advised. With excellent spirit does Lord John place upon record his abhorrence of enacting laws to suit a solitary case—laws 'which at once create the offence, regulate the proof, decide upon the evidence, and invent the punishment.' He asks if the Queen will escape from justice in the event of the bill not passing? Are the ministers afraid lest she may so defraud justice?—why, 'that the Queen has *not* fled from justice is not only the admission, but forms one of the chief charges, of her prosecutors.' Her prosecution, then, will not serve the State. Can the revelation of her alleged iniquity at Como or Athens serve or influence public morals in England? What is the situation of the Queen? asks Lord John, who thus replies to his own query: 'Separated from her husband during the first year of her marriage, she has been forced out of that circle of domestic affections which alone are able to keep a wife holy and safe from evil. For the period to which the accusation extends she has been also removed from the control of public opinion—the next remaining check the world can afford on female behaviour.' Lord John perhaps makes a low estimate of female virtue when he thus concludes that women cease to be 'holy and safe from evil' when they cease to have a share in domestic affections or to be controlled by public opinion. There is more sly humour in what follows than there is of correctness in the noble lord's estimation of female virtue. The drawer-up of the petition reminds the King that what most distresses him is 'the uncrowning a royal head without necessity. We see much to alarm us in the example, nothing to console us in the immediate benefit.' Not, says the petitioner, slyly, that we do not recognise the right of parliament to alter the succession to the crown. 'None respect more than we do the Act of Settlement which took away the crown from its hereditary successors and gave it to the House of Brunswick;' and, as the writer alludes to the possibility of the new subject of strife bringing the country to the verge of a civil war, he of course intimates that parliament may again be called upon to regulate the succession. The sum of the petition is to let the Queen alone. 'From her future conduct your Majesty and the nation will be enabled to judge whether the reports from Milan were well founded, or whether they were the offspring of curiosity and malice.' The prayer of the petition, therefore, is that parliament be prorogued, and 'thus end all proceedings against the Queen.'

Of course this petition was really a political pamphlet, introduced for no other purpose but the exposition of certain opinions. The Queen's replies to the popular addresses borrowed something of the tone of this document, and were partly sarcastic, partly serious, in regretting that an impartial tribunal was not to be found on this occasion in the House of Lords.

Her Majesty now once more changed her residence from Portman Street to Brandenburgh House, the old suburban residence of the Margravine of Anspach, on the banks of the Thames, near Hammersmith, where watch and ward were nightly kept by volunteer sentinels from among some of the more enthusiastic inhabitants of the vicinity. The distance, however, was too great to enable her Majesty to repair conveniently to the House of Lords when her trial should be in progress. The widow of Sir Philip Francis had compassion upon her, and made her an offer, promptly accepted, of the widow's mansion in St. James's Square. It was next to that of her great enemy, Lord Castlereagh; and to reach the House of Lords she would daily have to pass Carlton House, the residence of the husband who was so blindly bent upon consigning her to infamy.

In the midst of these preparations for a great event died a princess as unfortunate as Caroline, but one who bore her trials with more wisdom. The Duchess of York, the wife of the second son of Queen Charlotte, died on Friday, the 6th of August. Her married life had been unhappy, and every day of it was a disgrace to her profligate, unprincipled, and good-tempered husband. She endured the sorrows which were of his inflicting with a silent dignity and some eccentricity. In her seclusion at Oatlands this amiable, patient, and much-loved lady passed a brief career, marked by active beneficence. Her blue eyes, fair hair, and light complexion are still favourite themes of admiration with those who have reason to gratefully remember her. A great portion of her income was expended in founding and maintaining schools, encouraging benefit societies, and relieving the poor and distressed. But her benevolence had an eccentric side, and the indulgence of it was the only indulgence she allowed herself. She loved the brute creation, and had an especial admiration for dogs. Of these she supported a perfect colony; and daily might her canine friends, of every species and in considerable numbers, be seen taking their airing in the park, often with their benevolent hostess leading the way and taking delight in witnessing their gambols. She, perhaps, was the more attached to them because she had been so harshly used by man; and a touch of misanthropy was probably the basis of her regard for animals. The progeny of her established favourites were boarded out among the villagers, and in the park was a cemetery solely devoted as the burial-ground of her quadruped friends. They rested beneath small tombstones, which bore the names, age, and characters of the canine departed. In these things may be seen the weak side of her character; but it was a weakness that might be easily pardoned. Her character had its firm, and perhaps humorous, side. She had patronised a party of strolling actors, and sent her foreign servants, who could comprehend little, to listen to the moan of Shakspeare murdered in a barn. Shortly after, an earnest and itinerant Wesleyan hired the same locality, and the Duchess ordered the household down to listen to the sermon. The foreigners among them pleaded their ignorance of the language as an excuse for not going. 'No, no,' said the Duchess; 'you were ready enough to go to the play, and you shall also go to the preaching. I am going myself;'—and in the barn at Weybridge the official successor of John Wesley expounded Scripture to the lineal successor of Frederick the Great.

She had not the spirit of Caroline, and was all the happier for it. The latter, indeed, was more harshly tried, but she in some degree provoked the trial, and was now suffering the consequences of the provocation. The Queen gave a few days to retirement, in consequence of the death of the Duchess; and, this duty performed, she was again in public, working with energy and determination to accomplish the restoration of a name which had been tarnished by her own indiscretion. And indiscretion is perhaps one of the most ruinous ingredients in a character. It is a torch in the hand of the careless, firing the very garments of the bearer.

The addresses to the Queen now became greater in number and stronger in language. The replies to them also became more energetic and menacing in expression. They were still popularly ascribed to Dr. Parr, and, from whomsoever proceeding, the author very well kept in view the personage for whom and the circumstances under which he was speaking. Thus, to the deputation from Canterbury, one paragraph of the royal reply was in these words: 'When my accusers offered to load me with wealth, on condition of depriving me of honour, my habitual disinterestedness and my conscious integrity made me spurn the golden lure. My enemies have not yet taught me that wealth is desirable when it is coupled with infamy.' This was something of self-laudation; but in answer to the Norwich address the Queen directed attention from herself to the perils which menaced the State through her prosecution. The manner of that prosecution was described by her as ultimately threatening the vital interests of individual and general liberty. 'The question at this moment is not merely whether the Queen shall have her rights, but whether the rights of any individual in the kingdom shall be free from violation.' There was more dignity in this sentiment and language than in the Queen's letter addressed to the King. Of course this epistle was not the Queen's, but a mere manufacture, which the King, naturally enough, would not read, or at least would not acknowledge that he *had* read. 'Your court became much less a scene of polished manners and of refined intercourse than of low intrigue and scurrility. Spies, bacchanalians, tale-bearers, and foul conspirators swarmed in those places which had before been the resort of sobriety, virtue, and honour.' But the object of the letter was less to contrast the Regent's court with that of the Queen Charlotte than to protest against the constitution of the court before which she was to be tried. In that court, she said, her accusers were her judges; the ministers who had precondemned her commanded the majority; and the husband who sought to destroy her exercised an influence there perilous to the fair award of justice. She demanded to be tried according to law: 'You have left me nothing but my innocence,' she remarked, 'and you would now, by a mockery of justice, deprive me of the reputation of possessing even that.'

In the reply to the Middlesex address occurs the sole

admission of blame attaching to her through indiscretion. 'My frank and unreserved disposition may, at times, have laid my conduct open to the misrepresentations of my adversaries.' But 'I am what I seem, and seem what I am. I feel no fear, except it be the fear that my character be not sufficiently investigated. I challenge every inquiry. I deprecate not the most vigilant scrutiny.' Against the method of carrying on the scrutiny she continued to protest most heartily. 'In the bill of Pains and Penalties,' she replied to the address from Shoreditch, 'my adversaries first condemn me without proof, and then, with a sort of novel refinement in legislative science, proceed to inquire whether there is any proof to justify the condemnation.' To the more directly popular mind, to the address of the artisans, for instance, she delivered an answer in which there is the following passage: 'Who does not see that it is not owing to the wisdom of the Deity, but to the hard-heartedness of the oppressors, when the sweat of the brow during the day is followed by the tear at its close?' This was stirring up popular opinion against the King, of whom she invariably spoke as her 'oppressor.' She, however, as significantly directed the public wrath against the peers in her reply to the Hammersmith address, wherein she says: 'To have been one of the peers who, after accusing and condemning, affected to sit in judgment on Queen Caroline, will be a sure passport to the splendid notoriety of everlasting shame.' The married ladies of London went up to her with an address of encouragement and sympathy. Her answer to this document contained an asseveration that she was not unworthy of the sympathy of English matrons. 'I shall never sacrifice that honour,' she observed, 'which is the glory of a woman. . . . I can never be debased while I observe the great maxim of respecting myself.' An eye-witness well remembers seeing several of these ladies (principally wives of small shopkeepers) descend from the hackney coaches in which they were conveyed to Brandenburgh House. They descended the steps as a man comes down a ladder! The Queen's answer to them was, however, full of dignity. But her reply to the inhabitants of Greenwich had even more of the matter in it that would sink deep in the bosoms of mothers. After alluding to the period when she was living happily with her daughter, among those who were now addressing her, she added: 'Can I ever be unmindful that it was a period when I could behold that countenance which I never beheld without vivid delight, and to hear that voice which to my fond ear was like music breathing over violets? Can I forget? No; my soul will never suffer me to forget that, when the cold remains of the beloved object were deposited in the tomb, the malice of my persecutors would not even suffer the name of the mother to be inscribed upon the coffin of her child. Of all the indignities I have experienced, this is one which, minute as it may seem, has affected me as much as all the rest. But if it were minute, it was not so to my agonising sensibility.' But she observed in her reply to the Barnard Castle address: 'My conscience is without a pang—and what have I to fear?' Her Majesty at the same time seldom allowed an opportunity to escape of placing the King in, if the phrase may be allowed, a metaphorical pillory. 'To pretend,' she thus spoke to the Bethnal Green deputation, 'that his Majesty is not a party, and the sole complaining party, in this great question, is to render the whole business a mere mockery. His Majesty either does or does not desire the divorce which the bill of Pains and Penalties proposes to accomplish. If his Majesty does not desire the divorce, it is certain that the State does not desire it in his stead; and if the divorce is the desire of his Majesty, his Majesty ought to seek it on the same terms as his subjects; for in a limited monarchy the law is one and the same for all.' In the answer to the people of Sheffield the same spirit is manifested. 'It would have been well for me,' she exclaims, 'and perhaps not ill for the country, if my oppressor had been as far from malice as myself; for what is it but malice of the most unmixed nature and the most unrelenting character which has infested my path and waylaid my steps during a long period of twenty-five years?' Her complaint was, that during that quarter of a century her adversaries had treated her as if she had been insensible to the value of character. 'For why else,' she asks, in addressing the Reading deputation, 'why else should they have invited me to bring it to market, and let it be estimated by gold? But—a good name is better than riches. I do not dread poverty, but I loathe turpitude, and I think death preferable to shame.' Finally, she flattered the popular ear by placing all the authorities in the realm below that of the sovereign people. In her reply to one of the City Ward addresses occurs the assertion that, 'If the power of king, lords, and commons is limited by the fundamental laws of the realm, their acts are not binding when they exceed those limitations. If it be asked: "What then?—are kings, lords, and commons answerable to any higher authority?" I distinctly answer, *yes*. "To what higher authority?" "To that of God and of the people."' Lord John Russell, too, told the King that the crown was held at the will and pleasure of the parliament; and the Queen, speaking on that hint, now maintained that crown and parliament were, under certain contingencies, beneath the heel of the *peuple souverain*.

It perplexed many of the clergy that the Princess of Wales should be continued to be prayed for up to the period of George III.'s death, but that Queen Caroline should not be named in the Liturgy after the decease of the only true friend she ever had in the royal family. One military chaplain, a Mr. Gillespie, of a Scotch Yeomanry regiment, was put under arrest for daring to invoke a blessing upon her in his extemporary prayer for the royal family; but this was the only penalty inflicted for the so-called offence.

CHAPTER X.

THE QUEEN'S TRIAL.

The Queen's reception by the House of Lords—Royal progress to the House—The Queen's enthusiastic reception by the populace—Their treatment of the King's party—Marquis of Anglesea—The Duke of Wellington's reply to them—The Attorney-General's opening speech—Examination of Theodore Majocchi—The Queen overcome at the ingratitude of this knowing rogue—Disgusting nature of the evidence—Other witnesses examined—Mr. Brougham's fearless defence of the Queen—Mr. Denman's advocacy not less bold—His denunciation of the Duke of Clarence—Question of throwing up the bill entertained by Ministers—Stormy debates—Lords Grey and Grosvenor in favour of the Queen—Duke of Montrose against her—Ministerial majority—The Queen protests against the proceedings—The Ministers in a minority—The bill surrendered by Lord Liverpool—Reception of the news by the Queen—Her unspeakable grief.

THE Queen's trial, as the proceedings in the House of Lords were called, commenced on the 17th of August. 'Now we are in for it, Mr. Denman,' said her Majesty's Attorney-General to her Solicitor-General. With what spirit Brougham went in for it has been left on record by Lord Denman himself, in the 'Memoir' edited by Sir Joseph Arnould.

'Let me here state, once for all, that from this moment I am sure that Brougham thought of nothing but serving and saving his client. I, who saw him more nearly than any man, can bear witness that from the period in question his whole powers were devoted to her safety and welfare. He felt that the battle must be fought, and resolved to fight it manfully and " to the utterance."'

The Queen had signified her intention of attending

daily in the House during the proceedings, and suitable accommodation and attendance were provided for her. In the House, at all events, she was treated as Queen-consort, and she more than once adverted to the fact when about to take her seat on the throne-like chair and cushion placed at her disposal, near her counsel. Her usual course was to come up from Brandenburgh House early in the morning to the residence of Lady Francis in St. James's Square. From the latter place she proceeded, in as much 'state' as could be got up with her diminished means, to the House of Lords. On these occasions she was attended by Lady Anne Hamilton, her chamberlains, Sir W. Gell and Mr. Keppel Craven, and Alderman Wood, who invariably endeavoured to have the honour of escorting the Queen into the House, but was as invariably forbidden to pass in that way by the local authorities. The alderman, being a member of parliament, was compelled to pass through the entrance allotted to the 'Commons;' and the Queen, who was received with military honours, was usually led into the House, or to the apartment assigned to her use, by Sir Thomas Tyrwhitt and Mr. Brougham, each holding her by a hand.

The royal progress from St. James's Square to the House of Peers and the return were daily witnessed by a dense multitude, and hailed with acclamations. The Queen thought the popular sympathy for her far stronger than it really was. It did not indeed want for earnestness, intensity, or honesty, but it did not go deep enough to urge the multitude to make any serious demonstration in her favour. They cheered her as she passed, cheered the soldiers who saluted her, and hissed those who failed to show her that mark of respect. They hissed or cheered the peers on their arrival according as they knew that they were opponents or supporters of the Queen. They were especially delighted when they succeeded in compelling a lordly adversary to shout, or seem to shout, for the Queen. They strove mightily to bring the Marquis of Anglesea to this; but on his assertion that rather than do a thing against his inclination they might run him through the body, they laughed, cheered, and let him pass on. The Duke of Wellington served those who assailed him quite as characteristically: he was violently hissed on his way to the House on the first day of the trial; he checked his horse for a moment, looked round with a half-smile, as if the people had been guilty of some absurd mistake, and then quietly walked his horse onward. On another occasion, as he was returning from the House, the mob insisted upon his crying 'The Queen! the Queen!' 'Yes, yes!' was his reply; but his persecutors were not content therewith, and continued to assail him as he rode slowly forward. At length, wearied with their importunity, he is said to have turned to his assailants and exclaimed, 'Very well; the Queen then, and may all your wives be like her!'

Caroline was early in her attendance on the 17th of August. She entered the House at ten o'clock, while the names of the peers were being called over. She wore a black satin dress, with a white veil over a plain laced cap. The whole body of peers rose to receive her, and she acknowledged the courtesy with that dignity which she could well assume, and which she could so readily throw off.

It was not till the 19th of August that the case was actually opened by the Attorney-General. The preliminary proceedings were not, however, of much interest, save on the part of the Duke of Leinster, who attempted by motion to get rid of the bill at once, in which he failed, all parties being nearly agreed that there was now no possibility of retrocession. The second incident of interest was in the speech of Mr. Brougham against the bill, and the method by which it sought to crush his illustrious client. While praising her self-denying generosity, which induced her to refrain from all recrimination, he ably adverted to the anomaly of the accused person in a case of divorce being prevented from showing the guilt of her accuser.

On the 19th the Attorney-General opened his case. He professed his conviction that he should state nothing which he could not substantiate on proof, and, reviewing the general course of the Queen's life abroad, he deduced from it that she had been guilty of conduct which stamped her with shame as Princess and as woman. Caroline entered the House towards the conclusion of his speech, shortly after which he introduced the first of the batch of Italian witnesses lodged near the House, in Cotton Garden, and whose presence there was sufficient to render uneasy the spirit of the philosopher who gave his name to the spot, and the wreck of whose library is among the richest treasures of the British Museum.

The entrance of the first witness gave rise to an incident dramatic in its effect. He was the celebrated Theodore Majocchi, and he no sooner appeared at the bar than the Queen, overcome, as it would seem, at seeing one who owed her much gratitude arrayed against her, exclaimed '*Oh, traditore!* (oh, traitor!)' and, hurrying from the scene, took refuge in her apartment, from which she did not again issue except to return home. The chief points supposed to have been established by Majocchi were that on the deck of the polacca Bergami slept at night beneath the tent wherein the Princess also slept, and that the same individual attended her when she was in the bath. The tent was partially open in the hot climate beneath which the wayfarers were travelling, and in the bath the Princess wore a bathing dress, so that, if the indiscretion was undoubtedly great, indecorum was not (it was suggested) very seriously injured. Of the remainder of Majocchi's evidence it has been well remarked, by one who heard it, that 'all his subsequent assertions did not, in consequence of what he implied by this statement, weigh the worth of two straws with me, for it was of the nature of inference, and deduced by the imagination. Besides, I do think he was a knowing rogue, who forgot to remember many things which perhaps might have changed the hue of his insinuations. I do not say that what he did say was not sufficient to induce a strong suspicion of guilt itself in the members of an English society; but this is the very thing complained of. The Queen was in *foreign* society, in peculiar circumstances, and yet our state Solomons judge of her conduct as if she had been among the English.'[1] The remark is worth something, for even at so short a distance from town as Ramsgate Sands the law of modesty does not appear to be the same as it is in other parts of England; and as for the incident of the bath, our grandfathers and grandmothers, in the heyday of their youth, used to walk in couples in the 'Baths of Bath,' and no one presumed to take offence at the proceeding. The writer last quoted further remarks, as a matter worthy of observation, that Majocchi did not appear to be 'at all shocked or shamefaced at what he said.' The inference deduced is that the witness had been 'taught to dwell so particularly on uncomely things by one who did know how much they would revolt the English.'

It would indeed be revolting to go through all the evidence: it must suffice to tread our way through it as lightly and as quickly as possible. All the government witnesses deposed to an ostentation of criminality in parties who, if guilty, must have been most deeply

---

[1] Letter in 'Diary illustrative of the Court, &c., of George IV.'

interested in concealing all evidences of guilt, and one of whom at least knew that she was constantly watched and daily reported of. This contradiction very soon struck Lord Eldon himself, who intimated that some measures should be taken to punish perjury, if it could be proved to have been committed. It is certain that the King's case was materially damaged at a very early stage of the proceedings, not only by discrepancy in the evidence, but by the suspicious alacrity of the witnesses in tendering it.

A close watcher of Majocchi, when giving his evidence, says: 'I cannot understand why so much importance is attached to the evidence of Majocchi. He did not state any one thing that indicated a remembrance of his having put a sense of indecorum on the conduct of the Queen at the time to which he referred; and in this, I think, the want of tact in those who arranged the case is glaringly obvious. As men they could not but have often seen that it is the nature of recollected transactions to affect the expression of the physiognomy, and particularly of those kinds of transactions which the *traditore* knew he was called to prove; yet in no one instance did Majocchi show that there was an image in his mind, even while uttering what were thought the most sensual demonstrations. In all the most particular instances that pointed to guilt he was as abstract as Euclid; a logarithmic transcendent could not have been more bodiless than the memory of his recollections. I do not say that he was taught by others, but I affirm that he spoke by rote.'[1]

Many of the servants examined swore positively to much unseemliness of demeanour between Bergami and the Princess, and some went very much further than this. Of these, several confessed to being hostile to the courier;

[1] 'Diary,' &c.

some were jealous of him; but they all, despite some discrepancy of detail, kept to the leading points of their evidence, which was destructive to the reputation of the Princess.

Captain Briggs and Captain Pechell, with whom she had sailed, deposed to some folly, but no positive guilt. Something was attempted to be made out of the arrangement of the respective berths on board the ship commanded by the first officer, but with no remarkable success. The captain of the polacca gave evidence that was much more damaging, with reference to the unseemliness of sleeping on deck, beneath a tent—for which the heat of the atmosphere and the horses and mules that were below deck hardly offered sufficient authority. Again, there was testimony of such disgraceful conduct at inns that, if it be accepted, no other conclusion can be arrived at than that those guilty of it must not only have been lost to all sense of shame, but eager that their iniquity should be a spectacle to all beholders. 'As the whole case now is,' says a contemporary writer, 'by making it more gross than in all human probability it could be, the evidence, where it might otherwise be trusted, is rendered unworthy of credit.'

But there were incidents in the drama that were not all for the audience. 'Nature,' says the writer of the 'Supplementary Letters' annexed to the 'Diary Illustrative of the Court of George IV.,' 'often mixes up the sublime and the ridiculous helplessly, as it would seem; and I met to-day with a curious instance of her indifference. I forget how it happened, but I was driven accidentally against a curtain, and saw, in consequence, behind it Lord Castlereagh, sitting on a stair by himself, holding his hand to his ear, to *keep* the sound and words of the evidence which the witness under examination at the bar was giving. Notwithstanding the moody wrath of my ruminations, I could not help laughing at the discovery, and his lordship looked equally amused, and was quite as much discomposed. He smiled, and I withdrew. I met him afterwards in the lobby of the House of Commons, when he again smiled.'

Masons, painters, whitewashers, and waiters vied, or seemed to vie, with each other in the dirty character of their depositions. Rastelli, a groom, but discarded as a thief, did not go further, but both sides evidently considered him as an unmitigated scoundrel, and he was somehow permitted to disappear, as if either side was anxious to be rid of him. Scarcely more respectable was the woman Dumont, who dwelt on the abominations to which she swore as if she loved thinking of them. She was worse than the boatmen, bakers, and others with aliases to their names, who, however, deposed to circumstances sufficiently gross in character, and drew dreadfully strong inferences from generally slender but occasionally very suspicious premises.

The loathsome mass was got through by the 7th of September, when the House adjourned till the 3rd of October. The members needed breathing time, and all parties, the public included, stood in urgent need of that peculiar civet whose virtue, according to the poet, lies in its power to sweeten the imagination.

The course of the trial exhibited more than one trait illustrative of the English Bar, and also of individuals. Thus, in the interim between the closing of the King's case and the opening of the Queen's defence by Mr. Brougham, the last-named gentleman went down to Yorkshire to attend the assizes there. The chief advocate of one Sovereign against another was there engaged in a cause on behalf of an old woman upon whose *pig-cot* a trespass had been committed. The tenement in question was on the border of a common of one hundred acres, upon five yards of which it was alleged to have unduly encroached, and was therefore pulled down by the landlord. The poor woman sought for damages, she having held occupation by a yearly rental of sixpence, and sixpence on entering. The learned counsel pleaded his poor client's cause successfully, and, having procured for her the value of her levelled pig-cot, some forty shillings, he returned to town to endeavour to plead as successfully the cause of the Queen. The re-opening of the case took place on the 3rd of October. Before Mr. Brougham rose to speak, Lord Liverpool made severe introductory remarks, for the purpose of disavowing all improper dealing with the witnesses on the part of Government. He also expressed his readiness to exhibit an account of all moneys paid to the witnesses in support of the bill.

Mr. Brougham then entered on the Queen's defence in a speech of great boldness and power. The sentiments put forth in that oration were probably not endorsed by *Lord* Brougham. He declared, too, that nothing should prevent him from fulfilling his duty, and that he would recriminate upon the King if he found it necessary to do so. The threat gave some uneasiness to ministers, but they trusted, nevertheless, to the learned counsel's discretion. He would have been justified in the public mind if he had realised his promise. The popular opinion, however, hardly supported him in what followed, when he declared that an English advocate could look to nothing but the rights of his client, and that, even if the country itself should suffer, his feelings as a patriot must give way to his professional obligations. This was only one of many instances of the abuse of the very extensively abused and widely misunderstood maxim of *Fiat justitia ruat cœlum*.

Denman's famous speech, which many peers thought superior to Brougham's, was partly prepared, as to some of its points, at one of the 'Sundays' he used to spend at Holland House. There, Denman, after suggestions from Dr. Parr, resolved to draw a parallel between Caroline and Octavia, George and Nero. And this he did with such effect as regards George IV. that, veiled as the most personal allusion was, the King never forgot him who made it.

Mr. Denman, the Queen's solicitor-general, was not less legally audacious, if one may so speak, than his great leader. In a voice of thunder, and in presence of the assembled peerage of the realm, he denounced one of the King's brothers as a calumniator. Mr. Rush, who was present on the occasion, says, ' the words were, " Come forth, THOU SLANDERER!"—a denunciation,' he goes on to say, ' the more severe from the sarcasm with which it was done, and the turn of his eye towards its object.' That object was the Duke of Clarence; and in reference to the exclamation, and the fierce spirit of the hour generally, Mr. Rush says: ' Even after the whole trial had ended, Sir Francis Burdett, just out of prison for one libel, proclaimed aloud to his constituents, and had it printed in all the papers, that the ministers ALL DESERVED TO BE HANGED. This tempest of abuse, incessantly directed against the King and all who stood by him, was borne during several months, without the slightest attempt to check or punish it; and it is too prominent a fact to be left unnoticed that the same advocate who so fearlessly uttered the above denunciation was made attorney-general when the prince of the blood who was the OBJECT OF IT sat upon the throne, and was subsequently raised to the still higher dignity of lord chief justice.'

By the end of the third day of the defence the testimony had assumed so favourable an aspect for the Queen that ministers began to deliberate upon the question of throwing up the bill altogether. During the following fortnight, however, the subsequent testimony was not so decidedly contradictory of what the witnesses on the other side had sworn to, and the government then decided that the bill should take its course. The first witness was a Mr. Lemann, clerk to the Queen's solicitor. His deposition was to the effect that he had been sent to Baden to solicit the attendance of Baron Dante, the Grand Duke's chamberlain. The baron, who was proprietor of an estate in Hanover, and who consulted his memoranda before answering the solicitation, finally, and under sanction, if not order, of his ducal master, refused to attend as a witness. Colonel St. Leger simply proved that he did not resign his appointment in the Queen's household from any knowledge of her having conducted herself improperly, but on account of ill health. The Earl of Guildford spoke to the general propriety of the Queen's conduct abroad while under his observation; and Lord Glenbervie showed that the royal reputation had not been dimmed, in his eyes at least, during his residence in Italy, or otherwise he would not have permitted Lady Glenbervie to act, even for a brief time, as lady-in-waiting to the Princess. Lady Charlotte Lindsay deposed to having heard reports unfavourably affecting that reputation, but she had never seen anything to confirm them. Persons of inferior rank, in attendance on the Princess, deposed to the same effect. The testimony of Dr. Holland and Mr. Mills was of a highly favourable character, exact and decisive. The evidence of other witnesses was equally favourable to the character and conduct of the courier chamberlain; and, partly in answer to the evidence which spoke of her Royal Highness receiving strangers in her sleeping apartments, the Earl of Llandaff, who had resided in Italy with his lady and family, showed that such a circumstance was a part of the custom of Italy. Mr. Keppel Craven, who had originally engaged

Bergami for the service of the Princess, declared that the individual in question brought excellent testimonials with him, and that he was of respectable family and behaved with propriety. Mr. Craven added that he had heard much about spies, and that he had admonished the Princess touching the being seen with Bergami in attendance as a servant. This evidence was corroborated by that of Sir W. Gell. A writer, commenting upon the testimony of these witnesses and that given on the other side, remarks : that the witnesses on the King's side ' told improbable stories, and none of them had the look of speaking from recollection . . there is a visible difference between the expression of the countenance in telling a recollection and an imagination, especially such stories as they told.'

It was further proved that, if Bergami kissed the Princess's hand, he did no more than what was commonly done by respectable Italian servants by way of homage to their mistress.

This 'plain sailing' was, however, somewhat marred by the contradictory evidence of Lieutenant Flynn ; and even that of Lieutenant Hownam was sufficient to show that the Princess, if not the most gross, was certainly the most indiscreet, of ladies. Other witnesses spoke to dresses and dances, which had been described as disgraceful in their character, being really harmless ; and others again showed that certain unedifying sights could not have been seen by the witnesses who had sworn to having been spectators of them from the place in which they stood. Again, the evidence did not lack which proved the purchasing of testimony on the other side, and some excitement was raised when, on the presence of Rastelli being required, it was found that he had been permitted to leave the country. In the opinion of some,

[1] The 'Diary,' &c.

he had been conveyed away by the prosecuting party. A few thought he had disappeared with the connivance of both sides.

The entire evidence was closed on the 30th of October. Allusion has been already made to Mr. Denman's speech, which was ably made, now, in summing up the evidence for the defence. It closed rather unaptly in terms, the remembrance of which embittered many years of the speaker's life—for it seemed to undo all that had been previously said and done: 'This, my Lords, is the highest tribunal on earth; it can only be exceeded by that where all the world shall be judged, and the secrets of all hearts laid open. I invoke you, my Lords, therefore, to imitate the wisdom, justice, and beneficence of that high and sacred Authority who said to the woman brought before him : "If no accuser come forward, neither will I condemn thee. Go in peace, and sin no more." '

The Lords adjourned to the 2nd of November, from which day to the 6th the peers were engaged in debates upon the evidence, almost every member assigning reasons for the vote he intended to give. Mr. Rush describes the character of the debates as the case approached its close. It was 'stormy' in the extreme. 'Earl Grey declared that, if their lordships passed the bill, it would prove the most disastrous step the House had ever taken. Earl Grosvenor said that, feeling as he did the evils which the erasure of the Queen's name from the Liturgy (a measure taken before her trial came on) was likely to entail upon the nation, as well as its repugnance to law and justice, he would, had he been Archbishop of Canterbury, have thrown the Prayer-book in the King's face sooner than have consented to it. On the other hand, the Duke of Montrose said, even after the ministers had abandoned the bill, that, so convinced was he of her guilt, whatever others might think to do, he, for one, would never acknowledge her as his Queen.'

The bill, however, was not yet abandoned. The House divided on the 6th of the month, on the second reading, which was carried by 123 to 95, giving ministers a majority of 28. The Queen immediately signed a protest against the nature of the proceeding. The document terminated with these words: 'She now most deliberately, and before God, asserts that she is wholly innocent of the crime laid to her charge, and she awaits with unabated confidence the final result of this unparalleled investigation'—and as she signed the protest she exclaimed, with a dash of her pen, ' there, " Caroline *regina*," in spite of them.'

By a clever manœuvre of her friends the ministers were next cast into a minority. The House had gone into committee on the divorce clause. The clause was distasteful to some of the bishops. Dr. Howley, indeed, is said to have held that the King could do no wrong, even if he broke the seventh commandment. Others, however, thought that a man so notoriously guilty in that respect was not justified in seeking to destroy his wife, even if she were as guilty as *he* was. The clause was objected to by many peers, and *popularly* it was distasteful for something of the same reasons. The ministers, thinking to gain a point by abandoning a clause, moved the omission of this very clause of divorce. But the Queen's friends immediately saw that, by the retaining of the clause, the bishops and others who preferred the bill without it would be less likely to vote for the passing of the bill itself. They accordingly voted that the divorce clause should be retained, and the ministers, in a minority on this point, proposed the third reading of the bill with the clause in question in the body of it. One hundred and eight voted for it, and ninety-nine against it. The ministry were thus only in a majority of nine—exactly the number of the peers who were members of the cabinet—and after a short delay Lord Liverpool made a merit of surrendering the measure as an offering to popular feeling, although they had carried the bill—with too small a majority, as he confessed, to enable ministers to act upon it.

The Queen was in her own apartment in the House of Lords when the intelligence was brought her by her excited counsel that the bill of Pains and Penalties had been abandoned. She received the intimation in perfect silence, hardly seeming to comprehend the fact, or perhaps scarcely knowing how it should be appreciated. The ministers had carried their bill, but even their withdrawing of it would not prove her guiltless. 'I shall never forget,' says one present, 'what was my emotion when it was announced to me that the bill of Pains and Penalties was to be abandoned. I was walking towards the west end of the long corridor of the House of Lords, wrapt in reverie, when one of the door-keepers touched me on the shoulder and told me the news. I turned instantly to go back into the House, when I met the Queen coming out alone from her waiting-room, preceded by an usher. She had been there unknown to me. I stopped involuntarily. I could not, indeed, proceed, for she had a *dazed* look, more tragical than consternation: she passed me. The usher pushed open the folding doors of the great staircase; she began to descend, and I followed instinctively two or three steps behind her. She was evidently all shuddering, and she took hold of the bannisters, pausing for a moment. Oh, that sudden clutch with which she caught the railing! Never say again to me that any actor can feel like a principal. It was a visible manifestation of unspeakable grief—an echoing of the voice of the soul. Four or five persons came in from below before she reached the bottom of the stairs. I think Alderman Wood was one of them, but I was in indescribable confusion. . . I rushed past, and out into the hastily-assembling crowd. . . I knew not where I was; but in a moment a shouting in the balcony above, on which a number of gentlemen from the interior of the House were gathering, roused me. The multitude then began to cheer, but at first there was a kind of stupor. The sympathy, however, soon became general, and, winged by the voice, soon spread up the street. Every one instantly, between Charing Cross and Whitehall, turned and came rushing down, filling Old and New Palace Yards as if a deluge was unsluiced.'[1]

It was asked by many why Bergami himself had not been summoned to deny upon oath any charge of guilt with the Queen, but Mr. Denman had given sufficient reason in his speech. 'If,' he said, ' any *man* guilty of the charge was examined he would deny it. I firmly believe the feeling among mankind in such a case would triumph over morality. It would be found better to violate the oath than betray the victim.' This is, doubtless, true; but like the concluding sentence of Denman's speech, already quoted, it seemed to some persons to damage as much as defend. The Queen had said, in her fear of her attorney-general, ' If my head is placed on Temple Bar, it will be through Mr. Brougham.' She stood in greater peril from the studied words of Denman than from the unpremeditated and impetuous utterances of Brougham. The Queen's own utterances did not want for boldness. It is reported of her having said at the time of the trial that she was, perhaps, not altogether blameless, since she had certainly lived with Mrs. Fitzherbert's husband !

[1] 'Diary of Court, &c., of George IV.'

CHAPTER XI.

'TRISTIS GLORIA.'

The result of the Queen's trial advantageous to neither party—The Queen's application to Parliament for a residence—Lord Liverpool's reply—Royal message from the Queen to Parliament, and its discourteous reception—The Queen goes to St. Paul's to return thanks—Uncharitable conduct of the Cathedral authorities—Their unseemly behaviour rebuked by the Lord Mayor—Revenue for the Queen recommended by the King—Accepted by her—The Coronation of George IV.—The Queen claims a right to take part in the ceremony—Her right discussed—Not allowed—Determines to be present—The Queen appears at the Abbey, and is refused admittance—With a broken spirit retires—Her sense of degradation—The King labours to give *éclat* to his Coronation—The Coronation-festival in Westminster Hall described—Appearance of the Duke of Wellington—His banquet to the King—The King's speech on the occasion—True greatness of the Duke—Anecdote of Louis XIV. and Lord Stair—Regal banquet to the foreign ministers—The Duke of Wellington appears as an Austrian general—Incident of the Coronation—Lord Londonderry's banquet to the minister of Louis Napoleon.

THE Queen was in tears when the 'people' were rejoicing, less certainly for her sake than for the popular victory which had been achieved. There was nothing in the issue of the trial for any party to rejoice at. The ministry could not exult, for although they had carried the bill which declared the Queen worthy of degradation from her rights and privileges, rank and station, yet they refrained from acting upon it, because the popular voice was hoarse with menace, so unfairly had the case of the two antagonists been tried before the august tribunal of the peers.

The popular voice had been heeded, and was satisfied with the triumph. Caroline must have felt that she was really of but secondary account in the matter, that the victory was not for her, and that, righteously or unrighteously, her reputation had been irretrievably shaken into ruins.

Her great spirit, however, was as yet undaunted. The bill was no sooner withdrawn than she formally applied to Lord Liverpool to be furnished with a fitting place of residence and a suitable provision. The premier's reply informed her Majesty that the King was by no means disposed to permit her to reside in any of the royal palaces, but that the pecuniary allowance which she had hitherto enjoyed would be continued to her until parliament should again meet for the regular despatch of business. Caroline, determined to harass her husband, next sent the following note to the prime minister:—' The Queen requests Lord Liverpool to inform his Majesty of the Queen's intention to present herself next Thursday in person at the King's Drawing-room, to have the opportunity of presenting a petition to his Majesty for obtaining her rights.'

The following humiliating minute was accordingly made to guide the King:—' If the Queen should decline delivering her petition into any hands but the King's, the King should not be advised to permit her to come up to the Drawing-room, but should himself go down to the room where the Queen is, attended by such of his household and his ministers as may be there, and receive the petition.'

The then present parliament was about to be prorogued, and the Queen was resolved that, if possible, that body should not separate until it had granted her what, as Queen-consort, she had a right to demand. Her solicitor-general, accordingly, went down to the Commons with a royal message, which he was not permitted to deliver. The House probably never presented such a scene as that disgraceful one of the night of the 23rd of November. Mr. Denman stood with the Queen's letter in his hand; he was perfectly in order, but the Speaker chose rather to obey that brought by the usher of the black rod, summoning the members to attend at the bar of the Lords and listen to the prorogation. The Speaker hurried out of the House, and the Queen's message was virtually flung into the street. The public, however, knew that its chief object was to announce the Queen's refusal of any allowance or accommodation made to her as by ministerial bounty. She still claimed the restoration of her name to the Liturgy, and a revenue becoming her recognised rank as Queen-consort.

In the meantime she publicly partook of the Holy Communion at the parish church of Hammersmith, a proceeding which many persons considered as a new protestation of her innocence. The admirers of coincidences affected to have found a remarkable one in the first lesson for the day, on this occasion (Isaiah lix.); and particularly in the verse which declares that 'Judgment is turned away backward, and justice standeth afar off, for truth is fallen into the street, and equity cannot enter.' This was considered as applicable to the Queen's case, but, as its applicability presented itself in a double sense, every one construed it as he thought best.

Caroline's next step was to proceed to St. Paul's in solemn, public array, to return thanks for her escape from the meshes constructed for her by her enemies. Due notice was given of her Majesty's intention and object to the Cathedral authorities, and the day appointed by her was the 29th of November. The intimation excited in those authorities neither admiration nor respect. Even the dean, the mild and virtuous Van Mildert, seemed to think that it was highly unbecoming in the Queen to be grateful for the dispensations of Heaven. The whole chapter thought, or were taught to think, that there was no greater nuisance upon earth than for this woman to come to St. Paul's and thank God that he had not allowed her enemies to prevail over her. Those who may have any doubt as to these being the capitular sentiments are referred to the 'Life of Lord Sidmouth,' by Dean Pellew, who records with emphatic approval what the good, but mistaken, Van Mildert very uncharitably said and did upon the occasion.

The Corporation of London were anxious to facilitate the Queen's object; the Chapter of St. Paul's, under pressure from very high authority without, resolved to do all they could to impede it. They determined that nothing should be changed in the ordinary service; that the Queen's presence or purpose should in no way be recognised; that the doors should be thrown open to the rush of Queen and *canaille* indiscriminately; and that the mayor and corporation should be held responsible for the safety of the Cathedral.

The chief magistrate and his council soon, however, brought the chapter to a more proper sense of seemliness. The latter body indeed would not yield on any really ecclesiastical point; but they agreed that certain arrangements might be made by the mayor and his corporate brothers for the better maintenance of the decorum, dignity, and decency becoming so solemn an occasion.

The dean was satisfied that the unwashed artisans— the unclean public generally—would make of the day a 'saturnalia,' a festival of obscene desecration. The public, it is to be hoped, pleasingly surprised him. It generally comports itself with propriety when it descends in countless masses into the streets to form a portion of the solemnity, partly actors, partly spectators, on great occasions. The people never behaved with more decency than they did on this day.

The circumstance was really solemn, but there were matters about it that robbed it of some of its solemnity. It was solemn to see a Queen proceeding alone, as it may be said, but through myriads of people, to acknowledge publicly the mercies of Heaven. Lady Anne Hamilton was her solitary female English attendant; but every woman who witnessed her progress either praised or pitied her that day. Her 'procession' was made up of very slender material, though all her court followed her in the person of Mr. Vice-Chamberlain Craven. This little company, however, was swollen by numerous additions on the way; members of parliament, among others, Sir Robert Wilson, Mr. Hume, and Mr. John Cam Hobhouse, lent some dignity by their presence. Horsemen fell into the line, vehicles of every degree took up their following, and the 'trades' marshalled themselves, either in joining the march or drawing up to greet the pious Queen as she passed upon her way. Among these, perhaps, the solemnity most suffered. Some very ill-favoured individuals shouted for her Majesty beneath banners which declared, 'Thus shall it be done to the woman whom the people delight to honour.' The braziers added a joke to the occasion by raising a flag over their position at the end of Bridge Street, on which it was recorded that 'The Queen's Guards are Men of Metal.'

With the addition of the ordinary civic pomp the Queen arrived at the Cathedral, where she was received with affectionate respect by her friends, and with some show of courtesy by the ecclesiastical authorities, who had wiled away the time previous to her arrival by squabbling rather too loudly for the place and occasion with the corporation present.

The usual service was then proceeded with, and again the coincidence hunters sought for their favourite spoil. They found abundance of what they desired in the hundred-

and-fortieth and the following psalms. But of these the phrases cut both ways, and perhaps there was no passage more personally applicable to the Queen, and some of those friends less in deed than in word, than where it is written, 'Oh let not my heart be inclined to *any* evil thing; let me not be occupied in ungodly works with the men that work wickedness, lest I eat such things as please them. Let the righteous rather smite me friendly, and reprove me. *But* let not their precious balsam break my head; yea, I will pray yet against their wickedness.' No especial form of thanksgiving was made use of in her Majesty's name, but this was not needed. It was, however, imperative upon the clergy officiating to read the parenthetical clause in the General Thanksgiving prayer, which has immediate reference to the individual who desires to make an offering of human gratitude to God. This clause, however, was omitted! The Queen-consort of England was upon her knees upon the floor of the Cathedral, but the officiating minister virtually looked up to Him, and standing between Caroline and her Creator, exclaimed, 'Lord, she is not here!' The omission of the clause was tantamount to this. The people behaved better than the priests on that day; and yet it was one on which the priests might have found occasion to give valuable instruction to the people. Those of St. Paul's mistook their mission on the day in question.

This spiritual matter ended, the temporal welfare of the Queen had to be looked to. If she could have existed upon good wishes, she would have been wealthy, for never did congratulatory addresses pour in upon her as at the end of this year and the beginning of that which followed. But she needed something more substantial than good wishes, and the King himself acknowledged as much in a speech from the throne, delivered on the re-opening of parliament in January, 1821. His Majesty recommended that a separate provision should be made for the Queen-consort. She instantly declared her refusal of any provision that was not accompanied by the restoration of her name in the Liturgy, The condition was peremptorily declined by the government, and the income of 50,000*l*. a year was then accepted by the Queen. In this step she disappointed numberless friends, who would not have contributed a farthing to her maintenance. But stern necessity broke the pride of the poor lady, who was beginning to feel that a banker without 'effects' for her use was a worse thing than a Liturgy without her name. Her increased revenue enabled her to bear the expenses of a town establishment, which she now formed at Cambridge House, South Audley Street, but her favourite residence was still that on the banks of the Thames.

Early in May, 1821, the ceremony of the King's coronation began to be spoken of as an event that was about to take place. Caroline did not forget that she was Queen-consort. She immediately addressed Lord Liverpool, claiming to take part in the ceremony. The claim was made literally in these words:—'The Queen, from circumstances, being obliged to remain in England, she requests of the King will be pleased to command those ladies of the first rank his Majesty may think the most proper in the realm to attend the Queen on the day of the Coronation, of which her Majesty is informed is now fixed, and also to name such ladies which will be required to bear her Majesty's train on that day. The Queen, being particularly anxious to submit to the good taste of his Majesty, most earnestly entreats the King to inform the Queen in what dress the King wishes the Queen to appear in on that day at the Coronation.' The premier replied that, as his Majesty had determined that the Queen should form no part of the ceremonial of the coronation, it was his royal pleasure that she should not even attend the ceremony itself. Ever active when she could inflict annoyance on the King by claiming what she very well knew he would never concede, she succeeded in obtaining a hearing for her legal advisers in her behalf before the Privy Council. They served her to the best of their ability, but in truth they had no right upon their side, and the arguments which they raised to prove what could not be demonstrated fell down as rapidly as they were constructed. Mr. Brougham deduced a presumed right from a curious fact, from a circumstance of a law being passed in the year 784 *excluding* Queen Adelberga from the ceremony of being crowned Queen of the West Saxons, because she had murdered a former husband. The most early instance in which the title of Queen is given to a wife of a King of Wessex in any contemporary document occurs in the reign of Edmund, A.D. 945. The West Saxons, it will be remembered, had well-nigh dethroned Ethelwolf for crowning his wife Judith, on the ground that by so doing he had violated the laws of the West Saxons, made by them on the death of their King Bertric. 'It has been supposed,' says Lingard, in his History of the Anglo-Saxon Church, 'that Queens were crowned, because in some MSS. the order for the coronation of a Queen follows that for the coronation of a King; but this proves only that both orders were contained in the original from which the copy was made.' The same writer also states that the little Queen Judith was so beloved that the people ultimately acquiesced in her coronation without a murmur. Mr. Brougham never pleaded a cause more unsuccessfully than on this day. Mr. Denman, the Queen's solicitor-general, was, if not more successful, at least infinitely more reasonable. He grounded his application upon the simple and incontrovertible fact, that the Queen was in so unfortunate a position as to be unable to waive any right she considered she possessed without being exposed to the most injurious imputations. 'He begged to impress upon their lordships, as well as upon the country, that the claim of his illustrious client was put forth in self-defence, because her Majesty could not forego that claim without hazarding her reputation or sacrificing her honour, which, to her, was dearer than life itself.'

The King's attorney-general showed that, if claim there were, it rested solely on usage, and that here the law of usage was without application, as a coronation of a Queen-consort was not a right, but a mere favour conferred by the King. The Queen, in short, could no more *demand* her own coronation than she could that of the King. The Privy Council made a report accordingly; it was approved by the King, and a copy was transmitted to Viscount Hood. The purport of it was—that, as the queens consort of this realm are not entitled of right to be crowned at any time, it followed that her Majesty Queen Caroline was not entitled as of right to be crowned at the time specified in her Majesty's memorial. The conclusion was disagreeable, but it was inevitable. They who thought, however, that it would silence the Queen for ever, were much mistaken. If she could not form a part of the ceremony, she could mar it by her presence; and this she resolved to effect. An announcement was made to Lord Sidmouth of the Queen's intention to be present at the coronation on the 19th of July, and she demanded that a suitable place might be appointed for her accordingly. The noble lord, in a letter commencing 'Madam,' and terminating without the signature of the writer, informs the Queen that it was not his Majesty's intention to comply with the application contained in her letter.

The Queen was none the less bent upon appearing in the Abbey, and due notification of the fact was made to

the Duke of Norfolk, as earl marshal of England, with
the request added that his grace would order persons to
be in attendance to conduct the Queen to her seat. The
earl marshal transmitted the letter containing the notifi
cation and request to Lord Howard of Effingham, who
was the 'acting earl marshal' on the day in question,
and that official 'made his humble representations to her
Majesty of the impossibility, under existing circumstances,
of his having the honour of obeying her Majesty's commands.' Her Majesty, however, was not so easily got
rid of. She now addressed a note to the Archbishop of
Canterbury, informing him of her desire to be crowned,
some day after the King, and before the arrangements
for the previous ceremony had been done away with.
The lord primate humbly replied that he was the King's
servant, and was ready to obey any commands that he
might receive from his royal master. Thus foiled once
more, the Queen issued a protest against the proceedings.
This document was drawn up by the law-advisers of her
Majesty. It re-asserted that the Queen could claim as of
right to be crowned, and yet it admitted that there had
been cases in which the exercise of the right 'was from
necessity suspended, or from motives of policy checked;'
and though perhaps not in the sense in which it was
understood by the Queen's council, the King now saw
that there was a 'necessity' for the suspension of the
right claimed, and that there were 'motives of policy,'
as well as of personal feeling, for declining to authorise
the exercise of it. The protest was addressed to the
King, from whom, says the royal protester, 'the Queen
has experienced only the bitter disappointment of every
hope she had indulged;' but—and it was in such phrases
she was made to represent the nation as hostile against
the King—'in the attachment of the people she has found
that powerful and decided protection which has ever been
her ready support and unfailing consolation.'

Her Majesty's legal advisers supposed, at least they hoped, that she had now done enough for her dignity, and that with this protest would end all further prosecution of a matter which could not be carried further without much peril to that dignity and to her self-respect. But even *they* did not know of what metal she was made. On the coronation day she was up with the dawn, determined to penetrate into the Abbey, or resolved to test the popular attachment, the powerful and decided protection of the people, the ready support of the public, of which she boasted in her last protest, and see if, upon one or other of these visionary essences, she could not be borne to the end which she ardently desired. Her health had already begun to suffer from the effects of the unsettled and agitated career through which she had passed, but her resolution was above all thoughts of health. She was like the sick gladiator, determined to stand in the arena, trusting to the chance of striking an effective blow and yet almost assured that defeat was certain.

At six o'clock in the morning, the poor Queen, in a carriage drawn by six horses, and with Lord and Lady Hood and Lady Anne Hamilton in attendance upon her, proceeded down to Westminster. The acclamations of the people hailed her on her way, and she reached the front of Westminster Hall without obstruction. If many a shout here welcomed her as she descended from her carriage, there was something like fear, too, in many a breast, lest the incident, peaceful as it seemed, should not end peacefully. After some hesitation, Caroline, attended as above mentioned, advanced to the doors of the Hall, amid much confusion, both of people and soldiery—the first were eager to witness the result, the second were uncertain how to act, and their leaders appeared as uncertain how to direct them. The officer on guard respectfully declined allowing her to pass, even though she were, as she said, Queen of England. He could only obey his orders, and they were to this effect: to give passage to no one whatever who was not the bearer of a ticket. The Queen turned away, disappointed, proceeded on foot to other doors, and encountered only similar results. It was a pitiable sight to see her, hurrying along the platform by which her husband was presently to march in gorgeous array, seeking for permission to pass the way she would go, ejected alike wherever she made the application, forced back in one direction by officers in authority, and turned off the platform, not roughly, but yet turned off, by the common men; and not an arm of the multitude, upon whose aid she reckoned, was raised to help her to her end. They pitied her, perhaps, but as her presence there promised to mar the splendour of which they hoped to be spectators, they wished she were gone, and rather tolerated than encouraged her.

Never was Queen cast so low as she, when, flurried, fevered, now in tears and now hysterically laughing, she stood at the door of the Abbey haggling with the official who acted as porter, and striving to force or win her way into the interior. The chief of the 'door-keepers' demanded to see her ticket, but Lord Hood claimed exemption for her on account of her recognised rank: the door-keeper would not recognise the claim. 'This is your Queen!' said Lord Hood. 'Yes, I am your Queen; will you admit me?' The assertion and the request were repeatedly made, but always with the same effect. No passage could be given without the indispensable ticket. Lord Hood possessed one, and the Queen appeared for a moment inclined to pass in with that. But her heart failed her, and, half-laughing, to hide perhaps what she could not conceal, her half-crying, she declined to go in without her ladies. Finally, a superior officer appeared, and respectfully intimated that no preparations whatever had been made for the accommodation of her Majesty; upon which, after looking around her, as if searching for suggestions or help from the people, and finding no encouragement, she assented to Lord Hood's proposition, that it were better for her to enter her carriage and return home.

She had dared the hazard of the die: the cast had been unfortunate. She, for the first time, felt degraded, and she withdrew, still, like the gladiator from the arena, conscious of bearing the wound of which death must ultimately and speedily come.

Meanwhile, let us tarry for a moment at the Hall and the Abbey. It is not likely that England will ever again behold such a scene of coronation splendour as that of George IV., and it is quite certain that England would not care to do so. The national taste does not merely regulate itself by the national purse, but by general principle; and it is an incontrovertible fact, that the outlay of millions for the crowning of one man involves the violation of a principle which the nation desires to see respected.

Never did sovereign labour as George IV. laboured to give *éclat* to the entire ceremony. He passed days and nights with his familiar friends in discussing questions of dress, colours, fashions, and effects. His own costume was to him a subject of intense anxiety, and when his costly habits were completed, so desirous was he to witness their effect that, according to the gossip of the day, a court-gossip which was not groundless, his Majesty had one of his own servants attired in the royal garments, and the King contemplated with considerable satisfaction the sight of a menial pacing up and down the room in the monarch's garb. The man did his office with as much mock gravity as the dramatic King, Mr. Elliston, when he showered tipsy benedictions upon the public as he crossed the platform over the pit of Drury Lane.

But it is true in real things as it is in tragedies, that
'the King' is not necessarily the principal character.
Even in a ballet the sovereign is less cared for than the
chief dancer who cuts *entrechats* in his presence. So at
the coronation festival of George IV., although he was
first in rank and as princely as any in bearing, he was
very far from being the first in consequence or the foremost man in the people's love. This matter is admirably
put by Mr. Rush, the American ambassador to our court,
who witnessed the ceremony, and made a very nice distinction as to the true position of the principal actors in
it. In his account of the scene the amiable and accomplished diplomatist remarks that the chief splendour of
the day, where all wore an air of joy and animation, was
in the Hall. 'The table for the King's banquet,' he
remarks, ' was spread on the royal platform ; the foreign
ambassadors and ministers had theirs in the painted
chamber of the house of lords, a communicating apartment under the same roof—but we ran from it soon to
come into the hall, the centre of all attraction. The
peeresses, peers, and others associated with them had theirs
in the body of the hall. Here six long tables were laid,
three on each side, leaving a vista, or aisle, open in the
middle, which directly fronted the royal platform. The
platform and all the seats were covered with crimson,
which, with the peeresses richly dressed, and the plate on
the banqueting-tables, and the company all seated, with
the King at the head of his sumptuous table, shaped as a
crescent, so that he and a few seated on his right and left
faced the whole company, made the spectacle extremely
magnificent. The comptroller and clerk of the kitchen,
and purveyor of wines, had not, as may be imagined,
overlooked their duties. But when the Champion appeared
at the opposite extremity of the hall, directly in front of
the King, nothing seen at first but tufts of plumes waving

from his horse's head and his own helmet, startling emotions arose in every bosom. Curiosity was breathless to see what was coming. He was attended by Howard of Effingham, and by Anglesea, and by another greater than all—the DUKE OF WELLINGTON; and as these, all on horseback, entered abreast, the Champion heralding his challenge, and the horses seeming almost in contact with the outward line of peeresses at the table, yet obedient to the bit which they kept champing—as this equestrian train slowly advanced in martial grace and strength up the aisle towards the King, all eyes were seen turned upon one man in it. In vain did the declining sun through the vast old Gothic edifice throw beams upon the bright and heavy armour of the Champion; in vain was it, when the horses reaching by slow, impatient steps the top of the aisle, and proudly halting at the steps of the royal platform, that the stout-clad Champion again put forth his challenge, threw down his glove, received the cup *from* his sovereign, and drank *to* his sovereign—in vain all this; the beauty and chivalry at the banqueting-tables still looked at the Duke of Wellington; still kept their eyes on the man whose person and horse recalled, not war in romance, but its stern and recent realities. All were at gaze—fixed, silent. He was habited only as a peer, had only his staff as Lord High Constable, yet was he the observed of all. Nowhere was he more intently eyed than from the box where sat the assembled ambassadors of the potentates of Europe. Judging from opinion in that box, there was nothing in the elaborate grandeur of the day to rival the scene. It was the inherent pre-eminence of a great man exalting moral admiration above the show of the whole kingdom.' This was the imperative fact. The King was the great figure of the hour, but the Duke was the great hero of the age; and the truth was not lost sight of in the gorgeous splendour of the spectacle.

To do the King justice, it must be confessed that he was among the first to acknowledge the pre-eminence of the Duke as regarded his services and merits. At the dinner given by the Duke of Wellington, a few days after the coronation, in honour of the new sovereign, and with that monarch as chief guest, this acknowledgment was very gracefully made. At this splendid banquet, after the noble host had proposed the health of his royal guest—a toast that was drunk all standing and all silent, the King himself merely rising to bow his thanks to the company—George IV. in turn proposed, in a brief speech, the health of the Duke. 'The purport of his remarks,' says Mr. Rush, who was present at this interesting festival, was, 'that, had it not been for the exertions of his friend upon the left (it was so that he spoke of the Duke), he, the King, might not have had the happiness of meeting those whom he now saw around him at that table; it was, therefore, with particular pleasure that he proposed his health. The King spoke his words with emphasis and great apparent pleasure. The Duke made no reply, but took in respectful silence what was said. The King continued sitting while he spoke, as did the company, in profound silence under his words.'

The silence of the host was true courtesy. It has not escaped Mr. Rush's discernment. 'I thought,' he says, 'of Johnson, when George III. complimented him: the innate dignity of great minds is the same. In Johnson it was that of the rough, virtuous recluse—whose greatness was that of the author. In Wellington it was externally moulded into the will which armies and courts, and long association with the *élite* of mankind, may be supposed to give. Johnson did not bandy civilities with his Sovereign, whom he had never seen before; nor did Wellington, who saw him every day!' It is ever the same with true gentlemen.

It would seem, however, that all the nobles who shone at the coronation festivities of George IV. were not so perfect in politeness as the warrior-duke. King George IV. gave a banquet to the ambassadors specially sent to grace the high solemnity of the coronation. To this banquet the foreign ministers generally and the members of the cabinet were invited and were present. The American Ambassador sat next to Lord Londonderry, and the two discussed between themselves the power, pretensions, and infamy of Russia, Lord Londonderry affecting to trust to the moderation of the Muscovite—a moderation which has been more truly described by Lord John Russell as more menacing than the ambition of other powers. The conversation then fell upon English society; and while on this theme Lord Londonderry remarked, 'that the higher the rank and education, the better bred, as a general rule, their people in England—so he believed it was considered.' Setting aside the fact that this is only partially true, it was at the same time a most uncourteous remark to be made by one who was high in rank and education to a commoner. But the Stewart-Castlereaghs have ever been unlucky in their civilities, and with their precious balsams they have too often bruised the heads they would only have anointed. Witness the fact of the banquet given by the late Marquis of Londonderry to the ambassador of Louis Napoleon. Everything was well done but one, and that one thing, ill done, marred all besides that was well. The room in which the English host welcomed his French guest was decorated with pierced and battered French cuirasses, which had covered the breasts of gallant French enemies at Waterloo. The man who is fortunate enough to kill an adversary in a duel may, possibly, in after years, be reconciled with that adversary's brother, and perhaps entertain him at dinner; but he would hardly think of hanging up the dead man's clothes (purchased as a trophy from his valet) in his dining-room.

The grand banquet at Carlton House was given on the 26th July. The special and ordinary ambassadors and the ministers were present. The monarch's brothers were also among the guests—always excepting the Duke of Sussex, whose sympathies for Queen Caroline had been too markedly and publicly expressed.

'We were invited,' says Mr. Rush, 'at seven o'clock. As my carriage turned into Pall Mall from the foot of St. James's Street, the old clock at St. James's struck seven, and before I reached Carlton Palace all the carriages appeared to be entering or coming out through the double gates of the Ionic screen in front of the palace. Mine was among the last that drove up to the portico, and by a very few minutes past seven all the guests, save one, were assembled in the reception rooms. I had never before witnessed such punctuality at any dinner in England.

'The King entered a minute or two afterwards, and saluted his guests generally, then went the rounds, speaking to each individually. With the special ambassadors he paused longest. Time had now run on to more than a quarter past seven, still one of the guests had not yet arrived, and that one was the Duke of Wellington. The man not apt to be behind time when his Majesty's enemies were to be met was, it seems, in meeting his friends. Five minutes more went by, and still no Duke of Wellington; critical moments when each one seemed to count two. At length, in one of the rooms at a distance, the Duke was seen; he was dressed in the uniform of an Austrian field-marshal, a plain round-about jacket of white cloth and white under-dress to suit, relieved by scarcely anything but his sword. The dress, being tight and simple, gave to his person a thinner look than usual; and as he kept advancing with easy step, quite alone, and a general silence prevailing, the King separated himself from the group of ambassadors where he was standing, and when he got near enough stepped forward to meet him. With both hands he shook the Duke by both with great cordiality, saying something which the company could not hear, but which, from the manner, we took to be a good-natured rally upon his late arrival. The Duke received it with placid composure, made no reply, but bowed. When liberated from the friendly grasp of the King, he approached a circle of which I happened to be one. One of the ministers composing it said to him, " We hope you will forgive our little treason, my Lord Duke, but we have just been determining that, as some one of the company was to be too late, it was best to have fallen to your Grace's lot, who can so well bear it." With a half whisper and an arch smile, the Duke replied, " The King knows I could have been here sooner but for attending to some of his Majesty's business." This, considering the Duke as a cabinet minister and privy councillor, had doubtless been sufficient to excuse his delinquency, and secure for him the very cordial reception all had witnessed. . . The entire dinner-service was of gold. Each of the salt-cellars, as well as I could catch the design, represented a small rock in dead gold, on which reclined a sea-nymph holding in her hand a shell, which held the salt. One of these was before every two guests; so it was, as to number, with the gold coolers down the sides, containing wine. The whole table, sideboard, and room had an air of chaste and solid grandeur, not, however, interfering with the restrained enjoyments of a good dinner, of which the King seemed desirous that his foreign guests should in no wise be abridged, for we sat till past ten o'clock.' Contrasting this banquet with the one given by the Duke of Wellington, the same writer and guest remarks that the Duke's table-service was not only brilliant, but that it lighted-up better than the King's; for being entirely of silver, and very profuse, the whole aspect was of pure, glittering white, unlike the slightly-shaded tinges which candles seem to cast from gold plate. The dessert-service at the Duke's was of china, a present from the King of Prussia, and made emblematical of the life of the Duke, commencing with a view of Dangan Castle, the (supposed) birth-place of Arthur Wellesley, and going through a course of views of all the places rendered interesting by his presence or remarkable by his deeds, down to the porcelained pictorial representation of the crowning glory at Waterloo.

While all these matters were in progress, people who nursed superstition were prophesying some calamity to come; and certainly, among the incidents of the coronation of George IV., was one which would have been counted ominous in earlier days. The gallant Marquis of Anglesea was Lord High Steward on that occasion, and it was part of his office to carry the crown up to the altar before the Archbishop placed it on the King's head. It was heavier than the gallant Lord High Steward had reckoned upon, and the glittering crown, ponderous with gold, diamonds, and other precious stones, slipped from his hands. He dexterously recovered it, however, before it reached the ground. Among the medallic records of the time one was the work of an enemy of Caroline of Brunswick. A bronze medal of the time is extant which has the Queen's head, on the obverse, with the inscription: 'CAROLINE, D. G. BRITT. REGINA.' On the reverse is the head of Bergami, with the inscription: 'COUNT B. BERGAMI.'

CHAPTER XII.

A CROWN LOST, AND A GRAVE WON.

The Queen's agitation—Her illness—Her sufferings—Desires her diary may be destroyed—Her death—Sketch of her life—Her mother a foolish woman—Every sense of justice outraged by the King—Inconsistency of the Whigs—The Queen persecuted even after death—Disrespect shown to her remains by the Government—Protest against a disgraceful haste to remove her remains—Course of the funeral procession interrupted by the people—Collision between the military and the populace—Effort to force a way through the people ineffectual—The procession compelled to pass through the City—The plate on the Queen's coffin removed—The funeral reaches Harwich—The Queen's remains taken to Brunswick—Funeral oration—Tombs of the illustrious dead there.

THE coronation-day killed the Queen. The agitations and sufferings of that eventful day called into deadly action the germs of the disease under which she ultimately succumbed. Once only, between that day and her death, did she appear in public, at Drury Lane Theatre, and even then she may be said to have been dying.

On August the 2nd, the first bulletin issued from Brandenburgh House, by 'W. G. Maten, P. Warren, and H. Holland,' announced that her Majesty was suffering from internal inflammation and obstruction. Her sufferings were considerable, but they were borne with resignation; and she even expressed a cheerful readiness to be gone from a world in which she had endured more than she had enjoyed. Her own conviction, from the first, was that her malady would prove fatal. No whisper of hope appeared to deceive or to cheer her. She was determined, as it were, that she must die, and she prepared for the worst. Her feelings were natural to a woman of her disposition and character. She felt that, despite all solemn protestation, notwithstanding all as solemn assertion, she had failed in re-establishing the reputation which she enjoyed during the early years of her residence in this country. The abandonment of the Bill of Pains and Penalties had not rescued her from degradation; and the people, who were ready to offer her consolation as a woman who had been most deeply wronged and outraged, were by no means so ready to espouse her cause further than this. She had herself confessed to indiscretions, and when the confession applies to constant repetition of the offence, the public judgment, even with nothing more to warrant its exercise, will never be slow to hold her who acknowledges so much as being guilty of more. In her position, with a reputation so soiled, and torn, and trodden upon; which could not be made bright by any declaration (poor indeed) that she was not so debased as she was declared to be by her adversaries; for a woman so placed, to die is the sole joy left her, if she has made the peace with God which can never again exist between her and man. Her few friends were accustomed to say that in after years her good fame would be substantiated. After years—alas! Of what use to the drowned sailor is the favourable wind *after* shipwreck? Assuredly, her own character perished more by her own suicidal acts than by the assaults made upon it by those who were interested in damning it; just as 'Tom Paine' himself has said that a writer may destroy his own reputation, which cannot be affected by the pens of other writers.

To die then was now in the very fitness of things, and death made but brief work with his new victim. Between the second and the seventh of August the suffering never ceased sufficiently to warrant serious hope of amelioration.

During the intervening time she continued to express her willingness to depart. She signed her will, gave with calmness all necessary orders which she wished to be observed, spoke charitably of all, and little of herself. Among her last acts was one of sacrifice, and perhaps posterity will regret it. She ordered the diary, which she had long kept, and in which she had entered the characters of the most prominent persons with whom she had come in contact, to be burned. This is said to have been done in her presence; but so many things only seem to be done in a dying presence that our successors may not despair, hereafter, of becoming more intimate with Caroline, her thoughts and feelings, than she ever permitted her contemporaries to be. The great chance against posterity being allowed to read the scandalous chronicle or the justifying confessions of Caroline lies in the fact that the series of journals were burned by a foreign female servant, who knew nothing of their value. Such, at least, was the accredited report.

After nearly five days of intense suffering, the Queen sank into a stupor from which she never awoke. At half-past ten o'clock on the morning of the seventh of August, 1821, 'after an entire absence of sense and faculty for more than two hours,' Caroline Amelia Elizabeth of Brunswick, Queen Consort of George IV., expired almost without a struggle. In her supreme hour only her faithful friends, Lord and Lady Hood and Lady Anne Hamilton, were with her. Her legal and medical advisers, with Alderman Wood and one of his sons, were also near her person. She had completed fifty-three years and three months; of these she passed by far the happier and the more innocent half—happier because the more innocent—in Brunswick. Of the following nineteen years spent in England, eighteen of them were passed in separation from, and most of them in quarrelling with, her husband. For the first nine or ten years of this period she lived without offence and free from suspicion; during the remainder she was struggling to re-establish a fame which had been wrongfully assailed; but this was accompanied by such eccentricity and indiscretion that she seemed almost to justify the suspicion under which she had suffered. Then came the half-dozen years of her residence abroad, when she too often shaped her conduct as though she had alacrity in furnishing matter condemnatory against herself to the spies by whom she was surrounded. To say that they exaggerated her offences does not, unfortunately, prove her guiltless of great crime. Her return to England was a bold step, but it was one she was compelled to take. It failed, however, in its great purpose. She did not triumph. Justice, indeed, was not rendered her, for she was condemned before she was tried; and though the trial was not carried to its intended conclusion, he who would now stand forth as the champion of Caroline of Brunswick would be necessarily accounted of as possessing more generosity than judgment.

Nevertheless, for this poor woman there is something to be said. She was ill-educated; religiously educated, not at all; and never had religious principles as expounded by any particular church. Her mother was a foolish, frivolous woman, and her father, whom she ardently loved, a brave, handsome, vicious man, who made his wife and daughters sit down in company with his mistresses. With such an example before her, what could be expected from an ardent, spirited, idle, and careless girl? Much—if she had been blessed with a husband of principle, a man who would have tempered the ardour to useful ends, guided the spirit to profitable purpose, and taught the careless girl to learn and love the cares, or duties, rather, which belonged to her position. But by whom, and what, was that Princess encountered in England, whither she had come to marry a Prince who had condescended to have her inflicted on him, and bringing with her the memories of pleasant communings with more courteous wooers in Brunswick? She met a husband who consigned her to companionship with women more infamous than ever she herself became, and whose interest and business it was to render the wife disgusting to the husband. They speedily accomplished the end they had in view, and when they had driven the wife from the palace they endeavoured to prove her to be guilty of vices which she had not then, in common with themselves and her husband. If he ever justly complained of wrong, he at least took infinite pains to merit all that was inflicted on him. He outraged every sense of justice when, steeped to the very lips in uncleanness, he demanded that his consort should be rendered for ever infamous, for the alleged commission of acts for which he claimed impunity on his own account. She was not, perhaps, betrayed by the Whigs, but these rather took up her cause for the reason that it served them politically than put credence in its righteousness. They were, however, the voluntary champions of her virtue. Lord Holland was among the first of them, and yet in his contemporary Diary he says of her, 'She was at best a strange woman, and a very sorry and uninteresting heroine. She had, they say, some talent, some pleasantry, some good-humour, and great spirit and courage. But she was utterly destitute of all female delicacy, and exhibited, in the whole course of the transactions relating to herself, very little feeling for anybody, and very little regard for honour and truth, or even for the interests of those who were devoted to her, whether the people in the aggregate, or the individuals who enthusiastically espoused her cause. She avowed her dislike for many, *scarcely concealed her contempt for all*.'

(no wonder); 'in short, to speak plainly, if not mad, she was a very worthless woman.' So wrote one who had asserted directly the contrary.

But it was the lot of this unhappy Queen to be persecuted even after death. Her will, in which she bequeathed the little she had to leave to William Austin, the protégé, who did not long survive her, contained a clause to this effect: 'I desire and direct that my body be not opened, and that three days after my death it be carried to Brunswick for interment, and that the inscription on my coffin be, "Here lies Caroline of Brunswick, the injured Queen of England."'

The government, acting under alleged orders from the King, but influenced, no doubt, by a wish not to mar the festivities attendant upon the visit of George IV. to Ireland, by allowing the Queen's body to remain longer than needful in England, announced their intention to pay every sort of respect to the orders and wishes of her late Majesty, and to despatch the body to Harwich at once, for embarkation. The personal friends of Caroline protested against this unseemly readiness, on the part of the ministers, to obey the wishes of one who, when alive, never had a wish that was not thwarted. Lady Hood addressed a letter to Lord Liverpool, not so much, indeed, as she said to *him*, as to his heart. The letter pleaded for delay, on the ground of the Queen's ladies being unprepared; and it expressly protested against the intended military escort, as being an honour never allowed to the Queen when living, and one not certainly desired by her, who was sufficiently guarded by the people's love. Reply was made that the arrangements already resolved upon were irrevocable, and that, if the ladies were not provided with the necessary mourning, there would be nothing disrespectful in waiting behind till they had been furnished with what was necessary, and then joining in the procession anywhere on its route. There was a singular want of courtesy in all the communications made by the ministry to the friends of the Queen. The latter could not even learn by what route the body would be conveyed to Harwich. The most direct road was through the City of London, and the mayor and corporation had announced their intention to attend on the royal remains on the passage through the City. The government curtly intimated that the funeral *cortège* would not be allowed to pass through the City at all. From the same source it was subsequently learned that the coffin would be carried by the circuitous route of the New Road to Romford, and then by the direct road to Harwich. The popular disgust was justifiably great. Lord Liverpool asserted that he and his colleagues were influenced only by feelings which prompted them to show full respect to the wishes of the deceased Queen. How very little the noble lord was really influenced by the feelings in question may be seen in Dean Pellew's Life of Lord Sidmouth. In that work there is a letter from Lord Liverpool, in which the writer says that he would have despatched the body the whole way by water to Harwich, had he not been afraid of the passage at London Bridge! In other words, he would have paid it as much disrespect as was in his power, only that he feared a popular demonstration of unwelcome character at the bridge.

On the 14th of August, the government authorised the persons employed by them to remove the body from Hammersmith. There had been very scant ceremony displayed in a 'lying in state,' and the preparations now were but of a meagre description. A few tawdry escutcheons, a tinsel coronet, heralds in private dresses, and a military escort, looking mournful rather because of the rain, which fell in torrents, than for any other reason.

When Sir George Naylor, in his official tabard, and

Mr. Bailey, the undertaker, authorised by government to carry out the prescribed arrangements, entered the room where the body lay, in order to remove it, they were met by Dr. Lushington, who stood at the head of a small group of her Majesty's friends, and protested against the intended removal, on account of over-haste, and also against the attendance of the soldiery. 'I enter my solemn protest,' said the doctor, 'in right of the legal power which is vested in me by her late Majesty, as executor. I command that the body be not removed till the arrangements suitable to the rank and dignity of the deceased are made.' Mr. Bailey declared that, with the authority he held, the body must be removed. 'Touch it not, at your peril,' exclaimed Dr. Lushington. Mr. Bailey asked if he intended to use or to recommend violence. The legal executor answered that he would neither assist in nor recommend violence. Whereupon the government officer declared that he should discharge his duty firmly and, he hoped, properly.

But he had to encounter a second duel of words with the other executor, Mr. Wilde, who protested as Dr. Lushington had done, and to as little purpose. Mr. Bailey said that his orders were imperative, and he would take upon himself the responsibility and peril of removing the body.

The procession then set out, and never had Queen a funeral of such strange ceremony and circumstance. The mourners comprised those friends and legal advisers who have been so often named: some of them were not in the mourning coaches, but in their own private carriages. It was a strictly government funeral (the King, it was said, paid all the expenses); but there was a multitude who descended into the streets on that day. There were many among them who deemed that the funeral charges would, after all, be defrayed out of the public pocket.

They were accordingly determined that their own programme should be followed, and that the body of the Queen should be carried through the City of London. The ministers, unwisely, were as obstinately bent in dragging the dead Queen through the outskirts, and getting her to Harwich in as unceremonious a manner as possible. They professed great respect, but it is certain that they meant none, and it was because the people were convinced of this that they occupied the highways on that stormy morning, resolute to bear the inanimate Caroline, as it were, and as she had desired, on the popular shoulders, through the very centre of the great metropolis.

It was between seven and eight o'clock when the funeral procession, escorted by or rather partly made up of, cavalry, passed through Hammersmith. It met with no obstruction until it reached Kensington Church. At this point the first attempt to turn out of the direct road leading to the City, by conducting the *cortège* up Church Street into the Bayswater Road, was met by a hoarse cry of execration on the part of the people. They went further than protest. In a brief space of time the road was dug up, rendered impassable, and obstructed by a barricade that would have won the approval of a Parisian professor of tumults. The military escort kept their places and their tempers; but the Life Guards, with the chief magistrate of Bow Street, Sir Richard Baker, speedily appeared. They saw the uselessness of attempting to force a passage; and when the order was given to proceed in the direct route to London, there broke forth a thundering shout of victory about the hearse of the unconscious Queen, as though expressly raised to give her assurance that the people had compelled respect to her will.

In the Park the multitude had spent many of the morning hours in rushing from the south to the north side, from the north to the south; and again and again repeating the same movement, according as report reached them that the funeral would pass by one or the other line. The issue of the struggle at Kensington having been announced in the Park, the great body of the people there had now moved once more to the south side, and were pouring into the Knightsbridge Road. Meanwhile, orders had been received from ministers, by Sir Richard Baker and the commander of the Life Guards, to lead the procession through the Kensington Gate of Hyde Park into the Edgeware Road. But at the gate the scene which had been enacted at Church Street was replayed with some additions. The people forcibly held the gates closed, placed every impediment in the way which they could collect, and were so fiercely demonstrative with their cry of 'The City! the City!' that magistrate and military again yielded to the popular will, and the body, which had halted amid the tumult, was once again carried forward amid shouts of triumph.

The delay had afforded time to Sir Richard Baker to apply to ministers for fresh instructions. These were forwarded to him in a peremptory order to see that the procession was conducted into the Edgware Road, either by the east side of the Park or through Park Lane. At both points the suspicious and exasperated populace were ready for the expected contest. It was here that the matter assumed a more serious aspect than it had yet worn. The soldiery began to grow chafed at an opposition which, in its turn, began to be emphasised by the employment of missiles. The attempt to pass up the Park was made in vain; that to force Park Lane was equally ineffectual. But while the struggle was raging at the latter point the line of procession was broken, and that part of it near the gate turned into the Park, carrying the hearse with it. The military at Park Lane turned back, followed the successful Mr. Bailey and his followers, and closing the gates upon the public, the body of the Queen was borne, at an unseemly pace, onwards to Cumberland Gate. But the increasingly-excited people were light of foot, and when the head of the funeral line reached Cumberland Gate, with the intention to proceed, not down Oxford Street to the City, but up the Edgware and, subsequently, the New Road, there was a compact mass resolved to give no passage, and determined to carry the royal corpse through the metropolis. It was here that Sir Robert Wilson endeavoured to mediate between the multitude and the military. The commander of the latter had no discretionary power, and could only obey his orders. His men, hitherto, had exhibited great forbearance, but their patience was overcome when they found themselves fairly attacked by the populace at this point. Neither mob nor soldiers were really culpable. The blame rested entirely with the ministry, whose folly and obstinacy had provoked the conflict, and made victims on both sides. The military (by which is to be understood the Life Guards, and not the 'Blues,' who formed part of the procession, and were quiescent throughout the day) at last fired a volley, by which several persons were severely injured, and two men, Francis and Honey, were slain. Not a few of the military were seriously wounded by the missiles flung at them in return, but the hitherto victors were vanquished. They gave way, and across the blood that had been spilt, and among the wounded lying around, the people's Queen, as they called her, was once more carried on the way which the respectful feelings of the ministry taught them it was best for her to go.

The defeat and the victory seemed respectively accepted by the different parties. The individuals having the body in charge, and the escort, pushed hurriedly forward with the hearse towards the New Road. But several of the mourners here left a procession to form part of which was attended with peril to life. The multitude looked moodily on; but suddenly, as if by common impulse, perhaps at suggestion of some shout, they, too, rushed forward, determined to make one more attempt at achieving a victory for themselves and the unconscious Queen.

They who were conducting the body along the New Road towards Romford did not dream of further opposition, and their astonishment was great when, on arriving at Tottenham Court Road, they found all progress, east or northward, completely obstructed, and no way open for them but southward, towards the City. In this direction they were compelled to turn, hailed by the popular exultation, and met with shouts of execration and menace, as they sought, but vainly, at each outlet down the east side of Tottenham Court Road, to find a passage back into the suburban line. In the same way the procession was forced down Drury Lane, into the Strand. Sir Richard Baker did not yield to anything but compulsion, yet he lost his office, as Sir Robert Wilson did his commission, for endeavouring to do his duty under most trying and difficult circumstances. Once in the Strand, the people felt that their victory had been fairly and irrevocably achieved. When the royal body was carried under Temple Bar, its advent there was hailed with such a wild ' hurrah ' as had never met the ears of living sovereign. For seven hours that body had been dragged through wind, and rain, and mud—the King's will drawing it in one direction, the people in another. How much or how little the latter were influenced by earnest attachment to her for whom, dead, they made their demonstration, even to the shedding of blood, it is not easy to say. There is less difficulty in coming to the decision that they who professed to be carrying out the King's commands served him ill, and even perilled his crown on that day. The King himself, however, is known to have been exceedingly wroth against the government for not having employed more stringent measures in order to fulfil his commands. The triumph of a dead wife embittered more than one joyous banquet in the Irish capital.

The civil authorities of the City, hurriedly collected for the occasion, accompanied the royal remains as far as the eastern limit of the City's 'liberty,' Whitechapel. Thence to Romford the funeral train proceeded at a very varied pace, sometimes as slowly as became the solemnity of a funeral, at others the pace would have been counted lively enough for a wedding. At Romford, the mourners who had rejoined the *cortège* passed the night, but the royal corpse was carried on to Colchester, where it rested for the night, in St. Peter's Church.

It was during this night that the silver plate announcing the occupant of the coffin as 'the injured,' or, according to some, 'the murdered, Queen of England,' was affixed to the lid. Whenever this was done the plate was not allowed to remain. It was removed and replaced by another, inscribed simply with the deceased's name and titles and dates, in the usual form. They who have visited the vaults beneath the Church of St. Blaize, the patron of Brunswick, may remember that the marks of the nails which fastened the original plate are still visible.

The journey to Harwich was unmarked by any particular incident, save that everywhere along the route the feeling of curiosity to see the remains of Caroline pass to their last resting-place was accompanied by manifest evidences of respect. Off Harwich were awaiting the *Glasgow* frigate, two sloops of war, three brigs, and the *Pioneer* schooner. The coffin was conveyed to the latter, after being unceremoniously swung into a barge, and from the schooner it was transferred to the *Glasgow*. The little group of mourners followed. They consisted of Lord and

Lady Hood, Lady Anne Hamilton, Mr. Austin, Dr. and Mrs. Lushington, and Count Vassali. Her Majesty's remains were now in charge of Captain Doyle, who, when a midshipman, more than a quarter of a century before, had handed the rope to the royal bride, whereby to help her on board the *Jupiter*. The squadron set sail, under a salute from Languard fort, and at two o'clock p.m., on Sunday, the 19th, it anchored in the harbour of Cuxhaven.

The *Gannet* sloop of war conveyed the body up the Elbe to the mouth of the Schwinde, and up the latter it was carried, with a guard of marines and the mourners, by the boats belonging to the *Wye* sloop, as far as Stade. From this place to Brunswick the body of the unhappy Caroline was borne, by slow journeys, and amid profuse respectful demonstrations on the part of the people. One of its resting-places by the way was at Zell, in the church of which place the body lay for a night upon the tomb of the unfortunate sister of George III., Caroline Matilda Queen of Denmark.

At midnight on Friday, August 24, the last rites were performed over the deceased consort of George IV. The body had been removed from the hearse to a funeral car, which was drawn by some hundred Brunswickers to the cathedral gates. No extraordinary service was allowed to be celebrated at the side of the vault. The Duke of Brunswick was then a minor and an absentee, and the government of the country was administered by the King of England. But though the service was of the most ordinary character, the sexagenarian pastor, Woolf, pronounced an oration above the remains of the Queen. He thanked God for adorning her with high advantages of mind and body, for bestowing upon her a heart full of clemency and benignity, and for placing her where she could, and was resolved to, accomplish much good. But 'unsearchable, O Eternal, are thy ways!' was the perplexed pastor's cry as he adverted to her subsequent career—for terminating which the wisdom of the Almighty was again to be revered.

Among the range of coffins in the vault beneath the cathedral of St. Blaize, at Brunswick, Caroline rests between two which contain two heroic but far from faultless men—her father, who fell at Jena, and her brother, who, at the head of his Black Brunswickers, also fell in avenging him at Waterloo. Speaking of the latter, 'two small black flags,' says Russell, ' the one an offering from the matrons, the other from the maidens of Brunswick, are suspended above his coffin, and its gaudy gold and crimson are still mixed with the brown and withering leaves of the garlands which the love of his people scattered on his bier, when at midnight he was laid among so many of his race who had fought and fell like himself.' Between the coffins of these two lies that of Caroline of Brunswick, between father and brother slain. Her mother died in exile, yet in her own land; and the grave of her murdered sister Charlotte, the first wife of the Prince of Wurtemburg, would be sought for in vain. Surely here was a household sternly dealt with.

On the Sunday following the funeral the venerable pastor, Woolf, preached a sermon appropriate to the event, and which ended in a panegyric on the character of the Queen. The old man, with singular tenacity, clung to the assertion, that in early life 'her quick understanding eagerly received every ray of divine truth, and her warm heart and lively feelings were excited and elevated by piety.' He declared that her sense of religion increased to a confirmed faith, and that pious occupations were dear to her heart. ' I knew her,' said the aged advocate, 'as an enlightened Christian, before she left the country of her birth. She first received from my hands, with pious emotion, the holy Supper of our Lord, and the solemnity of her manner was like her precious devotions, an unsuspected proof of her sincere faith and pious feeling.' The panegyric would have been, like most articles of the kind, far above the merit of the subject, were it not for the strong qualifying sentence in which the preacher acknowledged that 'the sense of religion, it was true, did not always preserve her from infirmities and errors;' but, as he asked after the admission, 'Where is the mortal, where has there been a saint, who has been always perfect? And,' said he, aptly and truly enough, whether addressed to the friends or the foes of the poor, ill-used, and erring Caroline of Brunswick—' And he who erred less may conscientiously ask himself whether he owes that to himself or to his more fortunate situation and the undeserved grace of God?' It is a query which we are all bound to make when viewing a brother or a sister of the human family who is reputed guilty of offence towards God or man. The latter is ever ready to condemn his neighbour, but never ready to pass sentence on himself. Happy for all that with God there is not only judgment but mercy.

There has been some discussion as to whether Caroline of Brunswick was legally married to the Prince of Wales. There is no doubt, however, to be entertained on the matter. Her husband had, unquestionably, previously married a Roman Catholic lady, and that lady was living when the Prince married Caroline of Brunswick.

By the well-known statute of William and Mary, marrying a Roman Catholic entails exclusion from, and incapability ever to inherit, the crown of this realm.

The Prince clearly forfeited his right to the Crown by his marriage with a Papist.

But he married the lady (with the King's connivance, he said) without the King's consent; and, wanting that consent, the marriage (according to the 12th of George III.) was null and void.

This would set aside the marriage, but it would not release the Prince from the consequence of having entered into such a marriage. Horne Tooke was not justified in sneering at the 12th of George III., nor in writing 'legally, really, worthily, and happily for the country, Mrs. Fitzherbert is Her Royal Highness the Princess of Wales.'

The Roman See, it is said, satisfied Mrs. Fitzherbert's scruples by considering the marriage legal. That See never considered any other marriage between such (religious) parties, so celebrated, legal. Had there been issue of such an union, grave peril might have arisen. There was, indeed, a claimant to such honour, but he disappeared. He lacked the power of lying since manifested by Orton and some of the Orton gang. The monument to Mrs. Fitzherbert's memory at Brighton asserts the legality of her marriage with the Prince by the three rings on her finger. That she was as much respected as if her last marriage was as legal as the preceding two there is no shadow of doubt. As little doubt is there that the Prince of Wales was never legally married except to his wayward and unhappy cousin—Caroline of Brunswick.

ADELAIDE OF SAXE-MEINENGEN,
WIFE OF WILLIAM IV.

The pocket Duchy—Old customs—Early training—The Father of the Princess Adelaide—Social life at the ducal court—Training of the Princess Adelaide—Marriage Preliminaries—English parliament—The Duke of Clarence—Arrival in London of the Princess—Quaint royal weddings—At home and abroad—Duke and Duchess of Clarence at Bushey—'State and Dirt' at St. James's—William IV. and Queen Adelaide—Course of life of the new Queen Consort—King's gallantry to an old love—Royal simplicity—The Sovereigns and the Sovereign people — Court anecdotes — Drawing-rooms—Princess Victoria — The coronation—Incidents of the day—Coronation finery of George IV.—Princess Victoria not present—Revolutionary period—Reform question—Unpopularity of the Queen—Attacks against her on the part of the press—Violence of party-spirit—Friends and foes—Bearing of the King and Queen—Duchess of Angoulême—King a republican—His indiscretion—Want of temper—Continental press adverse to the Queen—King's declining health—Conduct of Queen Adelaide—King William's death—Declining health of the Queen—Her travels in search of health—Her last illness—Her will—Death—And funeral.

THE little Duchy of Saxe-Meinengen was once a portion of the inheritance of the princely Franconian house of Henneberg. The failure of the male line transferred it in 1583 to the family of reigning Saxon princes. In 1680 it fell to the third son of the Saxon Duke, Ernest the Pious. The name of this son was Bernard. This Duke is looked upon as the founder of the House of Meinengen. He was much devoted to the study of Alchemy, and was of a pious turn, like his father, as far as may be judged by the volumes of manuscript notes he left behind him—which he had made on the sermons of his various court-preachers.

The law of primogeniture was not yet in force when

Duke Bernard died, in 1706. One consequence was, that Bernard's three sons, with Bernard's brother, ruled the little domain in common. In 1746 the sole surviving brother, Antony Ulrich, the luckiest of this ducal Tontine, was monarch of all he surveyed within a limited space. The conglomerate ducal sovereigns were plain men, formal, much given to ceremony, and not much embarrassed by intellect. There was one man, however, who had enough for them all : namely, George Spanginburg, brother of the Moravian bishop of the latter name, and who was for some time *the* Secretary of State at the court of Saxe-Meinengen.

Antony Ulrich reigned alone from 1746 to 1763. He was of a more enlightened character than any of the preceding princes, had a taste for the arts when he could procure pictures cheaply, and strong inclination towards pretty living pictures, which led to lively rather than pleasant controversies at court. His own marriage with Madame Scharmann disgusted the young ladies of princely houses in Germany, and especially exasperated the aristocracy of Meinengen. They were scarcely pacified by the fact that the issue of the marriage was declared incapable of succeeding to the inheritance.

The latter fell in 1763 to two young brothers, kinsfolk of Antony, and sons of the late Duke of Gotha, who reigned for some years together. The elder, Charles, died in 1782. From that period till 1803 the other brother, George, reigned alone. He had no sooner become sole sovereign than he married the Princess Louisa of Hohenlohe Langenburg. At the end of ten years the first child of this marriage was born, namely Adelaide, the future Queen of England.

Eight years later, in the last year of the last century, A.D. 1800, a male heir to the pocket-duchy was born, and then was introduced into Meinengen the law which fixed the succession in the eldest male heir only. Saxe-Meinengen was the last country in Europe in which this law was established.

The father of the Princess Adelaide, like his brother Charles, was a man of no mean powers. Both were condescending enough to visit even the burgher families of Saxe-Meinengen; and Charles had so little respect for vice in high places that when a German prince acted contrary to the rights of his people the offender found himself soundly lashed in paper and pamphlet, the pseudonymous signature to which could not conceal the person of the writer—the hasty Duke Charles. If this sometimes made him unpopular over the frontier, he was beloved within it. How could the people but love a sovereign Duke who, when a child was born to him, asked citizens of good repute rather than of high rank to come and be gossips?

In the revolutionary war Duke George fought like a hero. At home he afforded refuge to bold but honest writers driven from more mighty states. He beautified his city, improved the country; and, without being of great mental cultivation himself, he loved to collect around him scholars, philosophers, artists, authors, gentlemen. With these he lived on the most familiar terms, and when I say that Schiller and John Paul Richter were of the number, I afford some idea of the society which Duke George cared chiefly to cultivate. He buried his own mother in the common churchyard, because she was worthy, he said, of lying among her own subjects. The majority of these were country folk, but George esteemed the country folk, and at rustic festivals he was not unwilling to share a jug of beer with any of them. Perhaps the rustics loved him more truly than the sages, to whom he proved, occasionally, something wearisome. But these were often hard to please. All, however, felt a honest grief when, on the Christmas night of 1803, Duke George died, after a brief illness, caused, it is said, by a neglected cold, and by rage at an urgent demand from the Kaiser of 60,000 florins, fine-money for knightly orders ducally declined.

The Duke left a young family, Adelaide, Ida, and his son and successor, Bernard, then only three years of age. The mother of these fatherless children took upon herself the office of guardian, with that of Regent of the duchy. The duties of both were performed with rare judgment and firmness, during a time of much trouble and peril, especially when the French armies were overrunning and devastating Germany.

On the young ladies, gently and wisely reared in this little court, Queen Charlotte had begun to look with the foresight of a mother who had elderly and wayward sons to marry. When the death of the Princess Charlotte of Wales threatened to interrupt the direct succession of the crown, the unmatched brothers of the Regent thought of taking unto themselves wives. Cumberland had married according to his, but to no other person's, liking, hardly even that of his wife. The Dukes of Kent and Cambridge made better choice, and there then remained but the sailor-prince to be converted into a Benedick. The Queen selected his bride for him, and he approved or acquiesced in the selection. He might, as far as age goes, have been her father, but that was of small account; and when Adelaide of Saxe-Meiningen was spoken of, men conversant with contemporary history knew her to be the good daughter of an accomplished and an exemplary mother.

The preliminaries of the marriage were carried out amid so much opposition that at one moment the accomplishment of the marriage itself wore a very doubtful aspect. The difficulty was of a pecuniary nature. The

Dukes of Kent and Cambridge were content, on the occasion of their respective marriages, to accept an addition to their income of 6,000*l.* The Duke of Cumberland was compelled to rest content, or otherwise, without any addition at all—save the expenses of a wife. With the Duke of Clarence it was different. He already possessed 18,000*l.* per annum, and ministers resolved, after a private meeting with their supporters, to request the Parliament to allow him an increase of 10,000*l.* On the 13th of April, 1818, a message from the Prince Regent to that effect was submitted to either House by Lord Castlereagh and the Earl of Liverpool. In the Commons the first-named Lord hinted at the dependence of our Princes on the liberality of Parliament since the time when the crown had surrendered its long uncontrolled disposal of revenues. But the House was not to be 'suggested' into a generosity which might be beyond justice. Tierney, the gadfly of his period, complained of the previous meeting of the friends of ministers, and the communication to them, before it was made to the House, of the amount to be applied for. Methuen insisted that before the Commons would grant a farthing they must be made acquainted with all the sources from which the King's sons derived their present revenue, as well as the amount of the revenue itself. Finally, Holme Sumner met the proposal of an additional 10,000*l.* by a counter-proposal of 6,000*l.* This was carried by a narrow majority of one hundred and ninety-three to one hundred and eighty-four, and when this sum was offered to the Duke he peremptorily declined to accept it.

Things did not progress more in tune with marriage-bells in the House of Lords. There, when Lord Liverpool stated what his royal client would be contented to receive, Lord King started to his legs and exclaimed, 'That the question was not what it might please the Duke of Clarence to take, but what it might please the people to give him!' They were not willing to give what he expected, and for a time it seemed as if there would consequently be no marriage with the Princess of Saxe-Meinengen. But only for a time.

'The Duke of Clarence is going to be married, after all,' was a common phrase launched by the newspapers, and taken up by the people, in 1818. If the phrase had but one meaning, it had a double application. In the former sense it had reference to the disinclination of Parliament to increase his income, without which he had expressed his determination not to marry. It was further applied, however, to the old course of his old loves. There were the years spent with Dora Bland, then 'Mrs. Jordan,' the actress—years of an intercourse which had much of the quiet, happy character of a modest English home—the breaking-up of which brought such great grief to the mother in that home that even every service subsequently rendered to her seemed to partake of the quality of offence. It has been registered as such by those who heard more of the wailing of the Ariadne than they knew of the groundlessness of it, when vented in reproaches for leaving her unprovided for as well as deserted.

Then the public remembered how this light-of-heart Duke had been a suitor to other ladies. He was the rival of Wellesley Pole for the favour and the fortune of the great heiress, Miss Tilney Long. That ill-fated lady conferred on this wooer of humbler degree the office of slaying her happiness, sapping her life, and ruining her estate. The other lady, who declined the Duke's offer of his hand or petition for her own, was Miss Sophia Wykeham, of Thame Park, daughter and *sole heiress* of an Oxfordshire 'squire. Each lady had merits of her own, and other attractions besides those which lay in the *beaux yeux de sa cassette;* but perhaps each remembered the clauses of the Royal Marriage Act; however this may have been, Miss Tilney chose between her two suitors, while Miss Wykeham, after turning from the prayer of the Duke, never stooped to listen to a lowlier wooer.

These were the 'antecedents' of the lover who, in mature age, took rather than asked for the hand of Adelaide of Saxe-Meinengen. Of all the actions of his life it was the one which brought him the most happiness; and with that true woman he had better fortune than is altogether merited by a man who, after a long bachelorship of no great repute, settles down in middle-life to respectability and content, under the influences of a virtuous woman, gifted with an excellent degree of common-sense.

In the dusk of a July evening, in the year 1818, this unwooed bride quietly arrived, with her mother, at Grillon's Hotel, Albemarle Street. She had but cool reception for a lady on such mission as her own. There was no one to bid her welcome; the Regent was at Carlton House at dinner, and the Duke of Clarence was out of town on a visit. Except the worthy Mr. Grillon himself, no person seemed the gladder for her coming. In the course of the evening, however, the Regent drove down to Albemarle Street; and at a later hour the more tardy future husband was carried up to the door in a carriage drawn by four horses with as much rapidity as became a presumed lover of his age, in whom a certain show of zeal was becoming.

The strangers became at once acquainted, and acquaintance is said to have developed itself speedily into friendship. The family-party remained together till near upon the 'wee sma' hours; there was much indulgence there, we are told, of good, honest, informal hilarity; and when the illustrious and joyous circle broke up, the easy grace, frankness, and courtesy of the Regent, and the freedom and light-heartedness of the Duke, are said to have left favourable impressions on both the mother and the daughter.

Quaintest of royal weddings was that which now took place in old Kew Palace. Indeed, there were two, for the Duke of Kent, who had gallantly fetched his wife from abroad, where he had married her according to Lutheran rites, was now re-married to his bride according to the forms of the Church of England. Early in the day there was a dinner, at which the most important personages in that day's proceedings were present. The old house at Kew seemed blushing in its reddest of bricks, out of pure enjoyment. The Regent gave the bride away; and, the ceremony concluded, the wedded couples paid a visit to the old Queen in her private apartment. She was too ill then to do more than congratulate her sons, and wish happiness to the married. The Duke and Duchess of Kent thereupon departed, but the Duke and Duchess of Clarence remained—guests at a joyous tea party at which the Regent presided, and which was prepared *al fresco* in the vicinity of the Pagoda. It must have been a thousand times a merrier matter than wedding state-dinners of the olden times, at which brides were wearied into suffering and sulkiness. A more joyous party of noble men and women never met in mirthful green-wood; and when the princely pair took their leave for St. James's, the Regent led the hilarious cheer, and sped them on their way with a 'hurrah!' worthy of his bright and younger days.

The Regent, undoubtedly, manifested a clearer sense of the fitness of things on this occasion than either of the managers of the theatres honoured by the presence of the newly-married couple soon after the union.

At Drury Lane was given the 'Marriage of Figaro,' and Covent Garden complimented the Duke and Duchess with the 'Provoked Husband.'

It cannot be said that the public looked with much enthusiasm on any of the royal marriages. Such unions, with rare exceptions, are unpleasantly free from sentiment or romance; and in the present instances there was such a matter-of-fact air of mere 'business' about these contracts and ceremonies, such an absence of youth and the impulses and the dignity of youth, that the indifferent public, even remembering the importance of securing a lineal succession to the throne, was slow to offer either congratulation or sympathy. The caricaturists, on the other hand, were busy with a heavy and not very delicate wit; and fashionable papers, uniting implied censure with faint praise, observed that 'the Duchesses of Kent, Clarence, and Cambridge are very deficient in the English language. They can scarcely speak a sentence. They possess most amiable dispositions.' They also possessed true womanly qualities, which won for them the esteem of their husbands.

After a brief residence at St. James's, and as brief a sojourn at the Duke's residence in Bushey Park, the Duke and Duchess of Clarence repaired to Hanover, and remained there about a year—no incident marking the time is worthy of observation. The issue of this marriage scarcely survived the birth. In March 1819, a daughter was born, but to survive only a few hours. In December 1820, another princess gladdened the hearts of her parents, only to quench the newly-raised joy by her death in March of the following year. The loss was the keener felt because of the hopes that had been raised; and the grief experienced by the Duke and Duchess was tenderly nourished, rather than relieved, by the exquisite art of Chantrey, which, at the command of the parents, reproduced the lost child in marble—sleeping for ever where it lay.

The household at Bushey was admirably regulated by

the Duchess, who had been taught the duties as well as the privileges of greatness. The fixed rule was, never to allow expenditure to exceed income. It is a golden rule which, when observed, renders men, in good truth, as rich as Crœsus. It is a rule which, if universally observed, would render the world prosperous and pauperism a legend. It was a rule the more required to be honoured in this case as the Duke had large calls upon his income. When those were provided for, old liabilities effaced, and current expenses defrayed, the surplus was surrendered to charity. There was no saving for the sake of increase of income—economy was practised for justice-sake, and the Duke and Duchess were so just that they found themselves able to be largely generous. With the increased means placed at their disposal by the death of the Duke of York, there was but trifling increase of expenditure. If something was added to their comforts, *they* benefitted who were employed to procure them; and, if there was some little additional luxury in the rural palace of Bushey, the neighbouring poor were never forgotton in a selfish enjoyment of it.

In 1824, the Duke and Duchess of Clarence had apartments in St. James's Palace, where, however, they seem to have been as roughly accommodated, considering their condition, as any mediæval Prince and Princess in the days of stone walls thinly tapestried and stone floors scantily strewn with rushes. The Duke cared little about the matter himself, but he gallantly supported the claims of his wife. In a letter addressed to Sir William Knighton, the King's privy purse, in 1824, he thus expresses himself —from St. James's Palace:—

'His Majesty having so graciously pleased to listen to my suggestion respecting the alteration for the Hanoverian office at the palace, I venture once more to trouble you on the point of the building intended for that purpose. To the accommodation of the Duchess this additional slip at the back of the present apartments would be most to be wished and desired, and never can make a complete Hanoverian office without our kitchen, which the King has so kindly allowed us to keep. Under this perfect conviction, I venture to apply for this slip of building which was intended for the Hanoverian office. I am confident his Majesty is fully aware of the inconvenience and unfitness of our present apartments here. They were arranged for me in 1809, when I was a bachelor, and without an idea at that time of my ever being married, since which, now fifteen years, nothing has been done to them, and you well know the dirt and unfitness for the Duchess of our present abode. Under these circumstances, I earnestly request, for the sake of the amiable and excellent Duchess, you will, when the King is quite recovered, represent the wretched state and dirt of our apartments, and the infinite advantage this slip would produce to the convenience and comfort of the Duchess. ... God bless the King and yourself, and ever believe me, &c.—WILLIAM.'

Though often as ungrammatical and inelegant, it was seldom the Duke was so explicit in his correspondence as he is in the above letter. Generally, he wrote in ambiguous phrases, very puzzling to the uninitiated; but when his Duchess Adelaide was in question, and her comfort was concerned, he became quite graphic on the 'state and dirt' in which they passed their London days, in the old, dingy, leper-house palace of St. James's.

With the exception of the period during which the Duke held the office of Lord High Admiral, 1827-28— an office which may be said to have been conferred on him by Canning, and of which he was deprived by the Duke of Wellington—with the exception above noted, this royal couple lived in comparative retirement till the 26th of June, 1830, on which day the demise of George IV. summoned them to ascend the throne. During his fatal illness, Mrs. Fitzherbert addressed a letter of sympathy to her old lover, if not husband. She affectionately tendered any service which might be of use to him in his extreme necessity. To this letter no reply ever reached her; but some vestige of human affection was nevertheless evinced by the King on his death-bed. 'He more than once expressed his anxiety,' the 'Memoirs' tell us, 'that a particular picture should be hung round his neck, and deposited with him in the grave.' It seemed to be the opinion of the Duke of Wellington that this portrait was one which had been taken of Mrs. Fitzherbert in early life, and was set round with brilliants. It appeared the more likely, as this portrait was afterwards missing when the others were returned to her. Mrs. Fitzherbert was possessed of an annuity of 6,000*l.*, settled on her by George the Fourth, which she enjoyed to the year of her death, 1833.

It is said that when the news of the death of George IV. was announced to the Duchess of Clarence the new Queen burst into tears. The prayer-book she held in her hand at the moment she conferred on the noble messenger, as a memorial of the incident and of her regret. The messenger looked, perhaps, for a more costly guerdon; but she was thinking only of her higher and stranger duties. If Queen Adelaide really regretted that these now had claims upon her, not less was their advent regretted by certain of the labouring poor of Bushey, whose harvest-homes had never been so joyous as since the Duke and Duchess of Clarence had been living among them.

The course of life of the new Queen was only changed in degree. Her income was larger, so also were her charities. Her time had more calls upon it, but her cheerfulness was not diminished. Her evenings were generally given up to tapestry work, and as she bent over the frame many of the circle around her already sorrowingly remarked that the new Queen, though not old in years, seemed descending into the vale of life.

The esteem of her husband for her was equal to her merits. His affection and respect were boundless; and when the senate granted her, on the motion of Lord Althorpe, 100,000l. per annum, with Marlborough House and Bushey Park, in case she survived the King, the good old monarch was the first to congratulate her, and was pleased to put her in office himself, by appointing her Perpetual Ranger of the Park, which was to become her own at his decease.

William IV. was not forgetful of his old loves, and Queen Adelaide was not jealous of such memories. She looked more indulgently than the general public did on the ennobling of his children of the Jordan family. If that step could have been met by objections in these later days, it was at least supported by that amazingly powerful but sometimes perilous engine, precedent. Though indeed there was precedent for the contrary; and perhaps the husband of Queen Adelaide would have manifested a greater sense of propriety on this occasion had he rather followed the decent example, in a like matter, of the scrupulous Richard the Third than that of Henry the Eighth or the Second Charles.

There was another ennobling, however, which the public as warmly approved as the Queen heartily sanctioned. In 1834, her husband raised to the dignity of a Baroness the lady who had declined to share with him whatever of higher or more equivocal honour he could have conferred by marrying her. In that year Miss Wykeham became, by the grateful memory and good taste of her old royal lover, Baroness Wenman of Thame Park, Oxon. This testimony of the memory of an old affection was an act to be honoured by a Queen, and to it that royal homage was freely tendered. Inquirers, on turning over the peerage books, may discover many honours conferred on women too ready to listen to the suit of a monarch; but here, for the first time, was a title of nobility presented to a lady who had declined to give ear to royal suit, paid in honesty and honour. Baroness Wenman bore her honours with grace and dignity till her death, in 1870.

There was something chivalrous in the bearing of the King towards ladies; hearty, but a courteous heartiness. This sort of tribute he loved to render to his wife; and there was nothing so pleasant to hear, in his replies to addresses after his accession, as the gallant allusions to the qualities of the Queen, who stood at his side serenely satisfied. This heartiness was not an affectation in him. It was of his nature; and another phase of his character was manifested by King William at the first dinner after he ascended the throne, at which his relations only were present. On that pleasant occasion, although it was a family dinner, he gave as a toast, 'Family peace and affection;' it was the hearty sentiment of a citizen King who loved quiet and simple ways, who walked the streets with his intimate friends, and often occupied the box-seat of his open carriage, turning round to converse with the Queen inside. King William took much interest in the first lady whom his brother, George IV., had married. Mrs. Fitzherbert resided some part of the year at Brighton. The King visited her, and invited her to the Pavilion. He authorised her to put her servants in the royal livery, and to wear widow's weeds for his late brother. On Mrs. Fitzherbert paying her first homage to Queen Adelaide, the King went down to her carriage to meet her, took her by the hand, and introduced her to his consort and all the members of his family who were present. Mrs. Fitzherbert told Lord Stourton that 'she was herself much surprised at the great composure with which she was able to sustain a trial of fortitude which appeared so alarming at a distance.' After this she was frequently a guest. Queen Adelaide was a gentle hostess, and the royal Sunday dinners were as elegant as they were comfortable. Mrs. Fitzherbert very decidedly declined being made a Duchess.

When Adelaide became Queen-consort some persons who would not have been ill-pleased to see her fail affected to fear that the homely Duchess would prove to be unequal to the exigencies of the queenly character. One exalted person hinted that, in this matter, she would not do ill were she to take counsel of the Princess Elizabeth of Hesse Homburg, 'than whom none could better record to her Majesty the forms and usages and *prescriptions* of the court of Queen Charlotte.' But Queen Adelaide needed no such instruction as the good daughter of George III. could give her. She observed the forms and usages that were worthy of observance; and as for *prescriptions*, she could prescribe readily enough when duty demanded the service, as the Church felt, with mingled feelings, when she declined to invite clergymen to her state balls or her dancing *soirées*. The dancing clergy had their opportunity for censure when the King and Queen gave dinner-parties on the Sunday.

The court was essentially a homely court. The two sovereigns fed thousands of the poor in Windsor Park, and looked on at the feasting. The Queen went shopping to Brighton fancy fairs, and when on one occasion she bent to pick up the 'reticule' which an infirm old lady had dropped, as much was made of it as of the incident of King Francis, who picked up (or did not pick up)

Titian's pencil, and handed it to that sovereign gentleman among artists.

Then the new sovereigns paid more private visits than any pair who had hitherto occupied the British throne. While the Queen called on Sir David and Lady Scott at Brighton, her royal husband, with whom she had just previously been walking on the Esplanade, would suddenly appear at the door of some happy but disconcerted old admiral, and invite the veteran and his wife to dinner. To the hearty 'Come along, directly,' if there was a glance from the lady at her toilet, the citizen King would encourage her by an intimation never to mind it, for he and his wife were quiet people; 'and, indeed,' as he once remarked, 'the Queen does nothing after dinner but embroider flowers.' Which, indeed, was true enough, and, to tell the truth, very dull did the finer people find it.

The consequence of this familiarity of the sovereigns with their humbler friends was a rather audacious familiarity ventured upon by people who left their queer names in the book at the King's door, and more than once successfully passed it, and penetrated to the Queen's drawing-room. This evil, however, was soon remedied. There were other matters Queen Adelaide was bold enough to, at least, attempt to remedy. Indecorousness of dress in a lady she would censure as sharply as Queen Charlotte; and if, when Mrs. Blomfield appeared at her first drawing-room in a 'train of rich immortal velvet,' as the fashionable chroniclers of the day called it, she did not even hint surprise, it was, perhaps, out of respect for the successor of the Apostles, of whom that good but richly velvetted lady was the honoured wife.

The letter-writers who dealt with court incidents at the period of the accession of this domestic couple tell of various illustrations of the simplicity of the new sovereigns. When the Duke of Norfolk had an interview with William IV. at Bushey, on the affair which had brought him thither being concluded, the King declared he must not leave the house without seeing the Queen; and, thereupon ringing the bell, he bade the official who answered the summons to 'tell the Queen I want her.'

This lady, at the time when her husband was Duke of Clarence and Lord High Admiral, had been accustomed, on her visits to Chatham, to be received and entertained by the daughters of the then Commissioner, Cunningham. As soon as the Duchess became Queen, among her first invited visitors to Bushey were these ladies. At the meeting they offered to kiss her Majesty's hand, but 'No, no,' said Queen Adelaide, 'that is not the way I receive my friends. I am not changed;' and therewith ensued a greeting less dignified, but not less sincere.

Queen Adelaide and King William kept a 'state' at Brighton which had a burlesque element in it. They were the last sovereigns who held a court or entertained friends at the Pavilion—that place of big and little domes, which made Lord Alvanley say of it that it looked 'as if St. Paul's had come down to the sea-side and pupped.' It was not etiquette for any guest (of an evening) to stir till Queen and King retired, which was at midnight. On one occasion, when Captain and Mrs. Marryat were present, and anxious to go to a second party, the King remarked that the lady often looked at the clock. Being asked the reason, she frankly told him. 'Why don't you go then?' said his Majesty. 'Sir,' answered the lady, 'we cannot move till her Majesty and yourself have departed.' 'Oh, d—n it!' rejoined the royal sailor, 'take my arm; I'll smuggle you out.' At the Pavilion balls, after the ladies had kissed the Queen's hand, the King kissed the ladies, who then passed into the ball-room, where one of the Fitzclarences used to greet them with : 'Well, has Dad bussed you yet?'

There are other stories told of incidents at Windsor which indicate the difference of the court going out from that of the court coming in. This change required the removal from the palace of a little household, the head lady of which reluctantly gave way to the new Queen. People generally rejoiced in seeing a 'wife' installed where 'queans' used to rule it; and, when William IV. was seen walking arm-in-arm with Watson Taylor or some other happy courtier, they added one incident to the other, and, comparing the new court with the old, exclaimed, 'Here is a change indeed!' No one ever dreamed at that moment that the time would come when party-spirit would stir up the 'mobile' against the sovereigns; that the Queen would be accused of plotting with the Duke of Wellington against reform; that stones would be cast at the royal carriage as it bore the King and his Consort from the theatre; and that, when matters went adversely to the humour of the ultra-chiefs of the popular movement, the first lady in the land should be marked out for vengeance by the famous cry in the *Times*, 'The Queen has done it all!'

The drawing-room at which good Mrs. Blomfield appeared in 'immortal velvet' was remarkable for another incident, related in 'Frazer's Magazine,' by John Wilkes, ex-M.P. for Sudbury, in his 'Regina's Regina':—'The drawing-room of her Majesty Queen Adelaide, held in February, 1831, was the most magnificent which had been seen since that which had taken place on the presentation of the Princess Charlotte of Wales, upon the occasion of her marriage. No drawing-room excited such an interest when compared with that as the one held by Queen Adelaide, at which the Princess Victoria was presented on attaining her twelfth year. It was on this occasion that the Duchess of Kent and her illustrious daughter arrived in state, attended by the Duchess of Northumberland, Lady Charlotte St. Maur, Lady Catherine Parkinson, the Hon. Mrs. Cust, Lady Conroy, La Baronne Letzen, Sir John Conroy, and General Wetheral. This was the first public appearance of the Princess Victoria at court. Her dress was made entirely of articles manufactured in the United Kingdom. Victoria wore a frock of English blonde, simple, modest, and becoming. She was the object of interest and admiration on the part of all assembled, as she stood on the left of her Majesty on the throne. The scene was one of the most splendid ever remembered, and the future Queen of England contemplated all that passed with much dignity, but with evident interest.'

Nearly three-quarters of a century had elapsed since a Queen-consort had been crowned in Great Britain. On the present occasion, such small pomp as there was was confined to the religious part of the ceremony. The procession to and from Westminster Hall, the banquet there, and the dramatic episode of the entry of the Champion were all dispensed with. There was an idea prevalent that the cost would be too great, and that the popular voice would be given to grumble—others thought that money spent in the country, and made to circulate rapidly through many hands, would be a public benefit rather than a public injury. The ministry, however, would only sanction the maimed rites which were actually observed; the privileged people were deprived of many a coveted perquisite which might have dipped deeply into the public purse, and the heir of Marmion and the owner of Scrivelsby kept his horse and his defiance at home in the domain of the Dymokes. The public, cheated of their show, called it a 'half-crownation.'

There was only one incident at this ceremony which

is worth narrating. The Queen-consort's crown was a rich little toy, sparkling but small. It would hardly fit a baby's head, and, accordingly, Queen Adelaide's hair was turned up in a knot, in order that on this knot the little crown might safely rest. The Archbishop of Canterbury, in place of fitting the crown down upon this knot of hair, only lightly placed the glittering toy on the top of it. Had the Queen moved she would have been discrowned in an instant, and all the foolish people whose footsteps go wandering on the borders of another world, instead of going honestly straightforward in this, would have had a fine opportunity of discussing the value of omens. But, in a case of adornment, the ladies had their wits about them, and were worth the whole episcopal bench when the matter at issue was surmounting a head of hair with its supreme adornment of a crown. Some of those in attendance stepped forward, saved their embarrassed mistress from an annoyance, and Queen Adelaide was crowned in Westminster Abbey by a couple of ladies-in-waiting!

It may be that the Archbishop was not so much to blame on this occasion. The little crown was made up at the Queen's expense for the occasion, by Rundell, out of her own jewels, and it may not have fitted easily. She had a dread of unnecessary outlay, and, perhaps, remembered that at George the Fourth's coronation the sum charged by Rundell merely for the hire of jewels by the King amounted to 16,000*l.*, as interest on their value. The whole expense of the double coronation of William and Adelaide did not amount to much more than twice that sum.

The Queen herself was not ill-dressed on this occasion, as will be seen by the record made by those who have registered the millinery portion of the ceremony:—
' Her Majesty wore a gold gauze over a white satin petti-

coat, with a diamond stomacher, and a purple velvet train, lined with white satin, and a rich border of gold and ermine. The coronet worn by Her Majesty, both to and from the Abbey, was most beautiful. It was composed entirely of diamonds and pearls, and in shape very similar to a mural crown.'

When the modest coronation of William and Adelaide was yet a subject of general conversation, the expensive finery of that which preceded it was actually in the market, and was subsequently sold by public auction. Out of the hundred and twenty lots 'submitted' by Mr. Phillips, the new King and Queen might have been tempted to secure a *souvenir* of their predecessor; but they had no taste for 'bargains,' perhaps small regard for their defunct kinsman. Nevertheless, so thrifty a lady as the Queen may have sighed at the thought of the coronation ruff of Mechlin lace going 'dirt cheap' at two pounds; and she may have regretted the crimson velvet coronation mantle, with its star and gold embroidery, which, originally costing five hundred pounds, fetched, when yet as good as new, only a poor seven-and-forty guineas. There was the same depreciation in other articles of originally costly value. The second coronation mantle of purple velvet fell from three hundred to fifty-five pounds; and the green velvet mantle, lined with ermine, which had cost the Czar, who presented it to the late King, a thousand guineas, was 'knocked down' at a trifle over a hundred pounds. Sashes, highland-dresses, aigrette-plumes—rich gifts received, or purchases dearly acquired—went for nothing; and, after all, seeing into what base hands coronation bravery is apt to fall, the economical King and Queen were not without justification in setting an example of prudence, which was followed at the next great crowning.

Perhaps not the least remarkable incident in connection with this coronation was the absence of the heiress-presumptive to the crown, the Princess Victoria. No place had been assigned to her, nor any preparation made in expectation of her gracing or witnessing the ceremony. It has been said that Earl Grey, the prime minister, obstinately opposed all idea of inviting the Princess to be present. But the grounds for such opposition are so unapparent that it is difficult to give credit to them at all. By others it has been asserted that the Duchess of Northumberland, the governess of the Princess, in the exercise of a superior and enlightened judgment, and in consideration of the then alleged delicate health of her young charge, advised that her pupil should not be present at the coronation of King William and Queen Adelaide. This reason seems hardly to account for the fact. In the absence of a better, it was accepted by those at least who did not throw the blame of that 'conspicuous absence' on Queen Adelaide herself and her royal consort; but, as an anonymous writer remarked, 'Who that knew the good King William and his incomparable Queen would believe that any slight was put by them on their well-beloved niece and the heiress-presumptive to the throne?' The same enemies also stated that 'the Duchess of Northumberland was seeking to give a political bias to the education of the Princess, and some uneasiness was therefore created in the palace.' The 'Times' asserted, with iteration, that the Duchess of Kent had 'refused to attend, yes, refused to attend,' and reproved Her Royal Highness, in the harsh terms which illustrated many of the controversies of the day, for the impertinence of the widow of a mediatized German Prince, in withholding her daughter from a ceremony at which she could never, at one time, have expected to see daughter of hers, as heiress-presumptive to the crown of England! Other papers made this alleged refusal rest on the course taken by Lord A. Fitzclarence, who, in marshalling the coronation procession on paper, had assigned a place to the Princess Victoria after the other members of the royal family, instead of next to the King and Queen. Finally, the 'Globe,' on authority, declared that the Duchess, having pleaded the delicate state of her daughter's health, had obtained the King's sanction to her absence— a version of the end of a story which began, nevertheless, more like the current report of it than would seem here to be indicated. As marked an instance of absence as that of the Princess was that of the whole of such members of the preceding administration as happened to be members of the House of Commons. This, however, little affected the King, who, at the subsequent dinner at St. James's Palace, gave, as a toast, 'the land we live in,' and declared that, except as a formality and memorial, the coronation was a useless affair, as far as he was concerned, for no oath he had there taken could bind him more stringently to fulfil his duty towards the people than he felt himself to be bound by as soon as the responsibility of his position had fallen upon him.

The land he now lived in speedily became agitated by that wave of revolution which was shaking many of the monarchies of Europe. England endured as great revolution as any of them, but with this difference, that here it was effected according to law, and, albeit not exempt from very vast perils, was carried through to its natural consequences, to the mutual advantage of the government and the governed.

When the first rumours began to spread of an opposition establishing itself at court against the progress of reform, the press manifested particular desire to exonerate the Queen from the charge of participating in or heading such a course. The 'Times' at first interfered to protect that lady from similar aspersions. Papers of less influence, but of like principles, had openly named Queen Adelaide, the two daughters of George III., Elizabeth (Princess of Hesse Homburg), and Mary (Duchess of Gloucester) as mischievously active in impeding the popular will. In answer to such accusations, the 'Times' (April 9, 1831), in a brief but spirited and courteous leader, denounced the falsehood, and showed the improbability and the unfairness of such allegations. On a like occasion, that paper fairly urged that, whatever opinions might be expressed by members of the household, they were not to be attributed to the mistress of that household. At the same time, on these members and on the fair frequenters of drawing-rooms who there gave utterance to sentiments which they carried into action elsewhere against the great consummation sought by the people, the pro-reform paper thundered its bolts and showered its sarcasm with unsparing hands. On most occasions, however, so much was made of the apparent heartiness of the King, that excess of praise in that direction took the form of censure on the lukewarmness, if not the hostility, of the Queen. Contrasts rather than parallels were the favourite medium for turning the public attention to the two sovereigns. The Ex-Chancellor Eldon was said to have assured Queen Adelaide that, if reform was carried, the days of her drawing-rooms were numbered, and that royalty would do well to follow a counsel which was given by Earl Grey to the bishops—namely, set its house in order. On the other hand, we hear of the new Chancellor Brougham attending the court with his huge official purse so full of petitions in favour of parliamentary reform that, as he continued to extract and present them, he apologized to King William for troubling him with such piles of the public prayers or demands. Whereupon the King is said to have remarked, in the hearing of the Queen, 'My Lord Chancellor, I am willing to receive anything from that purse, except the seals!' The wit was small, but the suggestiveness was considered important, and gossips, on both sides, jumped to conclusions which had questionable affinity with the premises.

While the Queen was thus treated with a certain degree of moderation by the press, she is said to have been seriously coerced by the liberal ministry of the day. The charge was distinctly made, after the Queen's death, in a funeral sermon, preached by the Rev. Mr. Browne, Vicar of Atwick. The occasion was so solemn that an honest man was not likely to be led even into exaggeration, much less into deliberate misrepresentation. These are the preacher's own words :—

'The Queen-consort had witnessed in her father-land some of the dreadful effects of the French revolutionary movements; and she was known to disapprove, out of womanly feeling and fear for her husband's safety, of popular tumults and agitations. With the narrow-minded and impure suspicion is proof, and is followed by resentment. This pure being was a sufferer by the machinations and exactions of the ephemeral favourites of the misguided populace. Her influence over her royal husband was too great to be trusted, and she was forbidden—I speak advisedly, and mean nothing less than "forbidden"—to have a kindred spirit near her during the agitation and intimidation by which the measure called the Reform Bill was supported and carried.'

It was when that bill was in jeopardy, when the King —who had made so many knights that the very pages called them the 'Arabians,' the 'Thousand and One'— hesitated to create a sufficient number of new lords to secure the passing of the bill in the Upper House; it was then that the press began to admonish the King and to menace the Queen. On one occasion, when they attended at the opening of the new Staines Bridge, where, by the way, they were so closely pressed upon by the mob that maids of honour and gentlemen-in-waiting had their pockets picked, the Conservative wits remarked that the King might make new bridges, but that he must leave the *peers* alone. The Whig party at once assumed that Queen Adelaide was at the head of a faction whose object was to give reality to such jokes, and thenceforward the Queen was little spared. The 'Times' asserted that it was by 'domestic importunity' alone that the free action of the King's mind was impeded. The Queen was compared to Queen Amata, in the 'Æneid,' cajoling or raging at her older consort, Latinus, because the latter preferred Æneas to Turnus as a husband for their daughter Lavinia. There was not much alike in the two cases, for Amata was a staunch Conservative, who detested the idea of a foreign prince obtaining the hand of her daughter, and exercising influence within the limits of Latium. But there were strong terms in the original which suited the purpose of the hour, and the Queen was pelted with them most unmercifully.

Occasionally, there was a truth mixed up with the harder words, which even ultra-Tories could not gainsay, as when the 'Times' remarked that 'a foreigner was no very competent judge of English liberties, and politics are not the proper field for female enterprise or exertion.' When this strong hint was taken to have failed, and Queen Adelaide was still supposed to be conspiring with the daughters of George III. to turn King William from his liberal views, this was the tone with which the royal lady was lectured by the press:—'There is a lady of high rank who must be taught a salutary, though a very painful, lesson. She may be bold as an amazon, be troublesome, importunate, or overbearing, but her present course is one from which can follow naught but final wretchedness. Why has she so eagerly, within these few hours, bidden her gossips *not to despair*? Why such haste to tell them, *all will be well*? *The King will do without the Whigs.* Yes, madam, but England will not. Still less will England do without the unmutilated Bill.'

At another time Queen Adelaide was reminded that if a female influence drove Necker from the court of Louis XVI., one of the consequences was the destruction of the most influential lady; another, the ruin of the country. The influence being assumed to be still active, allusion was made to the 'foreign woman whom the nation may have too easily adopted.' Reports were rife that intrigues were on foot, the object of which was to induce liberal peers to betray their party, and then the public censor showered imprecations on 'blandishments and entreaties, urged with a force and pertinacity which, coming from a monarch, are difficult to be refused.'

On the other hand, the Conservative press drew its own inferences and made its own accusations. When the cholera was raging, during the reform fever, Queen Adelaide's drawing-room happened to be very thinly attended. The real cause was lost sight of, and her Majesty was respectfully assured that the scanty attendance was entirely owing to Lord Grey's revolutionary government, beneath which all old English energy, vitality, and spirit had become so extinct that it was unequal to the exertion of even manifesting respect for an English Queen. As much injury was inflicted on Queen Adelaide by the Tories who blazoned her name on their banners and boasted of having her on their side as by the Whigs and Radicals who, by their calumny, exposed her to popular insult. When Lord Chancellor Brougham coerced the King to go and dismiss the unreformed and unreforming Parliament, one part of the royal remonstrance took the form of: 'What! Would you have me dismiss in this summary manner, a Parliament which has granted me so splendid a Civil List, and given my Queen so liberal an annuity, in case she survives me?' Lord Brougham answered that he would, and that he had taken upon himself to order out the Horse Guards to escort the King down to the House.

Old English qualities manifested themselves at a Conservative festival in Gloucestershire, where the health of 'the Queen' was 'received with great applause.' Upon which announcement the 'Times' significantly asked, 'Is that meant as a compliment to her Majesty, or will it sound as such in the ears of the unanimous people?' Then, when reiteration was made of the alleged co-operation of the sisters of William IV. with Queen Adelaide in efforts to overthrow the Reform Bill, the 'Times' stepped forward with the following testimony in favour of those ladies and their mother, with the accompanying admonition to the Queen:—'No one will be persuaded that any daughter of George III. could so mistake her position in this country or so disregard her duty. Queen Charlotte was advised by her mother, before she ever touched the shores of England, to make entire and religious abstinence from politics the rule of her life as a British Princess; and for twenty-eight years, till the question of the first Regency forced Queen Charlotte upon the stage as a reluctant actress, she had satisfied herself with being a modest spectatress, living in strict observance of maternal counsel; and what was the consequence? Down to the above-mentioned period of her wedded life, her Majesty enjoyed, in a degree not experienced by any Queen-consort for centuries past, the respect and good-will of the whole community. Is it then to be supposed that the leading maxim of her own mother was not impressed by that judicious and estimable woman upon the minds of her daughters, the six Princesses, two of whom still adorn the court of England with their constant presence? The Princess Augusta and the Duchess of Gloucester owe little to the gossips who thus abuse the delicacy of their illustrious names.'

Party-spirit was, doubtless, aggravated on either side by the tone of the press. Influential cities announced their refusal to pay taxes, and tavern-clubs possessing pictures of King and Queen turned them heels uppermost, with an intimation that they should be righted as soon as the originals had made themselves right with the people. If Tories of eminence talked of coercing the King, Whigs equally exalted hinted at the possibility of sending his Consort to Germany, and of rousing the men of the provinces in order to make an impression upon people in high places. One well-known 'man about town,' presiding at a public dinner, refused to propose the Queen's health, and among the lower caricature-shops she might be seen pictured wending her way, the ejected of England, to a dull, dreary, and unwelcoming Germany.

Publicly, however, she had her champions too. Mr. Baring, from his place in parliament, protested against the language of the Whig papers generally. His own description of it, as applicable to the Queen, was, that it comprised foul slander against the highest personage of a sex, from insulting which every manly mind would recoil. The gallant champion added, with less discretion, perhaps, that the full measure of scornful indifference and silent contempt with which the Queen repaid all the insults heaped upon her had elevated her in the hearts of those whose homage was a worthy tribute. Mr. Hume, ultra-reformer as he was, exhibited very excellent taste on this occasion, and pointed out in a few words marked by good common sense that the name of the exalted lady in question should never be dragged into the debates, the discussions, and the dissensions of that house.

Less, perhaps, by way of championship than in the character of consolers, did the bishops, or a certain number of them, with the Archbishop of Canterbury at their head, address Queen Adelaide. They had, previously, 'been up' to the King, who was just then being counselled in various ways by everybody, from wary old politicians to the 'prentice-boys of Derry. They brought to his Consort the usual complimentary phrases—but, in the present instance, they carried weight with the Queen, for amid the din of abuse with which she was assailed a few words of assurance and encouragement, of trust, counsel, and consolation, must have fallen pleasantly upon her ear. She said as much, at least, in a brief phrase or two, indicative of the satisfaction she experienced at hearing such words from such men, at a period when she was the object of so much undeserved calumny and insult.

The scene was, undoubtedly, made the most of by those who rejoiced most in its occurrence; perhaps too much was made of it; and this induced the ridicule of the opposite side. The 'Times' courageously denied its existence. The presentation of the prelates was admitted, but the Queen's speech was defined as a hoax. There was nobody by, it was said, but the knot of diocesans and a body of maids of honour—and, of course, any report emanating from such a source was to be received with more than ordinary suspicion.

Long before the press had commenced directing an undesired notice upon the Queen private circles were canvassing her conduct with regard, especially, to this matter of reform. 'By-the-bye,' says Moore in his diary, 'the Queen being, as is well known, adverse to the measure which is giving such popularity to her royal husband, reminds me a little of the story of the King of Sparta, who first gave his assent to the establishment of the Ephori. His wife, it is said, reproached him with this step, and told him that he was delivering down the royal power to his children *less* than he had received it. " Greater," he answered, " because more durable." This is just such an answer as William IV. would be likely to give to *his* wife. But the event proved the Spartan Queen to have been right, for the Ephori extinguished the royal power ; and if Queen Adelaide's bodings are of the same description, they are but too likely to be *in the same manner realized*'—a curious avowal from Lord Lansdowne's Whig friend.

There are few things which more forcibly strike a student of the political literature of this period than its wide difference from that which now generally prevails. It seemed, in those days, as if no public writer could command or control his temper. The worst things were expressed in the worst forms, and writers had not reached, or did not care to practise, the better style by which a man may censure sharply without doing undue wrong to the object of his censure, without losing his own self-respect or forfeiting that of his readers.

Taken altogether, the year 1832 may be said to have been the most eventful and the least felicitous in the life of Queen Adelaide. It was a year which opened gloomily for the court, both politically and personally. At one of the small festivities held at the Pavilion, the King's old friend, Mr. Greenwood, of the firm of Cox and Greenwood, Army Agents, was playing whist, after dinner, with the Queen for a partner, and the King and Sir Herbert Taylor for adversaries. During the progress of the game he was taken ill, became insensible, and, on being removed from the room by Sir Herbert and Lord Erroll, died in an adjoining apartment, within a quarter of an hour. The Queen was very much shocked at this incident, and the elder ladies about court, who thought it ominous of a fatal year—for already were movements hostile to monarchy becoming active—considered the next month's omen of unpleasant significance too, when the fog in London, on the night of the anniversary of the Queen's birth-day, was so dense that not a lamp of illuminations was visible through the mist. Then ensued, in the subsequent spring, the unpleasant feud with the Sefton family, in which Queen Adelaide's name was so prominent.

Soon after the temporary resignation of the Grey ministry, King William invited the Jockey Club to dinner at St. James's Palace. Among the invited was old Lord Sefton, who was a Whig *and something more*, and who was resolved to avenge on the King the wrongs inflicted, as he assumed, by that dissembling monarch on his friends of the late administration. Lord Sefton accordingly withdrew from the club. The unsuspicious King at once invited him as a friend, but Lord Sefton was ungracious enough to absent himself, and did not condescend to restore the sovereign to favour till Lord Grey was once more at the helm of the national ship—steersman and captain too. His lordship and family appeared at the ball given by the Queen in May, to which, of course, they had been all invited. Meanwhile, however, the King had learned how he stood in the estimation of the Earl, meeting whom in the Queen's ballroom, he turned his royal back upon him, publicly. Thence arose embittered feelings on the part of the offended peer. *Vivere sat, vincere,* 'to conquer is to live enough,' is the Sefton motto, and the bearers of it seem to have been determined to have this taste of life, by putting down the royal offenders, and appearing before them to enjoy their humiliation. 'Lord Molyneux' (Lord Sefton's son, says Mr. Raikes, in his *Diary*) 'has attended a public meeting at Liverpool, where he made a speech, and, actuated by his father's feelings, alluded very bitterly to the conduct of both the King and Queen. He afterwards came to town, and appeared, with his family, at the ball. On the following day, the King commanded Mr. W. Ashley, as vice-chamberlain to the Queen, to write to Lord Molyneux, and request he would not appear at court again. Nothing could be more just. This is only a slight instance,' adds the Tory Diarist, 'of Whig insolence and ingratitude. Sefton has been made a peer, and treated with the most marked courtesy and attention by the present King.'

In the following June, Lord Lichfield, master of the buckhounds, prepared a list of guests invited by him to meet the King, at the conclusion of Ascot races, at dinner, at Lord Lichfield's house, Fern Hill. The King expressly ordered that Lord Sefton should not be invited. Considering the offence, it was singular that any one should have thought of winning the Queen over to use her interest in influencing her husband to withdraw the command. Lady Lichfield, however, did so, intimating to her Majesty that, if the King had been moved by what was reported to have passed at the Jockey Club, she was enabled to say how that matter had been much misrepresented. The Queen confined all reply and comment to the words, coldly uttered, that she hoped it was so.

It certainly was not a period when Queens could expect to be cordial with people who insulted them, and whose speeches in public were exercising a very unwholesome influence on the more ignorant of the lower orders. At the above very Ascot races the King was grievously assaulted, in the Queen's presence, by a ruffian in the crowd. Their Majesties had just taken their seats in the grand stand, and the King had then risen to salute the people in view, when the ruffian in question flung a stone at him, which struck the King on the forehead, but did not inflict any serious mischief. The assailant was let cheaply off; but Queen Adelaide was much distressed by his act, and the impression it made upon her was only increased, a week later, when she appeared with the King at the review in Hyde Park. There she was treated with such incivility and rudeness that at the fête at the Duke of Wellington's, in the evening, where they held a little court, the Queen wore a spiritless and sorrowing aspect, while King William, his buoyant spirits all quenched, looked aged and infirm, weary of his vocation and vexations.

The season, certainly, was not one for monarchs to be abroad in with joyous exterior. In the summer of this year there passed through London a princess whose story bore with it a great moral to the wearers of crowns—the Duchess of Angoulême, the daughter of Louis XVI. She had experienced the widest extremes of fortune, but had been longest and most intimately acquainted with misfortune. She was again a fugitive and an exile—one never destined to behold her country again. The Queen visited her at her modest apartments in Charles Street, Grosvenor Square, and she took leave of that illustrious victim of many revolutions with evil forebodings of the issue of the spirit of the then present time. Her Majesty did not, indeed, lack a certain spirit of her own wherewith to meet the other and revolutionary spirit. Thus, when her friend and faithful servant, Lord Howe, was compelled to give up his office of chamberlain to the Queen, his mistress would never accept the nomination of any other person to the same post. Lord Howe remained in attendance upon his mistress unofficially; but he positively refused to be reinstated by Lord Grey, to whom his reply was, 'That he had been wantonly dismissed by him, and would receive no favour at his hands.' The act of Lord Grey was, probably, far more keenly felt at court than that of the two new radical members (Messrs. Wigney and Faithful) returned for the royal borough of Brighton, and who, ' under the very nose of the court,' as it was said, ' talked openly of reducing the allowance made to the King and Queen.' This was a foolish speech; but there was an even more indiscreet tongue within the Pavilion than those of the new radical senators without. In 1833, the King himself declared in favour of a republican form of government! What must the feelings of Queen Adelaide have been—she who had a horror of revolutions and a hatred for republicanism—on that never-to-be-forgotten Sunday evening, the 6th of January, 1833? The American Minister was a guest at the dinner table that evening. At the *dessert*, the King, instead of wisely going to sleep, as he was accustomed to do after his second glass of wine, *would* be lively and talkative. When he was in this vein he was addicted to make speeches, and on this occasion, before the ladies had retired, he delivered himself of a very notable one, considering the times and the speaker, in which he expressed his great regret that he had not been born a free, independent American, seeing that he entertained deep respect for the United States, and considered Washington to be the greatest man that ever lived. Queen Adelaide must have been astounded when listening to this profession of political faith, and to this eulogy of a man who had struck the brightest jewel out of the crown of his panegyrist's royal father!

To old royalists such a speech as the above savoured of that period which is called ' the end of the world.' Speculative individuals who heard of it were amazed. ' The aristocracy are hourly going down in the scale; royalty is become a mere cypher.' Well might Mr. Raikes make this entry in his journal, when a King of

England manifested a liking for 'rowdyism.' The influences of these passing events, even on men of intellect, are well marked by a contemporary passage in the diary of the merchant, whose commercial affairs were going the way he fancied the monarchy was tending. 'I was walking the other day,' he writes, in February 1833, 'round the Royal Exchange, the *enceinte* of which is adorned with the statues of all our Kings. Only two niches now remain vacant; one is destined to our present ruler, and that reserved for his successor is the *last*. Some people might say it was ominous.' So, indeed, it proved to be; half-a-year after the accession of Queen Victoria, when there were as many niches as there had been sovereigns, and room for no more, destruction ensued, but it was the Royal Exchange that fell (by fire), and not the monarchy. *That* has grown stronger. May it ever so flourish!

Meanwhile, it is to be observed that Queen Adelaide after this time began to re-conquer the popular esteem. When, in July 1834, she embarked at Woolwich as Countess of Lancaster, on board the royal yacht, for Rotterdam, in order to visit her relations in Germany, the spectators of the scene received her with demonstrations of great respect, and on her return, in the following month, she landed at the same place amid acclamations of loyalty and welcome.

It was after her return that the King began to bear symptoms of restlessness and fatigue, which betokened that decay which gradually made progress, and was ultimately accelerated in 1837, when his daughter, Lady de Lisle, died, to the grief of many, but especially to the heart of her father.

As the King's health began to give way, so also did his temper more easily yield before such provocations, and more freely did he indulge in that early acquired habit of using strong expletives which has been noted, in her diary, by Fanny Burney. William the Conqueror, it is said, used to ungallantly beat his wife, Matilda, of whom he was otherwise so fond. William the Fourth was guilty of an offence only next to it in criminality—by swearing in presence of his consort, Adelaide. There is a well-known instance of this told in connection with a visit to the Royal Academy, in 1834. The occasion was that of a private view, with a very large public attendance at Somerset House. The President of the Royal Academy received the illustrious visitors, and accompanied them through the rooms. In the course of their progress he pointed out to the King the portrait of Admiral Napier, who had recently been in command of the Portuguese fleet for Don Pedro. The King's political wrath was too strong for his infirmity, and, without forgetting the presence of his wife, nay, making such presence an excuse for not breaking forth into greater unseemliness, he exclaimed: 'Captain Napier may be d——d, sir! and *you* may be d——d, sir! and if the Queen was not here, sir, I would kick you down stairs, sir.' Such a scene indicated as much infirmity as bad taste on the part of the chief actor, and must have sorely tried the patience and shaken the dignity of the Queen. She now, perhaps, as much or more than ever, required the support of those nearest to her. The old prejudices of the reform time against her had not yet died out, and to these was to be added certain malignity in foreign papers; a malignity which culminated in 1835 in the 'Gazette de France,' which paper seriously asserted that England was endeavouring to revolutionize Spain and Portugal, with ulterior purposes of pursuing the same course in Germany and Italy as she had done in Belgium and in Greece; and that at the head of this conspiracy for reconstructing Europe were William the Fourth, the Duke of Wellington, and *Queen Adelaide!* Thus, the lady who had seldom during her life desired more than to be permitted to enjoy it tranquilly, and who had but little perplexed herself touching the ways of others, was held up, after being accused of being a political meddler at home, as being a political conspirator abroad.

When her royal consort's indisposition assumed an appearance of increased gravity, Queen Adelaide at once took her place by his couch, and never left but when compelled by gentle restraint put upon her by those who loved her, and who feared for her own health. 'Les reines' (says a French writer) 'ont été vues pleurantes comme de simples femmes,' and she was one of them. Her constancy only gave way, and she broke into profuse but silent tears, on the eve of the old King's death, as the Archbishop of Canterbury concluded the service of the sick, by pronouncing the solemn words of the benediction as contained in the Liturgy of the Church. The good old monarch looked with affection upon his sorrowing Queen, and with as cheerful a voice as he could put on, and almost in nautical phrase, begged her to be of good heart and to 'bear up! bear up!'

The Rev. Mr. Browne, Vicar of Atwick, rendering testimony to her conduct on this occasion, said in a funeral sermon: 'She was by the King's bedside, a being so full of devoted love and pious resignation, of such meekness, gentleness, and goodness, and sweetness, that an angel might have beheld her with satisfaction and delight, and *almost with advantage.*' She did her duty like a true wife and tender woman; and Mr. Browne thought that, altogether, Queen Adelaide might have afforded an useful hint or two even to angels! It is more than the good Queen ever dreamed of.

The Archbishop of Canterbury was in close attendance upon the King during the last days of his life, in 1837, and in the course of his ministrations saw more of Queen Adelaide than any other individual there present had the opportunity of doing. At a meeting of the Metropolitan Churches' Fund Society, the primate went fully, but tenderly and sensibly, into this solemn matter; and after rendering due, but not over-piled, measure of justice to the King, spoke in these words of his consort:—'For three weeks prior to his dissolution the Queen sat by his bedside, performing for him every office which a sick man could require, and depriving herself of all manner of rest and refection. She underwent labours which I thought no ordinary woman could endure. No language can do justice to the meekness and to the calmness of mind which she sought to keep up before the King, while sorrow was preying on her heart. Such constancy of affection, I think, was one of the most interesting spectacles that could be presented to a mind desirous of being gratified with the sight of human excellence.'

The spectacle at the close was one most touching of all, for old King William, threescore and twelve, died at last in a gentle sleep, as he sat up on his couch, his hand resting, where it had lain undisturbed for hours, on the shoulder of the Queen. Such had been her office at various times, daily, for the preceding fortnight; and when it shall have been a little more hallowed by time, it will be a fitting subject to be limned by some future artist competent to treat it.

Since the death of Charles II. no King of England had died under the same roof with his wife; and *then* there was no such touching scene as the above, but only a few words of decent reconciliation before the royal pair parted for ever, and the wife (leaving the husband to die at leisure and commend worthless women to his brother's protection) went to her chamber to receive the formal news of his death, and finally to receive the condolence of visitors, lying the while on a state bed of mourning, in a chamber lighted with tapers, the walls, floor, and ceiling covered with black cloth. Queen Adelaide stayed by *her* husband to the last, then laid his unconscious head upon the pillow, and, quietly withdrawing to her chamber, looked for consolation to other sources than the visits of courtiers shaping their faces to the humour of the hour.

The respect of the royal widow for the deceased King did not cease here. On Saturday night, the 8th of July, she attended the funeral ceremony, at Windsor, being present in the royal closet during the whole ceremony. She is the only Queen of England who saw a King, her consort, deposited in the tomb.

In the following month the Dowager Queen left Windsor Castle, to which the shouts of a joyous people welcomed her successor. From that time she may be said to have commenced her own course of dying. Her story is really, henceforward, but the diary of an invalid. The nation, through the legislature, condoled with her upon her bereavement, and as she descended the steps of the throne to resume her old unostentatious privacy there was not a man in the realm who failed, in some wise, to greet her, or who did not acknowledge that she had borne greatness with honour, and had won the hearts of a people who had been once forward to censure her.

From this period her life was one of suffering, but it was a suffering that never rendered her selfish. In her worst hours of anguish her ear was open, her heart touched, her hand ready to relieve her sisters in affliction, and to remedy the distresses of all who really stood in need of the royal succour. For nearly twelve years she may be said to have been dying. The sunniest and most sheltered spots in this country were visited by her, but without resulting in permanent relief. The winter of

1837-8 was spent at St. Leonard's. An attack of bronchitis, in the autumn of the latter year, drove her for refuge and remedy to Malta, where the church raised by her at Valetta—the cathedral church of the diocese of Gibraltar —at an expense of 10,000*l.*, will long serve to perpetuate her memory. On her return in May 1839, she became, for a time, the guest of various noble hosts in England. In 1840 she visited the lakes, and established her home, subsequently and for a brief period, at Sudbury. Her next homes—the frequent changes indicating increased virulence of disease—were at Canford Hall, Dorset; Witley Court, Worcester; and Cashiobury, near Watford: thence she departed on one short and last visit to her native home, from which she returned so ill that, in 1847, she repaired, as a last resource, to Madeira, whither she was conveyed in a royal frigate.

The progress of the sick Queen over water was not without its stateliness and solemnity, mixed with a certain joyousness, acceptable to, though not to be shared in by, the royal invalid. Before the squadron departed from Spithead, on Sunday, the 10th of October, full divine service was celebrated on board the *Howe*, the ship's chaplain reading the prayers, the Queen Dowager's preaching the sermon, on a text altogether foreign to so rare and interesting an occasion :—' But now the righteousness of God without the law is manifested, being witnessed by the law and the prophets' (Rom. iii. 21). After service, the squadron stood forth to sea, no incident marking its way till the following Tuesday. On that day, a bird winging from the Bay of Biscay fluttered on to the *Howe*, perched on the yards, and then flew from one point to another and back again, as if he had made of the gallant steamer a home. A sailor named Ward attempted to capture the little guest, in pursuing which into the chains, being more eager than considerate, he fell headlong over

into the waves, while the *Howe* pursued her forward way.
In an instant after alarm was given, however, the life-
buoy was floating on the waters, a boat was pulling lustily
towards the seaman, and the *Howe* slipped her tow ropes,
and made a circuit astern to pick up rescued and rescuers.
Ward, meanwhile, had by skilful swimming gained fast
hold of the buoy, and was brought on board little the worse
for his plunge and his temporary peril. Queen Adelaide
was more moved by this accident than the man was himself. On the following Sunday, the Queen was better
able than she had previously been to turn the accident
to some account for Ward's own benefit. Her Majesty
had attended the usual service on board, and had listened
to another sermon from the ship's chaplain, this time on
a subject as unappropriate as that of the preceding Sunday:—' And almost all things are by the law purged
with blood; and without shedding of blood is no
remission' (Heb. ix. 22)—the ship's company were
repairing to their respective quarters, when Ward was
told that the Queen Dowager requested to see him. If
this message disconcerted him more than his fall into the
Bay of Biscay, he soon recovered that self-possession
which no man loses long who has a proper feeling of
self-respect. Besides, the widowed Queen, in her intercourse with persons of humble station, wore habitually
that air—

—————— which sets you at your ease,
Without implying your perplexities.

She spoke to the listening sailor kindly on his late peril,
and the position in which it suddenly placed him near to
impending death. A few words like these, wisely and
tenderly offered, were likely to be more beneficial to a
man like Ward than a whole course of the chaplain's
sermons on doctrinal points in the Epistle to the Hebrews;
and I cannot but hope that the artists of the next genera-

tion, when Time shall have poetized the *costume* of the incident, will not forget this picturesque passage in the life of the Queen and the man-of-war's-man.

And now, as they glided by the coast of Portugal, on the evening of Monday, the 18th of October, there was dancing on board, and again on the Wednesday evening. Princesses waltzed with commanders, the Grand Duchess tripped it on the poop with a knight, and the midshipmen went dashingly at it with the maids of honour, while the gun-room officers stood by awaiting their turn. On the fore part of the quarterdeck as many of the ship's company as were so minded got up a dance among themselves; and the suffering Queen below heard the echoes of the general gladness, and was content.

On the following Friday, the *Howe* was close to Belem Castle, and was towed into the Tagus by the steam-frigate *Terrible*. The King Consort of Portugal came down in a state barge to receive the Queen, whom he escorted to the palace of the Necessidades, landing amid a roar of artillery, and welcomed by loyal demonstrations as the illustrious traveller passed on her way to the Queen regnant, Donna Maria.

By such progress did Queen Adelaide make her way towards Madeira, the climate of which could not arrest the progress of her malady, and she returned to England —for a time to Bushey, finally to Bentley Priory, near Stanmore, where she occupied herself in preparation for the inevitable end. There, on the 8th of May, 1849, the Queen Dowager may be said to have 'done a foolish thing,' in altering her will without legal assistance in the method of alteration. On that day, alone and unadvised, her Majesty took out her old and duly attested will of the 14th August, 1837, and inscribed on the back thereof this remarkable endorsement :—'This will is cancelled, 8th May, 1849. My heirs are my brother and sister, and their heirs after them. My executors, Lord Howe and the Hon. W. A. Cooper, are requested to pay off all that I directed in my codicil, and then to divide my property equally between my brother and sister. This is my last will and request.'

It was the will of a Queen, but it stood for nothing in the eye of the law. The endorsement was brought under notice of the Prerogative Court; the Judge, Sir Herbert Jenner Fust, declared it to be of no effect. It was a mere unattested memorandum, and he pronounced, as the legal phrase is, for the original will. Of greater interest is the subjoined document, which pleasantly contrasts with the wills of many of her lady predecessors, whose minds were engaged on the disposal of their state beds, their mantles, and their jewellery, to the exclusion of all other subjects. Thus wrote the dying Queen Adelaide:—

'I die in all humility, knowing well that we are all alike before the throne of God; and I request, therefore, that my mortal remains be conveyed to the grave without any pomp or state. They are to be removed to St. George's Chapel, Windsor, where I request to have as private and quiet a funeral as possible. I particularly desire not to be laid out in state, and the funeral to take place by daylight; no procession; the coffin to be carried by sailors to the chapel. All those of my friends and relations, to a limited number, who wish to attend may do so. My nephew, Prince Edward of Saxe-Weimar, Lords Howe and Denbigh, the Hon. William Ashley, Mr. Wood, Sir Andrew Barnard, and Sir D. Davies, with my dressers, and those of my ladies who may wish to attend. I die in peace, and wish to be carried to the tomb in peace, and far from the vanities and pomp of this world. I request not to be dissected nor embalmed, and desire to give as little trouble as possible.

'ADELAIDE R.'

The end soon came, and it was met with dignity. On the 22nd of November 1849, Queen Victoria and Prince Albert visited the Dowager Queen for the last time. On the last day of the month she calmly passed away. The above document was then produced, and it rendered kings-of-arms, heralds, gold sticks, and upholsterers powerless to exercise their absurd dignity in connection with death when so intelligible and sensible a protest as the above was in existence. Accordingly, on a fine December morning of 1849, there issued from the gates of Bentley Priory an ordinary hearse with a pall emblazoned with the Queen's arms, preceded by three mourning coaches. A scanty escort of cavalry accompanied them, more for use than show, their office being to see that no obstruction impeded the funeral march from Stanmore to Windsor. On its way the attitude of the spectators exhibited more of sympathy than curiosity.

The Harrow boys turned out in testimony of respect, and the country people at large *looked* like mourners, wearing more or less, but wearing *some*, outward manifestation of sorrow.

The Queen's body reached the Chapel at Windsor at one o'clock. In the south aisle, close to the porch, there had been standing, grouped together, silent and motionless, a group of seamen,—grave, bronzed, athletic sailors. Their demeanour showed them worthy of the office which the now dead Queen had asked at their hands. When all the royal, and great, and noble personages were in their respective places — while some indispensable officials effected a little more of their foolish calling in the presence of death than Queen Adelaide herself would have sanctioned—while princes, peers, and prelates, ladies-in-waiting, clergy, and choristers, proceeded passively or actively with their parts in the ceremony of the day—then those ten sailors advanced to accomplish the duty assigned them, and, standing by the platform on which the body was placed, gently propelled it to a position over the subterranean passage into which it was lowered, after one of the simplest services that was ever said or sung for departed Queen had been accomplished —most simple, save when Garter stepped forward to announce, what all men knew, that it 'had pleased Almighty God to take out of this life to His divine mercy' the departed Queen; and to assert, what that royal lady would assuredly have gainsaid, that she was a 'Most High, Most Mighty, and Most Excellent Princess.' With this, and one or two other formalities of that pomp and state from which she had asked to be spared, Queen Adelaide passed to the tomb—a tomb capacious enough to contain whole generations of kings and queens, princes and princesses yet unborn.

This event was followed by an unusual amount of execrable elegiac verse, which was powerless, however, to throw ridicule on what it affected to solemnize. It was painful to read an inconceivable amount of this trash, which, intended to be serious, was often irresistibly comic. Out of the reams written in professed honour of a most exemplary Queen there was not an appropriate line worth citing. One sample of the solemnly absurd Pegasuses set restive on this occasion will assuredly satisfy curiosity. The writer affects to see at the royal funeral the ghosts of departed great ones, who assemble to do visionary homage to their new sister in death. Among them is the incautious Bishop who died from the effects of a cold caught at the funeral of the Duke of York :—

> Lo! see the shade of a prelate pass by
> Who came to a night-burial to die;
> Standing too long expos'd to the chill air,
> Death aim'd his dart, and struck the mitre there.

Poor Queen Adelaide! A wish could save her from some of the empty pomps and vanities that linger about the open grave, but nothing could save her from the villainous poetasters. All the rhymers who rung metrical knells at her death deserved the fate, and for like reasons, invoked in Julius Cæsar on the so-called poet who made 'bad verses.'

The preachers, if honest chronicling is to be observed, did not on this occasion very much excel the poets. Very 'tolerable' indeed, and not at all to be endured, were most of the funeral sermons which have come under my notice. One clergyman, who had been the Queen's chaplain too, and who had composed a funeral sermon on William IV. reproduced not merely the substance, but in many parts, identical passages from the discourse on the dead King, and made them do duty in illustrating the demise of that sovereign's royal widow. Others were illogical, or were painfully simple or amusingly trite. In one I find an intimation that, 'after deducting the more needful expenses of her household, she gave away *all* she had, and died *poor;*' which seems an inevitable consequence of such liberality. None of these who took a dead Queen for the subject of a lesson on vanity, or for an example to be followed, wore the mantle of a Bossuet —grand and instructive when consigning La Vallière to the cloister, or Henrietta of Orleans to a tomb. They might at least have found something suggestive in the sermon on the latter occasion, by the 'Eagle of Meaux,' where he exclaims, after apt reflection on birth, rank, and their responsibilities: 'No! after what we have just seen, we must feel that health exists only in name, life is a dream, glory a deception, favours and pleasures dangerous amusements, everything about us vanity. She was as gentle towards death as she had been to all the world. . . . She will sleep with the great ones of the earth, with princes and kings, whose power is at an end, amongst whom there is hardly room to be found, so closely do they lie together, and so prompt is death to fill the vacant places. *Can we build our hopes on ruins such as these?*'

From beyond sea there did come echoes something like these, and fitting homage to the virtues of the deceased lady was rendered from many a church pulpit among a foreign people. In another hemisphere, at the Cape of Good Hope, a funeral sermon was preached in St. George's Cathedral, Cape Town, on the 24th February, 1850, by the Rev. W. A. Newman, at that time Senior Colonial Chaplain and Rural Dean, in which that learned and eloquent divine rendered a graceful tribute to the memory of the deceased Queen, of which the following paragraph is a portion:—'Of this excellent lady's large charities I can speak from evidence, and can, therefore, speak with a full heart. I have lived near to the neighbourhood where her less public bounty diffused itself. I know that the sick-room of the poor has been visited by her in person; I know that from her own table a portion has been sent, to call forth the coy appetite of disease; and I know that wherever she went many a heartfelt *God bless her* would follow.'

Such was Queen Adelaide, some seven years Queen Consort of Great Britain; a lady who will be remembered, if not as a great Queen, yet as one of the truly good women who have shared with a King regnant the throne of these islands—one who lived down calumny, and who, being dead, is remembered with respect and affection.

THE END.

www.ingramcontent.com/pod-product-compliance
Lightning Source LLC
Chambersburg PA
CBHW051854300426
44117CB00006B/386